THE NEW BOOK OF KNOWLEDGE ANNUAL

THE
NEW BOOK
OF
KNOWLEDGE
ANNUAL

The Young People's Book of the Year

Grolier Incorporated, Danbury, Connecticut

2000
Highlighting Events of 1999

ISBN 0-7172-0634-3

ISSN 0196-0148

The Library of Congress Catalog Card Number: 79-26807

 COPYRIGHT © 2000 BY GROLIER INCORPORATED

Copyright © in Canada 2000 by GROLIER LIMITED

STAFF

PUBLISHER
PHILIP FRIEDMAN

EXECUTIVE EDITOR
FERN L. MAMBERG

DIRECTOR, ANNUALS
DORIS E. LECHNER

DESIGNER
ELIZABETH DE BELLA

ASSOCIATE EDITOR
PATRICIA A. BEHAN

DIRECTOR, PHOTO RESEARCH
CINDY JOYCE

YOUNG PEOPLE'S PUBLICATIONS

EDITOR IN CHIEF	VIRGINIA QUINN MCCARTHY
MANAGING EDITOR	KENNETH W. LEISH
DESIGN DIRECTOR	NANCY A. HAMLEN
EDITORS	ELAINE HENDERSON DANIEL O. HOGAN SARA A. BOAK
PHOTO RESEARCHERS	JOAN R. MEISEL SUSAN J. FERRELLI
MANAGER, PICTURE LIBRARY	JANE H. CARRUTH
PRODUCTION EDITOR	CAROLYN F. REIL
INDEXER	PAULINE M. SHOLTYS
FINANCIAL MANAGER	JOSEPH CANTONE
EDITORIAL LIBRARIAN	CHARLES CHANG
DIRECTOR, PUBLISHING TECHNOLOGY	ADRIANNE BEAUCHAMP
PROJECT LEADER	GAIL G. DELL
SENIOR PUBLISHING SYSTEMS ANALYST	EMILIA URRA SMITH
COMPOSITOR	KAREN CALISE
STAFF ASSISTANTS	JOAN FLETCHER ROSEMARIE KENT AUDREY M. SPRAGG

MANUFACTURING

VICE PRESIDENT, MANUFACTURING
JOSEPH J. CORLETT

PRODUCTION MANAGER
BARBARA L. PERSAN

DIRECTOR, REFERENCE PUBLICATIONS
CHRISTINE L. MATTA

PRODUCTION ASSISTANT
KATHERINE M. SIEPIETOSKI

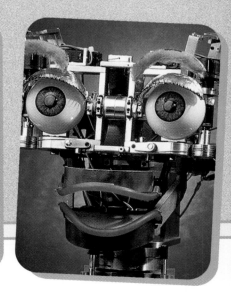

CONTENTS

CONTRIBUTORS

BOVE, V. Michael Jr.
Principal Research Scientist, MIT Media Laboratory, Massachusetts Institute of Technology

COMMUNICATION

BOWERS, Vivien
Author, *Crime Science: How Investigators Use Science to Track Down the Bad Guys*

FORENSIC SCIENCE

COOPER, Kenneth S.
Professor of History, George Peabody College for Teachers, Vanderbilt University; Author, *World Ways; The Changing Old World; Modern History*

GUILDS

FISHER, Marshall Jon
Coauthor, *Tube: The Invention of Television; Strangers in the Night: A Brief History of Life on Other Worlds*

TELEVISION

FREEMAN, John P.
Professor, Department of Radio-TV-Film, Texas Christian University,

TELEVISION

GREGORY, Paula
Director of Outreach and Education, Human Cancer Genetics, Ohio State University

GENETICS

HACKER, Jeffrey H.
Author, *Carl Sandburg; Franklin D. Roosevelt; Government Subsidy to Industry; The New China*

FOLLOWING THE LIGHT

HOWELLS, Cyndi
Author and Webmaster, *Cyndi's List of Genealogy Sites on the Internet; Netting Your Ancestors: Genealogical Research on the Internet*

GENEALOGY

JACKSON, Patrick
Professor, Sonoma State University; Editor, *Western Criminology Review*; Author, *The Paradox of Control*

JUVENILE CRIME

JESPERSON, James
Physicist, National Bureau of Standards; Coauthor, *Mercury's Web: The Story of*

Telecommunications; From Sundials to Atomic Clocks; Time and Clocks for the Space Age; The Story of Telecommunications; RAMs, ROMs, and Robots: The Story of Computers; From Quarks to Quasars: A Tour of the Universe; The Unseen Universe

TELEPHONE

KING, Nancy Jean
Professor of Law, Vanderbilt University

LAW AND LAW ENFORCEMENT

KURTZ, Henry I.
Author, *John and Sebastian Cabot; Defending Our Country: The U.S. Army; Captain John Smith; The Art of the Toy Soldier*

THE MAN WHO INVENTED SANTA CLAUS

MENDELSON, Karen
1997 Recipient, Intel Young Scientist Scholarship Award; 1998 Recipient, Glenn Seaborg Nobel Visit Award, International Science and Engineering Fair

SCIENCE FAIRS

PASCOE, Elaine
Author, *South Africa: Troubled Land; Neighbors at Odds: U.S. Policy in Latin America; Racial Prejudice; The Horse Owner's Preventive Maintenance Handbook; Freedom of Expression: The Right to Speak Out in America*

CELEBRATE THE CENTURY
AROUND THE WORLD

PIORKOWSKI, Nona
Editor, *Crafts 'n Things* magazine

POPULAR CRAFTS

SHERMAN, Heidi
Music Editor, *Seventeen* magazine

THE MUSIC SCENE

TESAR, Jenny
Author, *Endangered Habitats; Global Warming; Scientific Crime Investigation; The Waste Crisis; Shrinking Forests; The New Webster's Computer Handbook; What on Earth Is a Meerkat?; Spiders*

SPACE BRIEFS

VAN RYZIN, Robert
Managing Editor, *Numismatic News*, Krause Publications; Author, *Striking Impressions: A Visual Guide to Collecting U.S. Coins*

COIN COLLECTING

IN THE PAGES OF THIS BOOK . . .

How closely did you follow the events of 1999? Do you remember the people who made news during the year? What about the trends—what was in and what was out? Who won in sports? What were the top songs, films, and television shows? What important anniversaries were celebrated? All these helped make up your world in 1999—a year that was like no other.

Here's a quiz that will tell you how much you know about your world—about what took place during the past year and about other things, as well. If you're stumped by a question, don't worry. You'll find all the answers in the pages of this book. (The page numbers after the questions will tell you where to look.)

On January 1, 1999, eleven European nations adopted a common currency called the (toro/euro/ropo). (*45*)

The U.S. space shuttle *Columbia* completed a five-day mission in July. It was the first shuttle mission commanded by a woman. What was her name? (*56, 137–38*)

The 1999 Academy Award for best motion picture went to a romantic comedy called _____. (*250, 259*)

Balloonists Brian Jones and Bertrand Piccard soared into the record books on March 21, when they completed the first nonstop balloon flight (across the United States/over the North Pole/around the world). (*48, 204*)

In March, an archeological team in Peru climbed to the top of one of the world's tallest volcanoes and made an amazing discovery. What did they find? (*128*)

In women's basketball, _____ led the Houston Comets to their third straight Women's National Basketball Association (WNBA) championship. (*180*)

The (peregrine falcon/northern spotted owl/California condor) was officially removed from the U.S. list of endangered and threatened species in August. (*114*)

In September, more than 2.6 million people were ordered or urged to leave their homes in the Southeast. What was the reason for this evacuation—the largest in U.S. history? (*60*)

In June, Yugoslavia signed a peace plan with _____, agreeing to withdraw its troops from the province of Kosovo. (*54, 74*)

The New York Yankees won their second straight World Series. This was the (20th/25th/30th) time they had won the World series. (*174*)

Child-friendly monsters from Japan invaded North America—and collecting their cards turned into one of the biggest crazes ever. What are these little monsters called? (*236*)

According to a recent study, kids aged 9 to 11 spent more than _____ hours a week on homework. (*241*)

On April 1, Canada created a new, huge territory for the Inuit (Eskimos). It's called (Sumovut/Allovus/Nunavut). (*50, 72*)

With her album *Voice of an Angel,* a 13-year-old singer introduced opera to a new generation. Who is this young singer? (*225, 270*)

Three wildly popular children's books about _____ , a boy with a knack for magic, topped the bestseller lists. (*260, 297*)

Bill Clinton was the second president of the United States to be impeached. The first president to be impeached was (Andrew Johnson/Lyndon Johnson/Richard Nixon). (*70*)

Four of the world's greatest athletes—one each from basketball, football, hockey, and tennis—retired in 1999. Can you name them? (*195*)

In July, Americans mourned the death of _____ , who died along with his wife and sister-in-law in a plane crash. (*57, 381*)

On October 12, according to United Nations estimates, the population of the world reached (4 billion/6 billion/8 billion). (*62, 202*)

Which TV shows won 1999 Emmy Awards for best comedy and drama series? (*268*)

In September, a team of scientists reported that they had used genetic engineering to create a strain of "smart" _____. (*60*)

The year's most eagerly awaited movie was a science-fiction saga that was termed a "prequel" because it covered events leading up to the action in the earlier films. The movie was the fourth in the (*Star Trek/Star Wars/Starship Troopers*) series. (*263*)

For most people, September 9 was an ordinary day. But others noticed something odd about the date. Do you know what was different about that date? (*61*)

Teenage sisters Venus and Serena Williams brought a new brand of athleticism and power to the women's game of _____. (*191*)

Jazz fans marked the 100th anniversary of the birth of (Louis Armstrong/Duke Ellington/Cole Porter), one of the greatest jazz musicians ever. (261)

In March, the North Atlantic Treaty Organization (NATO) welcomed three new members. Can you name these three Eastern European countries? (*48*)

On August 11, millions of people across parts of Europe and Asia poured into the streets and stared at sky to see the last _____ of the 20th century. (*58*)

Young actor Haley Joel Osment won rave reviews for his performance in the film (*The Water Boy/The Smart Guy/The Sixth Sense*). (*243, 262*)

In Washington, D.C., visitors who went to see the famous cherry trees bloom in the spring found that one of them had been felled. George Washington didn't do it, so who chopped down the cherry tree? (*115*)

Pop music's newest sensation was 17-year-old _____. Her debut album and single, both titled . . .*Baby One More Time*, topped the music charts. (*271*)

Engineers are scrambling to save one of Europe's most famous landmarks from falling down. It is the (Leaning Tower of Pisa/London Bridge/Berlin Wall). (*140*)

The U.S. Women's National Soccer Team won the Women's World Cup. What team did they beat? (*173, 194*)

In 1999, the San Antonio _____ won their first-ever National Basketball Association (NBA) championship. (*178*)

At the stroke of midnight on December 31, 1999, millions of people around the world cheered the arrival of the year 2000. Among the very first to welcome in the new year were people (in Times Square in New York City/on the island of Fiji in the Pacific Ocean/at the Millennium Dome in Britain). (*198*)

CELEBRATE ★ THE ★ CENTURY

The 1969 Apollo 11 moon mission was one of the 20th century's most exciting events—perhaps the most exciting of all. On July 20, 1969, U.S. astronauts Neil Armstrong and Buzz Aldrin (below) became the first people ever to set foot on the moon. Armstrong stepped out first. His now-famous words were: "That's one small step for a man, one giant leap for mankind." In a century filled with amazing feats, the moon mission was a standout! But many things made the 20th century memorable. In the pages that follow, you will read about the events and trends that shaped our world and our lives in the past hundred years.

THE WORLD SCENE

U.S. marines on the Pacific island of Iwo Jima, during World War II. Two world wars marked the 20th century.

The 20th century witnessed two world wars and countless other conflicts. Nuclear bombs and other weapons of mass destruction changed the nature of war. But in spite of these developments, or perhaps because of them, there was also growing cooperation between nations. Here are some of the major international events that shaped the world during the century.

WORLD WAR I

World War I started with a conflict in the Balkans and soon engulfed Europe. Initially, it pitted Germany and Austria-Hungary against Britain, France, and Russia. Other nations joined in, and the fighting took a terrible toll.

At first, the war seemed remote to most Americans. But although the United States was neutral, Americans were in danger—especially on the high seas. Americans were furious when Germany sank the British passenger liner *Lusitania* in 1915 with nearly 1,200 people aboard, 128 of them Americans. By April 1917, five

American vessels had been sunk as well. President Woodrow Wilson asked Congress for a declaration of war. By the fall of 1918, the United States had nearly two million soldiers in France. They played a key role in the offensives that defeated Germany and brought an end to the fighting on November 11.

As the basis of a just peace, Wilson set out a list of goals, called the Fourteen Points. Although the Treaty of Versailles, the final peace accord, didn't include many of those points, one of Wilson's dreams did take shape. That was the League of Nations, an international organization that he hoped would prevent future wars. The U.S. Senate, however, rejected membership in the League, and it never became an effective force for peace.

THE RISE OF FASCISM

A severe economic depression brought hard times to much of the world in the 1930's. As people lost their jobs and worried about

The sinking of the passenger ship *Lusitania* in 1915 helped draw the United States into World War I.

Vladimir Lenin was the driving force behind the events that brought Communism to power in Russia.

The Russian Revolution

The years during and after World War I saw great social and political changes. The most dramatic change came in Russia. For centuries, Russia had been ruled by hereditary monarchs, the czars. There were huge differences between the rich and the poor, and by the early 1900's there was growing unrest. For many Russians, the suffering caused by World War I was the last straw. Early in 1917, Czar Nicholas II was forced to step down, and a provisional government was set up.

The new government was short-lived. On October 25, 1917, a faction known as the Bolsheviks seized control. Led by Vladimir I. Lenin, the Bolsheviks began the Communist dictatorship that would rule Russia for more than 70 years. The old order was swept away. Czar Nicholas, his empress, and their five children were executed. Private land and businesses were confiscated by the government. The old Russian empire became the Union of Soviet Socialist Republics (U.S.S.R, or Soviet Union).

After Lenin's death in 1924, Joseph Stalin came to power. He proved to be a brutal despot. Millions of people starved during his rule. Millions more were killed, victims of Stalin's infamous purges. They included military officers and Bolshevik leaders whom he thought might oppose him, writers, scientists, industrial managers who missed production targets, and thousands of ordinary citizens.

getting enough to eat, dissatisfaction grew. Germany was especially hard hit, and there dissatisfaction helped Adolf Hitler and his National Socialist (Nazi) Party come to power. Hitler gained support in general elections from 1930 to 1933 by presenting himself as Germany's last hope. In 1934 he gained total control and gave himself the title Führer (leader).

The Nazis established a Fascist regime, in which a powerful central government controlled every aspect of life, from newspapers to schools. They decreed that men should be workers and soldiers, and women should be housewives and mothers. Children were required to join Nazi youth organizations. A secret police force, the Gestapo, was set up to weed out opposition.

Hitler soon began to re-arm Germany, ignoring the Treaty of Versailles. In 1936 he reoccupied the Rhineland, territory from which German forces had been barred. In 1938 he invaded Austria, claiming it as part of a greater Germany. In March 1939 he occupied all of Czechoslovakia. It was clear his demands for more territory would only grow.

Fascist regimes also came to power in Italy and Japan. They allied themselves with the

Adolf Hitler, Nazi dictator of Germany, dreamed of conquest. The result was World War II and the Holocaust.

Nazis. Germany, Italy, and Japan—the Axis powers—set their eyes on conquest.

WORLD WAR II

World War II began in Europe on September 1, 1939, when Germany invaded Poland. Britain and France, allies of Poland, declared war on Germany. But Hitler conquered Poland in three weeks. In 1940, Denmark, Norway, the Netherlands, Belgium, and France fell to his armies. In 1941 the Nazis advanced through the Balkans, North Africa, and huge areas of the Soviet Union. Meanwhile, Britain was battered by a long air campaign. The leadership of Prime Minister Winston Churchill helped the British people hold on. The United States, which at first hoped to stay out of the conflict, soon began sending supplies across the Atlantic to aid Britain.

The event that finally brought the United States into the war occurred in the Pacific. There, Japan had gained control of much of China and was starting to invade Southeast Asia. The Japanese believed the United States stood in the way of their expanding empire. On December 7, 1941, they launched a devastating surprise attack on the U.S. naval base at Pearl Harbor, Hawaii. U.S. President Franklin D. Roosevelt immediately asked Congress for a declaration of war.

At first it seemed that the Axis powers might win. But gradually the tide turned. In Europe, Hitler failed in his attempt to conquer the Soviet Union. And on D Day, June 6, 1944, Allied forces under U.S. General Dwight Eisenhower invaded France, to begin the liberation of Europe. British and U.S. forces advanced on Germany from the west, while the Red Army closed in from the east. Hitler committed suicide on April 30, 1945,

The Holocaust

During World War II, Adolf Hitler carried out mass murder on a scale that the world had never seen. His victims were innocent civilians whose only "crime" was the fact that they were Jewish. This mass murder, known as the Holocaust, remains one of the darkest chapters in 20th-century history.

Hitler claimed that the Jews were responsible for Germany's defeat in the First World War, among other things. As his power grew,

Jews were increasingly persecuted. They were made second-class citizens and denied the right to vote, to own businesses, or to marry non-Jews. Beginning in 1939 they were forced to wear a yellow Star of David on their clothing.

Many Jews left Germany for Britain, France, or America. But when World War II began, it became hard to get out. Jews were forced into ghettos—walled, guarded areas within cities—and concentration camps, where many starved or were worked to death. This was only the beginning. In 1941, Hitler set up death squads whose job was to round up and kill Jews. The next year, the Nazis began to set up death camps. There, prisoners who didn't die of starvation were gassed to death by the hundreds.

Altogether, at least six million Jews were killed by the Nazis, along with more than one million gypsies and other people the Nazis considered undesirable. After the war, Nazi leaders were tried for these and other crimes by an international tribunal at Nuremberg, in Germany. Many of the top leaders were sentenced to death.

and Germany officially surrendered a week later.

In the Pacific, American forces advanced steadily until, in 1945, they were ready to invade Japan. Hoping to avoid the huge casualties that invasion would bring, the new U.S. president, Harry S. Truman, decided to use a new secret weapon—the atomic bomb. On August 6, an atomic bomb was dropped on the Japanese city of Hiroshima. A second bomb was dropped on Nagasaki three days later. The devastation was so great that Japan surrendered within a week. The end of the war thus marked the beginning of the atomic age.

U.N. headquarters in New York City. The organization was founded after World War II in the hope of preventing future wars.

NEW HOPES, NEW NATIONS

The postwar world began to take shape even before the Japanese surrender. On April 25, 1945, representatives of 50 nations met in San Francisco, California, to hammer out the framework of the United Nations. Their goal was a world organization that would provide a forum where international differences could be settled peacefully, while helping to fight hunger and disease worldwide.

One effect of the war was the growth of independence movements in areas of Africa and Asia that had been colonized by Britain, France, and other European powers. People who had fought against German and Japanese occupation during the war didn't want to return to colonial status. Sensing the inevitable, Britain pulled out of India in 1947. India and Pakistan became independent that same year. In other areas, colonial powers often tried to hang on. But by 1970 about 70 new nations, all former colonies, had gained independence.

Among the new nations was Israel, created by the United Nations in 1948 as a homeland for the Jews. Israel was carved from the for-

mer British territory of Palestine, and its founding was the realization of a dream long held by the Jewish people. But the Arabs of Palestine felt their land was stolen. Arab nations of the Middle East refused to recognize Israel and declared war on the newborn state. Israel survived that and several other wars, but conflict with Arabs would continue.

THE COLD WAR

There was a shadow on the hope for peace in the postwar world: the Cold War. That term refers to the tension between Western democracies, led by the United States, and Communist nations, led by the Soviet Union. Cold War rivalry caused postwar Germany to be divided into West

The leader of China in the postwar years was Mao Zedong, who led Communist forces to victory in a civil war.

Germany, where democracy flourished, and East Germany, where Communism ruled. Germany's former capital, Berlin, was likewise divided. In Eastern Europe, where Soviet troops had driven out the Germans, the Soviet Union set up Communist "satellite" regimes.

To block the spread of Communism in Europe, the United States and Canada joined Britain, France, and eight other Western European nations in a military alliance, the North Atlantic Treaty Organization (NATO). The United States also provided millions of dollars in aid, under the Marshall Plan, to help Europe rebuild. And the United States began to send military aid to nations elsewhere that were threatened by Communist movements. But in 1949, Communist forces led by Mao Zedong won a long-running civil war in China. That increased Western worries about the spread of Communism. As the Soviet Union began to develop its own nuclear weapons, fears of a devastating nuclear war mounted. An arms race began, with each side trying to develop more and more powerful weapons.

The Korean War was an outgrowth of Cold War tensions. In 1950, Communist North Korea invaded South Korea, which was allied with the United States. The United States led a U.N. action to defend the south. Chinese troops and Soviet aircraft aided the north. When the war ended in 1953, the invaders had been driven back. But the Korean peninsula remained divided.

In the 1960's the United States was drawn into war in Vietnam. This time the goal was to defend South Vietnam against Communist guerrillas and forces from North Vietnam. The effort failed; U.S. forces withdrew in 1973, and North Vietnam overran the south in 1975.

Other Cold War crises brought the two sides close to war. In 1956, Soviet troops crushed an anti-Communist rebellion in Hungary. In 1961, East Germans built a wall through the heart of Berlin, to prevent its citizens from escaping to the West. A year later the Soviet Union attempted to install missiles in Cuba, where Fidel Castro had established a Communist regime. In 1968, the Soviet Union crushed a reform movement in Czechoslovakia.

World War III didn't erupt over any of these crises because the United States and the Soviet Union realized that a full-scale nuclear war would wipe out both nations. Beginning in the 1960's, there were periods of détente, or easing of tensions. Several important arms-control agreements were signed. In 1972, U.S. President Richard Nixon visited China, a major step toward restoring relations.

THE COLLAPSE OF COMMUNISM

In the 1970's and 1980's, Communist governments faced growing pressures. The Communist economic system led to shortages and hardship, and people began to demand greater freedom.

In Poland, the labor union Solidarity gave voice to these demands in the early 1980's. At first, Solidarity was outlawed. But then the Communist world began to change. Soviet leader Mikhail Gorbachev began a series of reforms aimed at increasing economic and political freedom, and Eastern European nations followed suit. In Poland, the govern-

The Berlin Wall was a symbol of the Cold War. In 1989 it was torn down and became a symbol of the Cold War's end. And East and West Germany were reunited.

ment ended its ban of Solidarity and allowed free elections in 1989. Solidarity candidates won in a landslide, and Poland's Communist days were over. Communist regimes soon fell in other Eastern European countries. In Berlin, the hated wall dividing the city was torn down. And East and West Germany were reunited.

Meanwhile, the Soviet Union began to fall apart as its various republics declared their independence. By the end of 1991 the Communist system had collapsed, and the Soviet Union was no more. Russia began to build a democratic system, but it was crippled by economic and political problems. Only a handful of nations clung to Communism. One was China, where the government used military force to crush a pro-democracy student movement in 1989.

Nelson Mandela waged a lifelong fight against racial injustice in South Africa. He won, and in 1994 he became president of his country.

A NEW ERA

As Cold War tensions decreased, new problems appeared. The world faced growing threats from political terrorism and the spread of nuclear, chemical, and biological weapons. Religious fundamentalism became a force in world events. Fundamentalist Muslims in particular rejected the values of Western society, sometimes violently. In Iran, where fundamentalist Muslims took power in 1979, students took over the U.S. embassy in Tehran and held 52 Americans hostage for 444 days. In the Middle East, radical Muslim groups complicated efforts to bring peace between Israel and the Arabs. There was progress, though, as Egypt and other Arab nations gradually began to recognize and negotiate with Israel.

Regional conflicts continued to erupt. The United Nations played a growing role in settling these conflicts. In 1990, Iraq invaded its neighbor Kuwait and ignored U.N. demands to pull out. In January 1991, an international force led by the United States began military action in an effort to free Kuwait. After weeks of bombing and a four-day ground campaign, Kuwait was liberated in early March.

In Europe, conflict raged in Yugoslavia, which (like the Soviet Union) fell apart with the end of Communism. Ethnic rivalries were fanned into hatred by people such as Slobodan Milosevic, leader of Serbia and, later, all of what remained of Yugoslavia. The result was civil war and "ethnic cleansing"—in Bosnia and Herzegovina in the mid-1990's, and in Kosovo (a province of Yugoslavia) in 1999. In Kosovo, NATO resorted to bombing to stop Milosevic's forces from driving ethnic Albanians from their homes and killing them.

While some nations broke apart after Communism collapsed, others banded together for mutual benefit. For example, European nations had formed the European Economic Community in 1958. In the 1980's and 1990's, EEC members took steps that brought them closer to economic and political union.

Asia became the world's fastest growing region economically, with Japan leading the way. And from the 1970's on, democratic governments came to power in a growing number of countries worldwide. South Africa, where a minority white government had denied rights to blacks for years, finally shifted to majority rule when Nelson Mandela, who had devoted his life to the crusade for equal rights, was elected president in 1994. There and elsewhere, the growing strength of democracy was an encouraging sign for the 21st century.

AMERICA'S CENTURY

Immigrants in New York in the early 1900's. People from many lands shaped America in the 20th century.

Americans began the 20th century feeling good about themselves and their place in the world. In the 1800's, the United States had grown from a struggling little country on the eastern coast of North America to a sprawling nation that stretched to the Pacific. The country was prosperous. And war with Spain in 1898 had just given the United States its first overseas territories and, more important, a place as a world power. Many people believed that the 20th century would be America's century.

The bright outlook was clouded in September 1901, when President William McKinley was killed by an assassin. Theodore Roosevelt, his vice president, became president. With his energy, optimism, and forceful personality, Roosevelt turned out to be the ideal leader to take the country into the new century.

ROOSEVELT AND REFORM

Although many Americans were well off in the early 1900's, there were great gaps between rich and poor. Wealthy industrialists— "robber barons"—amassed huge fortunes, while workers lived in slums and worked long hours. There were few laws protecting workers or regulating businesses. Many politicians were corrupt, and people were beginning to clamor for reform. Reformers called "progressives" urged the government to take action against corrupt officials and harmful business practices. Journalists such as Upton Sinclair and Ida May Tarbell wrote books and articles exposing fraud and abuse in banking, meat packing, railroads, and oil.

In response, many states passed laws that improved working conditions. Child-labor laws were strengthened. Roosevelt supported many progressive measures. He worked especially hard to break the hold that trusts— groups of allied companies—had in railroads and other industries. Along with "trust-busting," he extended U.S. influence abroad. One of his most important acts was the creation of the Panama Canal, which allowed ocean ships to travel easily between the Atlantic and Pacific oceans. And he made

Energetic and popular, President Theodore Roosevelt set the nation's course in the century's early years.

conservation a national goal, bringing vast areas of land in the West under government protection.

A Republican, Roosevelt served two terms. His hand-picked successor, William Howard Taft, served one. Roosevelt actually ran against Taft in 1912, as a third-party candidate. Both were defeated by the Democratic candidate, Woodrow Wilson.

CHANGES IN THE TEENS

When Wilson took office in 1913, American society was in the middle of some big

Women campaigned for the right to vote with protests and marches. After years of struggle, they finally won the right to vote in 1920.

changes. Immigrants were pouring into the country from Italy, Russia, Poland, Greece, the Balkans, Mexico, and Japan. From 1900 to 1915, more than thirteen million immigrants arrived. At the same time, many African Americans were moving from the South to the North in search of jobs and freedom. Their desire for a better life was reflected by the founding, in 1909, of the National Association for the Advancement of Colored People (NAACP).

The temperance movement (against alcoholic beverages) was in full swing. And in 1919, this movement finally reached its goal. The 18th Amendment to the Constitution ushered in Prohibition, outlawing the manufacture, sale, or transportation of alcoholic beverages. Meanwhile, women were campaigning hard for the right to vote. They won that fight with passage of the 19th Amendment, which was ratified (approved by the states) in time for women to vote in the 1920 election.

By that time Woodrow Wilson was an invalid, having suffered a stroke. He had come to office with high ideals, but his presidency was overshadowed by World War I and his losing fight to bring the United States into the League of Nations. The end of his term seemed to mark the end of a period of idealism in America. Warren G. Harding, a Republican, followed him in office.

THE ROARING 20'S

In the 1920's, America turned its attention to making money and having fun. Calvin Coolidge, who followed Harding in the presidency, summed up a view held by many: "The business of America is business." The economy boomed, and stock prices went up and up. Many people saw stocks as a simple way to get rich quick. They borrowed money to buy shares without realizing that they could lose everything if stock prices fell.

The 1920's are known as the Roaring 20's and the Jazz Age for good reason. Young people adopted fashions, manners, and morals that shocked their parents. They listened to jazz music, kicked up their heels in dances like the Charleston, and tore around in automobiles. Meanwhile, Prohibition backfired. Thousands of "speakeasies"—illegal bars—sprang up. People drank smuggled "bootleg" whiskey or homemade "bathtub gin." Before Prohibition was repealed in 1933, gangsters and other criminals grew rich in the illegal alcohol trade.

By then the good times of the Roaring 20's had come to a close. In October 1929, prices on the New York Stock Exchange plummeted. Hard times were on the way.

When the stock market crashed in 1929, many Americans lost everything—including their cars.

THE DEPRESSION

Right after the stock market crash, many people predicted that America's economy would bounce back. Instead, the United States slipped into a major economic depression. Stock values continued to sink, wiping out the savings of many Americans. Those who had gone into debt to buy stock were ruined.

As the Depression deepened, businesses and factories shut down. Banks failed. Farm income fell. By 1932, about one out of every four people were out of work. With no income, many people were forced to leave their homes. Thousands took to the road in search of work, food, and shelter. In cities, people formed "bread lines" to get food donated by charities. Shantytowns sprang up around many cities. They were called "Hoovervilles," after President Herbert Hoover.

Hoover didn't believe that it was government's job to help the unemployed. He expected the economy to recover, and then people would be able to find jobs. But that didn't happen, and in the 1932 election Hoover lost to Franklin D. Roosevelt. A Democrat, Roosevelt promised a "New Deal" for Americans. Roosevelt set up a series of programs and agencies. They ranged from relief for the unemployed, to public works and conservation projects, to Social Security for retirees. Money spent on these programs helped "prime the pump" of the economy. But recovery didn't come quickly or easily.

Farmers were especially hard hit. In the Great Plains, severe drought added to their troubles. The southern Great Plains became known as the Dust Bowl. Huge dust storms there destroyed crops, harmed people and livestock, and ruined machinery. Several hundred thousand people packed up and left the region, most heading for California. They were called "Okies," although they came from Arkansas, Texas, and Missouri as well as Oklahoma. Most headed farther west to the land of myth and promise, California.

Roosevelt was re-elected in 1936, 1940, and 1944—the only president elected more than twice. By the time he won his third term, unemployment was down by more than a third. But eight million Americans were still out of work. The economy didn't fully recover until the United States entered World War II in December 1941.

THE HOME FRONT AND POSTWAR YEARS

Millions of American men and women were in uniform during World War II. Millions more supported the war effort at home. When men went to war, women filled jobs in factories, turning out thousands of tanks, planes, and other military needs. People recycled rubber and other materials needed by the army and got by with

Franklin D. Roosevelt led the nation through the Depression. He was the only president elected more than twice.

small rations of gasoline and other key items.

With the end of the war in 1945, Americans were eager for life to return to normal. And for many people, it did. By the 1950's, the economy was growing at a healthy rate. The United States was the richest country in the world. Dwight D. Eisenhower, a popular war hero with a homey manner, was elected president. But there were some worries that clouded the bright picture.

Many Americans felt threatened by the growing strength of the Soviet Union. They feared that Communists would undermine the United States. As a result, some people became determined to root out any sign of Communism in the country. In 1950, Senator Joseph R. McCarthy, a Republican from Wisconsin, caused a national uproar by claiming that he had a list of 205 known Communists in the State Department. He never produced evidence to back up his charges, but he became the leader of an "anti-Red" crusade. Through the early 1950's, in a series of Senate hearings, he charged high government officials and even army leaders with links to Communism. Careers and reputations were ruined with little or no evidence.

McCarthy's popularity waned after television brought the hearings into millions of homes, and Americans saw his savage tactics for themselves. The Senate eventually condemned him for his conduct.

THE 1960'S AND 1970'S

John F. Kennedy, a Democrat, was elected president in 1960. At 43, he was the youngest person ever to win the office. Kennedy's style and wit made him a popular president.

American women rolled up their sleeves and took factory jobs to help the nation meet World War II military needs.

Young people were especially inspired by his call: "Ask not what your country can do for you—ask what you can do for your country." But Kennedy's promise was cut short when he was assassinated on November 22, 1963, in Dallas, Texas. The nation was stunned.

Lyndon Johnson, Kennedy's vice president, carried on as president. Determined to fight problems such as racial discrimination and poverty, he built on programs begun by Kennedy and developed many of his own.

In the early 1960's, Americans were charmed by President John F. Kennedy and his wife, Jacqueline.

The Civil Rights Act of 1964 and other laws were the result. But Johnson's term was marred by the growing U.S. involvement in the Vietnam War. Young people especially began to protest the war. The antiwar movement became part of a youth "counterculture" that challenged many aspects of American life.

The war became an issue in the presidential election of 1968. Johnson didn't run. Robert Kennedy, John Kennedy's brother, was assassinated while running for the Democratic nomination. In the end, Richard Nixon, the Republican candidate, won.

Nixon is remembered for successes in foreign policy—opening ties with China, and reducing strain with the Soviet Union. But a scandal forced him from office. In 1972, men working for Nixon's re-election team broke into the offices the Democratic National Committee in the Watergate apartment complex in Washington, D.C. They were caught. Nixon tried to cover up his involvement and ordered the Federal Bureau of Investigation (FBI) not to investigate. But newspapers continued to dig for the truth, and the scandal continued to unfold. Congress opened hearings and began impeachment proceedings against Nixon. On August 9, 1974, he resigned to avoid almost certain impeachment.

The Watergate scandal left many Americans feeling disillusioned about government. Presidents Gerald Ford and Jimmy Carter, who followed Nixon, did their best to restore

The Civil Rights Movement

Most Americans enjoyed great prosperity in the 1950's. But most African Americans didn't share the good times. They faced segregation—laws and practices that kept them from getting the same education, jobs, housing, and services that whites enjoyed. The problems were most serious in the South. But African Americans dealt with discrimination everywhere.

During World War II, African Americans had challenged discrimination in the armed forces. In the 1950's, they began to demand equality in all aspects of life. The civil rights movement, as this push for equality became known, scored a major victory in 1954. The U.S. Supreme Court ruled in *Brown* v. *Board*

of Education of Topeka, Kansas, that communities couldn't send black children to separate schools.

Another victory came in 1955 in Montgomery, Alabama. Rosa Parks, a 42-year-old black seamstress who was also secretary of the state chapter of the NAACP, took a seat in the whites-only section of a bus. She was arrested, and that set off a boycott of the city bus system. Martin Luther King, Jr., a Baptist minister, led the boycott. It ended about a year later, when the Supreme Court ruled that bus segregation, like school segregation, was unconstitutional.

With boycotts, sit-ins, rallies, and other protests, African Americans worked to secure their right to vote and to end segregation in housing and other aspects of life. The movement reached its peak in the 1960's. The 1963 March on Washington brought more than 200,000 people to the capital for a huge rally. Martin Luther King's "I Have a Dream" speech inspired the nation.

Civil rights workers often faced violence, and some were killed. King himself was assassinated in 1968. But the movement succeeded in securing rights for African Americans and in making racial segregation against the law. It also inspired other minorities and women to seek greater equality. While minority groups still encounter discrimination, they have a better chance to share the American dream.

faith in the presidency. Both were known for their honesty and decency. But the country went through some rough times. Unemployment rose, and so did prices. Many people became nostalgic for the "good old days" of the 1950's. Ronald Reagan, who was elected president in 1980, appealed to them. A conservative Republican, Reagan promised to build up America's military strength while, at the same time, cutting government spending and reducing taxes.

Impeachment overshadowed the second term of Bill Clinton, the last U.S. president of the century.

NEW CHALLENGES

Reagan remained popular through his two terms, but some of his policies were controversial. He did cut taxes, and his administration spent huge sums on defense. But government spending grew, and the United States went deeply into debt. Reagan's vice president, George Bush, was elected president after him. He led the country through the short 1991 Persian Gulf War.

When that conflict ended, the United States found itself in a serious economic recession. Once again, Americans turned to new leaders to help. Bill Clinton, a Democrat, was elected president in 1992. He set out to trim the government's growing budget deficits. And he succeeded, thanks largely to an economic boom that began in the mid-1990's. Many Americans grew rich in the boom, especially by investing in stocks. Stock prices soared to unheard of levels.

But poverty and other social problems still plagued the United States. Clinton and Congress, which was controlled by Republicans, couldn't agree on how to solve them. Then, in 1998, Clinton became only the second president in U.S. history to be impeached. The impeachment grew out of a scandal over an improper relationship Clinton had with a young woman who had worked at the White House. The Republican-controlled House of Representatives charged the president with lying under oath about the relationship. In 1999, he was tried in the Senate and found not guilty. He would finish his term, but the scandal left a dark mark on his presidency.

Despite the scandals at home, Americans ended the 20th century the same way they had begun it—feeling good about themselves

The New York Stock Exchange. Soaring stock prices brought wealth to many people in the 1990's.

and their place in the world. The United States was the richest and most powerful nation in the world. And most Americans enjoyed a level of freedom and a way of life that were envied worldwide.

SCIENCE & TECHNOLOGY

Wonders such as this star, the brightest ever seen in the Milky Way, were discovered in the 20th century.

The 20th century saw more advances in science and technology than any other century in history. Thanks to those advances, many people today live longer, healthier, and more comfortable lives than people did a hundred years ago. They also know a lot more about their world.

HEALTH AND MEDICINE

In 1900, the average life span of a person in the United States was 47 years. Many women died in childbirth. Many children didn't survive to reach adulthood. Pneumonia and tuberculosis were among the leading causes of death, along with other deadly diseases—diphtheria, scarlet fever, typhoid fever, polio. In 1918–19, a worldwide flu epidemic killed nearly a million people.

Today the average American can expect to live to age 76. And many of the most-feared diseases of the past have been wiped out or controlled, thanks to modern drugs. Penicillin and other antibiotics, which fight typhoid, tuberculosis, and other bacterial infections, came into use in the 1940's. Doctors now have an arsenal of antibiotics on hand. And vac-cines can prevent many deadly diseases. Polio once killed and crippled thousands of people, mostly children, each year. Vaccines developed by Jonas Salk and Albert Sabin in the 1950's put a stop to that.

Blood transfusions saved many lives during World War II. Today "blood banks" keep a supply of blood on hand for use in emergencies and surgery. Surgery has made amazing steps forward, thanks to better anesthetics and surgical techniques. Open-heart surgery, hip replacements, and organ transplants are almost routine today. In 1900, these operations were unheard of.

Vaccines all but wiped out deadly diseases like polio, which once claimed thousands of lives each year.

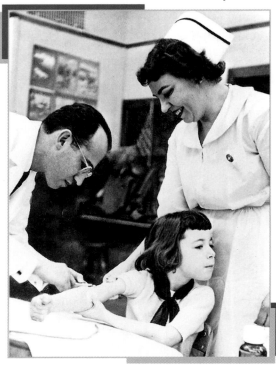

Doctors have new tools for diagnosing health problems. X rays were discovered in 1895, and early X-ray machines were in use in the 1920's. Today's machines are much more powerful, and other techniques, such as magnetic resonance imaging (MRI), allow doctors to see more details of the human body.

People also know a great deal more about staying healthy than they did in 1900. They understand the roles of nutrition, exercise, and sanitation in preventing disease. And research has shown the harmful effects of smoking and alcohol abuse.

Dolly, born in 1996, was the first clone ever to be created from an adult animal.

The war against disease isn't over, though. Some disease-causing bacteria have become resistant to antibiotics. And new health threats, such as AIDS, have appeared. Researchers are constantly working to find new drugs to overcome these health problems.

EARTH AND ITS LIFE

New tools and discoveries have helped scientists trace the history of Earth and its life. At the start of the century, most scientists thought the Earth was no more than 50 million years old. Then scientists learned to figure the age of rocks by measuring levels of uranium, which breaks down over millions of years. The Earth, it turned out, was more than 4.5 billion years old. Scientists also discovered that the Earth's continents are moving, and its crust is constantly changing. Research vessels probed the depths of the oceans, where molten rock bubbles up from deep trenches to form new crust.

New research also pushed back the date when scientists think life appeared on Earth. And scientists found that people evolved much earlier than had been thought. In Africa, Mary and Louis Leakey and other researchers found evidence that humanlike creatures lived 3.5 million years ago.

Some of the most amazing advances in life sciences were made in the lab. In 1953, biologists James Watson and Francis Crick worked out the structure of DNA (deoxyribonucleic acid). This molecule forms the genetic material inside living cells. It determines what traits are passed down from parents to their offspring. Understanding the structure of DNA led to the field of genetic engineering, in which genetic material is altered.

Today genetic engineering is being used to produce high-yielding, disease-resistant crops, to create medicines, and to fight hereditary diseases. Through other research, scientists in the 1990's found ways to clone animals—producing identical copies of individuals. Advances such as genetic engineering and cloning hold promise for the future, but they have also raised many ethical questions.

THE ATOM AND THE UNIVERSE

Many people consider Albert Einstein to be the greatest scientist of the century. Beginning in 1905, Einstein developed key theories

Scientist of the century: Many people think that Albert Einstein was the 20th century's greatest scientist.

about the relationship between matter and energy. His work laid the foundation for a fuller understanding of the universe and for the development of atomic energy. Another scientist, Marie Curie, won two Nobel Prizes for her work on radioactive substances. And Ernest Rutherford, Niels Bohr, and others explored the structure of atoms. Atoms were thought to be indivisible, the smallest particles of matter. But in 1934, Enrico Fermi successfully split uranium atoms.

As Einstein had predicted, splitting atoms released huge amounts of energy. The discovery led to the development of nuclear weapons and nuclear power. Like many 20th-century advances, nuclear energy holds both promise and danger. Nuclear weapons are a major threat to world peace. And even peaceful uses of nuclear energy are dangerous. The world was reminded of that in 1986, when an explosion at a Soviet nuclear power plant at Chernobyl spewed dangerous radiation over a wide area.

While some scientists were investigating the smallest particles of matter, others were exploring the vastness of space. Astronomers at the start of the century thought that the Milky Way, our home galaxy, was the entire universe. Then, in 1924, Edwin P. Hubble found a galaxy next door. Now we know that the Milky Way is just one of billions of galaxies in the universe.

Astronomers have also developed ways to measure the huge distances between stars. With powerful telescopes based on Earth and in space, they have found mysterious new objects—black holes, pulsars, neutron stars, even planets circling other stars.

Manned space flights made the biggest headlines of the century. But unmanned missions made some of the biggest discoveries.

Since 1970, unmanned craft have landed on Venus and Mars. Other probes have headed out for close views of Jupiter, Saturn, Uranus, Neptune, various comets and asteroids, and the sun.

A HIGH-TECH CENTURY

New technology has changed daily life in the 20th century. Many inventions such as electric power and light, the internal combustion engine, and the telephone were just curiosities in 1900. But people were quick to take up the new devices that promised a better, easier life. Change came with amazing speed. And technology itself drove the change forward, with each new development paving the way for the next.

The 20th century saw spectacular construction projects—skyscrapers, tunnels and bridges of daunting length, massive dams, engineering feats such as the Panama Canal. Machines reduced daily drudgery on farms and in factories, homes, and offices. Electrical lines brought cheap, reliable power to more and more homes and industries in the century's early years. That brought many changes, from lighting to electric motors that powered a new generation of home appliances. Electricity made possible an entire range of devices, from air conditioners to vacuum cleaners. The refrigerator/freezer replaced the old-fashioned icebox, and that (along with refrigerated rail cars and trucks) allowed the development of prepackaged frozen foods.

A reliable energy supply also gave a boost to manufacturing industries. In addition, new materials such as plastics and nylon and other synthetic fibers were developed and came into wide use. Manufacturers began to turn out a wide range of affordable consumer goods, from drip-dry clothing to disposable diapers.

But new technology advances also brought problems. Air and water pollution harmed plants and animals. Many scientists now believe that gases such as carbon dioxide, released by burning gasoline and other fossil fuels, are causing the world's climate to warm. If pollution isn't controlled, they warn, the world may pay a heavy price for the century's rapid development.

Protected by a space suit, an astronaut floats free in a "space walk." Space was the century's new frontier.

Into Space

The era of space exploration began when a tiny satellite named *Sputnik* was launched by the Soviet Union in 1957. *Sputnik's* launch also started a "space race" between the Soviet Union and the United States. A Soviet cosmonaut, Yuri Gagarin, was the first person to orbit the Earth, on April 12, 1961. About three weeks later, on May 5, U.S. astronaut Alan Shepard, Jr., became the first American in space. Soon after that, President John F. Kennedy set a new national goal for the United States: a manned mission to the moon by 1970.

That goal was achieved on July 20, 1969. Apollo 11 carried three astronauts to the moon. While Michael Collins waited in the main craft, the lunar lander *Eagle* carried Neil Armstrong and Edwin (Buzz) Aldrin to the surface. Armstrong stepped out first. His now-famous words were: "That's one small step for a man, one giant leap for mankind." The astronauts spent about two-and-a-half hours exploring the "magnificent desolation" of the moon. Then they returned to the command craft for the trip home.

In all, a dozen astronauts walked on the moon before the Apollo program ended in 1972. Manned missions since then have taken a different focus. The United States developed space shuttles, a fleet of reusable craft that take off and land like airplanes. The Soviet Union centered its space program on *Mir,* an orbiting space station. After the collapse of the Soviet Union in the early 1990's, the United States, Russia, and other countries began to work together to build a new space station—the *International Space Station*.

Since 1961, people have grown used to the idea of space travel. But tragic accidents have underscored how dangerous space travel is. The danger was brought home to Americans on January 28, 1986, when the space shuttle *Challenger* exploded just over a minute after takeoff. All seven crew members were killed. Among them was Christa McAuliffe, a teacher who had been chosen to be the first civilian in space. The *Challenger* crew and other space explorers will be remembered as some of the century's bravest pioneers.

The Model T was the first car that average people could afford. Millions were sold in the 1910's and 1920's.

copter and the jet airplane came into use, along with radar systems. As these and other developments found applications in the growing commercial aviation industry, air travel changed the way people thought about the world. Planes could reach the most isolated places, and as planes became faster and safer, travel times between continents shrank from days to hours. Today's fastest passenger jet, the supersonic Concorde, can fly faster than 1,300 miles (2,092 kilometers) an hour.

ON THE MOVE

At the start of the century, automobiles were luxury items—toys for the rich. That changed in 1913, when Henry Ford began assembly-line production of his Model T. More than fifteen million "Tin Lizzies" rolled off Ford assembly lines over the next fifteen years. Ford's assembly-line techniques changed automobile manufacturing forever and made cars something that average people could afford.

Developments in flight were even more dramatic. Until Orville and Wilbur Wright made the first successful powered flight in 1903, only gliders and balloons had carried people into the air. Improvements in airplane design then came so quickly that when World War I broke out in 1914, both German and Allied armies sent planes aloft to fight. The demands of aerial dogfights and bombing missions soon led to planes that were faster, more maneuverable, and more powerful. In 1927, Charles Lindbergh made the first solo transatlantic flight.

World War II brought more advances—the heli-

CAN WE TALK?

In 1901, Guglielmo Marconi, the inventor of radio transmission, successfully sent "wireless telegraph" signals across the Atlantic Ocean. A new era in communications was about to begin.

The development of the vacuum tube in the early 1900's gave that new era a jump start. The vacuum tube allowed electronic signals to be controlled and amplified, so it made long-distance telephone communication possible. With improved switching and other advances, telephone networks spread quickly, linking homes and businesses. The vacuum tube also brought radio—wireless signals that carried speech and music, instead of telegraphic beeps. Radio was first used to contact ships at sea. Radio telephone service spanned the Atlantic in 1924. Today this way of communicating has new importance, in the form of mobile cellular phones.

But radio's real potential was in broadcasting. Before the 1920's were out, there were 10 million radio sets in the United States, and inventors were developing the next electronic wonder—television. Television came into its own after

With wireless cellular phones, people can talk anytime, anywhere.

The early computer called **ENIAC** (*above*) filled a room but was far less powerful than today's laptops (*below*).

The Computer Revolution

The first entirely electronic programmable computer, the 1946 ENIAC (Electronic Numerical Integrator and Computer), covered 1,500 square feet (135 square meters) and had almost 18,000 vacuum tubes. Working at top speed, it added up 5,000 ten-digit numbers per second and used enough energy to dim the lights in an entire section of Philadelphia. Today's portable laptop computers are far more powerful—and they can run on batteries. Instead of bulky vacuum tubes, they have tiny silicon chips etched with thousands of miniaturized transistors.

As computers evolved from giants like ENIAC to desktop and portable units, they expanded their abilities to store and process information. And they changed the way products were designed and manufactured, the way people handled business and personal affairs, even the games people played. Since 1989 the Internet, the giant network of thousands of local computer networks, has linked millions of people and information resources around the world. And through electronic mail, computers provide a whole new way of communicating.

World War II—in 1949, there were one million TV sets in the United States; in 1959, more than 50 million. The medium evolved rapidly, with color broadcasting, satellite transmission (which relays telephone as well as broadcast signals worldwide), videotape recording, cable systems, and more.

Radio and television benefited from the 1948 invention of transistors, which quickly replaced bulky vacuum tubes. Another invention, the computer, benefited even more. Today the fields of telephone, broadcasting, and computer technology are merging. This is happening because the same digital code used for computer information can also carry telephone conversations and television shows, wirelessly or over fiberoptic cable. Telephone and cable television com-

The Internet, which links computer networks around the world, is the latest way to exchange information.

panies are rushing to create networks of fiberoptic cable with the "bandwidth" to deliver high-definition digital television (HDTV) signals while providing high-speed Internet access. In the near future these communications networks will link millions of people around the globe.

HOW WE LIVED

An American family of the 1950's. In most parts of the world, daily life changed greatly during the 20th century.

How did you start your day today? Chances are you woke up to the sound of a beeping electronic alarm or a clock radio. You jumped in the shower, dressed for school, and grabbed some breakfast—maybe orange juice and instant oatmeal, heated in the microwave oven. Then you headed out to catch the school bus.

Your day would have started very differently at the beginning of the 1890's. If you lived in the country, as many Americans did, you might have woken up to the sound of roosters crowing. You'd hop out of bed and scurry right outside, to visit the outhouse. On your way back, you'd stop at the woodpile to gather fuel for the kitchen stove. Instead of showering, you'd wash up with water pumped from a well and heated on the stove. You'd have time to do a few chores while your mother cooked breakfast. Then you'd start walking to school, several miles away.

In the early 1900's, it took a lot of hard work just to get through a day. Chopping wood, pumping water, and most other chores were done by hand. To get news and talk with neighbors, farmers walked, rode horseback, or drove a wagon to town once a week. Life was easier in the cities, but not for all people. The wealthy enjoyed indoor plumbing, for example, but thousands who lived in city tenements made do with a shared sink in a hallway or a common pump in a courtyard.

New technology has helped make daily living a lot easier since then. Life has changed in other ways, too. Schools, jobs, recreation, and even families aren't what they were in 1900.

AT HOME

At the start of the century, the average U.S. household had just under five members. America was filled with wide open spaces then. The U.S. population was about 76 million in 1900. More than half of those people lived in small towns with fewer than 3,000 people. Most of the rest lived in cities. There were very few suburbs. But that began to change as more people got cars. Cars allowed people to travel farther and faster, so they could live farther from their jobs.

Suburbs grew by leaps and bounds in the years after World War II. These were the years of the "baby boom," when the birth rate

The years after World War II saw Americans move in droves to new suburban developments like this one.

The Century in Style

In the 1900's and 1910's, women wore long skirts and always put on a hat and gloves to go out. Bowler hats were popular with men. Girls wore long dresses, like their mothers. Boys wore knickers.

In the 1920's young women called flappers (above) wore shocking styles—short skirts, rolled-down stockings, bobbed hair, and lots of makeup. But after the stock market crashed in 1929, hemlines plunged, too.

The zoot suit was what fashionable men wore at the jazz clubs of the early 1940's. It featured a long jacket with padded shoulders, and pants that ballooned out at the top and tapered to the ankles. Women favored slim, calf-length skirts and platform shoes.

Styles were more casual in the 1950's. Women wore full skirts that reached the calf or cropped pants called pedal pushers. Men went for plaid sports jackets and skinny ties. Blue jeans and sneakers were tops with kids.

The 1960's brought the miniskirt (right) and the hippie look—tie-dye T-shirts, bell-bottom pants, and long hair. In the 1970's, women adopted pants suits. Since then, fashion designers have offered up a mix of styles, many based on fashions of the past. Shoulder pads, mini-skirts, cropped pants, and platform shoes have all made brief returns to the style spotlight.

soared. People moved out of cities to new developments, where they could buy single-family homes and enough land for a lawn and garden. Supermarkets, shopping malls, fast-food restaurants, and other conveniences sprang up in these fast-growing towns. New highways were built to link cities and suburbs. People went almost everywhere by car.

Today there are more than 272 million people in the United States. Families are smaller, with an average of about three members. Suburbs have continued to grow. Almost 75 percent of Americans now live in metropolitan areas. The single-family home is still the dream of many Americans. More than 64 percent of Americans own their homes. Most people still travel by car, too. But over-development is a problem in many areas—wide open spaces are harder to find. Air pollution, much of it

caused by cars, is also a major problem. As the population continues to grow, these problems will have to be solved.

AT WORK AND SCHOOL

If you lived at the beginning of the century, you might be working right now instead of reading this book. Most children worked back then. On farms, they were expected to help out with planting, harvesting, and many other chores. In cities, kids in less well-to-do families often had steady jobs by the time they were in their teens. Many worked in factories, making about $3 a week. Even young children had to work to help the family make ends meet. But children from middle-class and well-to-do families could afford to stay in school.

There were public schools in all the states by 1900. Many children, especially those who had

At the start of the century, many children worked long hours in factories. Child-labor laws ended that practice.

scope. Homes were lighted by candles and oil lamps in the country, or by gaslight in the cities. In the 1920's and 1930's, with electricity in a growing number of homes, evenings at home might be spent reading or listening to the radio. Besides music and news, people tuned in to hear radio soap operas and dramas such as *The Shadow*.

By the 1960's, television had replaced radio as the major home entertainment. It also became the way most people heard the news. And the speed with which news could be transmitted by satellite and broadcast on television made viewers witnesses to history. Television reports helped shape public opinion about everything from the civil rights movement to the Vietnam War. And politicians increasingly relied on television to reach voters.

People had less leisure time at the start of the century. On most farms, a day off was rare. In cities, many people worked six days a week. But families sometimes got away for a day. They might ride the trolley line out to the country to enjoy a picnic or a visit to one of the new amusement parks that were being built near cities. A night out was a rare event for most families. In small towns, social activities centered around the community. A church supper or a harvest dance was an event that people looked forward to for months.

to work, received only an elementary-school education. Their lessons focused on reading, spelling, penmanship, arithmetic, and other basics. Many lessons were taught by rote, with students memorizing the material. But in the first half the 20th century, schools began to teach a wider range of subjects. And lessons emphasized the idea that kids learn by doing, not just by memorizing facts.

By mid-century, with child-labor laws limiting the age at which children could work, more kids were finishing high school. Today eight out of every ten American students complete high school, and seven out of ten go on to college. Women and minorities have more opportunities in education and careers than they did in 1900. That came about thanks to the civil rights and women's movements that flourished in mid-century.

By the 1930's, cars had made getting around easier, and there was more to do. A family might pile into the car and head to the local movie theater. Grownups went to clubs where they danced to jazz and swing tunes played by live bands and by jukeboxes.

HAVING FUN

The family of the early 1900's might have spent evenings playing musical instruments and looking at pictures through a stereo-

Kids and adults today have more time for fun—and they've found lots of ways to enjoy it.

Today styles have changed, but movies, music, and amusement parks are still high on the list of popular entertainment. People have a lot more free time, and they spend it pursuing a wide range of hobbies, sports, and outdoor activities such as hiking and cycling.

Milestones in Sports

Since 1900, professional sports have grown into a multi-billion-dollar industry. At the same time, amateurs have proved their mettle at the modern Olympic Games, which were started in 1896. And average people have taken up sports of all kinds, from tennis to windsurfing. Here are some highlights of the century.

1903 In baseball's first World series, the Boston Red Sox defeated the Pittsburgh Pirates.

1912 Jim Thorpe, one of the greatest all-around athletes ever, won two gold medals at the Stockholm Olympics. Thorpe, who was mostly Native American, had to give up the medals when it was learned that he had played minor-league baseball and thus was not an amateur. He went on to outstanding careers in baseball and football.

1919 In baseball's biggest scandal, the Chicago White Sox conspired to fix the World Series.

1923 The New York Yankees won the World Series for the first time, and stars like slugger Babe Ruth became heroes.

1932 Mildred "Babe" Didrikson Zaharias won two gold medals and one silver in track and field at the Los Angeles Olympics. Considered one of the greatest athletes of all time, she went on to win 31 Ladies Professional Golf Association titles.

1936 African-American track star Jesse Owens won four gold medals at the Berlin Olympics. The victories were a slap in the face for racist German dictator Adolf Hitler.

1939 Little League Baseball began.

1947 Jackie Robinson joined the Brooklyn Dodgers, becoming the first African-American player in modern major-league baseball.

1951 The Rochester Royals defeated the New York Knickerbockers to win the first National Basketball Association championship.

1956 Don Larson of the New York Yankees became the first person to pitch a perfect game (no batters reach first base) in the World Series.

1957 Fullback Jim Brown joined the National Football League's Cleveland Browns. In nine seasons he would rush for 12,312 yards, averaging a record-setting 5.22 yards per carry.

1962 Golfer Jack Nicklaus won the U.S. Open and would go on to win 17 other major championships, including six Masters.

1964 Muhammad Ali won the boxing heavyweight championship. He was stripped of the title in 1967 for refusing, on religious grounds, to be drafted into the army. But his rights were upheld by the U.S. Supreme Court. Ali would hold the heavyweight title four times.

1967 In the first Super Bowl, the Green Bay Packers of the National Football League defeated the Kansas City Chiefs of the American Football League.

1972 U.S. swimmer Mark Spitz won a record seven gold medals at the Munich Olympics.

1976 Fourteen-year-old Nadia Comenici of Romania became the first person to score a perfect 10 in Olympic gymnastics competition.

1978 Hockey star Wayne Gretzky joined the Edmonton Oilers. He would go on to set or tie 61 National Hockey League records.

1984 Michael Jordan joined basketball's Chicago Bulls. He would lead the Bulls to six National Basketball Association championships.

1994 Martina Navratilova retired from tennis after winning 167 singles titles—more than any other tennis player in history.

1966 Track star Carl Lewis won his tenth Olympic medal, nine of them gold.

1998 St. Louis Cardinal Mark McGwire hit a record-smashing 70 home runs in regular-season play. Sammy Sosa of the Chicago Cubs hit 66.

1999 The New York Yankees captured their 25th World Series, a record no other team even approaches.

ARTS & ENTERTAINMENT

The century's artists broke with tradition. This is *Sleeping Girl* by Pablo Picasso, a leader of the cubist movement.

In almost every field, the arts of the 20th century challenged traditions and overturned the past. In painting, architecture, and music, new styles first shocked people and then were accepted. And new technology—recordings, movies, and radio and television—gave rise to new forms of popular entertainment.

ART AND DESIGN

A series of movements swept the art world in the 20th century. In the century's early years, "modern" art developed several schools. Pablo Picasso and others advanced cubism, in which objects were portrayed as geometric shapes. Salvador Dali was among the surrealists, whose paintings seemed to capture disturbing dreams. Abstract artists turned away from portraying recognizable objects. Their works focused on the interplay of shapes, colors, and textures.

By the 1940's, the center of the art world had shifted from Europe to America.

Especially in New York City, new movements arose. Willem de Kooning, Jackson Pollack, and others painted huge canvases in the abstract expressionist style. In the 1970's pop art, which used images from popular culture, was the new thing. New movements in art didn't keep people from appreciating the past, however. Major museums in New York and other cities staged "blockbuster" exhibitions that drew thousands of people. Among the most popular were those that featured works by French impressionist painters and treasures from ancient Egypt.

Louis Sullivan, an architect at the turn of the century, decreed that "form follows function." That idea—that the shape of a building or object should reflect its use—guided many 20th-century architects and designers. Clean lines, geometric shapes, and materials such as concrete, steel, and glass were hallmarks of modern architecture. Frank Lloyd Wright, Mies van der Rohe, and Le Corbusier led in developing the new style.

REACHING FOR THE SKY

Medieval Europe had castles and cathedrals. And the 20th century had skyscrapers. These soaring towers now mark the skylines of all the world's major cities, dwarfing the buildings of earlier eras.

Skyscrapers such as the Sears Tower, in Chicago, dwarfed earlier buildings.

Skyscrapers were made possible by the invention of structural steel framing in the late 1800's. Until then, tall buildings were supported by walls of stone or brick. The taller the building, the thicker the walls had to be—and that set limits on building height. The first "high-rise" building with a steel frame was the Home Insurance Building, constructed in Chicago in 1885. It was 15 stories tall, remarkable for its day.

Engineers soon found ways to improve steel frames and build ever taller buildings. The Singer Building, at 612 feet (187 meters), set a record when it was built in New York City in 1908. But height records were set and broken time and again throughout the century. At 1,250 feet (381 meters), New York City's Empire State Building held

Swing was the thing in the 1930's and the 1940's. People of all ages danced to the "big band" sound.

the record from 1931 to 1972. It was eclipsed by the World Trade Center (also New York), at 1,368 feet (417 meters), and the Sears Tower (Chicago), at 1,454 feet (443 meters). In 1997 the Petronas Towers, in Kuala Lumpur, Malaysia, snatched the title with a height of 1,476 feet (450 meters).

POPULAR MUSIC

In the 1890's, people who wanted to hear music could go to a concert or stay home and play a musical instrument. The phonograph had been invented but wasn't in wide use. The early 1900's brought the wind-up phonograph and improved recordings. They were followed by electrical phonographs and vinyl records. And those developments were, in turn, replaced by tape and compact disc players, with multichannel sound.

Rock 'n' Roll

When rock 'n' roll burst on the music scene in the 1950's, parents dismissed it as noise—as in "turn off that noise!" But teenagers loved this music, with its hard-driving beat and snarling guitar sounds. Rock 'n' roll became the music of youth. And this new music's early stars started trends that would influence generations to come.

Elvis Presley was the "king" of rock 'n' roll. He probably did more to popularize rock than anyone. Chuck Berry drew on blues traditions but sang about things teens understood—cars and young love. Buddy Holly's songs showed that rock was more than beat. Little Richard's shrieks set new standards of outrageousness.

Rock 'n' roll was American music—until the mid-1960's. Then the Beatles, the Rolling Stones, and other British bands came to the fore. Musicians began to blend rock with folk, soul, and other musical styles. Disco, punk,

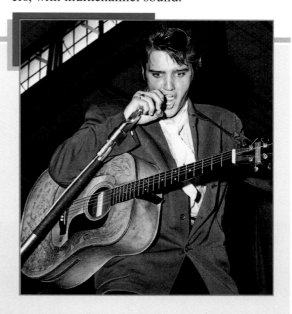

"heavy metal," alternative—rock developed in many different ways. And by the 1990's it was clear that rock was no longer the music of youth. It was everyone's music. The rock beat turned up in everything from commercial jingles to movie soundtracks.

Along with radio, the recording industry helped create pop music superstars such as Bing Crosby and Frank Sinatra. New styles of music also spread this way. Jazz developed out of African-American traditions and took the country by storm during the 1920's. That trend gave rise to the swing and "big bands" of the 1930's and 1940's. Jazz worked its way into serious musical compositions, too. For example, in the 1920's and 1930's, George Gershwin used jazz phrasing in symphonic works such as *Rhapsody in Blue* and the opera *Porgy and Bess.* Jazz, blues, country, and pop traditions blended to create rock 'n' roll in the 1950's. More recently, a new musical style—rap—has followed the path from the African-American community to the mainstream.

ON STAGE

Several outstanding American playwrights made their mark on the theater in the 20th century. Eugene O'Neill, Tennessee Williams, and Arthur Miller earned worldwide acclaim for their plays. The century also saw the heyday of American musicals. These stage shows were basically plays filled with music and dance. Most were light-hearted romances, but often there were serious themes underlying the

Clark Gable and Vivien Leigh starred in *Gone With the Wind,* one of the century's great films.

fun. Shows that were hits on New York City's Broadway went on the road or were restaged at smaller theaters around the country. Among the most famous were *Show Boat* (1927), *Pal Joey* (1940), *Oklahoma!* (1943) *Carousel* (1945), *South Pacific* (1949), *Guys and Dolls* (1950), *West Side Story* (1957), and *Fiddler on the Roof* (1964). In recent years shows from Britain, such as *Les Misérables* and *Cats,* have dominated musical theater.

AT THE MOVIES

At the start of the 20th century, motion pictures were a new invention. Films lasted just a few minutes, had no sound, and little story. But this new form of entertainment developed quickly. By the 1920's Hollywood film studios were turning out feature films starring the likes of Charlie Chaplin, Mary Pickford, and Rudolph Valentino. The first "talkie," *The Jazz Singer,* was made in 1927. Sound gave rise to a new flood of films and a new generation of stars. Color arrived in the late 1930's.

The big American film studios, based in Hollywood, California, churned out movies in large numbers to keep the public happy. They concentrated on certain types of films—Westerns, musicals, detective stories, romantic comedies. Among the great films from the studio era were *Gone With the Wind* (1939), with Clark Gable and Vivien Leigh; *The Wizard of Oz* (1939), with Judy Garland; *Casablanca* (1942), with Humphrey Bogart and Ingrid Bergman; and *High Noon* (1952), with Gary Cooper. The director Alfred Hitchcock became famous for chilling suspense films. Walt Disney pioneered in animated cartoons and feature films.

In the second half of the century, television began to compete with movies. Filmmakers turned to stereo sound, widescreens, and elaborate special effects to

American musical theater was at its peak in mid-century. Shows such as *Oklahoma!* were huge hits.

keep people coming to theaters. Special effects were a major draw for some of the most successful films of the era, including *Jaws* (1975), *Star Wars* (1977) and its sequels, *E.T.* (1982), *Jurassic Park* (1993), and *Titanic* (1997).

ON TELEVISION

By the 1950's, television had become something few U.S. homes could do without. Americans gathered in front of TV sets to watch comedians such as Sid Caesar and Milton Berle, quiz and game shows, Westerns, children's programs like the *Howdy Doody Show*, and situation comedies such as *The Honeymooners* and *I Love Lucy*. Until the late

Seinfeld was one of several shows that set new standards for television comedy in the 1990's.

1950's, they could also see original plays that were produced live in TV studios. That decade came to be known as the Golden Age of television.

Color broadcasts increased television's appeal in the 1960's. As television grew up and tastes changed, programs changed, too. In the 1950's sitcoms such as *Father Knows Best* presented "ideal" families—Mom, Dad, three clean-cut kids. Later sitcoms presented families of all kinds. And shows like *M*A*S*H* and *Seinfeld* set new standards for TV comedy. Many shows didn't reach their level, however.

Critics deplored what seemed to be growing levels of violence and crudity in television programming. But viewers kept tuning in.

During the 1980's and 1990's, television brought the growth of cable and satellite services. Because these services could deliver many more channels than broadcast networks, programs became more specialized. Viewers interested in cooking, home repair, and other specific fields now had access to programming tailored just for them.

TOP TOYS & GREAT GAMES

Kids played marbles and hopscotch at the start of the century. Toy soldiers and board games were popular. Dolls were fragile and fancy, with heads made of bisque (unglazed porcelain). By mid-century, model cars, trains, and planes were in big demand. With new materials like plastic, toy makers turned out a great variety of dolls and other toys. And every decade had its favorites—the toys kids just had to have.

● **1900's.** The Teddy Bear was named for President Theodore Roosevelt. In 1902, when Roosevelt was on a hunting trip, some of his friends captured a bear, tied it to a tree, and invited Roosevelt to take aim at it. He refused to shoot the helpless animal, and newspapers reported the story. That inspired a New York shopkeeper to create some stuffed toy bears and call

them Teddy Bears. Teddy Bears are as popular today as they were at the start of the century.

● **1910's.** The hot toys of the century's teen years were building sets. Kids spent hours building bridges and other metal structures with Erector Sets, frontier cabins and forts with Lincoln Logs, and all kinds of strange contraptions with wooden Tinker Toys.

● **1920's.** Two adorably soft and cuddly dolls, Raggedy Ann and Raggedy Andy, charmed kids in the 1920's. They were created by John and Myrtle Gruelle. John Gruelle, an illustrator, also cre-

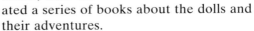

ated a series of books about the dolls and their adventures.

● **1930's.** The yo-yo was a huge fad in the 1930's. This toy originated hundreds of years ago in the Philippines, where it was first used as a weapon. Then Filipino children began to play with small versions. In the late 1920's, Pedro Flores, a Filipino living in the United States, started to manufacture the toys. He sold the rights to Donald F. Duncan, and the yo-yo fad took off.

times—now she has business suits, and her motto is "Be Anything." New Barbies with new "looks" have appeared every year. As a result, she's still the world's best-selling doll.

● **1940's.** In the 1940's, many kids dreamed of building a detailed model railroad—with trains, tracks, buildings, and landscape features all built to scale. Model railroading was a hugely popular hobby from the late 1930's through the early 1950's. Many adults and children still enjoy this hobby.

● **1970's.** What pet is cleaner, better behaved, and less expensive than a dog, a cat, or even a fish? A rock. As silly as it seems, "pet rocks" were a big item in the 1970's. People forked over money to buy a rock in a box—all in the spirit of fun.

● **1980's.** Video fever swept the country in the 1980's. Early video games such as Pac Man and Donkey Kong were simple by today's standards. But when they first appeared, people couldn't get enough of them. Video games didn't nudge traditional toys aside, though. Cuddly, chubby Cabbage Patch Kids came on the scene in 1983 and quickly became a craze. Each doll came with its own name, birth certificate, and "adoption papers."

● **1950's.** Who would ever have thought that a simple plastic hoop would turn into one of the biggest toy fads ever? The Hula Hoop was introduced in 1958. Kids figured out the game right away: Rotate your hips to keep the hoop spinning as long as possible. More than 100 million hoops were sold before the fad ended.

● **1960's.** Barbie was the must-have doll of the 1960's. Back then, Barbie was a glamorous fashion model, with lots of pretty dresses. But she, too, changed with the

● **1990's.** Beanie Babies and Pokémon were among the 20th century's final fads. Beanie Babies were introduced in 1994, and before long people were waiting in line to get them. Hundreds of millions of these squishy little bean-bag animals have been sold. Kids love them, and adults and kids collect them. Pokémon (the name is short for "pocket monster") started in Japan in 1996, with a video game. Pokémon games and cards then swept the United States.

THE WORLD IN 1999

Refugees from Kosovo, a part of Yugoslavia, cry as they wait to cross the Albanian border in a cart pulled by a tractor. They were among nearly a million ethnic Albanians who were driven from their homeland by Yugoslav forces in 1999. Most of Kosovo's people are ethnic Albanians, and their demands for independence caused Yugoslav President Slobodan Milosevic to launch a brutal crackdown against them. Yugoslav forces swept through the province, looting and burning homes and attacking Kosovars. In March 1999, after Milosevic refused to stop the campaign, the North Atlantic Treaty Organization (NATO) began air strikes against Yugoslavia. The air strikes finally forced Milosevic to end the crackdown in June. But by that time, hundreds of thousands of Kosovars were homeless, and an unknown number had been killed.

JANUARY

6 At the opening of the 106th Congress, Dennis Hastert of Illinois was sworn in as Speaker of the U.S. House of Representatives. He succeeded Newt Gingrich of Georgia, who had resigned after fellow Republicans blamed him for their party's unexpected loss of five House seats in the November 1998 elections. Initially, Robert L. Livingston of Louisiana had been chosen by the Republican majority to succeed Gingrich. But Livingston announced his resignation from Congress after admitting to inappropriate relationships.

7 The first presidential impeachment trial since 1868 opened in the U.S. Senate. The House of Representatives presented two charges, or articles of impeachment, against President Bill Clinton. One accused him of perjury, for lying under oath about his improper relationship with a young woman who had worked at the White House. The second accused him of obstructing justice, for encouraging others to lie about it.

25 A strong earthquake measuring 6.0 on the Richter scale of ground motion struck the coffee-growing heartland of western Colombia, in South America. The cities of Pereira and Armenia and most of the surrounding towns were devastated, leaving thousands of people homeless. More than 1,100 people were killed, and 4,700 were injured.

For more than 100 years, people have reported seeing huge, hairy ape-men roaming the forests of the Pacific Northwest. These creatures have been named Bigfoot and Sasquatch. Ever since this photo was taken in 1967, many people thought it proved that the legend of Bigfoot was really true. But in January 1999, a Canadian Bigfoot enthusiast announced that he had performed a series of computer enhancements on the photo, and saw a bell-shaped object swinging at the creature's waist. He concluded that the object was a fastener for a costume. Bigfoot was nothing more than a man in an ape suit!

Hundreds of people crowd around a huge euro symbol in Frankfurt, Germany.

The Euro Arrives!

On January 1, eleven European nations adopted the euro as a common currency, marking a big step on the road toward European unity. The nations—Austria, Belgium, Finland, France, Germany, Ireland, Italy, Luxembourg, the Netherlands, Portugal, and Spain—continued to have their own money. Euro prices were posted alongside prices in francs, marks, liras, and other national currencies.

In fact, there was no euro cash—no euro coins and notes. The new currency was being used in credit-card sales, electronic bank transfers, stock exchange transactions, and other "cashless" business. This situation is scheduled to change on January 1, 2002, when euro coins and notes are introduced. Once that happens, national currencies will be gradually withdrawn.

The nations that adopted the euro are all members of the European Union (EU). Other EU members—Great Britain, Denmark, Sweden, and Greece—may adopt the euro at some later time. Sharing a currency means that the nations agree to follow the same policies with regard to interest rates, national debt, and other economic factors. These policies will be set by the new European Central Bank, instead of by the central banks of the individual countries.

The participating countries expect that the single currency will make banking, travel, and trade much easier for them. And the Europeans hope that the euro will become more important than any of the individual European currencies presently in use. That, in time, could make the euro almost as important as the U.S. dollar.

Government changes in January: In **Turkey,** Bulent Ecevit became prime minister. He succeeded Mesut Yilmaz, who had been prime minister since July 1997.

FEBRUARY

6 More than 300 people drowned after the ship *Harta Rimba* sank in stormy seas in Indonesia, about 500 miles (800 kilometers) north of the capital, Jakarta. The ship, which was carrying about 325 people plus a cargo of timber, sank after it was hit by huge waves and its pumps failed.

12 The U.S. Senate acquitted President Bill Clinton of the two impeachment charges against him. The perjury charge was rejected by a vote of 55–45, with 10 Republicans joining all 45 Democrats in voting to acquit. The vote on the obstuction of justice charge was 50–50, with five Republicans joining the Democrats. (A two-thirds vote—that is, a miniumum of 67 votes—was needed to convict the president.) In the trial, the 100 U.S. senators made up the jury. William Rehnquist, the Chief Justice of the Supreme Court, served as the judge. Thirteen members of the House of Representatives acted as prosecutors, presenting the case against the president. And a team of lawyers presented Clinton's defense.

23 In Austria, a wall of snow more than 15 feet (4.5 meters) deep and 300 feet (90 meters) wide swept down on the Alpine ski resort of Galtür. The avalanche flattened buildings and killed at least sixteen people. It was the deadliest in a series of avalanches that claimed about 70 lives in the Alps during the winter of 1998–99.

In Seattle, Washington, a man scans a newspaper announcing President Bill Clinton's acquittal on February 12, following a five-week-long impeachment trial in the U.S. Senate.

The *New Carissa* Runs Aground

On February 4, the cargo ship *New Carissa* was caught in rough weather and ran aground just north of the entrance to Coos Bay on the Oregon coast. A few days later, the ship's fuel tanks cracked and began to leak thick, black oil. If the *New Carissa* stayed stuck in the sand, as much as 400,000 gallons (1,500,00 liters) of oil might leak into the water and onto beaches.

This part of the Oregon coast is home to rich ocean life and several rare bird species. Many of the people make their living by fishing, crabbing, and raising oysters. A large oil spill would be disaster for people and wildlife alike. To prevent such a disaster, the U.S. Coast Guard decided to break open the *New Carissa's* fuel tanks with explosives and burn off the oil. On February 11, this plan was put into effect with a fiery explosion that shot flames hundreds of feet into the night sky. The ship split in two, and its bow section drifted free of the sand (see photo above).

The fire burned up much of the oil, but thousands of gallons still remained in the bow section. This oil was too thick to burn easily. The Coast Guard then decided to tow the bow portion 300 miles (480 kilometers) out to sea, and sink it with the oil on board. The U.S. Navy blasted it with explosives, artillery shells—even a torpedo from a submarine. On March 11, the *New Carissa* finally went down, taking its oil with it.

Although the Oregon coast was spared the worst of the spill, a huge mop-up job remained. The oil spill fouled miles of beaches and killed hundreds of birds. The cleanup cost more than $16 million.

Government changes in February: In **Jordan**, Prince Abdullah became King Abdullah II, following the death of his father, King Hussein. Hussein, the longest-reigning ruler in the Middle East, had ascended to the throne in 1953.... In national elections in **Nigeria**, Olusegun Obasanjo was elected president—the nation's first elected president in fifteen years. Obasanjo succeeded Abdulsalam Abubakar, who had led the country since June 1998.

MARCH

12 Three Eastern European countries—the Czech Republic, Hungary, and Poland—joined the North Atlantic Treaty Organization (NATO), bringing membership in the military alliance to nineteen. NATO was created after World War II by the United States, Canada, and Western European countries to oppose the spread of Communism in Europe. At the same time, the Soviet Union and the Communist countries of Eastern Europe formed the Warsaw Pact, which was disbanded in 1991. The three new NATO members were the first former Soviet allies and Warsaw Pact countries to join NATO.

15 An Amtrak train traveling from Chicago, Illinois, to New Orleans, Louisiana, collided with a truck at a railroad crossing in Bourbonnais, Illinois. Eleven passengers were killed, and more than 100 were injured in the accident.

21 Bertrand Piccard of Switzerland and Brian Jones of Britain became the first people ever to fly around the world nonstop in a hot-air balloon. The two balloonists touched down in southern Egypt, completing a voyage of about 29,055 miles (46,760 kilometers). The voyage began on March 1 in Switzerland and lasted 19 days, 21 hours, and 55 minutes. Their balloon, the *Breitling Orbiter 3,* stood 180 feet (55 meters) tall when fully inflated. During their record-making flight, the men rode in an enclosed cabin that measured only 16½ by 10 feet (5 by 3 meters).

During a ceremony at the National Air and Space Museum in Washington, D.C., Bertrand Piccard (*left*) and Brian Jones are presented with a trophy—and a $1 million prize—for becoming the first hot-air balloonists to circle the globe nonstop. The prize money was offered by the Anheuser-Busch Companies.

The Melissa Virus

In late March, more than 100,000 computers around the world were infected with the Melissa virus—the fastest-spreading computer virus anyone had ever seen.

A computer virus is a small program attached illegally to existing programs and data files. The virus can reproduce itself and spread from one program to another. Hundreds of viruses are created and released onto the Internet every month. Most are harmless, but some are designed to be very destructive. They can erase files and do other damage when they infect computers.

Melissa reached a recipient as an attachment to a fake e-mail message. If the computer user opened the e-mail attachment, Melissa took over. Without the user's knowledge, the virus fired off the same e-mail message to the first 50 people listed in the computer's electronic address book. Each of those messages had a copy of the virus attached. And each of those 50 copies sent out 50 more copies as soon as it was opened.

Fortunately, Melissa didn't seriously damage individual computers. But because the virus spread so rapidly, it overwhelmed computer networks. Some companies had to shut down their networks, interfering with people's ability to work.

Investigators traced the Melissa virus to David Smith, a New Jersey software programmer, and he was arrested on April 2.

24 NATO began air strikes on military targets in Yugoslavia after Yugoslav President Slobodan Milosevic rejected an international peace plan for the province of Kosovo. Rebels in this province had demanded independence, and Milosevic brutally cracked down on the rebellion. (In the following weeks, NATO's bombing campaign spread to non-military targets, and efforts were made to aid nearly one million refugees driven out of Kosovo by Yugoslav forces.)

Government changes in March: In **Bahrain,** Hamad bin Isa al-Khalifa became head of state upon the death of his father, Isa bin Salman al-Khalifa, who had been the island-nation's ruler since 1961. . . .In national elections in **El Salvador,** Francisco Flores Pérez was elected president. He succeeded Armando Calderón Sol, who had been president since 1994. . . .In **Paraguay,** Luis González Macchi became president following the forced resignation of Raúl Cubas Grau. Cubas had been president for less than a year.

APRIL

1 Canada created a new territory—Nunavut. Carved from the eastern part of the Northwest Territories, Nunavut covers about 770,000 square miles (2,000,000 square kilometers), making it bigger than Alaska and California combined. Its capital is Iqaluit. The Inuit, the native people who make up about 85 percent of Nunavut's population, govern the territory. "Nunavut" is an Inuit word meaning "our land."

23 In Washington, D.C., the North Atlantic Treaty Organization (NATO) marked its 50th anniversary. NATO is the military alliance of seventeen European nations, Canada, and the United States. In addition to the leaders of NATO and its member nations, leaders of more than twenty other nations attended the ceremonies.

Scientists reported the discovery of fossils in Ethiopia of a previously unknown species that may be the connecting link between apelike ancestors and modern humans. The new species, which lived about 2.5 million years ago, was named *Australopithecus garhi*. It stood less than 5 feet (1.5 meters) tall and had long apelike arms. But it had long legs and walked upright like a human. It had an apelike face, a small brain, and surprisingly large teeth.

Leave town, Joe Camel! Bye-bye, Marlboro Man! On April 23, the era of billboard ads to sell tobacco came to an end as part of a 1998 agreement between tobacco producers and state governments. Some 3,000 of the oversized tobacco signs were replaced with antismoking ads.

Deadly School Shootings in Littleton

On April 20 in Littleton, Colorado, two high school seniors, Eric Harris and Dylan Klebold, went on a rampage at Columbine High School, firing shotguns and semiautomatic weapons and setting off explosives. They killed twelve students and one teacher. Then, as a police SWAT team closed in, they killed themselves. Twenty-four other people were wounded in the attack.

Police searched the school for hours after the attack. They found about 50 homemade bombs, including a propane tank bomb. A diary found at the home of Harris showed that the attack had been carefully planned. But police could only guess at the motives. At school, Harris, who was 18, and Klebold, 17, had been outsiders. They were fascinated with violent video games and with Nazi Germany. Harris's diary indicated that they chose April 20 for the attack because it was the birthday of Adolf Hitler, the leader of Nazi Germany. Harris and Klebold sought out as their targets athletes, racial minorities, and students who had made fun of them.

There were warning signs long before the attack. The boys had boasted about guns and bombs and threatened other students. Police even found gun and bomb parts in plain view in one boy's home. But no one had taken these signs seriously. This had been true in other school shootings, too. There have been a series of shooting incidents in U.S. schools in recent years, and in each one people ignored warning signs.

In the aftermath of the Littleton shootings, people across the nation searched for ways to prevent such violence from occurring again. Particular attention was paid to the easy access to guns that contributed to the shootings and to the widespread violence in video games, movies, and other forms of entertainment.

Government changes in April: In national elections in **Algeria** in which six of the seven candidates withdrew from the race, Abdelaziz Bouteflika was elected president. He succeeded Liamine Zeroual, who had been president since 1994. . . . In **Comoros,** Tadjidine Ben Said Massonde, president since late 1998, was ousted in a military coup. Azaly Assoumani, who led the coup, became president. . . .In **Niger,** President Ibrahim Bare Mainassara, who took office in a coup in 1996, was assassinated. A military junta led by Daouda Malam Wanke assumed power.

MAY

2   In Yugoslavia, President Slobodan Milosevic released three U.S. soldiers who had been captured by Yugoslav forces on March 31. The soldiers were the only Americans captured during the North Atlantic Treaty Organization's (NATO's) bombing of Yugoslavia, which came about because of the Kosovo conflict. The release came after American civil-rights leader Jesse Jackson went to Yugoslavia with a delegation of religious leaders and appealed for the prisoners' freedom.

3   A series of about 75 violent tornadoes ripped through Kansas, Nebraska, Oklahoma, Texas, and South Dakota, killing 49 people and injuring more than 700. The biggest of the tornadoes was 1 mile (1.6 kilometers) wide and 10 miles (16 kilometers) high. It packed winds of more than 300 miles (483 kilometers) per hour—and lasted four hours. Hardest hit were parts of Oklahoma and Kansas.

7   During the Kosovo conflict, a NATO plane mistakenly bombed the Chinese embassy in Belgrade, Yugoslavia. The incident sparked a wave of protests throughout China against the NATO bombing campaign in Yugoslavia.

12 Robert E. Rubin announced his resignation as U.S. Secretary of the Treasury. President Bill Clinton nominated Lawrence H. Summers to succeed Rubin. (On July 1, the U.S. Senate confirmed the nomination.)

A motorist tries to outrun a tornado that was racing toward Oklahoma City on May 3. The violent storms completely destroyed several small towns in Oklahoma and Kansas.

Chinese soldiers march past a missile on display at Beijing's Military Museum. The United States suspects that China stole nuclear secrets from U.S. weapons labs.

Did China Steal Nuclear Secrets?

On May 25, a committee of the U.S. House of Representatives released a report concluding that China had stolen secret information about nuclear-weapons design from U.S. weapons labs. The series of thefts, part of an intelligence operation that spanned twenty years, was believed to have helped the Chinese develop advanced missile warheads and, perhaps, more-deadly bombs.

U.S. officials became suspicious in 1995, when they discovered that China had miniaturized nuclear warheads that are very much like U.S. weapons. They began an investigation that led them to the Los Alamos National Laboratory in New Mexico. Suspicion fell on Wen Ho Lee, a Los Alamos computer scientist. He was fired in March for breaches of security. Meanwhile, Los Alamos and other U.S. weapons laboratories tightened security.

Government changes in May: In **Germany,** Johannes Rau was chosen president. He succeeded Roman Herzog, who had been president since 1994. . . .Following a military coup in **Guinea-Bissau,** Malan Bacai Sanha became president. He succeeded João Bernardo Vieira, who had been president since 1980. . . .In national elections in **Israel,** Ehud Barak was elected prime minister. He succeeded Benjamin Netanyahu, who had been prime minister since 1996. . . .In **Italy,** Carlo Azeglio Ciampi was chosen president. He succeeded Oscar Luigi Scalfaro, who had been president since 1992. . . .In national elections in **Panama,** Mireya Moscoso de Grubar became the first woman to be elected president. She succeeded Ernesto Pérez Balladares, who had been president since 1994.

JUNE

6 The U.S. space shuttle *Discovery* completed a ten-day mission. Its primary objective was to carry supplies to the new *International Space Station* being built in orbit around Earth. The crew consisted of Daniel Barry, Rick Husband, Tamara Jernigan, Ellen Ochoa, Kent Rominger, Julie Payette of Canada, and Valery Tokarev of Russia. Jernigan and Barry conducted an eight-hour spacewalk—the second-longest ever made—during which they attached cranes and other equipment to the space station's exterior.

9 Yugoslavia signed a peace plan with the North Atlantic Treaty Organization (NATO), agreeing to withdraw its troops from the province of Kosovo and allowing hundreds of thousands of refugees to return home. On June 10, following the start of the Yugoslav troop withdrawal, NATO ended its 78-day bombing campaign against Yugoslavia. NATO also authorized its forces to begin a peacekeeping mission in Kosovo.

Government changes in June: In **Latvia,** Vaira Vike-Freiberga was chosen president. She succeeded Guntis Ulmanis, who had been president since 1993. . . .In national elections in **South Africa,** Thabo Mbeki was elected president. He succeeded Nelson Mandela, who became president in 1994, when South Africa's first fully democratic elections ended that country's white minority rule.

Millennium Trails: The Lewis and Clark National Historic Trail (*below*) and the Freedom Trail (*opposite*).

National Millennium Trails

On June 26, the White House announced a list of sixteen National Millennium Trails. The trails—some already in existence, some yet to be completed—honor America's history and culture.

- **Unicoi Turnpike.** This ancient trail carried the Cherokee people and, later, European settlers over the Great Smoky Mountains into Tennessee.

- **Cascadia Marine Trail.** This water trail in the Pacific Northwest follows inlets and coves that originally marked a Native American water trade system.

- **Juan Bautista de Anza National Historic Trail.** This trail marks the route of Spanish exploration and settlement in California, from the Mexican border to San Francisco.

- **Freedom Trail.** This trail connects fifteen historic sites in old Boston associated with the American Revolution.

- **Lewis and Clark National Historic Trail.** This trail honors the Lewis and Clark expedition of 1804–06, from St. Louis, Missouri, to the mouth of the Columbia River in Oregon.

- **Underground Railroad.** This trail follows secret routes used by slaves escaping from the South in the days before the Civil War.

- **Civil War Discovery Trail.** This trail connects the battlefields, military routes, and other historical sites of the Civil War.

- **The International Express.** The No. 7 subway line, connecting immigrant neighborhoods in Queens, New York, represents all the people who have come to America from other lands.

- **Iditarod National Historic Trail.** Famous for its annual dogsled race, this Alaskan trail runs from Anchorage to Nome. It was used by goldminers in 1899, and by a dogsled team that rushed anti-diphtheria serum to Nome.

- **Appalachian National Scenic Trail.** Stretching from Georgia to Maine, this narrow footpath traverses the Appalachian Mountains.

- **Great Western Trail.** This trail follows the spine of the Rocky Mountains from the Canadian to the Mexican border.

- **North Country National Scenic Trail.** This trail links some 160 state parks, forests, and wildlife areas from New York to North Dakota.

- **Hatfield-McCoy Trail System.** This trail follows abandoned logging roads and old railbeds once used to transport coal from the coalfields of West Virginia and surrounding states.

- **East Coast Greenway.** Sweeping the Atlantic Coast from Maine to Florida, this trail will connect scores of currently disconnected local trails in fifteen states.

- **Mississippi River Trail.** This bicycling route will follow the nation's mightiest river from Minneapolis, Minnesota, to New Orleans, Louisiana.

- **American Discovery Trail.** When completed, this trail will cross the nation "from sea to shining sea," using country roads, forest lanes, railtrails, canal towpaths, and other routes.

JULY

27 The U.S. space shuttle *Columbia* completed a five-day mission. It was the first shuttle mission ever commanded by a woman, Eileen Collins. The highlight of the mission was the release of the Chandra X-ray Observatory, a telescope designed to detect X rays emitted by exploding stars, black holes, and other cosmic objects. In addition to Collins, the crew consisted of Jeffrey Ashby, Catherine Coleman, Steven Hawley, and Michel Tognini of France.

28 The U.N. Security Council approved the Pacific island-nations of Kiribati, Nauru, and Tonga as members of the United Nations, raising membership in the world body to 188 countries.

Government changes in July: Following national elections in **Belgium,** Guy Verhofstadt became premier. He succeeded Jean-Luc Dehaene, who had been premier since 1992. . . .In **Morocco,** King Hassan II, who had ruled the nation since 1961, died. He was succeeded by his eldest son, who became King Mohammed VI. . . .In **Papua New Guinea,** Mekere Morauta became prime minister. He succeeded William Skate, who had been prime minister since 1997.

Pennies are disappearing—according to a survey released in July. It seems that pennies don't buy very much these days, and people don't like to carry them around in purses and pockets. So they're stashing them away in piggy banks and other places. As a result, many stores and banks don't have enough pennies to conduct business, even though the U.S. Mint has made more than 312 billion pennies since 1970!

John F. Kennedy, Jr.: A Sad Good-bye

On the evening of July 16, a small plane took off from an airport in New Jersey. The pilot was 38-year-old John F. Kennedy, Jr. He, his wife, Carolyn Bessette Kennedy, and his wife's sister, Lauren Bessette, were on their way to Martha's Vineyard, a Massachusetts resort island. But the plane crashed into the Atlantic Ocean several miles from Martha's Vineyard. There were no survivors.

John F. Kennedy, Jr., was born in Washington, D.C. And Americans had followed his life ever since he was a child. He was just three days shy of his third birthday when his father, President John F. Kennedy, was assassinated in 1963. The sight of John, Jr., saluting his father's coffin captured the hearts of people around the world, and helped make ordinary Americans feel that he was part of their lives.

As John grew up, the assassination of his uncle Senator Robert Kennedy, and the deaths of his mother, Jacqueline Kennedy Onassis, and many other Kennedys also affected him greatly. But he made his life a decent and purposeful one. He became a lawyer, a crusader who helped impoverished children and the mentally disabled. He was also a founder and publisher of *George,* a political magazine.

"We dared to think," said his uncle Senator Ted Kennedy, "that this John Kennedy would live to comb gray hair, with his beloved Carolyn by his side. But like his father, he had every gift but the length of years."

AUGUST

2 Two crowded passenger trains crashed into each other at Gaisal in eastern India, about 250 miles (400 kilometers) north of Calcutta. Nearly 300 people were killed, and at least 500 others were injured. It was the ninth major railroad disaster in India in four years.

5 The U.S. Senate confirmed Richard C. Holbrooke as U.S. Ambassador to the United Nations. Holbrooke had been nominated by President Bill Clinton in June 1998 to succeed Bill Richardson, who became Secretary of Energy.

30 In East Timor, the eastern part of the island of Timor, people voted overwhelmingly for independence from Indonesia, which had controlled the area since 1975. (After the vote, anti-independence militia groups began a campaign of violence that tore East Timor apart for almost three weeks. Hundreds of people were killed. On September 20, an international force sent by the United Nations to restore peace began to arrive in East Timor.)

On August 11, millions of people across parts of Europe and Asia poured into the streets to see the last total solar eclipse of the 20th century. A solar eclipse occurs when the moon moves between Earth and the sun. The moon blocks the sun's light, casting a shadow that races from west to east across a narrow strip of Earth's surface. During the few minutes of total darkness, the sun's outer atmosphere can be seen as a beautiful white halo around the black disk of the moon.

A Powerful Earthquake Devastates Turkey

On August 17, a powerful earthquake rocked northwestern Turkey. The quake, which measured 7.4 on the Richter scale of ground motion, was one of the most powerful to occur this century anywhere in the world.

The earthquake struck at 3 A.M., hitting Turkey's most heavily populated region. It was centered on the industrial city of Izmit, with damage extending as far as Istanbul, Turkey's biggest city, 55 miles (89 kilometers) farther west. Since most people were sleeping, thousands were trapped, killed, or injured when their apartment buildings collapsed. More than 17,000 people were killed, another 30,000 were missing, and hundreds of thousands were left homeless. The high number of seriously injured people overwhelmed hospitals and emergency medical centers. Power was knocked out over wide areas, and food and water were in short supply.

Thousands of rescue workers from around the world poured into Turkey to help, and dozens of nations sent food, medicines, blankets, tents, and other desperately needed items. Survivors of the earthquake focused much of their criticism on builders and building inspectors. They charged that many of the deaths and injuries had occurred because builders used cheap materials and poor building techniques, and because inspectors didn't enforce construction codes.

Government changes in August: In **Guyana,** Bharrat Jagdeo became president. He succeeded Janet Jagan, who had been president since 1997. . . .In **Singapore,** S. R. Nathan was named president. He succeeded Ong Teng Cheong, who had been president since 1993.

SEPTEMBER

2 A team of U.S. scientists reported that they had used genetic engineering techniques to create a strain of "smart" mice. The scientists boosted mouse memory by adding a single gene to a fertilized mouse egg. This gene instructs brain cells to produce a protein that's involved in forming memories. Mice with the extra gene produced more of the protein—so they learned faster and remembered more. Since humans form memories in much the same way mice do, using basically the same protein, the scientists believe that their research might be used to improve human memory.

5 Israeli Prime Minister Ehud Barak and Palestinian Arab leader Yasir Arafat signed an agreement that offered the possibility of peace within a year. The Palestinians live in territory occupied by Israel and have long demanded a country of their own. The agreement called for Israel to turn over more land to the Palestinians. Also, formal negotiations for a permanent peace agreement were to begin, with the agreement scheduled to be completed by September 2000.

15–16 Hurricane Floyd roared up the East Coast of the United States, causing at least 23 deaths and millions of dollars in damage. As the huge storm approached the southeastern coast, more than 2.6 million people were urged or ordered to evacuate their homes—the largest evacuation in U.S. history. Particularly hard hit was North Carolina, where heavy rain caused widespread flooding that left hundreds of people stranded, many in trees or on rooftops.

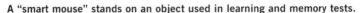

A "smart mouse" stands on an object used in learning and memory tests.

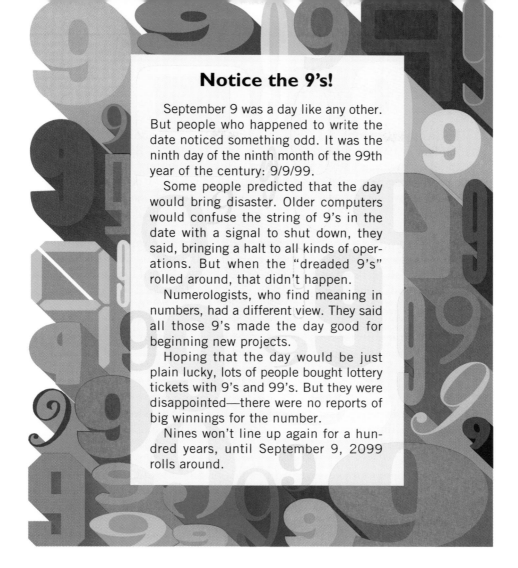

Notice the 9's!

September 9 was a day like any other. But people who happened to write the date noticed something odd. It was the ninth day of the ninth month of the 99th year of the century: 9/9/99.

Some people predicted that the day would bring disaster. Older computers would confuse the string of 9's in the date with a signal to shut down, they said, bringing a halt to all kinds of operations. But when the "dreaded 9's" rolled around, that didn't happen.

Numerologists, who find meaning in numbers, had a different view. They said all those 9's made the day good for beginning new projects.

Hoping that the day would be just plain lucky, lots of people bought lottery tickets with 9's and 99's. But they were disappointed—there were no reports of big winnings for the number.

Nines won't line up again for a hundred years, until September 9, 2099 rolls around.

21 A severe earthquake struck Taiwan, a populous island off the coast of mainland China. The earthquake measured 7.6 on the Richter scale of ground motion. More than 2,000 people died, thousands were injured, and some 100,000 were left homeless.

30 In Japan, an accident at a nuclear fuel processing plant in Tokai-mura, a city 90 miles (145 kilometers) northeast of Tokyo, exposed at least 55 people to deadly radiation. It was Japan's worst nuclear accident ever. The incident occurred when workers accidentally dumped a large amount of uranium into a container meant for a much smaller amount, setting off an uncontrolled nuclear chain reaction. Although some radiation escaped from the plant, emergency workers were able to stop the chain reaction before it produced an explosion.

Government changes in September: In **Malaysia,** Salahuddin Abdul Aziz Shah became king. He succeeded Jaafar bin Abdul Rahman, who had been on the throne since 1994.

OCTOBER

1 The People's Republic of China celebrated the 50th anniversary of its founding in 1949 by Communist leader Mao Zedong. In Beijing, China's capital, a huge parade featured a vast display of military hardware and floats showcasing the nation's achievements. Much of the celebration glorified the government, with posters and slogans praising past and present leaders.

12 The world's population officially reached 6 billion, according to United Nations estimates. Several factors were behind this population explosion, including high birth rates in many parts of the world and longer lives. If current trends continue, the world's population is expected to reach 7 billion in 2013.

21 Scientists announced the discovery of fossilized dinosaur jawbones that might be the oldest dinosaur fossils ever found. The fossilized remains were from two plant-eating dinosaurs, and they were found in Madagascar, an island-nation off the east coast of Africa. The dinosaurs lived about 230 million years ago. They were about the size of kangaroos, with small heads and long necks. Scientists believe they were early ancestors of giant plant-eating dinosaurs such as *Apatosaurus,* which lived some 100 million years later.

29 In India, a devastating cyclone with winds of 160 miles (260 kilometers) per hour struck the eastern state of Orissa. Almost 10,000 people were killed by the storm and by the extensive flooding that followed. About 10 million people were left homeless.

Chinese Communist Party leaders at a banquet celebrating the country's 50th birthday.

The 1999 Nobel Prizes

Chemistry: Ahmed H. Zewail of the United States, for finding a way to see how atoms in a molecule move during a chemical reaction. Zewail's technique, using ultra-short flashes of laser light, has helped scientists understand and predict important reactions.

Economics: Robert A. Mundell, a Canadian-born American, for his work on economic policy and exchange rates. Mundell showed how the flow of money across national borders can affect the way countries manage their economies. His theories influenced the development of the euro, Europe's new currency.

Literature: Günter Grass of Germany, for his novels and other writings. With novels such as *The Tin Drum* and *Cat and Mouse,* Grass helped revive German literature after World War II. The Nobel committee called his works "frolicsome black fables" that "portray the forgotten face of history."

Peace: Doctors Without Borders (Médecins Sans Frontières), for its humanitarian work worldwide, without regard to national boundaries or political considerations. Founded in France in 1971, the group provides aid to victims of war, famine, and natural disasters. The Nobel committee praised the group for calling attention to human-rights abuses and other causes of suffering. (Above: A Doctors Without Borders nurse plays with a child at a feeding center in Angola.)

Physics: Gerardus 't Hooft and Martinus Veltman of the Netherlands, for their work in particle physics theory. They devised ways to calculate how subatomic particles behave. Their method predicted the existence of several particles that have since been discovered.

Physiology or Medicine: Günter Blobel, a German-born American, for his discoveries about proteins produced by the body's cells. Blobel found that the proteins carry signals—like zip codes—that direct them to the correct places within the cell.

Government changes in October: In **Albania,** Ilir Meta was named premier. He succeeded Pandeli Majko, who had been premier for one year. . . .In national elections in **Argentina,** Fernando de la Rúa was elected president. He succeeded Carlos Saúl Menem, who had been president since 1989. . . .In **Indonesia,** Abdurrahman Wahid was chosen president. He succeeded B. J. Habibie, who had been president since 1998. . . .In **Pakistan,** Nawaz Sharif, who had been prime minister since 1997, was overthrown in a military coup. General Pervez Musharraf assumed control of the nation.

NOVEMBER

9   Berlin, Germany, celebrated the tenth anniversary of the fall of the Berlin Wall, which once divided the city. In 1961, East Germany, then a Communist state, built the wall through the heart of Berlin, to keep citizens from escaping to West Germany, a democratic republic. In 1989, change swept through the Communist world, and East Germans demanded more freedom. The government opened the borders, and East and West Berliners greeted the step with huge celebrations. They climbed on top of the Berlin Wall and even picked up sledgehammers and began to knock the Wall down. In the months that followed, East Germany and West Germany were reunited.

12   The second major earthquake of the year struck northwestern Turkey. The earthquake, which measured 7.2 on the Richter scale of ground motion, killed about 400 people and injured 3,000 others.

16–18   Skywatchers in many parts of the world enjoyed the Leonid meteor shower, a dazzling light show created as debris from Comet Tempel-Tuttle entered Earth's atmosphere and burned up. At the peak of the shower, more than 1,800 meteors an hour flashed through the night sky. (Meteors are commonly called shooting stars.)

23   In northeast China, near the port of Yantai, a ferry caught fire and capsized in rough, icy seas. About 300 people were killed.

Government changes in November: In **Croatia,** President Franjo Tudjman, who founded the nation following the breakup of Yugoslavia in 1991, was gravely

Skywatchers in Spain saw the Leonid meteor shower at its peak, with 1,800 meteors an hour flashing through the night sky. The intensity of the shower varies from year to year, depending on how close to Earth Comet Tempel-Tuttle is when it passes. Scientists say the comet won't be so close to Earth for a long time: Another great meteor show isn't expected for 100 years.

Giant pandas Yang-Yang and Lun-Lun play in their new home at Zoo Atlanta.

Panda Patrol

Panda-mania swept Atlanta, Georgia, after two giant pandas arrived at Zoo Atlanta on November 6. Lun-Lun, a female panda, and Yang-Yang, a male, were both two years old. They came from China and were on loan from the Chinese government for ten years. On November 20, the public got their first glimpse of the furry twosome, in a new habitat that Zoo Atlanta had built especially for them.

Giant pandas are among the rarest animals in the world and are in great danger of dying out, or becoming extinct. Only about 1,000 pandas remain on Earth, and more than 120 of those live in captivity. In the wild, they are found only in bamboo forests in China.

In addition to the Atlanta pandas, three other pandas live in the United States, at the San Diego Zoo in California. They are an adult male, Shi-Shi; an adult female, Bai Yun; and their baby girl, who was born on August 21 and became the first panda born in the United States ever to survive past four days. Following Chinese tradition, she wasn't named until the end of November, when she was 100 days old. She was given the name Hua Mei, which means both "splendid beauty" and "China USA."

One of the most beloved pandas in captivity was Hsing-Hsing, a gift to the United States from China in 1972. He lived at the National Zoo in Washington, D.C., until November 28, when he died at age 28, a very old age for pandas.

ill. The powers of the presidency were transferred to Vlatko Pavletic. (Tudjman died in December.). . .Following national elections in **New Zealand,** Helen Clark became prime minister. She succeeded Jenny Shipley, who had been prime minister since 1997. . . . In national elections in **Niger,** Namadou Tandja was elected president. He succeeded Daouda Malam Wanke, the leader of the military junta that had seized power in April. . . .In national elections in **Uruguay,** Jorge Batlle was elected president. He succeeded Julio Sanguinetti, who had been president since 1995.

DECEMBER

2   Britain ended direct rule over Northern Ireland, granting the province self-government. While Northern Ireland remains a part of the United Kingdom, authority over local affairs was transferred to a new provincial government in which Catholics and Protestants share power. It was hoped that the new era in Northern Ireland would bring an end to the "Troubles"—30 years of violence between Catholics and Protestants that killed more than 3,300 people.

15   In northern Venezuela, flooding and massive mudslides caused the nation's worst natural disaster of the century. At least 25,000 people were killed, and 150,000 were left homeless.

20   The Portuguese colony of Macao, on the coast of southern China, once again came under the rule of China. The Portuguese had ruled Macao since 1557. In 1987, they agreed that Macao would be returned to China in 1999; China said that Macao would be a self-governing unit, able to keep its own economic system and way of life.

27   The space shuttle *Discovery* completed an eight-day mission. The purpose was to make repairs to the Earth-orbiting Hubble Space Telescope. The crew consisted of Curtis Brown, Michael Foale, John Grunsfeld, Scott Kelly, Steven Smith, Jean-François Clervoy of France, and Claude Nicollier of Switzerland.

Welcome 2000! At midnight on December 31, people everywhere celebrated as the world entered not only a new year and a new century but also a new millennium. In London, England, the world's largest Ferris wheel—called the London Eye—was built as part of Great Britain's millennium celebration. Located on the Thames River, it will carry up to 15,000 passengers a day in glass-sided compartments.

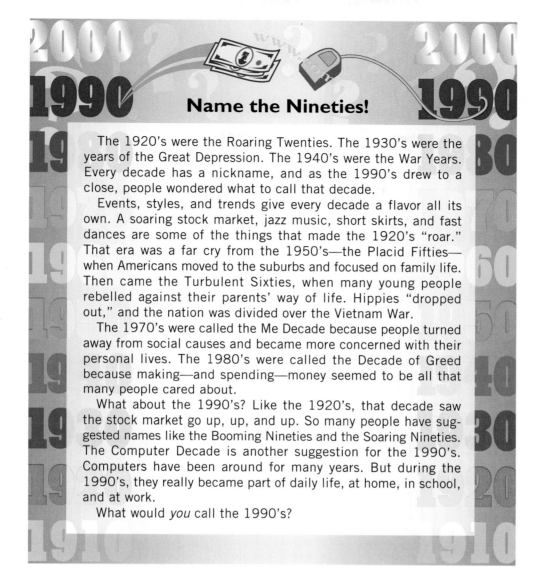

Name the Nineties!

The 1920's were the Roaring Twenties. The 1930's were the years of the Great Depression. The 1940's were the War Years. Every decade has a nickname, and as the 1990's drew to a close, people wondered what to call that decade.

Events, styles, and trends give every decade a flavor all its own. A soaring stock market, jazz music, short skirts, and fast dances are some of the things that made the 1920's "roar." That era was a far cry from the 1950's—the Placid Fifties—when Americans moved to the suburbs and focused on family life. Then came the Turbulent Sixties, when many young people rebelled against their parents' way of life. Hippies "dropped out," and the nation was divided over the Vietnam War.

The 1970's were called the Me Decade because people turned away from social causes and became more concerned with their personal lives. The 1980's were called the Decade of Greed because making—and spending—money seemed to be all that many people cared about.

What about the 1990's? Like the 1920's, that decade saw the stock market go up, up, and up. So many people have suggested names like the Booming Nineties and the Soaring Nineties. The Computer Decade is another suggestion for the 1990's. Computers have been around for many years. But during the 1990's, they really became part of daily life, at home, in school, and at work.

What would *you* call the 1990's?

31 In a surprise announcement, Boris Yeltsin resigned as president of Russia. He named Vladimir Putin, the country's prime minister, as acting president until elections are held in early 2000. Yeltsin had been president since 1991 and was credited with replacing Russia's Communist system with a democratic framework. Yeltsin said he was stepping down because "Russia must enter the new millennium with new politicians, with new faces, with new intelligent, strong, energetic people."

The United States turned over control of the Panama Canal to the nation of Panama. The canal, which connects the Atlantic and Pacific oceans, is one of the most important waterways in the world. In 1903, when Panama became independent, its leaders agreed to let the United States build and run the canal. In 1977, the United States agreed to turn the canal over to Panama in stages, with Panama assuming full responsibility for the canal by the end of 1999. The United States also gave up the Canal Zone, a strip of territory it controlled along the canal.

President Clinton walks back into the White House after making a statement about his acquittal in the Senate impeachment trial. "This can be and this must be a time of reconciliation and renewal for America," he said.

PRESIDENT BILL CLINTON IS ACQUITTED

In a historic vote on February 12, 1999, the U.S. Senate acquitted President Bill Clinton on charges of perjury (lying under oath) and obstruction of justice. The second presidential impeachment trial in U.S. history thus came to an end. It had divided the country along political lines, and most Americans breathed a sigh of relief when it was over. But it was still unclear what long-term effects the impeachment of Clinton would have on his legacy, on U.S. politics, and on the office of the presidency.

INVESTIGATION AND SCANDAL

The impeachment grew out of a complicated chain of events. It began with an investigation of the president and Hillary Clinton, his wife. The investigation was headed by Kenneth W. Starr, a judge and prosecutor, who was named an independent counsel in 1994. The job of an independent counsel is to make sure that high-level government officials, such as the president, aren't above the law. Independent counsels are appointed by a federal court, not by the president or other officials, so that they can investigate fairly and thoroughly.

Starr was appointed to examine the Clintons' business dealings during the 1980's, when Bill Clinton was governor of Arkansas. Specifically, he probed their involvement in Whitewater, an Arkansas real-estate venture. He later expanded his inquiry to pursue various rumors, but those leads turned up no evidence of wrongdoing on the part of the president or the First Lady.

Meanwhile, however, Clinton was also facing a civil lawsuit filed by an Arkansas woman, Paula Jones. Jones claimed he had made an unwelcome advance to her when he was governor. The suit was thrown out of court in 1998, but not before Clinton gave a deposition—a formal statement, made under oath. In his deposition he denied not only Jones's charge but also rumors of an affair with Monica Lewinsky, a 21-year-old former White House intern. Lewinsky also denied the rumors under oath. But she said otherwise to friends. And one of those friends, Linda Tripp, taped her conversations and gave the tapes to Starr. (Tripp later faced charges for illegally taping the conversations.)

Tapes in hand, Starr launched an investigation to learn if Clinton had committed perjury and urged Lewinsky to do the same. Although Clinton finally acknowledged his relationship with Lewinsky in August 1998, he denied that he had lied under oath or encouraged anyone else to do so. Starr didn't accept that. In his report, delivered to Congress in September 1998, he said Congress should consider removing the president from office.

IMPEACHMENT

The report set off a storm of controversy. Democrats said that Starr, a conservative Republican, had set out to trap the president. Clinton's opponents, especially conservative Republicans, called on him to resign. With Republicans holding a majority in both the Senate and the House of Representatives, Con-

gress began the lengthy process of impeachment—the act of bringing formal charges against the president.

The process began with an inquiry by the House Judiciary Committee. The committee's job was to decide if there was evidence of wrongdoing and, if so, whether the wrongs were grounds for impeachment. (The Constitution permits impeachment for "Treason, Bribery, or other high Crimes and Misdemeanors.") The committee voted along party lines to send articles of impeachment, or formal charges, to the full House for a vote.

On December 19, 1998, after bitter debate, the House passed two articles. Those articles charged Clinton with perjury before Starr's grand jury and obstructing justice by encouraging others to lie. This vote, too, split along party lines. Republicans

Key players in the events that led to the Senate trial: Kenneth Starr, the independent counsel (*left*); Monica Lewinsky, the former White House intern (*bottom left*); and Linda Tripp, who secretly recorded her telephone conversations with Lewinsky (*bottom right*).

nearly all voted for the articles, and Democrats nearly all voted against them.

Bill Clinton thus became only the second president in U.S. history to be impeached. (The first was Andrew Johnson, who was impeached and acquitted in 1868.) He would now be tried in the Senate. The stakes were high: If two thirds of the senators (67 of 100) voted to convict him, he would be removed from office—the first president ever to meet that fate.

THE SENATE TRIAL

The trial began on January 7, 1999. The 100 U.S. senators made up the jury. William Rehnquist, the Chief Justice of the Supreme Court,

The impeachment crisis dominated news headlines for more than a year as the nation's attention was riveted on the drama unfolding in Washington.

served as the judge. Thirteen members of the House of Representatives (called managers) were appointed to act as prosecutors, presenting the case against the president. And a team of lawyers presented Clinton's defense.

First, each side argued its case. The House managers said Clinton's alleged offenses were so serious that, under the Constitution, he should be turned out of office. A president, they said, should follow the highest standards of behavior. The president's lawyers countered that he hadn't broken the law, and that the offenses he was charged with—lying in a civil lawsuit that was thrown out of court—didn't meet the constitutional standard for impeachment. Besides, his actions involved his personal life, not his job as president, and didn't threaten the welfare of the nation.

The arguments were followed by questions from the senators. Then, on January 27, the Senate voted on two motions—one to dismiss the charges, and the other to continue the trial with testimony from witnesses. Both votes split along party lines. All 55 Republicans and just one Democrat voted against dismissal and for witnesses. So Republicans carried both votes, and the trial continued.

Beginning February 1, three witnesses were questioned. They were Monica Lewinsky; Vernon Jordan, a lawyer and a friend of the president's; and Sidney Blumenthal, a White House aide. Their statements weren't made public, but senators had a chance to see videotapes of the questioning. This marked the first time that videotaped testimony was ever presented in the Senate.

House managers next wanted the witnesses to give further testimony, in person, in the Senate. But many senators were eager to bring the trial to a quick end. Polls showed that most citizens also wanted the trial to end promptly. And the witnesses, all of whom had testified in earlier hearings, hadn't provided any new information. So after hearing final arguments from the prosecution and defense, the Senate closed its doors to debate the evidence in private.

Five weeks after the trial began, the moment of truth arrived. And when the vote was taken, both articles of impeachment fell far short of the two-thirds majority required to convict the president. The charge of perjury was rejected 55 to 45, with 10 Republicans joining all 45 Democrats in voting to acquit. The vote on obstruction of justice was 50 to 50, with five Republicans joining the Democrats.

The Watergate Scandal

In 1999, the United States experienced the second presidential impeachment trial in its history. It also marked the 25th anniversary of a scandal that *nearly* ended in impeachment. That was the Watergate scandal, which led to the resignation of President Richard Nixon in August 1974.

The events that ended Nixon's presidency began in 1972, when he was campaigning for a second term. Workers for his re-election committee broke into Democratic Party headquarters at the Watergate apartments in Washington, D.C., and were caught. Nixon and his aides tried to cover up their links to the burglary.

Nixon won re-election, but investigations into the Watergate burglary haunted his second term. Eventually his role in the cover-up and other campaign irregularities was discovered. In Congress, the House Judiciary Committee held hearings and voted to send articles of impeachment to the full House. Knowing that the House would almost certainly vote for impeachment, Nixon resigned.

THE AFTERMATH

Most Americans were relieved that the trial was finally over. The trial had lasted five weeks, but the scandal leading up to it had lasted more than a year. Throughout that time, polls showed that most citizens wanted Clinton to stay in office and finish his term, which runs through the year 2000. In fact, the rumors, investigations, and even impeachment didn't hurt Clinton's popularity much at all. Americans were disappointed in Clinton and thought less of him as a person, but they still approved of the job he was doing as president.

Many Americans saw the impeachment issue as a political fight between parties. Republicans, who control Congress, called for Clinton's removal from the beginning, and Democrats supported him. After the trial, Democrats and Republicans promised to put their differences aside. "This can be and this must be a time of reconciliation and renewal for America," Clinton said after the verdict was announced.

The months after the trial brought some footnotes to the case. In April, a judge found Clinton in contempt of court for not revealing his relationship with Lewinsky in his deposition for the Paula Jones case. He was the first sitting president ever to be held in contempt of court.

In June, the law that allowed appointment of independent counsels like Kenneth Starr expired, and Congress didn't renew it. Starr's four-year pursuit of Clinton and the $50-million cost of his investigation were major reasons. Some people felt that Starr's investigation had probed too deeply into Clinton's personal life. Presidents have had improper relationships in the past, they said, but those relationships weren't exposed by a prosecutor. Starr himself stepped down in October, leaving an associate to wrap up the investigation.

The Clinton impeachment trial was a historic event, and it seemed certain to leave some scars. After such a bitter fight, could Democrats and Republicans work together in government? Would the blot of impeachment overshadow Clinton's achievements as president? Had the trial and the scandal done lasting damage to the office of the presidency? These questions are left for future historians.

Arctic Rangers raise Nunavut's flag for the first time on April 1. The symbol on the flag is a pile of stones called *inukshuk*, which Inuit hunters once used to mark trails.

CELEBRATING NUNAVUT

Fireworks lit the night sky over the little town of Iqaluit, in northern Canada, on April 1, 1999. Their glow, reflected in the ice and snow, marked an important moment for Canada and its Inuit people. The map of Canada had been redrawn for the first time in 50 years, and a new territory—Nunavut—had come to life.

The name "Nunavut" means "our land" in Inuktitut, an Inuit language. The Inuit make up about 85 percent of Nunavut's people. Thus their votes control the territory's elected government. And that's cause for great celebration among the Inuit.

OLD WRONGS MADE RIGHT

Nunavut was carved from the eastern 60 percent of the Northwest Territories to settle a dispute over land that the Inuit claim. This was the latest in a series of settlements between the Canadian government and native peoples. And it was the biggest such settlement in Canadian history.

The Inuit lived in the region that's now Nunavut long before European explorers and traders arrived in the 1500's. For centuries, they moved from place to place in this land, hunting and fishing. The region became part of Canada in the 1800's, but the Inuit never signed a treaty with the Canadian government. In the 1970's, they began to call for old wrongs to be put right by the creation of a new territory. The Canadian government finally agreed in 1993.

The agreement between the government and the Inuit has other provisions. The Inuit agreed to give up claims to all other lands. They will also get payments totaling $1 billion, spread over fourteen years. But the creation of Nunavut was the most important part. Canada hasn't seen so big a change since Newfoundland joined the country in 1949.

As in other Canadian territories, Nunavut and its government are open to everyone. A person doesn't have to be Inuit to live there, and residents don't have to be Inuit to vote. But since so many of Nunavut's people are Inuit, this is an Inuit territory.

Inuit heritage is reflected in Nunavut's official symbol, which appears on the territorial flag. The symbol is a pile of stones, called *inukshuk,* which Inuit hunters once used to mark trails. Even the new building for the territorial legislature reflects pride in the Inuit past. The building has a domed ceiling designed in the shape of an igloo. Legislators sit on sealskin seats.

LOTS AND LOTS OF ICE

Nunavut is huge, covering about 770,000 square miles (2,000,000 square kilometers). That's bigger than Alaska and California combined! On a map, the new territory looks like Texas flipped upside down. Its southern border touches Manitoba, and its northern border extends above the Arctic Circle.

Nunavut's capital, Iqaluit, is a small frontier town that doesn't even have traffic lights. But Iqaluit's new building for the territorial legislature reflects Inuit heritage with a modern design. The domed ceiling represents an igloo, and the legislators sit on sealskin seats.

Rocky islands make up most of the land. During the long winters, they are covered with snow and linked by thick ice.

Only about 27,000 people live in this harsh land. In fact, caribou are said to outnumber people by more than 25 to 1! There are few paved roads and only 12 miles (19 kilometers) of highway in the entire territory.

The territory has just 28 communities, including Iqaluit, the capital. Iqaluit is the largest town, with about 4,500 people. It's the northernmost capital city in North America—but it isn't Nunavut's northernmost community. That honor goes to tiny Grise Fiord, with only about 130 people. Well north of the Arctic Circle, Grise Fiord gets round-the-clock sunshine in June—and round-the-clock darkness in December.

Poverty is one of the biggest problems facing Nunavut. Jobs are hard to come by, and Nunavut has more than its share of unemployment. But this part of the world is the traditional Inuit homeland. Many of today's Inuit hunt and fish, as their nomadic ancestors did, and that helps them get by.

And now that Nunavut is a separate territory, a small boom has started. New buildings are going up in Iqaluit. There are still no traffic lights, but Iqaluit has banks, take-out restaurants, even tanning salons. People can get Internet and even cellular phone service. The people of Nunavut may rely on Inuit traditions, but they also make use of modern technology.

Nunavut's new government is gradually taking on the duties previously carried out by the government of the Northwest Territories. The transfer will be complete by 2009. The government hopes to encourage the growth of industry and tourism, to create jobs. Meanwhile, Nunavut's people are taking pride in their homeland. They know they face problems, but now they are in control of their future.

Thousands of ethnic Albanians flee their homes to escape Serbian forces in the Yugoslav province of Kosovo.

ETHNIC CONFLICT IN KOSOVO

The part of Europe known as the Balkans has a long history of ethnic conflict. In the spring of 1999 the latest outbreak of Balkan violence raged in Kosovo, a remote region in southern Yugoslavia. Thousands of Kosovars were killed and nearly a million were driven from their homes in a brutal campaign of "ethnic cleansing" carried out by the Yugoslav government.

Tiny Kosovo suddenly became the focus of world attention. Concerned that ethnic violence might spread to surrounding regions, the United States and European nations tried to stop the fighting. When diplomacy failed, they turned to force.

A HISTORY OF HATRED

Kosovo is a province of Serbia, the main republic of Yugoslavia. About the size of the state of Connecticut, Kosovo borders the nations of Albania and Macedonia. Before the

1999 conflict began, more than 2 million people lived in Kosovo. Ninety percent of them were ethnic Albanians (their ancestors came from Albania, and they shared the same culture, language, and religion).

Strain between the ethnic Albanians and the Serbs, who make up most of Yugoslavia's people, goes back to the Middle Ages. Serbs controlled Kosovo in the 12th and 13th centuries. But in 1389 they were defeated by the Turks in a battle on the Field of Blackbirds, near Pristina, Kosovo's capital. During the more than 500 years of Turkish rule that followed, many Albanians became Muslims, while Serbs held on to Christianity. And tensions between Serbs and Albanians grew.

In the early 1900's wars swept through the Balkans, and the Turks lost control of the region. Albania became an independent nation. But Kosovo, on its northern border, became part of Serbia and Montenegro.

Kosovo's Serbs celebrated; Kosovo's Albanians were bitter. After World War I, when Serbia became part of Yugoslavia, Albanians faced increasing discrimination. That continued when Yugoslavia became a Communist country after World War II.

In 1974, the Yugoslav leader Tito granted autonomy, or self-government, to Kosovo. Albanian language and culture flourished. But after Tito's death, discrimination returned. Leaders such as Slobodan Milosevic whipped up Serbian nationalism with speeches recalling the years of Turkish rule. In 1989, Milosevic ended Kosovo's autonomy. But by the mid-1990's, Yugoslavia was breaking up into separate countries. Kosovars began to dream of independence. And some of them started a guerrilla movement, the Kosovo Liberation Army (KLA).

In 1998, President Milosevic sent forces into central Kosovo, where the KLA was strong. He turned his tanks and artillery on ethnic Albanian homes and villages, attacking families that were accused of helping the KLA. Thousands of ethnic Albanians fled to the mountains. European nations, the United States, and other countries called on him to stop. He didn't.

Slobodan Milosevic: Serbian Strongman

Yugoslav president Slobodan Milosevic earned a place in history in 1999, but it wasn't one he could be proud of. He became the first sitting head of state to be indicted by an international criminal tribunal. The tribunal, created by the United Nations, charged Milosevic with crimes against humanity for his brutal campaign against Kosovo's ethnic Albanians.

Long before the violence of 1999, Milosevic had made an issue out of the Serb domination of Kosovo. It was one of the tools he used to fan nationalist feelings among Serbs. Serbian nationalism brought him to power and kept him there.

Born in 1941, Milosevic grew up in Yugoslavia under Communism. He developed good connections within the Communist Party and obtained good jobs as a result. By 1987, he was head of the governing committee in the Yugoslav republic of Serbia. When Serbs in Kosovo began to demonstrate against the Albanians there, he was sent to quell the unrest. Instead, he delivered a speech that inflamed Serb feelings.

Serbs who felt victimized by other ethnic groups, in Kosovo and elsewhere, rallied to Milosevic. Their support allowed him to take full control of Serbia. In 1989, as Serbia's new president, he warned that Serbs might have to fight other groups.

In the early 1990's, Yugoslavia broke apart. The republics of Slovenia, Croatia, Macedonia, and Bosnia-Herzegovina declared independence. Milosevic became president of what remained of Yugoslavia—Serbia and the smaller republic of Montenegro. Ruling as a dictator, he backed Serbian militias that fought to grab territory in Croatia and Bosnia. In Bosnia, Serb militias carried out a brutal campaign of ethnic cleansing. Bosnia ended up divided into ethnic regions when fighting ended in 1995.

Milosevic's popularity dropped after that war, and he was nearly driven from power early in 1997. But in 1998 he once again used the issue of Kosovo to boost his own popularity. This time the plan backfired, bringing NATO air strikes to Yugoslavia and a criminal indictment to its leader.

An elderly Kosovar woman huddles under a blanket at a refugee camp in Macedonia.

NATO STEPS IN

As Milosevic's crackdown continued, there were fears that the violence would threaten the stability of Europe. The North Atlantic Treaty Organization (NATO) warned that Yugoslavia would face military action if the fighting didn't stop. But in March 1999, Milosevic rejected a peace agreement that had been worked out with the support of the United States and other countries. Ignoring repeated NATO threats, his forces continued their attacks.

On March 24, NATO began air strikes against Yugoslavia. The goal was to force Milosevic to end the crackdown and accept the international peace plan. Instead, Milosevic stepped up the violence and expanded it throughout Kosovo. His campaign had two goals: to crush the KLA, and to change the ethnic balance of Kosovo by driving the ethnic Albanians out. Yugoslav armed forces and bands of Serb paramilitaries swept through the province, looting and burning homes and killing ethnic Albanians. Those who weren't killed were forced to hide or flee.

Hundreds of thousands of people poured across the borders to refugee camps in neighboring Macedonia and Albania, taking only what they could carry. Those countries were hard pressed to care for them. International aid agencies stepped in to help. The United States agreed to give shelter to some 20,000 Kosovar refugees. Other NATO countries took an additional 100,000. Still, conditions in the camps were desperate, and food, water, and medicine were in short supply.

The refugees brought tales of atrocities—civilians killed or beaten, or used as "human shields" to protect the Yugoslav military from air strikes. In early May, the U.S. State Department estimated that some 900,000 Kosovars had been driven out of the province, and 500,000 more were displaced inside Kosovo. An international tribunal formally charged Milosevic with war crimes for his campaign of "ethnic cleansing."

Meanwhile, NATO planes continued to pound Yugoslavia. U.S. and British planes carried out most of the strikes. But planes from other nations also took part; German planes flew their first combat missions since World War II. Military installations, power plants, bridges, and fuel depots were among the targets. NATO tried to avoid civilian targets, but there were mistakes. In one, planes attacked a refugee column, thinking it was a military convoy. In another, the Chinese embassy in Belgrade was bombed, in the belief that it was a Yugoslav command post. That touched off angry protests in China.

NATO casualties were very light. Yugoslav gunners brought down two U.S. planes, but in both cases the pilots escaped unharmed. However, crews of two U.S. helicopters were killed when their aircraft crashed in training exercises. Three U.S. soldiers based in Macedonia were captured near the Yugoslavian-Macedonian border soon after the air strikes began. They were released on May 2.

By late April, NATO had used 14,000 bombs and missiles and claimed to have destroyed a third of the tanks and other heavy military equipment in Kosovo. But Milosevic's campaign continued. People began to wonder if NATO would have to send ground forces into the province to end the fighting. Then, on June 3, Milosevic finally accepted a peace plan. The bombing stopped.

AN UNEASY PEACE

Under the peace agreement, Yugoslavia withdrew all its 40,000 troops from Kosovo. Kosovo was divided into five sectors, each under the control of a leading NATO member. An international force of 50,000 troops from more than 30 nations moved in. The United States sent 7,000 soldiers as part of that force. Russia, which helped negotiate the peace, also sent troops. At first, Russia demanded to control its own zone in northern Kosovo, and that caused some friction with NATO. Russia eventually dropped the demand.

As soon as Milosevic's forces pulled out, the ethnic Albanians who had fled Kosovo to escape Serb military forces began to flood back. Many found little or nothing left of their homes. And mass graves and other evidence of killings were discovered. It seemed that at least 5,000 people had been killed. But the true number may never be known.

Some ethnic Albanians took revenge by looting and burning the houses of Serbs and, in some cases, killing them. Now Serb civilians began to flee the province. While the peacekeeping forces tried to stop this violence, they were only partly successful.

Under the peace accord, the United Nations was to set up a temporary government and police force for Kosovo, until elections could be held. But the U.N. government was slow to take charge. Instead, the KLA quietly took control. KLA fighters were supposed to turn in their weapons, but many

didn't. There was concern that they would try to rule Kosovo by force.

Continued violence was only one of Kosovo's problems. In addition to the damage done by Serbian burning and looting, the weeks of bombing damaged roads, bridges, electricity, and water supplies in the province and elsewhere in Yugoslavia. The United States and other nations promised aid. But, they insisted, the Yugoslav government would get no help as long as Milosevic stayed in power. And opposition to Milosevic spread through Yugoslavia in the weeks after the war. In several cities there were demonstra-

How do you say "cheeks" in Albanian? A U.S. Air National Guardsman and an 11-year-old refugee try to communicate. The boy was one of hundreds of Kosovar refugees who arrived in the United States in May.

tions demanding that he resign. But by year's end, he was still in power.

The Kosovo conflict is only one aspect of the Balkan problem. On July 30, U.S. President Bill Clinton and 38 other national leaders met to discuss this problem in Sarajevo, Bosnia-Herzegovina—another Balkan land torn by ethnic fighting. They pledged to encourage economic and democratic reforms for the Balkans. Clinton said, "It is not enough to end the war. We must build the peace."

SHOPPING IN CYBERSPACE

Your favorite music group just came out with a new CD. You've saved the money to buy it. Where will you find it? You could wait for the weekend and your next trip to the music store at the local mall. Or you could buy the CD right now—in cyberspace. Just sit down at your computer, go online, and find the CD on the Web site of an Internet vendor.

The Internet is the hottest trend in shopping, and it isn't hard to see why. Imagine a huge mall where you can check out thousands of items from all over the country and even abroad, and you have an idea of what Internet shopping can be like.

CLICK AND BUY

Specialty retailers were the first to recognize the possibilities of cybershopping. Book lovers quickly discovered Amazon.com, an online bookstore that started in 1995. That site's success encouraged other booksellers, as well as online music, electronics, and video stores, to open on the Internet. For mail-order companies, going online was a natural step—

they were already selling to distant customers through catalogs. Now big department stores and other traditional retailers are jumping into cyberspace, afraid of losing business to this trend.

Why are people going online to shop? There are three big advantages.

• **Selection:** Instead of being limited to the merchandise in your local store, you can search the Net and come up with items from all over the world. Many online vendors offer a huge selection. Online book and music sellers, for example, list thousands more titles than typical stores can stock. The wide choice is especially attractive for people in rural areas who don't have access to lots of big stores.

• **Convenience:** You can shop on line anytime, even at night in your pajamas. There are no crowds, no lines, no traffic jams, no hunting for a parking spot.

• **Simplicity:** Buying online is easy—you click your mouse on the items you want, enter your credit-card number and shipping address, and you're done.

SMART SHOPPING

In fact, buying online may be *too* easy. Some people overspend and buy things they don't really need. There are other drawbacks, too. For example, many people are uneasy about giving out credit-card information online. They worry that the information may fall into the wrong hands, and strangers will start to run up bills using their credit.

In addition, when you shop online you don't get to see or touch the items you're buying. That may matter less for a book or CD than for clothing.

Seeing a picture of a sweater online isn't the same as touching it and trying it on. If there's a problem with your purchase, there's no store to go back to. You deal with the online vendor's customer-service department, and some are more helpful than others.

Experienced cybershoppers know there are ways to avoid these problems:

• Don't buy items you don't need, and set a budget for your shopping.

• Buy only at Web sites that offer secure connections, which protect your credit-card information.

• Know what you're buying—pick items and brands that you're familiar with.

• Deal with established online vendors, and check out their customer service before you buy. What's their policy on returning merchandise? Is there a phone number you can call if there's a problem?

Many people expect that this new way of shopping will grow tremendously in the years ahead. They predict that it won't be long before the Internet's World Wide Web becomes a World Wide Mall.

Cybermalls for Teens

Teens who want to shop online quickly run into a roadblock. To pay for items sold by Internet vendors, you need a credit card. And that's something very few kids have.

Some new online services offer a way around the roadblock. They allow parents to establish online accounts, with "electronic money" that their children can spend. Kids like the idea because it allows them to shop online. Parents like it because it allows them to control where their children shop and how much they spend.

Here's how it works: Suppose you save $50 from a babysitting job. Instead of taking the cash to local stores, you turn it over to your parents. They use a credit card to put $50 worth of electronic money in an online account with the service of your choice. You can then log onto the service, which offers connections to various Internet vendors.

Several such services started up in 1999. They include:

iCanBuy (www.icanbuy.com)
DoughNET (www.doughnet.com)
RocketCash (www.rocketcash.com)

All offer links to many different vendors. Some also give kids a chance to donate to charities and set up savings accounts.

What Teenagers Buy Online

36.2%	25.1%	20.3%	17.9%	16.4%	13%	9.7%	8.7%
Music	Books	Electronic Equipment	Computer Games	Software	Concert Tickets	Travel	Health & Beauty Aids

(These figures represent the percentages of teen shoppers who bought items in each category.)

As the year 2000 began, the Panama Canal in Central America changed ownership: On December 31, 1999, the United States turned control of the canal over to Panama.

AROUND THE WORLD

The year 1999 was one of turmoil and transition in many parts of the world. Here is an overview of some of the events that made headlines during the year.

PANAMA'S CANAL

On December 31, 1999, the United States turned over control of the Panama Canal to the nation of Panama. That action ended an important chapter in the history of both countries.

The Panama Canal provides the major water route between the Atlantic and Pacific oceans. It cuts through Central America at a narrow point, the Isthmus of Panama. In 1998 about 14,000 ships passed through the Panama Canal. They carried 228 million tons of cargo—about 4 percent of the world's oceangoing trade.

The United States built the canal in 1914. And, under a treaty with Panama, the United States controlled the canal for the next 85 years. But Panamanians came to resent U.S. control of the canal. In 1977, after long nego-

tiations, the two nations signed a pair of new treaties. The agreements called for Panama to take a growing role in operating the canal until 1999, when it would take over full control. Also under these treaties, the United States gave up the Canal Zone, a strip of territory it controlled along the canal. And it agreed to withdraw U.S. soldiers stationed in Panama to protect the canal. However, the United States kept the right to take any actions necessary to keep the canal neutral.

As the moment of transfer neared, both nations had some lingering concerns. The United States was worried by drug trafficking in the region and wanted to keep some soldiers in Panama. Panama wanted the United States to do more to clean up after its past military operations. Panamanians were especially concerned about unexploded bombs dropped in the jungles during target practice.

U.S. President Bill Clinton met with Panamanian President Mireya Moscoso in October to discuss these and other concerns. Moscoso, Panama's first woman president, had been sworn in only the month before. The daughter of a teacher, she was the widow of former Panamanian President Arnulfo Arias. Moscoso had won a sweeping victory in the country's May 1999 presidential election by promising to fight poverty and corruption. She also promised to work to revive the nation's spirit. The return of the canal would be a key step in that effort.

Some Americans were against giving up the canal. They feared that opponents of the United States might gain control of it. Others thought giving control to Panama was the right thing to do. They remembered that the United States itself once fought to control its own land—during the Revolutionary War.

And Panamanians were thrilled to finally have full responsibility for the canal. The Panama Canal brings in $700 million in revenue each year, but much of the money goes toward operating and maintaining the 50-mile (80-kilometer) waterway. More important was the sense of national pride Panamanians gained. The transfer marked the start of a new era for their country.

HOPES FOR PEACE IN THE MIDEAST

Ehud Barak, the Labor Party leader, was elected prime minister of Israel in a landslide on May 17. He defeated Benjamin Netanyahu, leader of the conservative Likud Party, who had been prime minister for three years. Those years had seen growing divisions among Israelis and between Israelis and Arabs. The voters who cast their ballots for Barak hoped he would steer the country on a new course—toward peace with its Arab neighbors and with the Palestinian Arabs.

The Palestinian Arabs live in territory occupied by Israel and have long demanded a state of their own. For years, they carried out a campaign of war and terrorism. But in 1993, Israel and the Palestinians signed the Oslo accords. This agreement gave the Palestinians control over land in the Gaza Strip and parts of the West Bank, territories occupied by Israel in 1967. It also allowed them to set up their own government.

Further negotiations were to decide the question of an independent Palestinian state. But those talks broke down in 1996, after Netanyahu's conservative government came to power in Israel. Israel and the Palestinians

At a summit meeting in September, Israeli Prime Minister Ehud Barak and Palestinian leader Yasir Arafat shake hands after signing an agreement to restart the peace process.

King Hussein of Jordan

The world lost a voice for peace on February 7, 1999, with the death of King Hussein of Jordan. King Hussein, who had been ill with cancer for some time, was 63 years old. He was the longest-reigning ruler in the Middle East. And he had guided his nation through some of that region's most difficult times.

When Hussein was born on November 14, 1935, the nation that is Jordan today was Transjordan, a British protectorate. It became independent in 1946, and Hussein's grandfather Abdullah became its king. Just four years later, Abdullah was assassinated. Hussein's father, Talal, became king. But he suffered from mental illness, and in August 1952, Hussein was named king in his place. He was just 16.

Hussein was soon nicknamed the PLK—the "plucky little king." Risk never bothered him. He flew stunts in jet planes and raced cars and motorcycles across the desert. He survived several assassination attempts—and many setbacks. One of the worst setbacks came in 1967, when Jordan joined Egypt and Syria in a war against Israel. Jordan lost the West Bank and half of the city of Jerusalem, territory it had taken in a previous war. Then, in 1970, King Hussein faced a civil war with Palestinians, who make up more than two thirds of Jordan's people.

After each setback, the king bounced back. He came to realize that the troubles in the Middle East could only be solved through peace. Even while Jordan was still formally at war with Israel, he met with Israeli leaders in secret to find common ground. Hussein also became a strong ally of the United States and other Western countries. In 1994, Jordan finally made formal peace with Israel. Hussein considered that the greatest accomplishment of his reign. Even after he became ill with cancer, he continued to work for peace. In October 1998, he helped forge a new peace agreement between Israeli and Palestinian leaders.

King Hussein's death was met with deep grief in his country, where he was much loved. In Amman, the capital of Jordan, people wept in the streets. President Bill Clinton and leaders from all over the world attended his funeral. Hussein's eldest son, Abdullah, became king on his death. Around the world, people wished Abdullah success in carrying on his father's legacy.

did sign a pact in 1998, under which Israel was to turn over more of the West Bank to the Palestinians. But that agreement wasn't fully carried out. The May 17 election was a clear call for the peace process to go forward. After taking office, Barak moved to restart the Israeli-Palestinian peace process. And on September 5, he and Palestinian leader Yasir Arafat formally signed a new agreement. Under its terms, Israel would turn over more land in the West Bank to the Palestinians, and formal negotiations for a permanent settlement would begin. Israel and the Palestinians were to have a rough agreement by February 2000 and a final agreement by September 2000. They would have to solve serious issues—the final borders of a Palestinian state, the future of Jewish settlements in the West Bank, and the status of Jerusalem, a city to which both groups have claims. But the September 5 agreement was a sure sign that the on-again, off-again Mideast peace process was back on track.

IRAN'S TUG OF WAR

Iran seemed to be caught in a tug of war through much of 1999. On one side were religious conservatives who wanted to keep tight control of society. On the other were moderates who wanted to allow greater freedom. And when protests and demonstrations brought the conflict into the open, the result was a setback for the moderates.

Iran is ruled by an Islamic government. The most powerful person in the country is the spiritual leader, Ayatollah Ali Khamenei, a Muslim cleric. He and his supporters want Iran to be governed by religious law and kept free of Western influences. Personal freedom is very restricted, especially for women.

But in 1997, Iranians elected a moderate as president. Mohammad Khatami hoped to bring more freedom and openness to the country. He also hoped to improve the economy. However, the president doesn't hold as much power as the spiritual leader and the conservatives, so reform turned out to be difficult. And that added to the growing frustration among Iranians.

Protests erupted in July 1999. Students in Tehran, the capital, demonstrated against a new law curbing press freedom and banning a popular moderate newspaper. In response, security forces stormed a university dormitory, beating students. At least one student, and possibly as many as eight, died. Many people were outraged. Over the next few days, protests grew and spread to other cities. The protesters wanted conservatives to resign from government, and Khatami and other moderates to take full control.

At first, the government simply urged the protesters to show restraint. But on July 13, the security forces cracked down. Police and bands of Islamic militants attacked the protesters with tear gas and clubs, breaking up the crowds. The violence closed businesses in whole sections of Tehran. Even the city's huge bazaar shut down. Later, government officials said that people arrested for protesting against the government would be charged with crimes that, under Islamic law, usually carry a death sentence.

Iran's conservatives kept the upper hand. But many expected the tug of war to continue.

INDIA AND PAKISTAN: UNEASY NEIGHBORS

Tensions between India and Pakistan were high in 1999, thanks to longstanding disputes over territory along the border these countries share. The disputes go back to 1947, when Britain granted independence to its Indian colonies. The Indian subcontinent was divided into two countries—India, mostly Hindu; and Pakistan, mostly Muslim. Almost immediately, the two nations went to war over the territory of Kashmir. Tucked in the snow-capped Himalayas where India, Pakistan, and China meet, this region was claimed by both nations.

The fighting settled nothing. India and Pakistan went to war again in 1965 and in 1971–72, over border and other issues. The 1972 war ended in a cease-fire, with Pakistan in control of the northern part of the region and India in control of the south. Indian and Pakistani troops have continued to trade shots

A Pakistani tea delivery boy gazes at a poster of General Pervez Musharraf, the army chief of staff who declared himself the country's leader in October.

across the cease-fire line from time to time. And since 1990, Muslim guerrillas have rebelled against India's control of southern Kashmir.

From mid-May to late July 1999, Indian forces battled hundreds of Muslim fighters who had sneaked into India's part of Kashmir. India said that they were Pakistani soldiers, while Pakistan insisted that they were Kashmir rebels. The fighting brought the two nations to the brink of all-out war when, at the urging of the United States, Pakistan got the infiltrators to agree to withdraw. But soon new tensions flared. On August 10, India shot down a Pakistani naval aircraft with sixteen people aboard. Pakistan said the plane was on a routine flight and had been "ruthlessly" shot down in Pakistani skies. India said the plane had provoked the attack and flown into Indian territory.

Worries over border conflicts increased in October, when Pakistan's army overthrew the government and took control of the country. The coup took place after Pakistani Prime Minister Nawaz Sharif tried to fire General Pervez Musharraf, the army chief of staff. Instead, army troops took over airports and television and radio stations and arrested Sharif. Musharraf declared himself the country's leader. He imposed martial law, suspended the constitution, and dismissed the legislature.

Countries all over the world condemned the coup and urged the army leaders to give power back to civilians. Many people wondered if the coup would lead to new conflict over Kashmir. Pakistan's military leaders had opposed the agreement under which the Kashmir infiltrators withdrew. And because both India and Pakistan have nuclear weapons, people worried that any war between them might become a nuclear war.

A billboard in Shanghai, China, advertises the film *Notting Hill*. Under a new U.S.-China trade agreement, more American films will be distributed in China.

CHINA IN THE SPOTLIGHT

"Chilly" was the word that best described relations between the United States and China through much of 1999. These two powerful nations didn't see eye to eye in important areas such as human rights and security. But despite their disagreements, China and the United States reached an important agreement on trade late in the year.

The United States has long been critical of China's record on human rights. The Chinese government is run by the Communist Party, and that party has never allowed opposition. Dissidents—people who disagree with the government—have been put in jail for speaking out politically. In the past, protesters have even been killed.

In 1999, a number of people who tried to form an independent political party were jailed. And Chinese officials cracked down on a semi-religious movement known as Falun Gong. Falun Gong's followers include students, retirees, and everyone in between. In April 1999, they staged a silent vigil in Beijing, to protest government criticisms of their movement. The government responded by banning the movement, saying its leaders had a secret political agenda. Through the summer and fall thousands of Falun Gong followers were arrested.

U.S. officials were also concerned about China's nuclear weapons program. China has developed advanced nuclear weapons, and U.S. officials suspect that China may have stolen information needed to make these weapons from the United States. China also has missiles that can carry weapons. The United States is considering setting up a missile defense system in East Asia, to protect its allies. And Chinese leaders don't like the idea. They're especially concerned that the system might be used to defend Taiwan.

China's problem with Taiwan, an island off the Chinese coast, goes back to 1949. That's when the Communists defeated the Nationalists, China's previous leaders, after a long civil war. The Nationalists fled to Taiwan and set up a government there. But ever since then, Chinese leaders have viewed Taiwan as a breakaway province. They have warned Taiwan not to declare independence. And they see U.S. protection of Taiwan as a threat.

Despite these differences, China is the fourth largest U.S. trading partner. And on November 15, China and the United States reached a major agreement on trade. Under this agreement, China would ease restrictions on foreign goods and services, so U.S. products could be sold more freely in China. In exchange, the United States agreed to help China become a member of the World Trade Organization (WTO), an international group that governs trade between member nations. Joining the WTO would make it easier for China to sell its products worldwide.

American business groups favor the new trade deal because, with 1.2 billion people, China offers huge markets for products of all kinds. But the agreement must be approved by Congress before it takes effect.

South Africa: End of an Era

Nelson Mandela, South Africa's first black president, stepped down in June 1999. His retirement marked an important transition for this nation.

Mandela, 80, had campaigned all his life to end apartheid, the system under which a minority white government had ruled the nation. Under apartheid, everything— housing, jobs, education, services—was segregated by race. Blacks couldn't vote and weren't even considered citizens, even though they formed the overwhelming majority of South Africans.

Mandela was a leader of the African National Congress (ANC), an anti-apartheid group. Because of his opposition, he spent 27 years in prison. But in the 1990's protests and pressure from other countries finally brought change. Mandela was freed. Black and white leaders worked together to develop a new multiracial government. In the nation's first all-race elections, in 1994, Mandela and the ANC were swept into power.

By 1999, Mandela was ready to retire. And Thabo Mbeki, who was deputy president and leader of the ANC, was ready to take on the presidency. Voters showed their support: In elections on June 2, the ANC won about 65 percent of the vote. That gave the party a huge majority in parliament. And parliament then elected Mbeki, 56, the nation's next president.

Thus leadership passed to a new, younger generation. South Africa faced many problems. But Mbeki pledged to continue the fight against poverty, racism, corruption, and crime. South Africans were hopeful for the future.

INDESIA IN TURMOIL

For Indonesia, 1999 was a year of turmoil. A nation made up of thousands of islands and many ethnic groups, Indonesia struggled with political crisis, an economic slump, and several rebellions. Its actions in East Timor, on the island of Timor, brought worldwide criticism.

The political crisis began in 1998, when riots and protests forced Indonesian President Suharto to step down. Suharto had ruled as a dictator for more than 30 years. B. J. Habibie was named to take his place until elections could be held. And in January 1999, Habibie made a surprising statement about East Timor, a former Portuguese colony that Indonesia had invaded in 1975. The East Timorese had fought Indonesian rule, and the United Nations hadn't recognized it. Now, Habibie said, East Timor might be allowed to vote on independence.

But many members of the Indonesian military didn't want to release their hold on East Timor. They organized militia groups that began a campaign of violence, to keep people from voting for independence. Still, when the vote was held on August 30, under U.N. supervision, nearly 99 percent of eligible East Timorese turned out to vote. And more than 78 percent of them chose independence. However, even before all the votes were counted, furious violence engulfed East Timor. The militias, with the clear support of the military, went on a spree of killing, looting, and burning. Hundreds of people were killed. Tens of thousands fled Dili, the capital, and other towns to escape the violence.

Finally, on September 12, Habibie asked the United Nations to send an international force to restore peace to East Timor. Peacekeeping troops began to arrive on September 20 from Australia, Britain, Thailand, and more than a dozen other countries. Aid groups rushed to help East Timorese refugees. And Indonesia agreed to a U.N. transition plan that would bring independence to the shattered country.

Meanwhile, in June 1999, Indonesians went to the polls and elected members of a new national assembly. And in October, the assembly chose a new president—the first democratically elected president in Indonesia's history. He was Abdurrahman Wahid, 59, a Muslim leader.

Wahid's victory was a surprise because his supporters didn't have the most seats in the assembly. The biggest vote-getter in the June elections had been the Indonesian Democratic Party for Struggle, led by Megawati Sukarnoputri—the daughter of Indonesia's founding president, Sukarno. Many people thought Megawati would be the next president, but she couldn't put together a majority in the assembly.

Wahid immediately took steps to unify the country, naming Megawati as his vice president. He promised to revive the economy, end corruption, and work to end several rebellions that threatened to tear the country apart.

RUSSIA'S MANY WOES

For Russians, 1999 brought a continuation of hard times. Their economy was in a major slump, their government was in

East Timorese march in a religious procession in Dili, the capital of East Timor, after peace was restored.

It was a tumultuous year in Russia. Left: Russian soldiers patrol a village in the rebellious province of Chechnya. Below: Russian President Boris Yeltsin shocked the world by resigning on December 31.

turmoil, and there was new fighting in the rebellious province of Chechnya. And at year's end, Russian President Boris Yeltsin startled the world by resigning.

Yeltsin was a leader in the events that brought about the collapse of Communism and the breakup of the Soviet Union in 1991. Back then, he promised democracy and a free market economy, and he was very popular. But economic reforms didn't take hold, and most Russians remain poor. Corruption and crime have risen.

Former Communists in the State Duma, the lower house of the Russian parliament, led a drive to remove Yeltsin from office in May 1999. But the effort failed. Meanwhile, Yeltsin went through three prime ministers during the year. He replaced Yevgeny Primakov with Sergei Stepashin in May, and then replaced Stepashin with Vladimir Putin in August. And Yeltsin continued to have serious health problems.

Russians also found themselves embroiled in a new war in Chechnya. From 1994 to 1996, fighting had raged in this region in southern Russia, as Russian troops tried—and failed—to put down a rebellion there. Chechnya became a lawless place, where warlords and criminal gangs ran unchecked. The 1999 military action began after Muslim militants based in Chechnya invaded a neighboring region, Dagestan, in August. The militants' goal was to create an Islamic state in south-

ern Russia. Russian leaders also blamed these militants for a series of terrorist bombings in Moscow and other cities in September.

Russia responded with air strikes against targets in Chechnya. Then, at the start of October, Russian troops rolled into the region. By December, they were closing in on Grozny, the capital. Meanwhile, more than 200,000 Chechen refugees fled the region. The military action was criticized abroad, but many Russians supported it.

Support for the war in Chechnya helped Yeltsin in December, when elections for the Duma were held. Parties that supported him made big gains. With that support behind him, Yeltsin stepped down and named Prime Minister Putin his successor. Presidential elections were scheduled for March 2000, and Putin was expected to be a strong candidate.

In an elegant ceremony on June 19, 1999, Britain's **Prince Edward married Sophie Rhys-Jones** at Windsor Castle, outside London. Edward, 35, is the youngest son of Queen Elizabeth II. The wedding was a simple one by royal standards. Just 550 friends and family members filled St. George's Chapel at Windsor. But millions of people watched the ceremony live on television. And thousands of people lined the streets outside to see the newlyweds pass through the castle grounds in a horse-drawn carriage, on their way from the chapel to the wedding reception. Edward's older brothers, Charles and Andrew, were his "supporters"—the equivalent of best men. The bride's ivory silk dress was covered with hundreds of thousands of cut-glass and pearl beads, and she wore a pearl necklace and earrings that Edward designed for her as a wedding present. He wore a gift from her: a gold pocket watch and a gold chain.

Edward and Rhys-Jones, 34, had known each other for six years before they decided to get married. The marriage was unusual for royal circles because Rhys-Jones was a "commoner"—not a member of the aristocracy. The daughter of a salesman, she headed a public relations firm in London. Edward, for his part, was a television producer. Both planned to stay at their jobs after their wedding. But they went back to work with new titles, as the Earl and Countess of Wessex—honors given by the queen as a wedding present.

Maxilla and Mandible Ltd. is a New York City shop stuffed with natural history treasures—bones, animal sculptures, and other curiosities. You might find anything there. But even Henry Galiano, the shop's owner, was astounded when a major archeological discovery turned up. In March 1999, Galiano bought a carload of items from Indonesia. They were being sold to settle the estate of a collector. And among them was a nearly complete **fossil skull.** The skull turned out to be that of an early human ancestor, and it may shed light on how modern humans evolved. Galiano turned the skull over to scientists, to be returned to Indonesia.

In May 1999, twenty-one-year-old **Nancy Mace** became the first woman graduate of The Citadel, a famous military college in Charleston, South Carolina. The Citadel was an all male college until 1995, when a court ruled that the state-supported school had to admit women.

Adrienne Clarkson, 60, was named Canada's new Governor General in September 1999. She's the first Asian and first immigrant to hold the country's highest ceremonial post. Clarkson arrived in Canada as a refugee in 1942, when she was 3 years old. She and her family had fled when the Japanese invaded Hong Kong, her birthplace. (Hong Kong was then a British colony on the coast of China.) It was a big adjustment, but Adrienne's parents and teachers encouraged her. She ended high school at the top of her class and went on to college and graduate school. Clarkson had a long career in television broadcasting, as a producer and host of cultural programs. As Governor General, she has no real political power. But she plans to use the office to promote "a Canada for all of us."

One minute, **Maria Grasso** of Boston, Massachusetts, was a live-in baby-sitter. The next, she was a multi-millionaire. In April, Grasso won a $197 million jackpot in the six-state Big Game lottery—the biggest lottery prize ever won by one person. The odds of winning the drawing were 76 million to 1. Grasso, 54, came to the United States from Chile in 1971. She became a U.S. citizen in 1984 and worked as a teaching assistant for the mentally handicapped, as well as a baby-sitter. Not a regular lottery player, she bought her winning ticket in a Boston supermarket because the jackpot was so big. Grasso chose to take her winnings in a lump sum instead of 26 annual payments. After income taxes were taken out, she received a check for $70.2 million. She said she would use some of the money to help her family and handicapped children.

Ehud Barak, 57, was elected prime minister of Israel in May 1999. The leader of the Labor party, Barak won in a landslide over Benjamin Netanyahu, leader of the Likud party, who had been prime minister for three years. Barak was known for his intelligence, bravery, and keen attention to detail. Born on a kibbutz (an Israeli collective farm), he had spent 35 years in the army, rising to chief of staff. Along the way he became the most decorated soldier in Israel's history. In the most famous of his many daring missions, he led an antiterrorist squad that freed a commercial airliner and 97 hostages from Palestinian terrorists. Later, he served in government under Israeli prime minister Yitzhak Rabin, who was assassinated in 1995. Like Rabin, Barak believed that Israel must make peace with its Arab neighbors and with the Palestinian Arabs. The Palestinian Arabs live in territory occupied by Israel and have long demanded a state of their own. Under Netanyahu, there had been growing divisions among Israelis and between Israelis and Arabs. The voters who cast their ballots for Barak hoped he would steer the country on a new course toward peace.

This fabulous feline is a Maine coon cat. The Maine coon breed originated in Maine in the 1850's. At that time, some people thought the cat's long, fluffy fur made it look like a raccoon—so they called it a "coon" cat. The Maine coon cat's thick coat keeps it warm in northern winters. And its gentle nature has helped it become the second most popular breed of cat in the United States.

Cats rule! Cats have clawed their way to the top of pet popularity polls as more people than ever before now share their homes with one or more of these purr-fectly captivating creatures.

CRAZY OVER CATS

Cats have been charming people for thousands of years. It's hard not to be captivated by these graceful animals, with their intelligence, tidy habits, and amusing ways. Today more people than ever share their homes with one of these purr-fect pets—and many people have more than one. In fact, cats now outnumber dogs in the United States. According to a paw count conducted by a pet industry group, there are about 66 million cats in American homes, compared to about 58 million dogs.

Of all God's creatures there is only one that cannot be made the slave of the lash. That one is the cat. If man could be crossed with a cat it would improve man, but it would deteriorate the cat.

Mark Twain

Cat lovers often say that they don't own their cats. Instead, they say, the cats own them! Cats seem to agree. They are famous for their independence. And in the eyes of cat lovers, that independence is just one more delightful trait to cherish.

FROM WILD TO PET

The domestic cats of today are descended from wild cats that lived in Europe and Africa. About 4,000 years ago, some of these cats consented to live with people. And people

94

were honored to have them, or so it seems. Cats were considered sacred by the ancient Egyptians. Archeologists have uncovered lots of cat mummies in Egypt. Other ancient societies also honored cats. In ancient China, for example, people believed that cats could drive away evil spirits. And early Norsemen had great reverence for the cat. Their goddess of fertility, Freyja, traveled in a chariot pulled by two cats.

But cats haven't been held in such high esteem in all times and places. In Europe during the Middle Ages, cats were associated with witchcraft—and that was bad news for cats. In the 1300's, many cats were put to death by people who believed that these animals were really witches in disguise. However, fewer cats meant more rats—and that was bad news for people. Rats helped spread plague, a deadly disease that wiped out 25 percent of Europe's population.

Domestic cats came to America with European colonists. The colonists valued these animals not just as pets but as pest controllers; colonial cats caught mice and rats, keeping these rodents from gobbling up stores of grain. Farmers still keep barn cats and value their talents as "mousers." But today most cats are house cats, valued as pets and companions.

A PURR-FECT LIFE

House cats have a good life. They spend about 70 percent of the day sleeping, and another 15 percent grooming themselves. A cat stays clean by licking itself all over with its rough tongue. Along with dirt, the tongue whisks away loose hairs—which the cat may swallow. Cats sometimes throw up little balls of this fur.

> *Nature breaks through the eyes of the cat.*
> Irish Proverb

When a house cat sleeps during the day, it isn't being lazy. It's just doing what comes naturally. In nature, most cats rest during the day and hunt at night. And cats are excellent hunters. A cat stalks its prey in silence and will sit motionless for ages, waiting for the right moment to come. Then, with a quick pounce, the cat strikes.

Black Cats

Is it bad luck for a black cat to cross your path? That's an old superstition, a belief that has no basis in fact.

The idea that black cats bring bad luck probably goes back to the Middle Ages. People of that time associated cats with witches

and black with evil—so, they figured, a black cat must be *really* bad news! But this old belief hasn't been shared by everyone. In ancient China, black cats were thought to bring good luck. And in Britain today, many people still consider a black cat to be a good-luck charm.

Sit, Kitty

Unlike dogs, which are eager to please people, cats aren't very interested in what their people think of them. That independent nature means that it's hard to train a cat to sit, fetch, or perform other tricks on command. But some animal trainers have found that there is a way to train cats—by offering food as a reward.

Want to train your cat to sit on command? Try this: Scoop up a bit of cat food with a spoon. Move the spoon up over your cat's

head, saying "sit" as you do (see photo above.) As the spoon moves overhead, your cat will look up to follow it and, in the process, automatically sit. (If the cat doesn't, you can gently press its hind end down—but don't push hard.) The instant the cat sits, say "good sit" and give a bit of the food as a reward. After many repetitions, your cat will make the connection between your command, the action of sitting, and the reward of food. When that happens, the cat will sit on command.

Of course, for this method to work, your cat must want the food you offer. And with independent-minded cats, you can't always be sure of that!

Speed is one reason why cats excel at hunting. Cats are very fast. The African cheetah is the world's fastest land mammal, reaching speeds of nearly 70 miles (113 kilometers) an hour. But even a house cat can run as fast as 30 miles (48 kilometers) an hour. That's a little more than 2 miles (3 kilometers) an hour faster than the fastest human runners!

With food provided for them, house cats don't have to hunt. But they do hunt, acting on the age-old instincts that kept their ancestors alive. If your cat goes hunting, it may surprise you with a little gift—a dead mouse or other prey. Bringing prey home is another instinct. It's your cat's way of making sure *you* don't go hungry!

CAT CHAT

Cats mew, meow, hiss, and yowl. Some big wild cats—lions, tigers, jaguars, and leopards—roar. But the sound cat lovers like to hear best is purring. Scientists aren't completely sure how cats purr, but they know that this rumbling, humming sound is amplified by a bony structure in the cat's throat. Kittens as young as one week old purr while they nurse, and cats of all ages make this noise when they're content. But cats also purr when they're sick or injured. Some scientists think purring may help cats relieve stress.

If you really want to know what your cat is thinking, you'll need to learn to interpret its body language as well as the sounds it makes. Are your cat's ears perked up, and its tail relaxed? The cat is probably happy and relaxed. Are the ears flat back? The cat may be frightened or in pain. Is the tail held high, with the tip flicking back and forth? The cat may feel threatened. When a cat feels really threatened, it may even strike a Halloween pose—it arches

Authors like cats because they are such quiet, lovable, wise creatures, and cats like authors for the same reasons.

Robertson Davies

What does a cat do all day? A cat spends most of its day sleeping in any comfortable spot—or position—it finds. A cat also spends a great deal of time cleaning itself with its rough tongue. And after a nap and a grooming session, a cat might like to go on a hunt; as it silently stalks its prey, a cat waits for just the right moment to pounce.

its back and puffs out the fur on its back and tail. The pose makes the cat look bigger than it actually is, so it may scare off an enemy.

When your cat runs to greet you and rubs against your legs, it may seem to be showing affection. In fact, the cat is laying claim to you. The cat has scent glands on its head. As it presses its head against you, some of the scent rubs off. You may not notice it, but other cats will. They'll know that you "belong" to your cat! In the wild, a cat uses its scent to mark its territory, rubbing

Top Cat

At cat shows, cats are judged on their appearance and on how well they represent the characteristics of their breed. And the top show cat of 1999 was Nobu, the winner of the highest award at the International Cat Show, held in New York City in March.

Nobu is a Japanese bobtail, a slender, medium-size breed with a short, bunny-like tail that looks like a pom-pom. The bobtail has a triangular head, large ears, and slanted eyes, and it may be white, black, red, or a combination of those colors. Japanese bobtails are unusual in America, but they are well known in Japan. There, many people believe that the bobtail brings good luck. And luck was certainly with Nobu. He bested 273 other felines of various breeds to win his award.

against objects or clawing them (there are also scent glands in the cat's paws).

Clawing is something that cats do naturally, and smart cat owners provide a scratching post so their pets won't wreck the furniture. Here, too, cats are just obeying their instinct to stretch their claws and leave their mark.

Cats also "knead" soft objects—such as a pillow, or your lap—by pressing with their paws over and over again. Kittens do these "paw presses" while they nurse to help the mother's milk flow. When adult cats do them, it usually means they're content.

> *Cats seem to go on the principle that it never does any harm to ask for what you want.*
> Joseph Wood Krutch

THE TOP TEN

Among cat breeds, the elegant, longhaired Persian cat has clawed its way to the top of the popularity polls. These fancy felines are famous for their fluffy fur, which may be white, black, red, blue, or cream, and solid or parti-colored. Persian cats, as you might guess, are thought to have originated in Persia many years ago. They are sturdy and broad-chested under all that fur.

Second in popularity is the Maine coon cat. This breed originated in Maine in the 1850's, when long-haired cats from abroad mated with local short-haired cats. With thick, shaggy coats and long bushy tails, the offspring of that cross looked a little like raccoons—and that gave rise to the name "Maine coon." Maine coons are large, muscular, rugged cats, but they are also gentle and good natured.

In third place is the Siamese, a graceful, streamlined cat with slanting, brilliant blue eyes. The Siamese cat has a short, glossy coat, pale buff or cream in color, with dark "points" on the face, ears, feet, and tail.

Rounding out the top ten most popular registered cat breeds are the Abyssinian, exotic

Among cat fanciers, the top breeds include the fluffy, longhaired Persian (*top*); the unusual lop-eared Scottish fold (*center*); and the graceful, blue-eyed Siamese (*bottom*).

shorthair, Oriental shorthair, Scottish fold, American shorthair, Birman, and ocicat. There are lots of unusual breeds, too. The Rex cat is an example. This odd-looking breed was developed in Britain in the 1950's. It has huge ears and a short, curly coat, and it wags its tail like a dog when it's happy! For that reason (and its curly coat) the Rex is sometimes called the "poodle cat."

Of course, lots of cats aren't registered and don't belong to any particular breed. They're mixed breeds—alley cats—but they're loved by their owners just as much as any purebred cat.

A white SNAKE is easy to spot coiled on the dark forest floor. This snake doesn't have the black and brown pigments that help others of its kind blend in. But you can see that it has traces of a pattern in its scales. Such ghostly patterns are common in albino snakes.

PEACOCKS are famous for their colorful, shimmering feathers. But this albino peacock's pure white display is a knockout, even without those colors. In the wild, white feathers would make the bird an easy mark for predators. But the peacock is a domestic bird, and people protect it from danger.

COLOR ME WHITE!

A cream-colored alligator? A pink and white koala? You might expect to see such animals in a toy store, not in nature. Yet these animals are real. They are albinos—animals that look as if they've just taken a swim in a tub of white paint.

Albino animals lack pigments, the substances that produce color. Pigments are made by cells in skin, fur, feathers, and eyes. One animal differs from another in color depending on the amount and kind of pigments these cells contain.

But albinos can't produce pigments. True albinos have pale skin, pure white coats or feathers, and pink eyes. Most white animals aren't albinos. Polar bears, for example, have plenty of pigment in their skin and eyes. An albino is white when it shouldn't be—it's normally meant to be another color. Some animals are only partly albino. They may lack color in some parts of the body. Or they may be extremely pale, but not pure white, all over.

An albino KOALA snoozes in a eucalyptus tree. Its fluffy white fur and pink nose make it look like a stuffed toy. But this cute koala has some real problems to worry about. That white fur is easy for predators to see. And that pink nose—well, without pigment, the koala could get a very bad sunburn. Better stay in the shade!

This albino ALLIGATOR doesn't have to worry about predators—it is one. But how can a 'gator sneak up on prey when it's glow-in-the-swamp white? Without pigment, the alligator could also be harmed, even killed, by too much sun. That's a problem for albino alligators and other reptiles because they are cold blooded and need the sun's warmth.

Albinism is inherited. That is, it's passed from parents to offspring by the genes inside cells. Animals that aren't albino can have albino babies if both parents carry the gene for albinism. That's because genes work in pairs. If an animal has the gene for albinism paired with a gene for color, it will be colored. But what if this animal mates with another that carries the gene for albinism? Their offspring may get two albino genes—one from each parent—and be white.

Albinism can occur in just about any species. Besides the animals shown here, it has been found in catfish, frogs, gorillas, lobsters, penguins, porcupines, trout, turtles, and many others—including people.

Albino animals have a hard life, and it's often a short life. Their pale color makes them easy for predators to spot. And without pigment to act as a sunscreen, their eyes are very sensitive to light. They often have poor vision.

People have long been fascinated by albinos. In American Indian beliefs, white deer and buffalo were held sacred. It's easy to see why—there is something magical about these rare and wonderful creatures.

SAVE THE SEA HORSE

If you set out to invent a fantasy animal, you couldn't come up with anything wilder than a sea horse. A little of this, a dash of that—it's almost as if this odd-looking fish borrowed its body parts from other animals. The sea horse has the fins of a fish, but its head might be on loan from a horse. It can change color like a chameleon. Its long tail could belong to a monkey—because the sea horse can wrap its tail around a piece of seaweed the way some monkeys wrap their tails around tree branches. Oddest of all, the male sea horse has a pouch like the pouch of a female kangaroo.

But the sea horse is unlike all those animals in one big way. It's the male sea horse, not the female, that gets pregnant and gives birth to babies!

Of all the strange fish that swim in the oceans, the sea horse may be the strangest. It's certainly one of the cutest. Today, however, the number of sea horses is shrinking worldwide, mostly because of overfishing. But people are taking action to protect sea horses. They want to be sure that these weird and wonderful fish don't join the lists of extinct and endangered animals.

BOBBING IN THE WEEDS

There are about 35 kinds, or species, of sea horses. They range in size from less than 2 inches (5 centimeters) to more than 12 inches (30 centimeters) long, but most are about 6 inches (15 centimeters). They're found in shallow waters, among beds of seaweed and sea grass, in temperate and tropical regions. Sea horses live off both coasts of North America. The greatest variety is found along the coasts of Southeast Asia and Australia.

The number of sea horses is shrinking worldwide, so many people are working to save these wonderfully weird fish.

Besides their "borrowed" body parts, sea horses have some other special features. Sea horses are close relatives of pipefish, and like pipefish they don't have scales. Instead, a sea horse's skin is stretched over a series of bony plates and rings. The plates and rings give it a knobby look, as if it had been carved from wood. But there's lots of variety in the sea-horse family. The hedgehog sea horse, for example, which lives off Australia, is covered with spines.

It can be difficult to spot a sea horse in a bed of seaweed. Most of the time, sea horses blend right in with their weedy surroundings. Some sea horses are nearly white, and some are red or purple. But drab green and brown are the most common sea-horse colors. And like chameleons, many sea horses can change color to match their surroundings. Several species also have skin tendrils that sprout like little branches from their bodies, so they look even more like seaweed. This

The sea horse spends much of its life clinging to plants with its long prehensile tail. Its grasping tail also plays a part in the sea horse's courtship rituals; some "romantic" sea horses hold tails and twirl up and down stalks of seaweed together.

The sea horse is the only fish that carries its head at right angles to its body. And it swims with its body upright, rapidly waving its back fin to push through the water. When a sea horse hits top speed, its back fin is just a blur. But sea horses aren't strong swimmers. A sea horse spends its life in the same patch of seaweed, bobbing in the currents or clinging to plants with its long prehensile (grasping) tail.

camouflage makes it hard for predators to find the sea horse.

The sea horse itself is a predator. Swimming or resting, it's always on the lookout for the tiny ocean animals it likes to eat. When it spies a meal, the sea horse snaps it up or sucks it in through its tubelike snout. The sea horse is like a chameleon in another way: Its eyes protrude from its head, and it can swivel them independently in all directions. Like a chameleon, a sea horse can look ahead with one eye, and back with the other!

"MR. MOM"

Sea horses may look different, but it's their family life that *really* sets them apart. Among many kinds of sea horses, males and females form long-lasting bonds. It's believed that some mate for life. Sea-horse courtship actually seems quite romantic. The male and female "blush" when they meet, changing color from drab to glowing. They don't hold hands, of course (they don't have hands), but some sea horses do hold tails. And some dance, twirling up stalks of seaweed and bobbing through the water together.

Finally the male bobs and bows to the female and puffs out his brood pouch by filling it with water. That tells her that he's ready to mate. The female uses a small tube called an ovipositor to squirt her eggs into the brood pouch on the male's belly. The opening to the brood pouch closes, and she swims away.

Inside the brood pouch, the eggs are fertilized and begin to develop into baby sea horses. They get nourishment through the walls of the brood pouch, and the male's belly swells like a balloon as they grow. The male's pregnancy lasts about a month, depending on water temperatures and on the species. During that time the female stops by to visit her partner every morning, and the pair performs a greeting dance.

One day the male wraps his tail around a strand of seaweed and begins to pump his body like an accordion. A baby sea horse pops out of his pouch with each push. Small

Left: It's easy to tell the male sea horse from the female—the male is the one with the belly pouch that's puffed up like a balloon. And in the pouch are some 200 infants! Right: When the babies are ready to be born, the male tightens his muscles and the little sea horses shoot into the water.

sea horses generally give birth to ten or fewer babies at a time, while larger kinds may have several hundred. A Caribbean sea horse called James once gave birth to 1,572 babies!

The newborn sea horses are perfect copies of their parents, but they are only about half an inch (1 centimeter) long. They swim off on their own and right away begin to eat microscopic ocean animals. They grow quickly—if they aren't devoured by bigger fish and other predators. Sea horses generally live about three years in the wild.

SEA HORSES AND PEOPLE

The scientific name for the sea horse is *Hippocampus*. That name comes from Greek words that mean "horse" and "sea monster." And like a legendary sea monster, the sea horse is the subject of many odd beliefs. In ancient times, people put sea-horse ashes on their heads as a cure for baldness. Dried, powdered sea horses were thought to prevent rabies and cure other diseases. They were an ingredient in love potions. But mixed with wine, they were said to be a deadly poison.

Today, sea horses are still widely used in traditional Chinese medicine. Chinese herbal practitioners prescribe powdered sea horse for everything from sore throats to asthma. Dried sea horses are also sold as souvenirs. At least 20 million wild sea horses are taken from the ocean for these uses every year, and the number is growing. Several hundred thousand more are taken live—sea horses are popular aquarium specimens, but they don't live long in captivity and must be replaced frequently.

At the same time, the shallow coastal waters where sea horses live are threatened by pollution and shoreline development. Facing all these threats, sea-horse populations have declined by more than 50 percent since the early 1990's. But now scientists, conservationists, and concerned individuals are banding together to protect these one-of-a-kind fish. The sea horse may look quirky, but it's one of nature's greatest wonders.

Project Sea Horse

Amanda Vincent, a biology professor at McGill University in Canada, began to study sea horses in 1986. The more she learned about the unusual animals, the more she was charmed—and alarmed. Fishermen were catching more and more sea horses every year. Sea-horse populations were shrinking dramatically. What could be done?

Vincent's answer was to join with other scientists to found Project Sea Horse, in 1996. This international group is working to save sea horses before their numbers decline so much that they are in danger of dying out. Here are some of the actions they are taking:

Research: Learning more about these unique fish is the first step in saving them. Scientists want to know more about where they live, what they eat, and how they grow and reproduce.

Captive breeding: Sea horses often don't thrive in captivity. But researchers hope to improve survival rates and get more captive fish to reproduce. It may even be possible to raise sea horses commercially.

Reducing fishing: Project Sea Horse is helping fishermen become less dependent on income from sea horses by finding other ways for them to earn money. Some areas have set up reserves where sea-horse fishing isn't allowed.

Reducing demand: Project Sea Horse is also encouraging practitioners of Chinese medicine to use fewer sea horses. And they are asking people not to buy sea horses for aquariums.

Animals use their tails to do many things—and sending messages is one of the most important. When you see a skunk lift its black-and-white tail. . .watch out!

ANIMAL TAILS

The longest tail ever measured belonged to a dinosaur known as *Diplodocus*. One of the shortest tails belongs to people. In between, tails range from a pig's skinny twirl to a peacock's dazzling train.

A skeleton of *Diplodocus* is on view at the Carnegie Museum of Natural History in Pittsburgh, Pennsylvania. The dinosaur's neck measures 22 feet (7 meters), its body 15 feet (5 meters), and its tail 50 feet (15 meters). The tail alone is longer than a city bus. *Diplodocus* probably used its gigantic whiplash tail as a bone-crushing weapon against enemies.

Humans have barely a hint of a tail. It's a small bone at the base of the spine, shaped like a cuckoo's beak. It's called the *coccyx* (KOK-siks), from the Greek word for "cuckoo."

Short or long, plain or fancy, tails are important. Some animals can't get along without them. They're used for flying, jumping, running, swimming, sitting, eating, hunting, fighting, keeping warm or cool, warning friends, scaring enemies, and flirting with the opposite sex.

TAILS THAT SEND MESSAGES

When a beaver hears or smells anything suspicious, it smacks the water with its large, paddle-shaped tail. This danger signal sounds like a sharp gunshot. And it warns all the beavers within hearing to quickly race for safety.

The beaver's tail has other uses, too. In the water, it serves as a rudder—a beaver lowers its tail when it dives and raises it when it swims back to the surface. On land, the tail becomes a sturdy prop—when a beaver sits upright to feed or to cut down a tree, it supports itself with its broad, flat tail.

A white-tailed deer sends a silent warning signal with its tail. At the first sign of danger it flicks its tail upward. The top of the deer's tail is dark, but the underside is pure white—the only white patch on the animal's body. The sight of this white patch flashing in the woods instantly alerts all the deer in the herd.

Some tails are used to scare off enemies. A rattlesnake shakes its tail when it feels threatened. As the rattles at the tip of the tail click together, they make a buzzing sound—a warning that the rattler is ready to strike. The rattle isn't a signal to other rattlesnakes, since snakes are almost deaf. A rattler can't even hear its own rattle. Instead, its rattle may save the snake from being stepped on or attacked.

A skunk also depends on its tail to keep enemies at a distance. When you see a skunk lower its head and lift its black-and-white tail like a battle flag, it means that the skunk is getting ready to fire. If you don't retreat fast, the skunk will twist into a U-shaped position, aim both head and tail at its target, and let go with its stinking spray.

Some birds use their tails to send a different kind of message. Male birds often have large, colorful tail feathers that they show off during courtship displays. When a peacock spreads his long tail feathers, or train, he wants to attract the attention of females. He opens his train by shaking himself until the brilliant feathers rise behind him and spread out like a lacy fan. Then he turns again and again, jumping forward and stepping back, snapping his tail closed, then spreading it open again. During this dance, he sings the lyre bird's melodic courtship song and also imitates the songs and calls of many birds and other animals.

TAILS FOR MOVING ABOUT

Without tails, birds would have a hard time flying. In the air, a bird drives itself forward with its wings, but it steers and balances with the help of its tail. When a flying bird turns, it spreads its tail like a fan

What a show-off! Male peacocks have large, colorful tail feathers that they display while courting. When a peacock wants to attract the attention of females, he spreads out his tail like a lacy fan and struts about.

struts about, clattering his quills together, screaming loudly, and turning around slowly as the peahens watch.

The Australian lyre bird gets its name from its big lyre-shaped tail. During his courtship display, a male lyre bird not only shows off his tail, he also sings, dances, and does imitations. As a female watches, he spreads his tail wide, throws the tail over his head, and turns in a half-circle. Then he stands on tiptoe and shakes his tail feathers.

and twists the tail in one direction or the other to help swing its body around. When it moves upward or downward, it bends its tail up or down. As it lands, it lowers its widely spread tail, which acts as a brake.

Long-tailed birds like swallows can turn sharply at high speeds as they dart about chasing insects. Short-tailed birds like ducks can't steer nearly as well. They never make quick turns while flying. Short-tailed birds are also poor landers, since they find it dif-

Like most fish, this fairy basslet uses its tail as a propeller to glide in the water.

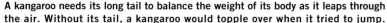

ficult to slow down. A duck usually lands on water, pushing its webbed feet forward and skidding to a stop.

Most fish would be helpless without their tails. A fish uses its tail as a propeller. It swims by twisting its body and beating its tail fin from side to side. A fast swimmer like a marlin or swordfish has a large forked tail fin, which it beats back and forth with great force.

A fish's tail fin is upright, or vertical. Whales, dolphins, and porpoises have tails that are flat, or horizontal. They beat their tail flukes up and down, like the flippers on a skin diver's feet, as they dive down into the depths, rise to the surface to breathe, or swim straight ahead.

On solid ground, tails help many animals keep their balance as they run and jump.

Fast runners like wolves and cheetahs must constantly twist and turn as they chase their dodging prey. They bend their long tails in the direction they want to turn, just as speeding bicycle riders lean inward while turning to keep their balance.

Powerful jumpers like kangaroos also need their long tails for balance. A kangaroo's outstretched tail balances the weight of its body as it leaps through the air, covering 30 feet (9 meters) with a single bound. Without its tail, the kangaroo would topple over when it tried to jump. Like a beaver, a kangaroo also uses its sturdy tail as a support when it sits upright.

The long tails of many tree-dwelling animals help them maneuver through the treetops. A squirrel uses its bushy tail to keep its balance as it races along branches and

A kangaroo needs its long tail to balance the weight of its body as it leaps through the air. Without its tail, a kangaroo would topple over when it tried to jump.

runs headfirst down tree trunks. When it leaps to the ground from a high branch, its tail serves as a parachute and a brake. Flying squirrels spread their wide tails like sails as they glide long distances from one tree to the next.

Some tree dwellers have long prehensile (pre-HEN-sul) tails— tails that can grasp a limb or other object and hang on. A prehensile tail is like a long arm with one strong finger at the end, in place of a hand. South American spider monkeys, woolly monkeys, and howlers have such powerful prehensile tails that they can swing from branches, supporting their entire body weight with just the tips of their tails.

A spider monkey can reach out with its tail and grab a piece of fruit hanging at the end of a branch. It can wrap its tail around a branch and hang on while it sleeps. If it misses its mark as it leaps from tree to tree, it can check its fall by seizing a branch with the tip of its tail. Even a baby spider monkey uses its prehensile tail, to hang on to its mother.

Another animal with a strong prehensile tail is the opossum, which also hangs upside down from branches. An opossum often uses its tail as a safety belt, anchoring itself to one end of a branch while reaching with its paws for ripe fruit at the other end. When baby opossums are big enough to leave their mother's pouch, they climb onto

The opossum's strong prehensile tail allows it to dangle securely upside down from a tree branch.

her back and cling to her fur with their tiny feet and their little prehensile tails as she climbs trees in search of food.

TAILS FOR HUNTING

Alligators and crocodiles often hunt with their tails. A crocodile will lie in wait along a riverbank waiting for deer or pigs to come and drink. Once an unsuspecting animal gets close enough, the crocodile lashes out with its powerful tail, hurling the victim into the water and then attacking with its toothy jaws.

The thresher shark uses its tail to catch fish. The upper part of its tail fin is longer than the shark's body and is curved like a scythe. Lashing the water with its long, curved tail, the shark herds schools of small fish into a tight bunch, so it can easily gulp them down.

The Willie wagtail is a bird that's native to Australia. When it's hungry, it swishes its long tail feathers through the grass, stirring up insects in the process. As the insects fly up from the ground, the wagtail grabs and eats them.

TAILS FOR SELF DEFENSE

Few animals are foolish enough to attack a porcupine. Buried beneath its long fur, a porcupine has more than 30,000 sharp quills, and lots of those quills are in its tail.

If a porcupine is threatened, it raises its quills, turns it back to the enemy, and lashes

A porcupine's tail contains sharp quills that act like fishhooks when slapped against an enemy.

stick out along each side of its tail, like the blades of a double-edged sword. A pangolin's lashing tail can rip into an enemy.

In the sea, stingrays have tails like whips, armed with poisonous spines as sharp as daggers. When a stingray is disturbed, it flicks its tail from side to side or snaps the tail over its head, driving its spines into the enemy. Some stingrays have two or three poisonous spines on their tails. And some of those spines are more than a foot long.

The tropical surgeon fish is armed with a pair of small switchblades, one on either side of its tail. Each blade is as sharp as a surgeon's scalpel. Normally the blades are flattened shut against the fish's tail fin. But in an emergency, the surgeon fish can snap open the blades and strike sideways with its tail.

The tail of an electric eel packs a real jolt. In the eel's tail are bundles of special cells that build up electricity. As the eel swims through South American rivers, it gives off a weak electric current. When it finds food or is alarmed, it can deliver a strong electric shock of 650 volts. It uses the electricity in its tail to stun the fish and frogs it feeds on, and to jolt enemies like alligators.

Some tails save the lives of their owners by breaking off if they are grabbed by an enemy. Many lizards have long tails that snap off easily. Often the tail will wrig-

out with its tail. A single slap of that bristling tail can drive hundreds of barbed quills into the enemy's flesh. Like fishhooks, the quills catch under the victim's skin. After attacking a porcupine once, most animals learn their lesson. They never try it again.

Another dangerous tail belongs to the African pangolin, or scaly anteater. A pangolin looks like a walking pine cone. It's covered with flat, sharp-edged scales from the top of its head to the end of its long tail. The scales

A stingray's whiplike tail is armed with sharp, poisonous spines.

110

The Gila monster stores fat in its tail, just as a camel is able to store body fat in its hump. This helps the lizard to survive in desert regions where food is often scarce.

gle violently on the ground after it breaks off, holding the enemy's attention while the lizard quickly escapes. In a short time, the lizard grows a new tail that may save its life again.

MORE TAILS

Cows and horses use their tails as fly swatters. You've probably seen two horses standing side by side, facing in opposite directions, flicking their tails as they shoo flies from each other's faces.

Songbirds sometimes use their tails as umbrellas for their nestlings. During a rainstorm, a robin will spread its wings and tail feathers over its nest, keeping the nest and the chicks dry.

A lizard called the Gila monster is one of several animals that store food in their tails. Gila monsters live in desert regions where food is often scarce. When they have a chance, they eat more than they need. The extra food is changed to fat and stored in the Gila monster's tail for future use, just as a camel stores body fat in its hump.

Tails can also keep their owners warm or cool. Foxes and squirrels wrap their furry tails around their faces while sleeping in winter. In summer, animals like mice, beavers, and muskrats sweat through their nearly naked tails. Without such tails, the body heat in these thick-furred animals would build up to dangerous temperatures.

TAILS THAT EXPRESS FEELINGS

A tail can sometimes tell you how an animal feels. Squirrels flick their tails when they're nervous. The more nervous they become, the faster their tails flick.

A frightened mouse vibrates its tail. And when a cat is frightened or angry, its tail swells up to three times its normal size as the tail's fur stands on end.

Members of the dog family express several emotions with their tails. A dog holds its tail high when it feels confident. If it feels playful, it wags its tail slowly, with wide sweeps. If it wants approval, it holds its tail lower, and wags it more quickly. And if it is being scolded, it hides its tail between its hind legs.

ANIMALS IN THE NEWS

You're strolling down a rain-forest path, surrounded by tropical trees and vines. Suddenly, you stop short. There, just a few yards away, stands a big silverback gorilla! There's no need to worry, though. This is the new **Congo Gorilla Forest** exhibit at the Bronx Zoo, in New York City. And there's a thick glass window between you and the gorilla.

Congo Gorilla Forest, which opened last summer, focuses on the Central African rain forests. Its goal is to help people learn about the rich plant and animal life in these forests. And the $3 exhibit admission fee goes to conservation projects in Africa. The projects are run by the Bronx Zoo's parent organization, the Wildlife Conservation Society (WCS). The WCS, which was founded as the New York Zoological Society in 1899, marked its 100th birthday in 1999.

All together, the exhibit covers 6.5 acres (2.6 hectares). It includes a variety of habitats for animals—shady forests, treetop lookouts, rock outcrops, streams and pools, bamboo thickets, and meadows. Visitors follow a trail that takes them through indoor and outdoor areas. Along the way there's a chance to see some 75 different kinds of animals. Near the end of the trail, visitors enter a glass-walled tunnel. It leads through the heart of the rain forest. There they meet the exhibit's stars—its 22 lowland gorillas. For zoogoers, it's a thrill to come face to face with these urban gorillas. And the gorillas seem just as curious about people as people are about them!

When **squirrels bury acorns** in the fall, do they know what they're doing? To find out, researchers tested eastern gray squirrels. They set out acorns from white oaks, which sprout soon after they drop; and acorns from red oaks, which lie on the ground all winter before they sprout. The squirrels ate most of the white-oak acorns right away. And they buried most of the red-oak kind.

Once acorns sprout, they're no longer such good squirrel food. Do squirrels know that the white-oak acorns will sprout quickly, while the red-oak acorns will last? That's doubtful. A squirrel has a brain the size of a bean. But something tells squirrels to eat one acorn and bury another. In the winter, the squirrels find and eat only some of their buried nuts. Those they lose grow into oak trees in the spring.

Is this duck awake or asleep? Both answers are right. Scientists have discovered that **birds can sleep with one eye open**—and their brains half awake. A bird's brain, like yours, is divided into halves, called hemispheres. But a bird can close one eye and let one hemisphere sleep. Meanwhile, the bird's other eye stays open, and the other hemisphere stays alert. This trick is called unihemispheric slow-wave sleep (USWS). It lets a bird "keep an eye out" for predators even in its sleep! (This duck's right eye is closed; its eyelid is white.)

On August 20, 1999, the **peregrine falcon** was officially removed from the U.S. list of endangered and threatened species. Once in danger of dying out, the graceful peregrine was placed on the list in 1970. It made an amazing comeback—proof that threatened species can be saved.

Kirby weighs just 6 pounds (3 kilograms). But small size didn't keep this little dog from big things. Kirby won the top award at the 1999 Westminster Kennel Club Dog Show, the most important dog show in the United States. The little furball of energy was so pleased with himself that he jumped right into his silver trophy!

Kirby's full name is Champion Loteki Supernatural Being. He's a papillon, and he's the first of his breed to take top honors at Westminster. The papillon is a dainty dog with long fur. Its big ears stick out to the side, and when the little dog prances along they wave like the wings of a butterfly. In fact, that's how the breed got its name. *Papillon* is French for "butterfly."

The famous cherry trees around the Tidal Basin in Washington, D.C., were just reaching peak bloom in April 1999. Then disaster struck. Visitors and park rangers arrived one day to find a bare stump sticking up from the ground. One of the beautiful trees had been felled.

Who chopped down the cherry tree? Not George Washington! The culprit was a beaver—actually, **a family of beavers.** Beavers toppled ten trees, including four cherry trees, around the Tidal Basin. Four more cherry trees were damaged by the animals, whose big teeth and strong jaws can chop through wood like axes.

The beavers may have been planning to build a log dam or lodge in the Tidal Basin. Or they may just have wanted to snack on the trees' tender spring leaves and twigs. Either way, National Park Service rangers didn't give the beavers a chance to settle in. They wrapped tree trunks with wire mesh for protection. And they set traps to catch the beavers. The traps were designed not to hurt the animals. Once the furry culprits were caught, they were moved out of town—to a place where they could chew on trees that weren't national treasures.

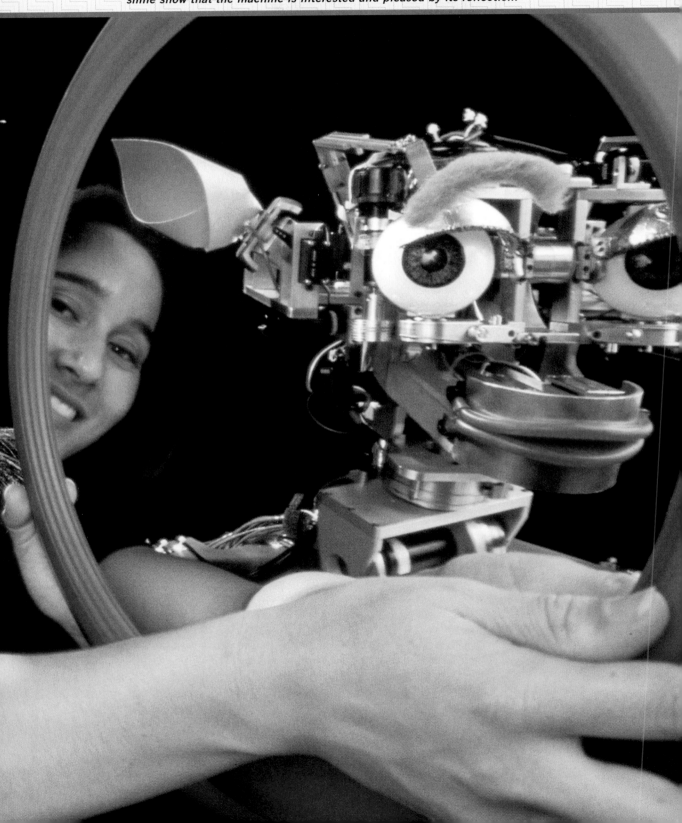

Who's the fairest of them all? A robot named Kismet looks in a mirror—and it clearly seems to like what it sees! Even humans have to agree that Kismet is cute. This robot is programmed to express feelings like happiness, boredom, fear, and surprise. Perky pink ears, raised eyebrows, and a little smile show that the machine is interested and pleased by its reflection.

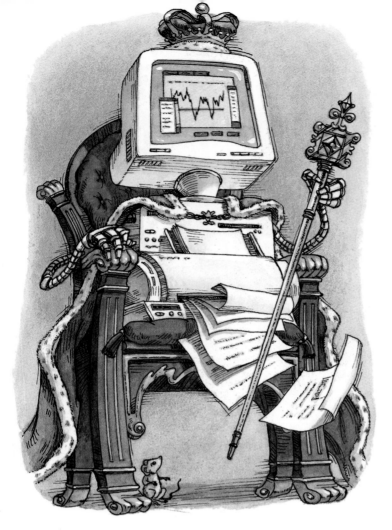

INTO THE FUTURE

You've had a hard day, and you're ready to relax. You flop down on the sofa, put your feet up, and make three wishes: "Dim lights. TV on. Popcorn." Instantly, the lights go down, the TV switches on, and the microwave oven starts popping your favorite snack. There's no magic, and no flock of servants waiting for your commands. In the high-tech world of the future, automated systems may do all this and much more.

The year 2000 marks the beginning of a millennium—a thousand-year period. And as the world gears up for the next millennium, people are looking ahead and wondering what life will be like in this new era.

Futurists—people who are experts at making predictions—have been especially busy as the new millennium approaches.

Futurists keep an eye on trends and technology, and then they try to imagine where new developments might lead in years to come. These experts know that their predictions may not be right. The farther ahead in the future you look, the less accurate the predictions are likely to be. But who can resist taking a peek at the futurists' crystal ball? Here's just a sampling of what may lie ahead in the new millennium.

COMPUTERS WILL RULE

Computers are already important. In the next millennium, they'll be essential. Computers will be involved in just about everything people do, futurists agree.

The computers of the future will be different from those of today. They'll be smaller and more powerful, and they'll probably be wireless. That is, instead of using cables to carry signals to printers, monitors, and other devices, the computers will transmit radio signals. Wireless technology is already here, in the form of wireless keyboards and mice. Experts say the trend will grow, and that tangle of cables behind most computers will be a thing of the past.

Some of the biggest changes may be in home computers. For example, your home may have a central computer that keeps the family records, links you to the Internet, acts as a game unit, controls your TV, VCR, and sound system—all at the same time! This central computer will have several display screens in different parts of your house. They'll be flat screens mounted on the walls, and they'll receive signals wirelessly from the central computer.

You'll still have keyboards, mice, and remote controls, but you won't use them so often. Computers of the future will be controlled by voice. The computer will recognize your voice and understand your speech. Say "check my bank balance," and the computer will tell you how much money is in your account.

HIGH-TECH HOMES AND GADGETS

The home of the future, experts say, will be totally automated. Automated systems, controlled by one computer or several, will do everything from turning out lights to adjusting temperatures. You'll tell the computers what to do by speaking—and they'll talk back. Using sensors placed all around the house, a central computer may monitor your home and tell you if the roof is leaking or the heating system needs service, for example. In the kitchen, you'll have computer-controlled appliances that talk, too. When you open the refrigerator, it may announce that you're running low on milk.

Your high-tech home's sensors may even monitor you. If you lie down for a nap, the computer will thoughtfully dim the lights and close the blinds. Outside, while you're relaxing, a robot lawnmower will cut the grass. Infrared sensors will keep it from slamming into trees or running over flowerbeds.

Want to find out what's going on in the world? Say "watch the news," and your home computer will switch on the television and select the program you want. When it comes to entertainment, high-definition digital television will provide super-sharp pictures and quality sound. Watching TV will be as exciting as going to the movies today.

But the real excitement will come from virtual reality. When you want to play a video game, you'll put on a headset and special sensors that give you the sensation of actually being inside the game. Computer connections will let you interact with other players—even if they're hundreds of miles away.

With no cables and better batteries, computers will go on the road—they'll be able to work much longer away from a power source than portable computers can today. And as computers go wireless, they'll begin to merge with other electronic devices—like wireless (cellular) telephones. You'll carry a single hand-held device that will let you make phone calls, send and receive faxes, or check the Internet for news and e-mail. Or you'll be able to finish up a report, and then transmit it to your printer at school, work, or home.

You'll be able to send and receive pictures as well as sound and text. So when you make a phone call, you'll be able to see the person you're talking with. You'll take pictures with a hand-held digital camera, then transmit them wirelessly to a printer or modem or send them over the Internet to your friends. You may even be able to create and send holograms—three-dimensional images—by scanning an object with a special device connected to your computer.

SMART CLOTHES FROM CYBERSPACE

Will future fashions look like the outfits worn in science-fiction movies? No one can really guess what the styles will be hundreds of years from now. But whatever they look like, tomorrow's clothes will be "smart." They'll be made of high-tech fabrics that will be able to sense the temperature and adjust to make you comfortable. They'll keep you cool in hot weather and warm in cold weather.

Clothes may even double as computers. Tiny, lightweight microprocessors will be embedded right in the fabric, and you'll enter commands by tapping a pattern on your shirt! Eyeglasses may double as computer screens, allowing you to see your wearable computer's output while you look through to the world.

Whether you're in the market for computerized glasses or an old-fashioned sweater, you'll do most of your shopping by computer. Millions of people already shop by way of the Internet, and the trend is expected to grow. And the days of waiting for graphics and documents to download will end—high-speed cable connections will bring everything to your screen 100 times faster than standard dial-up modems do today.

The Internet will feature more pictures, video, animation, and sound. It may even deliver the sensation of touch. A device that can do this is already being developed. It translates the surface texture of an object—a sweater, for example—into digital code. The code is sent over the Internet. You put your finger into a thimble-like device attached to your computer, and feel how soft the sweater is.

Sophisticated software will help you make use of these new tools. For example, software "agents" or "bots" will surf the net for you, searching out the best price for that new CD or whatever you're looking for. When you find it, you'll pay with a credit card or a debit card, which automatically deducts money from your bank account. Old-fashioned cash may become a thing of the past.

DRIVING INTO THE FUTURE

Cars of the future will produce little or no pollution. They'll run on electricity or hydrogen fuel cells, like those used to power spacecraft today. And they'll be stuffed with high-tech features.

Built-in navigation systems will make sure you get where you want to go. Each car will carry a computer chip that communicates with global positioning satellites. If you're lost, just ask. The car's computer will understand your voice, tell you exactly where you are, and give you directions to your destination.

Meanwhile, sensors on the car will monitor traffic, road, and weather conditions and alert you to dangerous conditions ahead. Using laser beams or radar, other sensors will constantly measure the distance to the car ahead of you and warn you if you're getting too close for safety. For night driving, infrared vision systems will help you detect things you might not see, like a dog running into the road. The infrared system will detect the dog's warmth and warn you, giving you time to avoid it.

ual minitrain. Just tell the train where you want to go, and it will take you there.

STARTLING SCIENCE

Scientific breakthroughs will bring still other changes to daily life. For example, the foods of the future may not look or taste very different from today's foods. But nutritionally, they may be very different. Scientists are already tinkering with genes (the structures in cells that determine the traits of all living things). In the future they may be able to pro-

Future cars may also be equipped with drowsiness detection systems. Mounted on the dashboard, this device will monitor the driver's eyes for signs of sleepiness—and sound a loud wake-up call if the driver starts to nod off.

City transportation systems may take new forms in the future, too. One possibility is called personal rapid transit. Instead of taking a train with hundreds of other people, and perhaps changing trains several times to reach your destination, you'll step into an individ-

duce a potato with more vitamin C than an orange and more protein than a steak. Fry the potato in fat-free oil, and you'll be eating french fries that are actually good for you.

Genetically altered foods may play a big role in feeding the world's future population. The number of people in the world will continue to grow, and providing everyone with enough to eat will be a challenge. With farmland in short supply, researchers will need to develop crops that produce higher yields per acre. More crops will be grown hydroponi-

cally—that is, in nutrient-rich water rather than in soil—and under artificial light. Multistory hydroponic farms may rise in the middle of cities.

Genetically altered foods may also have a role in health care. Genetically altered cows might produce milk that contains medicine, for example. And as scientists learn more about genes, experts predict, they'll be able to cure diseases that are caused by genetic defects.

That's good news, because genes are involved in many disorders. Doctors of the future may be able to harness infectious agents, such as viruses, in the fight against these diseases. To counteract a defective human gene, for example, a copy of a normal gene might be inserted into a harmless virus. The virus would then "infect" the person who has the defective gene, and correct the defect.

To make sure people get the health care they need, a computer chip may be implanted under each person's skin. The chip would carry information about that person's medical history. It might also carry other information—driver's license, social security number, and so on. Like the computer chips in cars of the future, this personal chip could even link up with global positioning satellites. With a system like this, lost children would be found easily.

FAMILY, SCHOOL, AND MORE

If current trends continue, experts say, you'll marry later than your parents did. You'll be older than they were when you have children. But your children may start school at a younger age than you did, perhaps attending a free public preschool.

From kindergarten right through college, your children will be using computers. They may spend more time with computers than they do with teachers! In fact, a lot of learning may take place long-distance, as students log on at home and meet up with their teachers and classmates in cyberspace.

Those heavy books you tote around in your backpack will be a thing of the past. Instead of textbooks, students of the future will have e-books—hand-held notepad-size computers stuffed with thousands of pages of text and pic-

Faulty Forecasts

Anyone can make a prediction. But how often are predictions correct? Even experts are wrong much of the time, as these examples show.

◆ The famous inventor Thomas A. Edison thought the phonograph was just a clever gadget. In 1880, he predicted that few people would want one. He couldn't have been more wrong—a hundred years later, people were snapping up phonograph records at the rate of about 240 million a year! Now CD's have replaced vinyl records. But recorded music is still part of daily life everywhere.

◆ In 1901, Wilbur Wright flatly announced that it would be at least 50 years before anyone invented a successful flying machine. He proved his own prediction wrong just two years later, when he and his brother Orville made their historic first flight at Kitty Hawk, North Carolina.

◆ The noted physicist Albert Einstein predicted in 1932 that people would never succeed in splitting the atom. But in 1938, scientists figured out how to split atoms and release the tremendous energy inside.

◆ The discovery of atomic energy led to all kinds of predictions. In the 1950's, for example, the Ford Motor Company predicted that this new energy source would power future cars. Once people discovered just how dangerous atomic energy can be, that idea was shelved.

◆ When the IBM company developed the first computers, Thomas J. Watson, the head of the company, thought only about five customers worldwide would want the machines. That was in 1949, when computers were so big that they filled entire rooms. Now, thanks to microchip processors, computers fit anywhere, and millions are sold every year.

tures. One little e-book will be all a student needs for a full term of classes. At the end of the term, students will just erase their e-books and download new text and pictures for the next term.

There are lots of other predictions for the new millennium. People may learn to communicate with animals. They may establish colonies on the moon or on Mars, living under huge glass domes.

It's hard to see 30 years into the future, let alone 1,000. Certainly people who lived 1,000 years ago could never have imagined our world. Horses were their fastest transportation, and candles were their only artificial lighting. Our jet aircraft, electric lights, telephones, and televisions would have seemed like magic to them. Who can say? The next millennium may hold things that we can't even dream about.

Dolly, the first clone of an adult mammal, gave birth to triplets in 1999. She made news again when studies of her chromosomes revealed a strange finding—and refueled the debate over cloning.

CLONING: THE NEXT GENERATION

What if you had a perfect double—another person exactly like you? What if there were three or four or forty more, all exact copies of you? It's a wild idea. And so far, it's just an idea. But one day such things may be possible, through cloning.

Cloning is an exciting new area of science. It's also very controversial. Researchers are just beginning to learn how to produce clones, or perfect copies, of animals. They haven't figured out how to produce clones of people, and right now they aren't trying to. But the day of human clones may come.

DOUBLE TAKE

Just a few years ago, clones existed only in science fiction. Experiments in cloning frogs and other animals had shown promise, but the results were mixed. Then, in July 1996, a lamb named Dolly arrived. Dolly was the first clone ever created from an adult animal.

The Scottish scientists who produced her caused quite a stir when they announced their success in 1997.

What made Dolly so special? Her genes. Genes are coded instructions that determine the physical traits of all living things. They decree whether an animal is a cat or a cow, and whether a cat is black or calico. Your genes determine your hair color and eye color and all your other physical traits. Genes are formed of chemical DNA. They are arranged in strings called chromosomes inside the nucleus, or center, of each body cell.

In all animals that reproduce sexually—such as sheep, cats, cows, and people—offspring get half their genes from each parent. A sperm cell from the male fuses with an egg cell from the female, and their genetic material is combined.

A strand of DNA. A clone is produced using the genetic material from only one "parent."

Then the fertilized egg begins to divide, forming a many-celled embryo. The offspring that results is unique—it has some of the traits of both parents, but it's not identical to either.

A clone, on the other hand, has only one "parent." The clone grows from a single cell, with no mating and no mixing of genetic material. It's identical in every way to its parent. Animals don't reproduce this way in nature. So, unlike all sheep before her, Dolly didn't result from a mating between a ram and a ewe.

The Scottish scientists used new laboratory methods that allowed them to manipulate microscopic structures inside cells. They started with a cell from the udder of one sheep. They took an egg cell from another sheep and removed its nucleus, complete with genes. Then they fused the two cells with a little jolt of electricity. The fused cell began to divide and develop into an embryo. It was placed in the womb of a third sheep. And the result was Dolly, a perfect copy of the first sheep.

HERE COME THE CLONES

Was Dolly just a fluke, or could the feat of the Scottish scientists be repeated? The answer wasn't long in coming. Other scientists soon announced that they, too, had produced clones.

In July 1998, scientists in Hawaii reported that they had cloned adult mice, using a technique similar to that of the Scottish scientists. Then they cloned the clones, producing dozens of identical mice. In Japan, scientists cloned an adult cow. Eight calves were born in December 1998, all identical to the first. There have been other reports of cloned cows in Japan and New Zealand.

Cloned sheep, cloned mice, cloned cows—these animals have proved that cloning is possible. And they have shown that the scientific techniques

Three generations of cloned mice: Each one is an exact copy of the mouse on top.

for cloning are developing rapidly. What will be next?

Maybe a dog. One wealthy couple has given more than $2 million to scientists to produce a clone of their pet dog, Missy, a husky-border collie mix. They really love their dog! The scientists hope that if they're successful, their methods will be used to clone endangered wolves and wild dogs.

In China, scientists are trying to clone a giant panda. If they succeed, cloning could help save the pandas, which are in danger of dying out. Only about 1,000 giant pandas remain in the wild, and experts say the species could become extinct in less than 25 years.

Some Japanese scientists are involved in an even wilder project. They hope to clone a woolly mammoth—a huge, elephantlike animal that died out 3,800 years ago. They are searching for frozen mammoth remains in Siberia, in Russia, where the ground in some places never thaws. If they find what they need, they'll extract the genetic material from mammoth cells and try to produce a clone.

The idea of bringing an extinct animal back to life may seem far-fetched. And the Japanese scientists are a long way from succeeding in their mammoth project (no pun intended). Most researchers are interested in cloning for its potential to help people directly.

Cloning could be a great help to ranchers. A sheep that produces lots of wool or a cow that produces lots of milk might be cloned. Its identical offspring would also produce lots of wool or milk, so ranchers could raise herds of super-producers. Cloning could help scientific researchers, too. Using identical animals such as cloned mice in laboratory experiments would simplify research. There would be no individual variation to cloud the results.

Combined with a technique called genetic engineering, cloning may also play a role in producing medicine for people. Here's how: First, scientists would alter the genetic code in cells from an animal, such as a sheep or a cow. For example, they might insert genes that prompt the animal to produce certain proteins and chemicals in its milk—substances that could be extracted and used as medicine. Then that sheep or cow could be cloned. The result would be a herd of medical milk-makers.

A wealthy couple has given researchers more than $2 million to clone their dog, Missy.

HUMAN CLONES?

If animals such as sheep and cows can be cloned, so can people, scientists say. No one has done it yet. But scientists in South Korea announced in December 1998 that they had cloned a cell from an adult woman. They stopped the experiment when the original cell had developed into a four-cell embryo. They said they didn't want to produce a human clone because there's great debate over whether cloning humans would be right or wrong.

Human cloning could have benefits, especially in medicine. For example, if a person had kidney disease, that person's clone could donate a kidney because the two clones' tissues would match perfectly. But cloning could change the way we think of ourselves.

Suppose you were cloned, and there were a hundred other clones like you in the world. Chances are you wouldn't all be exactly alike because people are shaped by their experiences as well as their genes. But you'd be enough like the others so it would be hard to think of your-

An international team of scientists hopes to clone a woolly mammoth—a creature that died out 3,800 years ago.

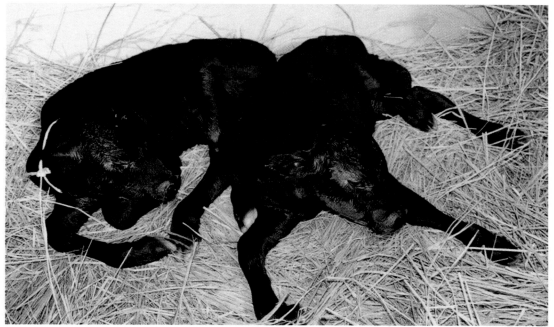

Eight calf clones were born in Japan in late 1998. But four of the clones died within days after their birth, and scientists don't know why. Are cloned animals weaker than animals born naturally?

self as a one-of-a-kind individual. You'd be one of a set. What would that be like?

The idea of cloning people raises lots of other troubling questions. Would clones be treated as the equals of "originals"—people who were conceived naturally? How would family relationships work? For example, what if your mother was actually your "original" and thus also your twin? Would your mother's father also be your father? And who would decide which people would be cloned? What if everyone, even criminals, could choose to be cloned?

DOUBLE TROUBLE

It may be many years before people have to answer these questions—or before they see real benefits from cloning. One reason is that the techniques that are used to produce clones are complicated and difficult. For every clone that's successfully produced, there are scores of failed attempts.

Many clones also die young, and researchers don't know why. For example, four of the eight calf clones born in Japan in 1998 died within days of their birth, of various causes. Does some step in the cloning process cause cloned animals to be weaker than others of their kind?

Does the genetic mixing that takes place when animals mate naturally somehow make offspring stronger? No one knows.

Some clones may have problems even after they grow up to be adults. Dolly has grown into a healthy adult sheep. She's even had offspring of her own—she gave birth to a lamb in 1998 and triplets in 1999, all fathered by a ram named David. But studies of Dolly's chromosomes have shown something odd.

Chromosomes end in structures called telomeres. Telomeres normally become shorter with age. But Dolly's telomeres seem to be about 20 percent shorter than those of other sheep her age. Why? Perhaps because the udder cell from which Dolly was cloned came from a 6-year-old sheep. However, scientists just don't know. They also don't know if Dolly's shortened telomeres will have any effect on her health or her lifespan. So far she shows no signs of premature aging.

While researchers hunt for solutions to these problems, the debate about cloning goes on. A number of countries and some U.S. states have banned research into cloning humans, at least until the problems are sorted out. But many scientists believe it's just a matter of time before human cloning arrives.

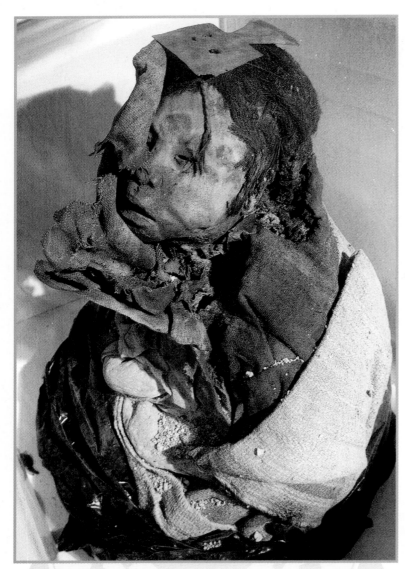

A 500-year-old mummy of an Inca girl—one of three amazingly well-preserved human sacrifices discovered in Argentina.

INCA ICE CHILDREN

On the snow-capped top of a volcano in western Argentina, researchers made an amazing discovery in 1999. They uncovered three frozen mummies, all so well preserved that they seemed to have died just recently. In fact, the mummies were 500 years old! They were the bodies of three Inca children—two girls and a boy—who had met their deaths on the mountain in a religious ceremony.

ON THE SACRED MOUNTAIN

Until the Incas were conquered by Spain in 1532, they ruled an empire that stretched along the Andes Mountains from Colombia to central Chile. Mountains were important in their lives, and they considered mountains sacred. The higher the mountain, the more sacred it was. Mount Llullaillaco, where the mummies were found, was a very sacred site. At 22,000 feet (6,706 meters), it is one of the world's tallest volcanoes.

As part of their religious beliefs, the Incas sometimes sacrificed humans to honor their gods. The three children, who were probably between the ages of 8 and 15, met their deaths in such a sacrificial ceremony. Researchers think the children were probably from noble families. The Incas believed it was a great honor to be sacrificed and sometimes promised a child to the gods at birth. The children were dressed in fine clothes, and one of the girls was wearing a white feathered headdress.

The children didn't die violently. On the day of the ceremony, priests and others probably took them to the mountain summit. There they were probably drugged with a powerful drink, so that they became unconscious. Their bodies were placed on a burial platform and covered with rocks and earth, as an offering to the god of the mountain. They lay there, undisturbed, for 500 years.

AN AMAZING FIND

A team of archeologists from the United States, Argentina, and Peru discovered the mummies in March 1999. Johan Reinhard, an American archeologist, led the expedition. Reinhard had found Inca ruins farther down the mountain. He reasoned that those ruins might mark the site of a sort of "base camp," where Incas stopped on their way to the summit. And he suspected there might be ceremonial burial sites on the mountaintop.

The team struggled through snow and very strong winds on the summit. But they kept searching. On March 16, they found the first mummy, under about 5 feet (1.5 meters) of earth and rock. A worker was lowered into the pit by his ankles to pull it out. Then the other two mummies were found.

In earlier expeditions, Reinhard had found other mummies on South American mountaintops, all victims of sacrifices. One, a frozen Inca mummy he discovered in Peru in 1995, had become known as the Ice Maiden. But none of these earlier finds was as well preserved as the mummies found on Mount Llullaillaco.

Researchers believe that the bodies froze soon after they were buried. They were curled up as if they were sleeping peacefully. One of the mummies had been damaged by lightning, but the others were perfectly preserved. All their internal organs were intact, and blood was still present in their hearts. Even the fine hair on their skin could be seen.

The ruins of Machu Picchu, the ancient Inca city, in Peru. Mountains were sacred in Inca culture.

CLUES TO A MYSTERY

The mummies weren't the only remarkable discovery on the mountaintop. Around them was a wealth of artifacts, which were left with the children as gifts to the god. There were small statues made of gold, silver, and shell. There were moccasins and bundles of fine patterned cloth made of alpaca wool. And there was beautiful pottery, some of which still contained food.

The archeologists wrapped the mummies in ice and insulation and carried them down the mountain. They were rushed to the city of Salta, where they were kept refrigerated for further study. Then the researchers headed back up Mount Llullaillaco, in search of more discoveries.

Because the mummies are so well preserved, they are expected to reveal many secrets. Researchers will analyze their tissues to learn about the Incas' diet, health, and heredity. Tissue samples from the mummies may contain undamaged DNA, the cell protein that carries genetic information. The DNA may help researchers answer the question of how and when people first arrived in the Americas.

The mummies and the artifacts found with them are also expected to tell much about the Incas' life and beliefs. The Incas had no written language. The only accounts we have of their civilization were written by the Spanish who conquered them. Thus the Incas' history and their way of life are shrouded in mystery—a mystery that the Inca ice children now may help solve.

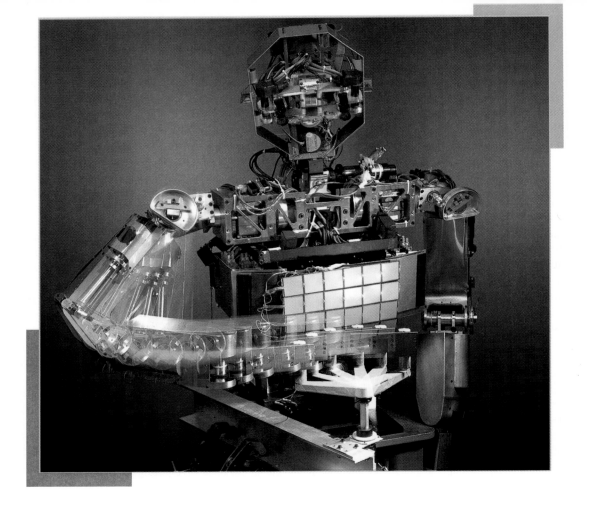

THE "SMART" ROBOTS ARE HERE!

Two of the most popular characters in the wildly popular *Star Wars* movies aren't humans. They aren't even aliens. They're robots! C3PO and R2D2 are intelligent machines that can understand speech, perform all sorts of amazing tasks, and even seem to have personalities.

The *Star Wars* films are science-fiction fantasies, and no one has yet made a real robot as clever and capable as these fictional ones. But real robots are getting better and smarter all the time, with more powerful computers for "brains," sensors that allow them to see and hear, and other technical improvements. The day may even come when you have one of these "smart" machines at your house—a personal "bot" to do your bidding.

ROBOTS AT WORK

Robots are already performing lots of jobs for people. They're perfect for assembly-line work, which is really boring. In car factories, for example, a worker stands in place as partly assembled cars roll by, bolting or welding the same part in place on each car. A robot can do the same thing, and it won't mind doing it over and over again.

A typical factory robot is little more than a giant arm. It's programmed to do one thing, and one thing only. But more complex robots are tackling other work. Robots are most use-

Cog (*above*), a robot programmed to think and reason as humans do, works a lever by using its visual system to guide the movements of its hands. Today, "smart" robots are no longer just science fiction!

ful for dangerous jobs, such as detecting explosives. Instead of risking their lives, soldiers can send remote-controlled robots to check an area for buried land mines. Robots are also used to find terrorist bombs. These robots have sensors that can detect explosives, and they disarm or blow up some bombs.

A robot called Hazbot III goes to work when dangerous chemicals are spilled. The robot rolls onto the site of the spill to assess the danger, so that people can figure out how to clean up the spill without putting their health at risk. Robots are also at work cleaning up the site of the world's worst nuclear accident, which occurred in 1986 at the Chernobyl nuclear plant in the former Soviet Union.

Robots are also exploring places where people can't go. Underwater robots called AUVs (for Autonomous Underwater Vehicles) can scout the bottom of the ocean. A robot called Dante II has explored the crater of an active volcano, unfazed by heat and deadly gases. And a robot named Sojourner has explored parts of Mars.

PERSONAL ROBOTS

When people think of personal robots, they usually imagine a mechanical servant—a bot that will serve meals, do the dishes and laundry, clean the house, mow the lawn, and take care of any other chores that need doing. Such wonderful machines aren't available yet. But robot experts are making progress.

Cye, a little boxlike robot, is one of the newest personal robots on the market. It comes with special computer software and a radio transmitter, so you can operate it with a personal computer. You plot the robot's route on your computer screen, and the computer radios instructions to the bot. Cye is

Robots at work: A factory robot (*right*) welds auto parts on an assembly line. Dante II (*below*) explores areas like volcanoes where people can't go. An explosives-detecting robot (*below right*) searches for a land mine.

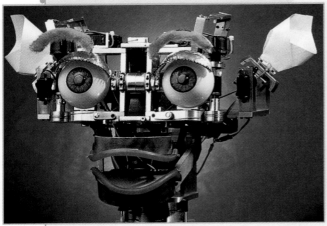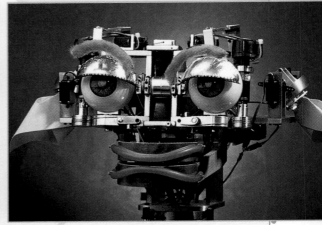

Kismet is a robot that's programmed to have "moods," which it shows in "facial expressions." Its eyes, ears, and mouth can change to express emotions, such as surprise (*left*) and anger (*right*).

available with a small cart (so it can carry things) and a vacuum-cleaner attachment (so it can clean floors).

Personal robots like Cye are still curiosities. They don't perform enough tasks to be really useful. In fact, even a complex robot like the Mars Sojourner is more like a backhoe than like C3PO. That's because building a machine that can mimic human actions and intelligence is enormously complicated.

Suppose you want your personal robot to go to the kitchen and get you a banana. It would need to understand your command, navigate to the kitchen without banging into furniture or tipping over, locate and recognize bananas, pick one up without squashing it, and find its way back to you. Powerful computer chips, voice-recognition software, video and pressure sensors, and other advances may make all this almost possible, but the machine that can do it isn't available yet.

However, robot experts have lots of plans. Some researchers are developing robots that can stand and move on two legs. For example, P3, a robot being developed in Japan, can walk, wave, bow, shake hands, pick up objects, and go up and down stairs.

Other experts are working on robots that can recognize individuals and facial expressions and perform complicated tasks. Two experimental robots developed at the Massachusetts Institute of Technology (MIT) are already doing some of these things. Cog is a robot programmed with artificial intelligence (AI). It can learn new tasks like playing the drums. It can also make decisions and learn from its mistakes. Kismet is programmed to have "moods," which it shows in "facial expressions." Kismet looks around constantly, hoping to make "eye contact" with a person. If you talk to this robot, it smiles!

The MIT robots seem almost human. And in as little as 30 years, some researchers say, robots will be able to "think" like people.

ROBOT CHALLENGE

How well can a robot serve hors d'oeuvres? Beeping and whirring, mechanical contestants gathered in Orlando, Florida, to answer that question in July 1999. They were on hand with their human handlers for the eighth annual Mobile Robot Competition and Exhibition, an event sponsored by the American Association for Artificial Intelligence (AAAI).

The exhibition gave robot experts a chance to see the latest developments in robotics. And the competition gave them a chance to show off their best efforts.

In the hors d'oeuvres contest, robots were waiters at receptions. They were judged on their ability to find and stop at people (not plants or furniture), offer the food without dropping or throwing it, cover the entire serving area, and recognize people who hadn't been served. The robots also had to sense when they needed to refill the serving tray, communicate with people, and navigate through the room without banging into people. Personality was a plus!

The second contest was a scavenger hunt that sent robots off to find items on a list. The list was designed to draw on a variety of sensory abilities, including hearing, range finding, and vision. Examples included finding the source of a tape recording being played, a corridor of a given width, objects with certain colors or shapes, and a person wearing a shirt of a given color.

In addition to the competition and exhibition, the event organizers issued a challenge to robot experts: Build a robot that can take part in a future AAAI conference. To do this, the robot will have to be dropped off at the front door of the conference site, register itself as a student volunteer, perform various tasks as assigned, and talk at a session!

Building a robot that can do all that will require input from experts in several areas of robotics and artificial intelligence. It will probably take many years. But the AAAI hopes that the challenge will encourage researchers to make big strides in developing robots for the future.

Robopets

It walks like a dog. It barks like a dog. But it's definitely not a dog! AIBO is a robot that looks like a pet puppy—a puppy made of plastic. The Sony company, which makes AIBO, designed this little robot strictly for fun and entertainment. They sold quickly in 1999—for about $2,500 each!

AIBO is about the size of a Chihuahua. It can walk, sit, beg, stretch, yawn, raise a paw, and even dance a little hula. If you pat it on the head, it wags its tail. It can chase a little pink ball that's sold with it. But the chase is slow—AIBO's top speed is 18 feet (5 meters) a minute.

The robot can also mimic six emotions—happiness, sadness, anger, surprise, fear, and dislike—through body language and musical tones, and by flashing its eyes. The eyes flash green when AIBO is happy, and red when the robot is displeased. And AIBO can "learn." Over time, its behavior changes, based on how its owners play with it.

A computer chip gives AIBO all these amazing abilities. Electronic sensors allow the robot to interact with the world around it. A touch sensor detects a pat on the head. Distance sensors help the robot avoid obstacles. A color camera lets it search for colors it likes—the

pink ball, for example. Balance sensors alert the robot when it falls over, and it rights itself.

AIBO can also be operated by remote control to do a variety of motions. Microphones in the robot pick up the musical tones that are sent out by the remote-control unit. One day, Sony hopes, AIBO may be able to respond to voice commands.

The name "AIBO" was created by combining the letters AI (for "artificial intelligence") and BO (from ro*bot*). But "AIBO" also means "companion" in Japanese. Other electronics manufacturers are betting that people will like the idea of having a robot pal. For example, Matsushita Electric plans to bring out a robot cat called Tarna in 2001.

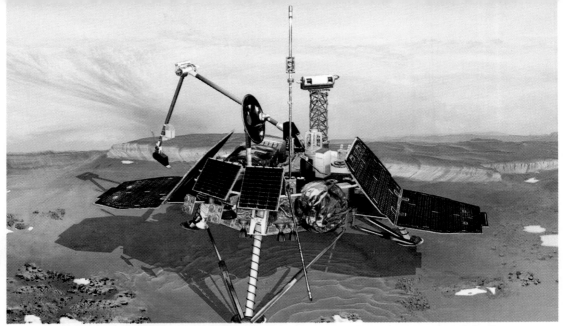

As 1999 ended, the fate of *Mars Polar Lander* (*in drawing above*) remained a mystery. Scientists lost communication with the spacecraft just as it was about to land on the Red Planet. The loss of the *Lander* was a great disappointment in a year marked by many exciting discoveries in space.

SPACE BRIEFS

As the new millennium begins, we can look back at one of the most exciting developments of the previous millennium: the launch of the first artificial satellites and space probes, and the start of human travel into space. Each year of the late 20th century brought exciting discoveries, with highlights of 1999 including new revelations about planets, moons, and stars. But even as scientists gain a better understanding of the universe, they are discovering that there's still a lot to learn as we enter the 21st century.

SOLAR SYSTEM NEWS

Mars. It was to be the highlight of the year in space. Instead it was 1999's biggest disappointment. *Mars Polar Lander,* a spacecraft that was to set down near the south pole of Mars on December 3, failed to return signals to Earth. Did it pass through the Martian at-mosphere and reach the surface? Did it crash upon landing? Were only its transmitters disabled? Scientists may not know for months, if ever.

Mars Polar Lander was launched by the National Aeronautics and Space Administration (NASA) on January 3, 1999. Everything seemed to work properly during the craft's 470-million-mile (750-million-kilometer) journey to Mars. Then on December 3 it entered the Martian atmosphere. . .and wasn't heard from again.

The loss was especially disappointing because it came after an earlier failure. In September 1999, the *Lander's* companion craft, *Mars Climate Orbiter,* disappeared as it approached the planet. Investigation showed that the loss resulted

Using measurements taken by *Mars Global Surveyor,* scientists put together the first-ever topographic map of Mars.

Looking for Water

Life on Earth began in water, and life as we know it cannot exist without water. Space scientists have long searched for water elsewhere in the solar system, hoping it might lead to signs of life—or at least to a better understanding of how life can begin. Several interesting developments occurred during 1999.

Meteorite. In March 1998, seven boys were playing basketball in Monahans, Texas, when a fiery object streaked down from the sky and hit the ground nearby. Investigating, the boys found a grapefruit-size meteorite, still warm from its fall. This would be remarkable enough. But in September 1999, scientists from the Johnson Space Center made a startling announcement: Locked inside the meteorite, named Monahans 98, were tiny amounts of water—the first liquid water ever found in an object from space.

The scientists had cracked the rock open and found crystals of halite, or rock salt. And trapped inside the halite was salty water. The halite is believed to be 4.5 billion years old. That means that the trapped water could be older than Earth. How did water get in the meteorite? The rock may have broken off an asteroid that had water. Or it may have been brushed by an icy comet. Either way, the discovery shows that water was present when the solar system formed.

Moon. The first evidence of ice on our moon was discovered in 1998 by the spacecraft *Lunar Prospector* as it orbited 20 miles (30 kilometers) above the moon. By mid-1999, *Lunar Prospector* had successfully completed its mission of mapping the moon. NASA scientists decided to intentionally crash the spacecraft onto the moon, near the south pole, where sunlight never reaches the bottoms of some deep craters. The crash, on July 31, created a huge cloud of dust and other debris. The scientists hoped that tele-

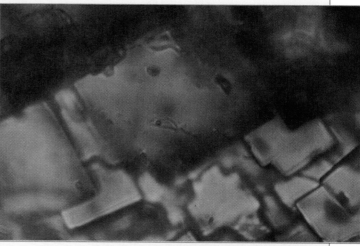

Crystals of halite in this meteorite contained the first liquid water ever found in an object from space.

scopes on Earth and in space would detect the presence of water in the debris. No such evidence was found. But this doesn't mean that there aren't large amounts of water buried in the moon's craters, brought there by comets that crashed onto the surface.

Jupiter. A thick crust of ice covers Europa, one of Jupiter's moons. Unusual markings that look like fracture lines decorate the ice. Scientists suggested that these lines may indicate that an ocean of liquid water once lay beneath the ice, and may still be there. As tides caused by Jupiter's pull moved the water up and down, the ice would have been repeatedly bent, causing the formation of ridges and cracks. If the ocean still exists, it may contain some forms of life.

from a mathematical mismatch. For nine months, as *Mars Climate Orbiter* sped toward Mars, it was sending information to NASA using metric measurements. But engineers on the ground were replying in the non-metric English system. As a result, the spacecraft was on the wrong path as it entered the Martian atmosphere.

The good news from Mars came from *Mars Global Surveyor,* which since 1998 has been

Pluto and its moon Charon. In February, Pluto traded places with Neptune to once again become the most distant planet in the solar system.

circling Mars to take detailed measurements of the planet's surface features. Using those measurements, NASA scientists put together the first-ever topographic map of Mars. It revealed some fascinating facts about the Red Planet:

● Mars is slightly pear-shaped, with its southern hemisphere bulging up higher than its northern hemisphere.

● Scientists believe that Mars once had lots of water. Since the Martian surface is higher in the south, they now know that water must have flowed south to north. And there's a big flat basin in the north that may once have been an ocean.

● The Hellas basin, in the middle of the southern hemisphere, may be the solar system's biggest impact crater, formed by an asteroid that crashed into Mars early in the planet's history. The basin is more than 1,300 miles (2,000 kilometers) across and 6 miles (9.7 kilometers) deep.

● Mars has the tallest known volcano in the solar system: Olympus Mons, which stands about 17 miles (27 kilometers) high.

Pluto. Unlike the other planets, Pluto has an exceptionally elongated orbit that makes its distance from the sun vary. Usually, it's the farthest planet from the sun. But once every 248 Earth years, Pluto passes inside Neptune's orbit. For 20 years, it's closer to the sun than Neptune. Then it travels outside Neptune's orbit again. That happened on February 11, 1999. Once again Pluto became the most distant planet in the solar system.

But is Pluto really a planet? It has been ranked as a planet ever since its discovery by astronomer Clyde Tombaugh in 1930. Some astronomers, however, have suggested that Pluto—the smallest of the planets—should be classed with asteroids and comets. These smaller objects, sometimes known as minor planets, also orbit the sun. In fact, Pluto has a lot in common with a group of minor planets called Trans-Neptunian Objects. More than 80 of these chunks of ice and rock have been discovered, orbiting beyond Neptune. But in 1999 the International Astronomical Union, the final authority on astronomical matters, ruled that Pluto was indeed a planet.

Your Name Can Be Out of This World!

Have you ever signed up to get a free gift. . . to join a club. . .to go on a field trip? Now you can sign up to send your name out of this world.

NASA is planning to launch the *Mars Surveyor 2001 Lander* in April 2001. NASA expects it to land on Mars in January 2002. The *Lander* will take pictures of the Martian terrain and carry out experiments.

The *Lander* will also carry a CD with millions of names on it, which will be left on Mars. *Your* name can be one of them! All you have to do is go to this Web site:

http://spacekids.hq.nasa.gov/2001/

Sign up, and in 2002 a little bit of you may become part of the Red Planet!

Comet Dust. Can a sprinkling of stardust help unlock the secrets of the Earth's beginning? A little spacecraft called *Stardust,* launched on February 7, 1999, may find out. *Stardust* is on a long, long journey. In January 2004, the spacecraft will rendezvous with Comet Wild-2. If all goes as planned, *Stardust* will return to Earth in January 2006 with a cargo of interstellar dust. It will gather some of the dust on its way to the comet and some from the comet itself.

Tiny grains of interstellar dust exist throughout the seemingly empty spaces of the universe. Scientists think that our solar system formed when a gigantic cloud of this dust collapsed about 4.6 billion years ago. Most of the dust formed the sun and, later, the planets. But some of the dust is contained in icy, dusty bodies called comets. And some dust—including a recently discovered flow of particles passing through our solar system from interstellar space—drifts free in space.

When a comet nears the sun, the sun's heat causes some of its ice to vaporize, or turn to gas. As this gas forms a cloud around the comet, it takes some of the comet's dust with it. When *Stardust* enters the dust and gas cloud around Comet Wild-2, it will flip out a cosmic dust collector. This device is shaped like a tennis racket and is covered with a glass foam called aerogel. The collector will capture comet dust, while special shields protect the rest of the spacecraft from flying particles. Then *Stardust* will fold its collection device into a return capsule, take a final trip around the sun, and make a parachute landing in the Utah desert.

SHUTTLES AND SPACE STATIONS

Shuttle Missions. NASA's first space shuttle mission of 1999 began on May 27, when *Discovery* was launched. Its objective was to rendezvous with the *International Space Station,* which is being built over a period of more than five years. After docking with the space station, mission astronauts spent six days unloading supplies and making repairs. Then, on their way home, they released a mirror-covered satellite called *Starshine.* During the following six months, students from eighteen countries tracked *Starshine*'s twinkles. In the process, they learned some basic principles of physics.

Columbia was launched on July 23. It was the 95th shuttle mission, and the first to be led by a woman. Eileen Collins, a 42-year-old Air Force colonel and a former test pilot, was in command. The *Columbia* crew accomplished their main goal on the first day of the mission. They released the Chandra X-Ray Observatory from the shuttle's cargo bay—the largest payload ever carried by the shuttle. Chandra

Stardust was launched on February 7, on a mission to rendezvous with Comet Wild-2. If this cosmic game of tag goes as planned, the prize will be a cargo of interstellar dust returned to Earth in 2006.

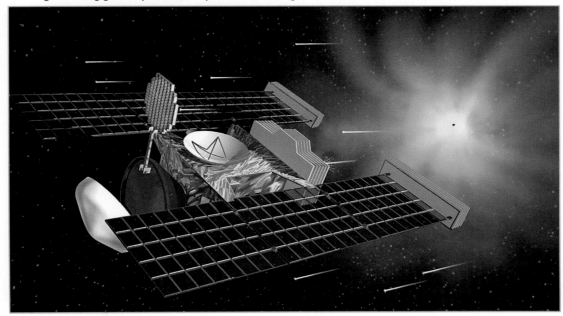

Eileen Collins, the first woman to command a space shuttle, led the *Columbia* mission that released the Chandra X-Ray Observatory into space in July.

was designed to detect X rays emitted by exploding stars, black holes, and other objects in the universe. It soon began sending spectacular images to Earth. Its first pictures showed the remnants of a supernova called Cassiopeia A. Astronomers think this object is a star that exploded 320 years ago. The images show clouds of hot gas boiling around the explosion, created by material blasting into space at millions of miles per hour.

On December 19, *Discovery* was launched again and rendezvoused with the Hubble Space Telescope, which needed repairs. The crew used the shuttle's robot arm to grab Hubble and bring it into the shuttle's cargo bay. During the next few days the crew installed various replacement parts, including six gyroscopes needed to correctly point the telescope. Hubble was then released back into space, and *Discovery* returned to Earth.

Mir. On February 19, 1986, the Soviet Union launched the space station *Mir* ("Peace"). It became the world's longest-operating space sta-

tion. During 13½ years *Mir* made more than 77,000 orbits of Earth, had 135 human visitors, and made a great many contributions to our understanding of space and space travel. But by 1999, it was time to abandon the aging craft. The last crew departed *Mir* on August 27, traveling to Earth in a *Soyuz* capsule. "With grief in our soul. . . we're abandoning a piece of Russia," said the crew commander, Viktor Afanasyev.

China. In November, China took a major step toward putting people in space. It launched and recovered an unmanned capsule named *Shenzhou* ("Magic Vessel"). *Shenzhou* was similar to the capsules used by the United States and the Soviet Union for manned space flight during the 1960's. It was launched atop a Long March rocket from northwestern China, completed fourteen orbits of Earth, and parachuted to a landing in Inner Mongolia. Chinese officials said that they would conduct additional test flights before sending astronauts into space.

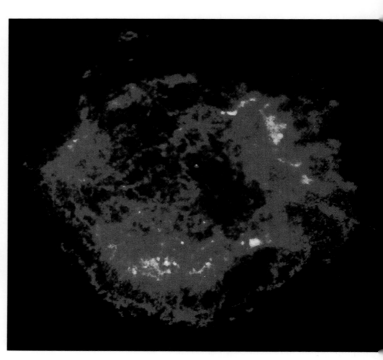

Chandra's first pictures were images of supernova Cassiopeia A—a star that astronomers think exploded 320 years ago.

Looking for E.T?

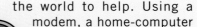

For years, in a project known as SETI—the **S**earch for **E**xtra**T**errestrial **I**ntelligence—a group of astronomers has been looking for intelligent life elsewhere in the universe. In 1999, the astronomers began to enlist the help of thousands of home-computer users.

Astronomers have long used the giant Arecibo radio telescope in Puerto Rico to collect data from the universe. The telescope sweeps the sky, gathering radio signals naturally produced by distant stars. SETI researchers use computers to analyze the data. They look for unusual signals and patterns that cannot be produced naturally. Such signals could be signs of life in outer space. After all, radio and TV signals escape from Earth's atmosphere all the time. Maybe similar signals are being sent by aliens!

The Arecibo telescope produces so much data that SETI researchers cannot keep up with the flow. So they established a project called SETI@home to allow people around the world to help. Using a modem, a home-computer user can download a chunk of telescope data and a program to analyze it. The program works on its own, kicking in whenever the computer isn't busy. It takes up to two days for the program to process the data. Then the person returns the results to the SETI researchers.

SETI@home was launched on May 17. By October, more than 1.2 million people had participated. All together, in less than five months, they logged more than 81,000 years of processing time! No one had yet picked up beeps from aliens. But the project was already considered a success because it opened up a new method of doing research via the Internet.

If you would like to be part of this project, visit the researchers' Web site at:

http://setiathome.ssl.berkeley.edu

OUT IN THE UNIVERSE

Birth of a Star. The Hubble Space Telescope has used its infrared camera to peer deep into the heart of our galaxy, the Milky Way. Here, new stars are born as vast clouds of gas collide. Hubble has photographed two immense clusters of young stars. In a few million years, the clusters will be pulled apart by gravitational forces. But right now, they are the brightest star clusters in our galaxy. The Arches Cluster includes 150 of the brightest stars known in the Milky Way. At least a dozen of the stars are 100 times more massive than our sun. The Quintuplet Cluster is older, and its stars are more scattered. They include the Pistol Star, which is the brightest known star in the Milky Way.

Extrasolar Planets. Since the mid-1990's astronomers have detected more than 25 planets around nearby stars. They haven't actually seen these planets. Rather, they inferred the planets' existence from the stars' wobbles. The wobbles, they believed, had to be caused by the gravitational pull of large orbiting planets. In 1999, astronomers for the first time saw direct proof of an extrasolar planet. They saw the shadow of the distant planet pass in front of its star. Telescopes recorded the dimming in the amount of light coming from the star as the planet crossed between the star and Earth. The star, HD 209458, is in the constellation Pegasus.

JENNY TESAR
Author, *Global Warming*

139

Workers attach steel braces to the Leaning Tower of Pisa before beginning work to save the famous structure from falling down.

THE LEANING TOWER OF PISA STRAIGHTENS UP

The bell tower of Pisa Cathedral is one of Italy's most famous landmarks. It isn't known for its height (187 feet, or about 58 meters) or even for its 207 marble arches. It's famous because it leans. In fact, it's been leaning for more than 800 years, tilting just a tiny bit more each year. And in 1999, engineers were scrambling to save the famous tower—because it was in danger of falling down.

PISA'S PROBLEM

The base of Pisa's bell tower was built in the 1170's, during the late Middle Ages. Workers dug down about 10 feet (3 meters) to lay the foundation, but they didn't hit bedrock. They set the foundation stones on soil and started to build. But by the time they reached the fourth story, the tower was already starting to tilt. The problem was that the ground under the tower was softer on the south side. As more stones were added, the tower's foundation began to sink on that side, producing the tilt.

Work on the tower stopped in 1178 and started again almost 100 years later. At that time, workers tried to even out the tilt by building up the south side. That gave the tower a slight curve, like a banana. But it didn't fix the tilt.

The last straw was the bell chamber, which was added to the top of the tower in the 1360's. The extra weight of the bell chamber doubled the angle at which the tower leaned. Still, the tilt was slight—the top of the tower was just 5 feet (1½ meters) off center. The tower wasn't in danger of falling.

Things took a turn for the worse in 1838. That's when workers began to lay a walkway around the base of the tower, so that people could admire it from all angles. Their digging disturbed the foundation, and the tower lurched into a steeper tilt. But the tower didn't collapse, and its steeper angle only made it more amazing.

Over the years, the people of Pisa discovered that their Leaning Tower was a blessing in disguise. It became one of Italy's top tourist attractions! Millions of people visited Pisa and climbed the 300-step spiral staircase leading to the top. They marveled at the tower. Why didn't it fall down?

Galileo's Experiment

The Renaissance scientist Galileo Galilei supposedly found a good use for the Leaning Tower of Pisa. In the early 1590's, in an experiment dealing with the scientific laws governing falling objects, Galileo is said to have dropped balls of different weights from the tower.

Galileo was born in Pisa and taught mathematics at the university there. In his day, physics wasn't a science, and people knew little about the laws of motion. They simply accepted the ideas of the ancient Greek philosopher Aristotle. Among other things, Aristotle believed that falling objects travel at speeds proportional to their weight. That is, a heavy ball falls faster than a light ball.

Galileo questioned that. He thought that objects of different weights would fall at the same speed, and he is said to have proved the point in a demonstration at the Leaning Tower. Balls that he dropped from the tower together hit the ground at the same time, regardless of their weight.

Although later proved correct, Galileo's ideas offended other scholars, who didn't think Aristotle should be questioned. In 1592, Galileo left Pisa for the University of Padua, where he was free to pursue his ideas.

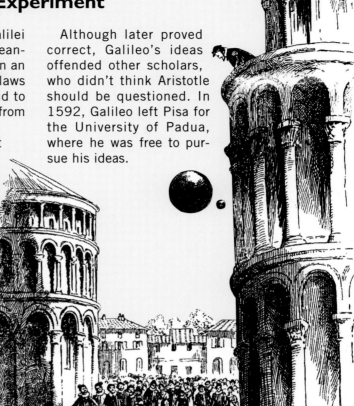

SAVING THE TOWER

In fact, by 1990 the Italian government was worried that the tower *would* fall down. It was tilted more than five degrees to the south, so that the top was roughly 16 feet (5 meters) off center. On the south side, the base had sunk about 10 feet (3 meters) into the ground. And the tower was leaning a little bit more each year. With the enormous weight of the stone tower bearing down unevenly on the south side, the structure was becoming weak.

So the tower was closed, and huge lead weights were placed around the base to counter the tilt. Engineers were asked to come up with a permanent plan to save the tower. Many ideas were considered. In the end, the engineers came up with a simple plan: Carefully remove soil from under the north side, to counter the settling on the south. The tower was braced with huge steel cables for this work, which started in December 1998. Over the months that followed, workers gradually dug out about 8 inches (20 centimeters) of soil from under the tower's north side.

The idea wasn't to make the tower perfectly straight. That couldn't be done—the tower had been built with a banana-shaped curve and could never be straight. Instead, the engineers hoped to straighten the structure about half a degree—just enough to keep it from tumbling down. Then Pisa would once again welcome visitors to its famous Leaning Tower.

Due to a summer-long drought, a normally picturesque pond in Pennsylvania is nothing more than a mud-patched hole. Dry conditions reached emergency levels in parts of the United States in 1999.

EARTH WATCH

We depend on the natural world—and often our actions affect nature as much as nature affects our lives. At times, that can be easy to forget. But in 1999 there were several sharp reminders of our close links with the environment.

Water Woes. Shriveled crops. Dry wells. Brown lawns. Those were some of the effects of a serious drought that hit parts of the United States in 1999.

The dry conditions actually started in 1998 and peaked in the summer of 1999. The Northeast and Mid-Atlantic regions were hardest hit. From Virginia to New England and westward to the Ohio Valley, 1999 rainfall was 20 to 40 percent below normal through the summer. Many rivers and streams were at record low levels. In four states—Rhode Island, New Jersey, Delaware, and Maryland—the drought was the worst on record. Drought hit other portions of the United States, too. Water levels were low in all five Great Lakes. In the West, from Idaho across northern Nevada and into northern California, rainfall was well below normal. Alaska and Hawaii were also dry.

In drought-stricken areas, towns placed restrictions on water use. Many private wells ran dry. And crops shriveled in the fields. Crop losses in the Mid-Atlantic states alone were expected to top $800 million. The U.S. Department of Agriculture declared a farm disaster in ten states and in parts of ten more. Farmers in those areas were eligible for special aid.

Luckily, rain was plentiful in most of the central states, the nation's biggest farming region. The summer there was one of the hottest on record. But the heat eased before crops died, and farmers had good harvests.

Harmful Hitchhikers. Today, people think nothing of traveling around the globe. Products and even fresh foods can be shipped anywhere in a matter of hours or days. But there's a downside to today's speedy transportation. The airplanes and ships that carry people and cargo sometimes carry hazards. Fast travel has made it easier for pests and diseases to reach new parts of the world.

Americans were reminded of that in September 1999. A new disease popped up in the Northeast, around New York City. The disease was a form of encephalitis, which is caused by a virus. But it wasn't a form that had been seen in the United States before. It was like a form of the disease found in Asia and Africa. This type of encephalitis affects birds as well as people. It's spread by mosquitoes. A mosquito picks up the virus when it bites a bird, for example, and then transmits it to the next animal it bites.

How did the virus get to America? Perhaps it came with a traveler from Africa. Perhaps someone smuggled an infected bird into the country. Health officials didn't know. But they moved quickly to squelch the disease, so only about 60 people actually came down with it.

Earlier in the year, officials were on the lookout for another hitchhiking hazard. The Asian long-horned beetle burrows into trees and kills them. In China, it has destroyed whole forests. Some of these inch-long black beetles arrived in North America in 1992. They were hidden in wood containers used for iron and steel pipes. Since then, they have turned up in Chicago; New York; Vancouver, Canada; and a few other places. These beetles can't be killed by pesticides. The only way to get rid of the beetles is to cut down the infested trees and burn them. The beetles are a huge threat because many industries depend on the forests.

Most countries take steps to block imported hazards like these. U.S. and Canadian officials now require packing materials from Asia to be treated to kill Asian longhorned beetles before they arrive. Imported foods are also carefully checked, and some are treated to kill pests. Animals that are brought into the country are checked and often quarantined, to make sure they aren't carrying diseases. And officials check baggage to make sure people aren't trying to sneak pets or restricted foods into the country. They even use specially trained dogs to sniff out hidden food.

The Monarchs and the Killer Corn. Beautiful orange-and-black monarch butterflies are one of the delights of summer. You can see

Buster sniffs cargo at Honolulu International Airport, in Hawaii. He is part of a beagle patrol charged with keeping out unwanted species of animals and plants.

The Big Stink!

Standing more than 6 feet (1.8 meters) tall, the flower of the *Titan arum* really is a titan. So when one of these rare jungle plants bloomed in August 1999 in southern California, thousands of people lined up to see it. They were impressed by more than the size of the bloom. The *Titan arum* is equally famous for its knockout scent. Some say it smells like dirty, wet socks. Others say the odor is more like rotting garbage.

The *Titan arum* is native to Sumatra, an island of Indonesia in the Indian Ocean. Its "flower"—one of the world's largest—is really a cluster of flowers. The bloom releases a smelly mix of chemicals designed to attract insects, which pollinate the plant. What kinds of insects are drawn to the odor of decay? Mainly dung beetles and carrion beetles. In Sumatra, the *Titan arum* is known as the corpse flower.

The *Titan arum* that flowered in August is only the eleventh of these plants to bloom in the United States. It's in the collection of the Huntington botanical gardens in San Marino, California. The plant was on display for 19 days while its flower developed, growing 4 inches (10 centimeters) a day at its peak. After the huge flower fully opened, the *Titan arum* flopped over in a smelly pile!

them fluttering around meadows and farm fields, searching for milkweed—the plant on which they lay their eggs. But in 1999 it seemed that monarchs faced danger in those fields.

The danger came from a new kind of corn that was being planted throughout the Midwest. This corn was developed to resist insect pests that can destroy crops. Through genetic engineering, scientists gave the corn the ability to produce Bt, a toxin that's normally produced by certain soil bacteria. Bt is lethal to some insects, like the corn borer. Farmers like the new corn because they don't have to spray it with pesticides. And that's good for the environment as well as for the farmers.

But researchers discovered that there's a downside to Bt corn: When monarch caterpillars eat pollen from these corn plants, they die or don't develop properly. Monarch caterpillars hatch on milkweed plants and eat only milkweed—but milkweed grows in and around cornfields throughout the Midwest, and the plants are often covered with a dusting of corn-plant pollen.

Bt-producing cotton and potatoes have also been developed. As yet, no one knows how great the danger from these new crops really

Monarch butterflies lay their eggs only on milkweed plants. Pollen from genetically engineered corn often dusts the plants—and this can harm the butterflies.

is. Most scientists think that it's probably less than the danger from spraying with pesticides. The monarch isn't in danger of dying out. But other moths and butterflies may be at risk, too. And scientists warn that these new crops may have other dangers. They may encourage insect pests that are resistant to Bt, for example.

Lighthouse on the Move. Each year, ocean waves and storm winds carve away sections of the U.S. Atlantic coastline. It's a natural process that

The Cape Hatteras lighthouse, off the coast of North Carolina, moved to a new, safer home in June.

threatens many manmade structures. And in 1999, extraordinary steps were taken to save one historic structure—the Cape Hatteras lighthouse, on the Outer Banks of North Carolina.

The Cape Hatteras beacon is the tallest lighthouse in the United States, at 208 feet (63 meters) tall. Back in 1870, when it was built, it was about 1,500 feet (457 meters) from the ocean. But over the years, storms and currents wore away the shoreline, and the Atlantic Ocean crept closer. In 1999, waves came within 100 feet (30 meters) of the tower. If the lighthouse wasn't moved, waves would begin to erode its foundation. It would fall into the sea.

How do you move a 208-foot (63-meter) tower? Very carefully. First, workers braced the interior of the structure. Then they dug into the foundation and inserted steel beams and hydraulic jacks under the base. The jacks lifted the lighthouse, and steel rollers were placed underneath. On June 17, hydraulic jacks started to slowly push the tower inland over a mat of steel beams. Its new site was 1,600 feet (488 meters) from the shore, but because of the curving shoreline the lighthouse had to travel 2,900 feet (884 meters) to get there.

The trip took about three weeks. Finally the historic tower was settled onto a new foundation. When powerful hurricanes swept up the Atlantic coast later in the year, it weathered the storms safely.

MAKE & DO

Paper can be folded, bent, cut, pieced, and curled to create wonderful things. Making masks from paper is especially fun. ...and challenging. Begin with a basic form—a square, circle, or oval—for the face. Add hair, facial features, whiskers, and other details. Try different shapes for the eyes and mouth. You'll find that even small changes can produce amazingly different expressions.

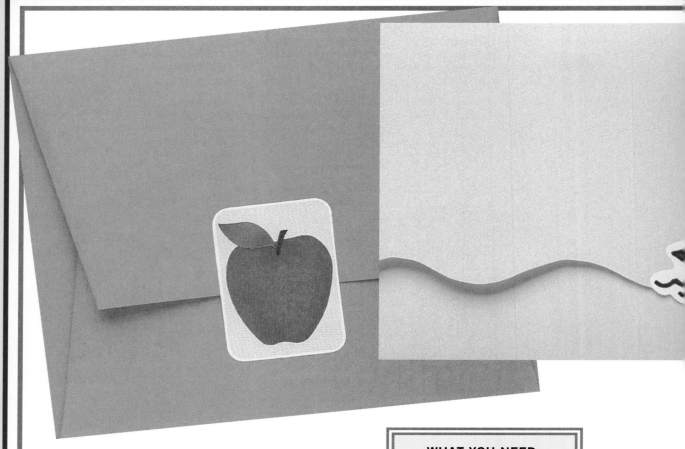

SEALED IN STYLE!

Make beautiful envelopes to fit all of your special cards. Use writing paper, colored construction paper, or the inside of a paper grocery bag! If you are going to mail your envelope, use shelf-lining paper (you can buy it at a supermarket). It's light and sturdy, and it won't get hurt if it gets wet.

WHAT YOU NEED:

Writing paper or colored construction paper

Scissors

White glue

Stickers

1. Lay your card in the middle of a big piece of paper. Fold the two sides of the paper in over the card.

2. Fold the bottom edge up over the card. Fold the top edge down. The card should fit perfectly inside.

3. Open the folds of the paper envelope. Cut out the corner rectangles, as shown here.

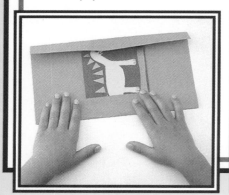
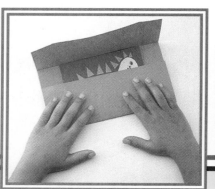

◄ This looks like an envelope. But it's really a letter folded in thirds and held together with a sticker.

Make a fancy envelope for a square card. Cut four flaps like flower petals. Fold them over the card, one flap at a time. Hold the flaps together with a colorful sticker.

4. Carefully fold slanted flaps on the top and bottom parts of the envelope.

5. Fold the sides of the envelope in. Fold the bottom up, and glue the flaps to the sides of the envelope.

6. Slip the card inside, and fold the top of the envelope down over it. Fasten with a favorite sticker.

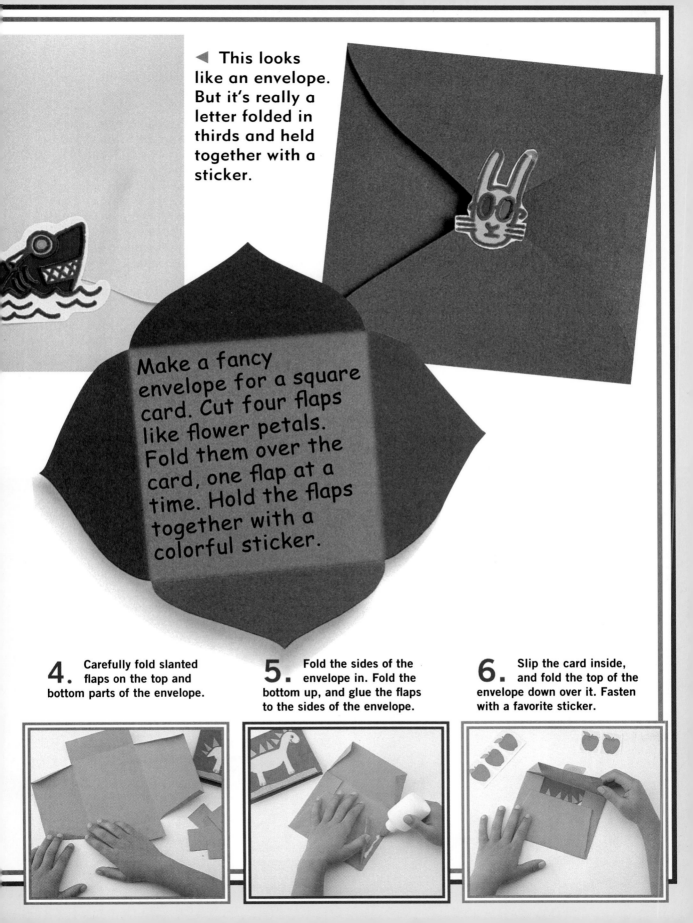

STAMP COLLECTING

The last year of the 20th century was a great one for stamp collectors. New issues from countries all over the world meant that there was plenty to choose from. In addition, many countries produced special stamps celebrating highlights of the century.

U.S. STAMPS

North America includes a wide range of wildlife habitats, from the cold Alaskan wilderness to the hot deserts of the Southwest. That great natural variety was showcased in several groups of stamps released by the United States Postal Service (USPS) during 1999.

The USPS launched a new commemorative series, "Nature of America," with ten self-adhesive stamps showing plants and animals of the Sonoran Desert. This desert stretches from southeastern California across southern Arizona and into Mexico. Featured on the 33-cent stamps were the saguaro cactus and a host of desert creatures, from the Gila monster to the cactus wren. The stamps came in

a pane that featured a complete desert scene, with the individual stamps forming parts of the design.

Insects and spiders crawled all over a pane of 20 stamps designed to appeal to young collectors. Sixteen insects, from beetles and butterflies to the scary-looking scorpionfly, were shown. They were joined by four spiders, including the poisonous black widow. The highly detailed artwork for these 33-cent stamps was created on a computer. The same computer technique was used for another group of 33-cent stamps released in 1999. This set showed four colorful tropical flowers—the gloriosa lily, bird of paradise, royal poinciana, and Chinese hibiscus.

Arctic animals were depicted on five 33-cent stamps. Pictures taken by wildlife photographers showed the snowy owl, polar bear, arctic hare, gray wolf, and arctic fox. And blueberries, strawberries, blackberries, and raspberries looked good enough to eat on new 33-cent self-adhesive definitive stamps. Unlike

1999 STAMPS FROM AROUND THE WORLD

commemorative stamps, which are issued to mark specific events, definitive stamps may be reprinted at any time to meet demand.

A duck was featured on a popular 33-cent stamp—but this was no duck found in nature. Daffy Duck, the spluttering star of countless cartoons, was the latest addition to the Looney Tunes series. Previous stamps in this series showed Bugs Bunny and Sylvester and Tweety. In the new stamp, Daffy was shown leaning on his mailbox—and looking annoyed because the letters inside have Bugs and Tweety stamps.

The 1999 U.S. Love stamps, issued around Valentine's Day, appeared in a new format. These self-adhesive 33-cent and 55-cent stamps showed hearts formed of flowers and paper lace. The stamps were die-cut in shapes that matched the outline of the designs—the first U.S. stamps to take this approach.

The glassmaker's art was honored with a set of 33-cent stamps showing four types of American glass: art glass, freeblown, mold-blown, and pressed. Other U.S. stamps included a stylized rabbit, issued to mark the start of the Year of the Rabbit in the Chinese lunar calendar.

And "Xtreme" sports—skateboarding, BMX biking, snowboarding, and in-line skating—were featured on a set of four 33-cent stamps. Each of these stamps carried a hidden slang word that could be seen only with a special decoder lens.

STAMPS AROUND THE WORLD

Canada's map was redrawn on April 1, 1999, when the new territory of Nunavut was created. Formerly part of the Northwest Territories, Nunavut is home to about half of Canada's Inuit (Eskimos). So it was fitting that a new 46-cent stamp, issued by Canada Post to mark the event, featured portraits of five Inuit children. Below the portraits was a landscape with two stone figures, called *inukshuk*. The *inukshuk* are symbols of guidance and welcome.

The Pan American Games were held in Winnipeg, Manitoba, in the summer of 1999. To celebrate the games, Canada Post released a block of four 46-cent stamps showing some of the sports at this international competition. Each stamp depicted athletes competing in three events, with one of the three showcased in a large central image.

Canada's wild orchids were featured in a group of four 46-cent stamps. The flowers were portrayed in delicate Chinese brush paintings. They included the greater yellow lady's slipper, which is found throughout Canada; and the round-leaved orchid, which thrives in damp coniferous forests and swamps.

Among the anniversaries marked by Canadian stamps was the 50th birthday of *Le Theatre du Rideau Vert* (the Theater of the Green Curtain). Founded in 1949, this troupe was Canada's first professional French-language theater company. Canada was also among several countries that marked the 50th anniversary of the North Atlantic Treaty Organization (NATO) by issuing a stamp.

Since 1993, the United Nations has been releasing stamps that highlight the plight of endangered animals. The 1999 stamps in this series included four 33-cent stamps, issued for use at U.N. headquarters in New York City. They featured the tiger; the secretary bird, an African bird of prey; the green tree python; and the long-tailed chinchilla of South America. Also in the group were 90-centime stamps,

issued for use in Geneva, Switzerland, and 7-schilling stamps, issued for use in Vienna, Austria. They showed animals ranging from the hyacinth macaw to the caracal, a lynx-like cat found in parts of Africa and Asia.

Holidays were the occasion for colorful stamps from many countries. The Czech Republic had one of the boldest designs for Easter—a brightly colored rooster covered with folk-art designs. Finland released a pair of Greetings stamps that had collectors guessing. Each stamp featured two animals that were natural enemies sitting side by side. But only the animals' tails were shown, so people had to guess what they were.

Ireland's Greetings stamps showed popular pets, drawn in a whimsical style. A Love stamp—showing a puppy and a heart—was part of this group. So was a stamp marking the Year of the Rabbit in the Chinese lunar calendar. Uganda also marked the lunar new year, with two stamps that carried delicate watercolor paintings of rabbits. These stamps were part of a thirteen-nation omnibus issue—stamps issued by many countries to mark a single event.

A TOPICAL COLLECTION OF MILLENNIUM STAMPS

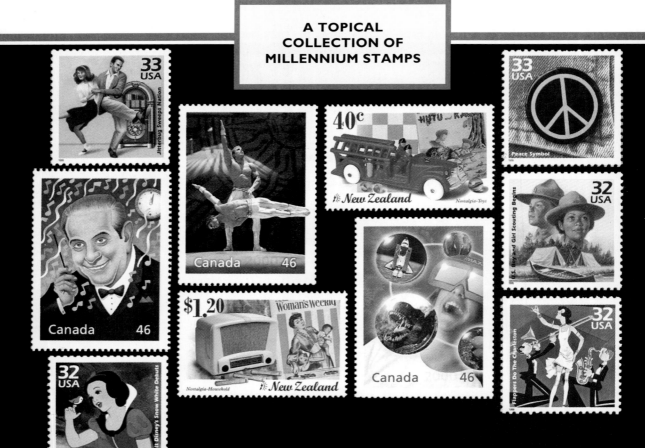

Many European countries take part each year in another omnibus issue, the Europa series. The Europa theme for 1999 was national parks and reserves. Guernsey, in the English Channel, produced some of the most interesting stamps in the group. They showcased the little island of Herm, a haven for wildlife. Each stamp featured a scene or an animal found on Herm.

Among the year's many other exceptional issues was a French art stamp, reproducing one of the impressionist artist Claude Monet's famous Water Lilies paintings. The Pacific island of Palau showed insects from various parts of the Pacific region on a sheet of 20 stamps. Also in the Pacific, the Marshall Islands released a sheet of sixteen stamps honoring famous American Indian leaders.

A TOPICAL COLLECTION FOR THE YEAR 2000

A topical collection is built around a single theme. And with the year 2000 beginning, this would be an excellent time to build a collection highlighting events of the past 100 years—or even the past 1,000 years. Many countries have issued stamps on this theme.

The United States is producing a series called Celebrate the Century. It features fifteen stamps for each decade of the 20th century, focusing on the styles, trends, and events of that ten-year period. Stamps covering 1900 through 1970 are already out; those for the 1980's and 1990's will be issued in 2000.

Canada's 68-stamp Millennium series salutes people, institutions, and events that defined the nation. Many of the stamps honor people who made an impact on modern life, such as inventor Alexander Graham Bell. There are entertainers such as band leader Guy Lombardo and the famous Cirque du Soliel troupe. The infant cereal Pablum, Saturday night broadcasts of hockey games, and Imax movies are among the wide-ranging subjects included in this series.

New Zealand's Millennium stamps are grouped by subject. Groups of stamps highlighting discovery, immigration, and cities were released in 1997 and 1998. A fourth group, released in 1999, took the theme of nostalgia. It featured six subjects—toys, the household, the garden, transportation, food, and collectibles.

IT'S GAME TIME...

ALL THAT JAZZ!

In 1999, the world celebrated the 100th anniversary of one of the century's best musicians. He was not only a fabulous pianist and orchestra leader but also the most prolific composer in jazz history. He wrote more than one thousand pieces of music, many of which were hits. Among the most famous was the concert piece, *Black, Brown and Beige.*

To learn this musician's name, you need a pencil and a sheet of paper. Carefully follow the directions given below. Hint: It will be easier if you rewrite the complete words at each step. (The solution is on page 414.)

1. Print the words BLACK BROWN AND BEIGE. Leave the words separated unless told otherwise.

2. Change the L to a D.

3. Remove the letter that comes after V in the alphabet.

4. Combine the third and fourth words by putting the third word between the I-G combination.

5. Replace the R with a T.

6. Find the first vowel of the last word. Move it to the end of the first word.

7. Substitute a U for the A in the first word.

8. Eliminate the third letter from the right.

9. Insert two Ls between the G-E combination.

10. Remove the second vowel from the right.

11. Erase all the Bs.

12. Combine the second and third words by putting the second word to the right of the G.

13. Reverse the last three letters. Move them to the start of the second word.

14. Take out the letter that is the second consonant in the alphabet.

This composer wrote his first piece of music— "The Soda Fountain Rag"—at the age of 16.

ANIMALS ON VACATION

All the animals decided to take a vacation. They wanted to travel and see new places. The lamb went to LAMBach, Austria. The llama went to PaLLAMAna, Australia. And the ox went to KnOXville, Tennessee. Can you figure out where the following animals went? (You may want to use maps to help you.)

The hen went to Greece's capital.
         _ _ HEN _

The bat flew to a city in Morocco.
         _ _ BAT

The mite hiked through a national park in California.
         _ _ _ _ MITE

The asp slithered north from Maine into Quebec.
         _ ASP _
         _ _ _ _ _ _ _ _

The dove flew along England's white cliffs.
         DOVE _

The ape swung through this city in South Africa.
         _ APE _ _ _ _

The ram visited the capital of California.
         _ _ _ RAM _ _ _ _

The rat relaxed in a spa in New York.
         _ _ RAT _ _ _
         _ _ _ _ _ _

The horse galloped to the Yukon Territory. . .or did it go to South Dakota?
         _ _ _ _ _ HORSE

The cow grazed its way to the capital of Russia.
         _ _ _ COW

The otter swam to one of the biggest cities in the Netherlands.
         _ OTTER _ _ _

The cat went to the east coast of Mexico.
         _ _ CAT _ _

The ant crawled to a city in Texas.
         _ _ _ ANT _ _ _ _

The hare hopped through the capital of Romania.
         _ _ _ HARE _ _

ANSWERS: Athens, Rabat, Yosemite, Gaspé Peninsula, Dover, Cape Town, Sacramento, Saratoga Springs, Whitehorse, Moscow, Rotterdam, Yucatan, San Antonio, Bucharest.

ORIENTEERING: CUNNING RUNNING

Pat was lost. A thick clump of trees loomed darkly a short way ahead, beyond a pile of small boulders. To the right, the ground rose steadily up a rooted and rocky slope. Which way to go? Pat looked at the compass, then studied the map. A "topographic" map, it showed every detail of the forest, the complete lay of the land.

"Okay—I've got it," thought Pat. "Here's the pile of boulders, and here's the slope that rises to the south. I've got to go north, down the slope. The map says there's a stream at the

bottom. . .I see it." And Pat was off at a fast trot, hopping over fallen logs, toward the stream, no longer lost. "Control point number five should be just west of that willow," she said to herself.

Pat isn't just a hiker in the woods; Pat is a participant in orienteering, a sport that combines the skills of navigation and cross-country running. For that reason, orienteering is sometimes called "cunning running."

In orienteering races, the idea is to travel through unfamiliar woodland areas as quickly

as possible. But unlike other races, the competitors—who are called "orienteers"—don't have to follow the same route. Each must, however, reach a series of landmarks, or control points, in a particular order. The winner is the person who reaches the control points, and the finish line, in the shortest time. But how the participants get to each control depends on their ability to read a topographic orienteering map and use a compass.

If you become an orienteer, you'll never get lost in the woods! And you'll experience the excitement of a sport that combines the skills of navigation and cross-country running. As orienteering has grown in popularity, people of all ages are getting involved in this physically—and mentally—challenging sport.

THINKING ALL THE TIME

To "orient" yourself means to find your bearings, to understand where you are in relation to your surroundings. That's why in orienteering, a map and a compass are indispensable. While orienteering is a physically demanding sport, it's just as demanding mentally. A good orienteer is thinking all the time, consulting the map, checking the compass, looking for landmarks—often while moving at top speed in the direction of the next control.

The topographic maps used in orienteering are called "O-maps." They are much more detailed than the average road map. Lakes, streams, rivers, ponds, swamps, wooded areas, and clearings are all represented, as are hills and valleys, trails and roads, and vegetation. Contour lines indicate the lay of the land—close together, they signify steep ground; farther apart, they mean the slope is more gradual. O-maps will often identify such tiny details as boulders and small caves and ditches. And O-maps will also point out human-made objects such as fences, cabins, and power lines. Of course, the control points are marked too.

In the woods, the control points are usually designated by orange and white flaglike markers. But even with the map, the controls aren't easy to find. They aren't supposed to be; otherwise, it would be too easy for you to accidentally happen upon one.

In addition to map and compass, every orienteer carries a scorecard. To prove that you have reached a control, you must use the special hole punch that's kept at each checkpoint and punch the card—in much the same way that a train conductor punches a ticket. Then it's back to the map and compass and the search for the next control.

Here's where the heavy brainwork starts. Examining the map, you realize that control point number six is just beneath a low ridge about a half mile to the east. The route

straight to the ridge looks like flat ground, through the woods, of course, but otherwise easy to cover.

But wait: The map says that some wetlands lie in there, perhaps even a mosquito-infested swamp. Would it be better to take the direct route, which might mean sloshing through a lot of muck? Or would it be faster to take the roundabout route that goes through higher and drier ground?

A quick decision is needed—you're losing time! "It hasn't rained much lately. Maybe the wetlands have dried out a bit. . . ." And off you go toward the swamp. Thinking, always thinking, you approach the wet ground and look for vines hanging from trees that may help you swing across. And as you dash onward, you're watching for your landmark, the low ridge.

In the meantime, some other orienteer has chosen the high ground, reaching the ridge by circling in from the north. It's a longer run, but there's little chance of getting bogged down with a bunch of frogs! Which route would *you* have chosen?

YOU CAN COMPETE, AND YOU CAN HAVE FUN

Orienteering developed in Sweden in the early 1900's, and to this day, many of the world's best competitors are from Scandinavian countries. The sport remains so popular in Sweden that an event lasting several days can attract thousands of participants.

Orienteering reached North America in the 1940's, but it didn't receive much attention for two decades. People in the military, however, saw the value of orienteering in the training of soldiers—it was a means of learning survival skills and the ways of the wilderness. In 1970, the first United States orienteering championships were held, and five years later, the first North American championships took place.

Orienteering has grown enormously in popularity. People of all ages are drawn to the

Every orienteer must use a special map and compass to reach a series of landmarks, or control points. The control points are designated by orange and white markers. When you reach one, you must use a special hole punch to punch your scorecard.

A good orienteer is thinking all the time, consulting the map, checking the compass, looking for landmarks—often while moving at top speed in the direction of the next control point.

sport, and there are clubs for both young people and adults. And not all orienteers are racers. Today orienteering is a recreational pastime as well as an intensely contested sport. Many participants enjoy just navigating and walking through orienteering courses. A hike in the woods is an invigorating exercise, and the mental stimulation of deciphering an O-map adds considerably to the fun. (Other types of orienteering involve travel by horseback, bicycle, cross-country skis, canoe, and even wheelchair.)

What about bad weather? In this sport, there's no such thing. Orienteering events are rarely canceled. They have been held in furious rainstorms and even blizzards. If you're going to venture into the wilderness to confront nature, you've got to be ready to face all it has to offer, whether mild or unforgiving.

What's the best way to practice for orienteering competition? If you're going to become a serious contender, you must be in good shape, since the physical side of the sport requires stamina and speed. Cross-country running is a recommended exercise. The mental side of orienteering is just as important: A good runner who can't read an O-map will spend a lot of time running around in circles. So of equal value to physical conditioning is technical training—learning to read and interpret O-maps.

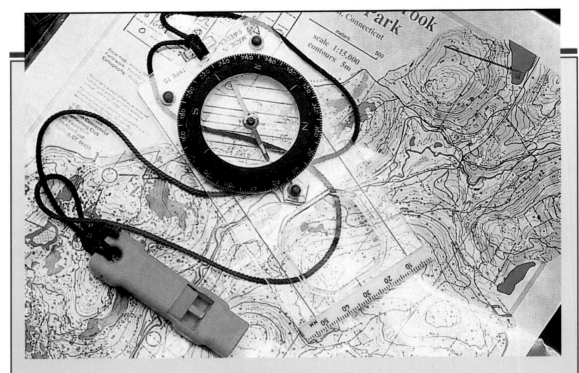

Be Prepared!

When you go into the woods, it's wise to pay heed to the Boy Scout motto: "Be prepared." You've got to bring suitable gear. But "being prepared" can mean different things: A hiker on the Appalachian Trail probably requires a large backpack, including tent, sleeping bag, clothing, an extra pair of shoes, cooking stove, and plenty of food. An orienteer, on the other hand, needs just an O-map, a compass, and proper clothing.

● **O-map.** All orienteers carry O-maps of the area in which they are competing. Highly detailed, these maps are extremely accurate representations of the territory.

● **Compass.** All orienteers use special compasses. The baseplate type of compass, in which the needle rests in a clear plastic baseplate, allows you to set a course from your current location to where you want to go. Another type of orienteering compass hooks onto your thumb; it's easy to use because you can hold it on the map as you are moving through the woods. But you can't set your course with it.

● **Clothing.** Competitive orienteers frequently prefer nylon running suits, gaiters (lightweight shin guards, which provide extra protection for the lower legs), and a sturdy pair of running shoes. If you aren't racing, but are just in the woods for an orienteering hike, then choose any loose, comfortable clothing and a pair of hiking boots. Shorts usually aren't recommended—they aren't protective enough. It's also a good idea to carry a whistle, to signal for help in case of injury.

You can sharpen your ability by running over orienteering courses while reading your map. You can also sit at home studying a map and trying to picture in your mind exactly what the locality looks like. One top competitor received a lot of technical training when he was an O-map maker. His job was to take a "base map," a general map of a proposed orienteering area, and walk through the woods and fill in all the details. In this way, he learned how to pick out significant landmarks, how to read the rises and falls of a region, how to gauge the density of brush and forest.

TYPES OF COURSES

Because more and more people of different ages and levels of ability have taken up orienteering, six different types of orienteering courses have been laid out.

The beginners' course enables participants to become used to reading maps, by finding and following easily located streams and trails. Advanced beginners must be able to leave the streams and trails now and then to find a control point, and then return to the original course they were following. On these courses, the controls are usually located at boulders, trees, or other large landmarks. On the third

Competing on cross-country skis adds to the thrill of orienteering in winter.

type of course, orienteers must move successfully cross-country while searching out large landscape features, such as a vast rock formation.

The top three courses are all equally difficult, but they vary in length, ranging up to 10 miles (16 kilometers). The world's best orienteers often compete on courses with few major terrain features, so very advanced skills are necessary, including the ability to identify subtle changes in landforms. The control points are usually located farther away from each other and in spots that are harder to find. At this level, you've got to be good—and even the top orienteers get lost occasionally.

When it comes right down to it, orienteering is a simple sport, requiring only that you get from "here" to "there." You're usually on your own, too, unless you're orienteering in a team. In an orienteering race, you may not even see any of the other competitors: Everyone starts at a different time, to eliminate the possibility of contestants following each other.

If you are pleased with yourself when you reach the finish line, you have a right to be. You've accomplished something. Plus, you've had the pleasure of experiencing nature in the most basic way—finding your way through a wilderness on foot. As one orienteer said, "I love the outdoors. Orienteering gives me one more way to go to the woods and enjoy myself."

THE NICKNAME GAME

Do you have a nickname? One you like? Or one you wish had never been given to you? In either case, you have something in common with many famous people.

Some people love their nicknames. Consider, for example, George Wagner, a well-known wrestler of the early 1950's. One night he was wrestling in Eugene, Oregon, when a woman in the audience cried, "Isn't he gorgeous!" The nickname stuck, and the wrestler liked it so much that he legally changed his name to Gorgeous George.

On the other hand, it's a safe bet that America's second president, John Adams, didn't like his nickname. Because of his excessive weight and his tendency to act like a king, critics called him His Rotundity (plumpness).

The names of 20 famous people are listed below, in the left column. Match each to his or her nickname, in the right column.

1. Andrew Jackson (U.S. president)
2. Wayne Gretzky (hockey player)
3. Clara Bow (actress)
4. Willie Mays (baseball player)
5. Jesse Ventura (governor of Minnesota)
6. Erwin Rommel (Nazi general)
7. Abraham Lincoln (U.S. president)
8. Benny Goodman (jazz musician)
9. William H. Bonney (outlaw)
10. Joe DiMaggio (baseball player)
11. Jimmy Durante (comedian)
12. Margaret Thatcher (British prime minister)
13. Ernest Hemingway (author)
14. Zachary Taylor (U.S. president)
15. Thomas Jackson (U.S. Civil War general)
16. Louis Armstrong (jazz musician)
17. Bette Midler (singer)
18. George Herman Ruth (baseball player)
19. Theodore Roosevelt (U.S. president)
20. Julius Erving (basketball player)

a. Divine Miss M
b. Great Emancipator
c. Schnozzola
d. Old Rough and Ready
e. Iron Lady
f. Old Hickory
g. The Babe
h. King of Swing
i. Papa
j. Dr. J
k. Desert Fox
l. Stonewall
m. Say Hey Kid
n. Trust Buster
o. Satchmo
p. Yankee Clipper
q. The Great One
r. The Body
s. It Girl
t. Billy the Kid

ANSWERS: 1.f; 2.q; 3.s; 4.m; 5.r; 6.k; 7.b; 8.h; 9.t; 10.p; 11.c; 12.e; 13.i; 14.d; 15.l; 16.o; 17.a; 18.g; 19.n; 20.j.

20

BCDE

Next, go on a hunt. All 20 nicknames are hidden in this search-a-word puzzle. Try to find them. Cover the puzzle with a sheet of tracing paper. Read forward, backward, up, down, and diagonally. Then draw a neat line through each name as you find it.

B	R	O	T	A	P	I	C	N	A	M	E	T	A	E	R	G
C	I	B	E	D	I	V	I	N	E	M	I	S	S	M	U	L
H	R	R	I	S	A	T	N	S	P	N	N	A	U	Q	L	E
V	O	L	D	R	O	U	G	H	A	N	D	R	E	A	D	Y
E	N	A	D	T	H	C	H	I	V	Y	B	R	W	H	A	R
R	L	D	I	H	A	I	O	W	R	A	H	E	O	P	E	O
A	A	E	K	E	R	N	B	A	J	L	N	E	A	Z	D	K
L	D	S	E	G	A	D	O	E	D	O	Q	P	Y	E	Z	C
O	Y	E	H	R	V	E	T	F	T	R	O	U	R	K	Y	I
Z	U	R	T	E	U	R	H	S	A	R	J	B	I	F	I	H
Z	R	T	Y	A	N	K	E	E	C	L	I	P	P	E	R	D
O	F	F	L	T	B	O	B	Y	I	N	C	H	L	R	N	L
N	H	O	L	O	K	I	O	M	H	C	T	A	S	N	Y	O
H	E	X	I	N	A	R	D	L	G	O	O	A	O	N	T	S
C	A	S	B	E	B	Y	Y	I	E	B	A	B	E	H	T	E
S	L	P	O	R	E	T	S	U	B	T	S	U	R	T	A	W
E	K	I	N	G	O	F	S	W	I	N	G	R	Y	S	M	Z

MANY FRIENDS COOKING

BERRY SHAKE
from Finland

Red lingonberries, yellow cloudberries, blueberries, deep red raspberries—colorful and delicate berries of all kinds are grown and eaten in Finland. Fresh berries are mixed into desserts or drinks like this Berry Shake. Use strawberries for your first shake. Then create a berry shake of your own.

INGREDIENTS

- 10 fresh strawberries or
- 6 tablespoons frozen sliced strawberries in syrup (thawed)
- 2 cups cold milk
- 1½ tablespoons sugar or honey

EQUIPMENT

paring knife
measuring spoons
measuring cups
small bowl
egg beater
2 glasses

HOW TO MAKE

1. Wash the strawberries (if fresh) and cut out the stems.
2. Cut the strawberries into small pieces. (If you're using frozen strawberies, drain the syrup into a small bowl or cup and save it for step 4.)
3. Pour the milk into the mixing bowl. Add the strawberries.
4. If you're using fresh strawberries, add the sugar or honey. If you're using frozen strawberries, add 3 tablespoons of the strawberry syrup instead of sugar.
5. Beat with the egg beater for one minute.
6. Pour the drink into the glasses.

This recipe serves 2 people.

ORANGE CHICKEN
from Cuba

A rainbow of citrus fruits ripens in the blazing sun of this tropical island. You can almost taste Cuba's sunshine in this tangy chicken bake. Add rice to the dish, invite friends to the table, and you'll all enjoy a delicious Latin American meal.

INGREDIENTS

1 chicken (3 to 3½ lbs.) cut into serving pieces
2 teaspoons salt
1 teaspoon pepper
½ teaspoon garlic salt
2 cups orange juice
1 lime

EQUIPMENT

small mixing bowls
paring knife
measuring spoons
measuring cups
baking pan

HOW TO MAKE

1. Measure salt, pepper, and garlic salt into the small bowl.
2. Sprinkle both sides of the chicken pieces with this mixture.
3. Measure the orange juice.
4. Cut the lime in half and squeeze the juice into the orange juice.
5. Place the chicken pieces in the baking pan and pour the orange-lime juice over the chicken. Marinate the chicken in the juice for 1 hour, then turn the pieces and marinate 1 hour longer.
6. Remove the chicken from the pan. Pour the juice off into the bowl.
7. Preheat the oven to 350°F.
8. Return the chicken to the baking pan and add ½ cup of the juice.
9. Bake for 30 minutes, then baste with 1 cup additional juice. Bake 30 minutes more or until the chicken is tender.

This recipe serves 4 to 6 people.

POPULAR CRAFTS

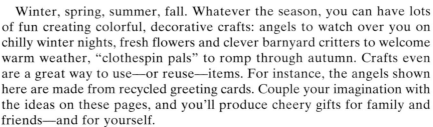

Winter, spring, summer, fall. Whatever the season, you can have lots of fun creating colorful, decorative crafts: angels to watch over you on chilly winter nights, fresh flowers and clever barnyard critters to welcome warm weather, "clothespin pals" to romp through autumn. Crafts even are a great way to use—or reuse—items. For instance, the angels shown here are made from recycled greeting cards. Couple your imagination with the ideas on these pages, and you'll produce cheery gifts for family and friends—and for yourself.

WINTER ANGELS

Making paper angels to decorate gift packages or to hang as ornaments is a great project to share with a friend on a snowy afternoon.

To make a winter angel, you'll need an angel cookie cutter for the pattern (or use a copying machine to enlarge one of the angels shown here). You'll also need old greeting cards, white glue, fine-line markers in various colors, felt, construction paper, bits of ribbon, and gold metallic thread.

Trace the angel onto a greeting card, and then decorate it. You might apply glue to the wings and sprinkle on gold glitter. Add a halo, button face, and ribbon bow. Paint a row of buttons or attach a lace ruffle at the bottom of the dress. When you are finished, cut out the angel along the traced lines.

Make a hanging loop for your angel by knotting together the ends of a length of gold metallic thread. Glue the knot to the back of the angel's head.

Now glue the angel to some background material, such as construction paper or felt. Trim the excess material, leaving a colorful edge around the angel.

In addition to greeting cards, you can make angels from other kinds of paper or from felt. And instead of angels, you can make trees, stars, and animals—just check out your supply of cookie cutters!

WELCOME SPRING!

Billie Bee and Timmie Turtle are eggxactly what you need to shout "It's spring!"

To make one of these critters you'll need a wooden egg, white watercolor paper, acrylic paints, acrylic spray matte sealer, a black marker, white glue, and a gold puffy heart for Billie or a sprig of flowers for Timmie.

Billie Bee and Timmie Turtle

Begin by sanding the egg and wiping it with a clean cloth. Apply two coats of the base color to the egg—yellow for Billie, green for Timmie. Always be sure to let one layer of paint dry completely before adding new paint.

Paint on stripes, facial features, and other details. Draw arms and legs on the watercolor paper, and paint them to match the critter's body. Cut out the arms and legs, crease each about 1/2 inch (1.2 centimeters) from the end, and glue each crease onto the body. Spray the entire critter with clear matte sealer. To add the finishing touch, glue on the puffy heart or flowers.

How about some egg-y friends for your critter? Make your own unique Priscilla Pig, Freddie Frog, or Betty Bunny!

FRESH FLOWERS

One of the wonderful things about spring and summer is the abundance of beautiful flowers and greenery. You can collect and press dry these materials, and then use them to create this lovely flower candle.

To make this candle, you will need fresh flowers and leaves, a pillar candle, non-coated paper, white glue, and clear acrylic sealer.

Here's the simplest way to press flowers and leaves: Take a sheet of poster board and cover it with a sheet of non-coated paper. Carefully arrange the flowers on the paper. Place a second sheet of non-coated paper over the flowers, followed by a second piece of poster board. Cover with heavy books. Let the flowers dry for about three weeks (the thicker the flowers, the longer the drying time).

Pressed flowers are very delicate. To avoid breaking them, handle them with tweezers.

Plan how you would like your candle to look by arranging the flowers on a sheet of white paper, moving them around until you have a pleasing design. Then apply a small dot or two of glue to the back of a flower and attach it to the candle.

Work on one section of the candle at a time. After you've attached several flowers, use a

small paintbrush to gently cover the flowers with a coat of acrylic sealer. Brush the sealer beyond all the edges of the flowers. Let the area dry before beginning to work on the next section of the candle.

When you've finished decorating the candle, you can place it on a candleholder. Or you can glue the bottom of the candle to a lace doily purchased in a craft store.

Your pressed-flower candle will make a perfect gift for Mother's Day!

A SUMMER BARNYARD

Need a decorative place to store all those little trinkets that clutter your pockets and tabletops? Then make room for this colorful barnyard trio.

You'll need three round, wooden boxes of different sizes, acrylic paints, a black fine-line permanent marker, and clear acrylic spray sealer.

Cover each box with two coats of acrylic paint—red for the chicken, pink for the pig, white for the cow. Make certain that the first coat is dry before you add the second coat. You can also paint the inside of the box.

Using the fine-line marker and the acrylic paints, create the faces and features of each animal—the cow's muzzle and spots; the chicken's beak, comb, and wattle; and the pig's rosy cheeks and dark hooves.

When you have finished, spray the boxes with sealer. Let the pieces dry completely before putting the lid on each box, or before stacking the boxes.

AUTUMN PALS

Autumn brings a nip in the air, and this charming sweeper and penguin are dressed for the season!

To make this whimsical pair, you'll need two wooden clothespins with stands, acrylic paints, fabric strips, a black fine-line permanent marker, twine, glue, and decorative items such as a small wooden button and a miniature spool, hat, broom, and basket.

For the sweeper, paint the clothespin and stand light beige. Give the sweeper an antique look by dry brushing the stand and opening edges of the pin. To dry brush, dip a brush in brown paint, then stroke it back and forth on paper until it's almost dry. Then lightly streak the paint onto the wood.

When dry, glue the clothespin into the stand. Use the   marker to draw

ter back of the neck. To finish the sweeper, glue a strip of fabric around the hat and tie a fabric scarf around the neck.

To make the penguin, you'll need two wooden "teardrops" for the wings. Paint them black. Draw light lines on the front of the clothespin separating the light and dark areas. Paint the light area beige, and the dark area black.

Glue the teardrop wings, tips down, to the center back of the clothespin. Dry brush brown paint onto the clothespin opening, the edges of the wings, and the stand.

A whimsical pair of clothespin pals celebrate autumn.

the face. To make the sweeper's hat, paint a mini spool and wooden button black. Glue one end of the spool to the button. Glue the hat to the head.

Now give the fellow a broom and some twine arms. Tie the center of a length of twine into a knot around the top of the broom handle. Glue the loose ends of the twine to the cen-

When completely dry, glue the pin into the stand. Add facial features. Glue on a straw hat and a basket of flowers. Tie a fabric strip around the hat and a scarf around the neck.

Your clothespin pals are ready to romp through the autumn leaves!

NONA PIORKOWSKI
Crafts 'n Things magazine

COIN COLLECTING

Rabbits frolicked, wolves howled, alligators snapped, and kangaroos hopped on 1999 collector coins from mints throughout the world. For its part, the U.S. Mint introduced a new series of quarters honoring the 50 states.

U.S. COINS

The new "state" quarters are being released five a year through 2008, in the order the states joined the Union. First up in 1999 were Delaware, Pennsylvania, New Jersey, Georgia, and Connecticut. Each coin showed George Washington on the obverse and a state-picked design on the reverse.

The famous geyser Old Faithful gushed up on a new silver dollar, one of three commemorative coins issued by the U.S. Mint in 1999. This silver dollar marked the 125th anniversary of Yellowstone National Park, the nation's first national park. An image of First Lady Dolley Madison graced the front of another commemorative silver dollar. This was the first U.S. coin ever designed by a private firm, New York jeweler Tiffany & Co., and it bore the company's hallmark. George Washington appeared on the face of a $5 gold coin, marking the 200th anniversary of his death. The design for this coin had originally been planned for use on circulating quarters.

U.S. "state" quarters representing Delaware, Pennsylvania, New Jersey, Georgia, and Connecticut.

Delaware chose Caesar Rodney, who in 1776 galloped all night to reach Philadelphia in time to cast Delaware's vote for the Declaration of Independence. Pennsylvania selected a figure of Commonwealth, based on a statue on the state capitol dome. New Jersey showed a key moment in the Revolutionary War, reproducing a version of Emmanuel Leutze's famous painting *Washington Crossing the Delaware.* Georgia presented a peach. And Connecticut showed the Charter Oak. Legend has it that Connecticut's charter was hidden in this tree, to keep it out of the hands of British agents.

The five circulating quarters were minted at both the Philadelphia and Denver mints. So collectors need to add ten coins to their collections to have a complete set of the 1999 state quarters. To help promote the new coins, the U.S. Mint signed Kermit the Frog as its official "spokesfrog." The Mint also launched a Web site to help kids learn about coins:

http://www2.usmint.gov/kids/index.html

The Mint continued its "Vistas of Liberty" designs for the platinum American Eagle bullion coin. These designs show the bald eagle in settings that represent the country's regions. The 1999 coin honored the southeastern United States by featuring an alligator and wetlands, with the eagle flying overhead.

WORLD COINS

Canada began a two-year series of 25-cent millennium coins with twelve designs focusing on the nation's past. In 2000, twelve more coins will look to its future. Designs were

U.S. silver dollar coins honoring Yellowstone National Park and First Lady Dolley Madison.

170

Canada's millennium coins honoring the nation's railroad system, and showing people holding hands in a gesture of peace and friendship.

tralia showed a "mob," or family, of kangaroos on a silver dollar. And since 1999 was the Year of the Rabbit in the Chinese lunar calendar, rabbits were featured on coins from many nations. Among them were Canada, Australia, Singapore, China, Laos, and Macao.

British royalty reigned over the coins of several nations. Gibraltar traced the history of English kings and queens on a twelve-coin crown set in various metals. The June 1999 marriage of Britain's Prince Edward to Sophie Rhys-Jones was the subject of coins from the Isle of Man, Sierra Leone, and Seychelles. The life of Britain's Queen Mother was celebrated on a twelve-coin set from Gibraltar. Britain itself released a memorial 5-pound coin for Princess Diana, who died in 1997.

A total eclipse of the sun that took place on August 11, 1999, was commemorated on coins from the Channel Island of Alderney. A 2-pound coin showed the eclipsed sun over an Alderney scene. In the foreground

selected in a nationwide contest that attracted more than 60,000 entries. The winners honored everything from Canada's early days, to its vast railroad system, to native art. Ten-year-old Claudia Bertrans, of Beauport, Quebec, became Canada's youngest coin designer when her coin was released in September. It showed people holding hands in a gesture of peace and friendship.

Canadian coin collectors could also choose from a number of commemorative coins. The design for Canada's 1999 $200 gold

The Isle of Man's coin featuring a British blue cat; Australia's silver dollar showing a family of kangaroos; and Macao's coin marking the Year of the Rabbit.

coin was inspired by ancient Mi'kmaw drawings found in Nova Scotia. Canada also released a $350 gold coin showing the delicate lady's slipper orchid, native to the wetlands of Prince Edward Island. Four sterling silver 50-cent coins joined Canada's series on "firsts" in sports, featuring yachting, golf, football, and basketball. And four felines appeared on another set of silver 50-cent coins, called Cats of Canada.

Many other countries issued coins with animal themes. The Isle of Man continued its platinum Manx cat series with a coin showing a British blue cat. South Africa added new coins to its flora and fauna series. Aus-

were a pair of gannets, ocean birds that had roosted when the eclipse turned day into night. A 5-pound coin showed the moon passing across the sun, with shadows cast over southern England and Alderney.

Rounding out the year were traditional 50-pence Christmas coins from the Isle of Man and Gibraltar. A Victorian family decorated a Christmas tree on the Isle of Man coin. Gibraltar's coin showed Santa Claus, helped by two of Gibraltar's famous Barbary apes, working to get presents wrapped in time for the holiday.

ROBERT VAN RYZIN
Editor, *Coins* magazine

What a kick! The U.S. women's soccer team jumps for joy after defeating China, 5–4, to capture the Women's World Cup. The July 10, 1999, final game was a hard-fought contest, decided by a shootout (penalty kicks) in overtime. More than 90,000 fans, including President Bill Clinton, packed the Rose Bowl in Pasadena, California, to see it—the largest crowd ever for a women's sporting event in the United States.

The strong arm of relief pitcher Mariano Rivera helped the New York Yankees sweep the Atlanta Braves in the World Series. Rivera was named World Series MVP.

BASEBALL

The New York Yankees, the most successful team in baseball history—and perhaps in any sport—continued their winning ways in 1999. They won their second straight World Series, and their 25th overall, sweeping the Atlanta Braves in four games.

In the regular season, manager Joe Torre piloted New York to a first-place finish in the Eastern Division of the American League (AL). The Boston Red Sox were four games behind the Yankees, and qualified for the playoffs with the fourth-best record in the league. The Texas Rangers were first in the Western Division, and the Cleveland Indians led the Central Division.

In the division series (the first round of the playoffs), New York swept Texas in three games. Boston, meanwhile, outlasted Cleveland, 3 games to 2. In the American League Championship Series (ALCS), the Yanks rolled over the Red Sox, 4 games to 1. Right-

handed pitcher Orlando Hernandez, nicknamed "El Duque," won the deciding game for New York and was named Most Valuable Player (MVP) of the ALCS.

With the best regular-season record in either league, Atlanta captured the crown of the National League (NL) Eastern Division. The Central Division champs were the Houston Astros, and the Arizona Diamondbacks topped the Western Division. Earning the NL wild-card berth were the New York Mets, who finished second in the East to the Braves.

Atlanta ousted Houston, 3 games to 1, in the division series, while the Mets trumped the Diamondbacks, also in four games. In the National League Championship Series (NLCS), the Braves eliminated the Mets in six games; Atlanta catcher Eddie Perez batted .500, banging out 10 hits, including two home runs, and was named the MVP of the NLCS.

Game 1 of the World Series, played in Atlanta, matched Orlando Hernandez against the Braves' superb right-hander, Greg Maddux. Both hurlers were masterful. Hernandez yielded only one hit in the seven innings he pitched—a home run to Atlanta's Chipper Jones. Maddux, meanwhile, shut out New York through the seventh. But in the top of the eighth, the Yanks pushed across four runs, and New York wound up winning, 4–1. The Yanks' ace reliever, Mariano Rivera, got the save, and New York was up, 1 game to 0.

In Game 2, also contested in Atlanta, the Yanks jumped on Atlanta starter Kevin Millwood for three runs in the first inning. Behind David Cone's one-hit, shutout pitching over seven innings, New York mounted a 7–0 lead. Bernie Williams had three hits for the victors, Paul O'Neill collected one, and Chuck Knoblauch, Derek Jeter, Tino Martinez, Scott Brosius, and Ricky Ledee added two apiece. The final score was 7–2, and the "Bronx Bombers" returned home with a comfortable lead of 2 games to 0.

Game 3, at Yankee Stadium, saw Atlanta go ahead 5–1, but on home runs by Chad Curtis, Martinez, and Knoblauch, New York eventu-

1999 WORLD SERIES RESULTS

		R	H	E	Winning/Losing Pitcher
1	New York	4	6	0	Orlando Hernandez (W)
	Atlanta	1	2	2	Greg Maddux (L)
2	New York	7	14	1	David Cone (W)
	Atlanta	2	5	2	Kevin Millwood (L)
3	Atlanta	5	14	1	Mike Remlinger (L)
	New York	6	9	0	Mariano Rivera (W)
4	Atlanta	1	5	0	John Smoltz (L)
	New York	4	8	0	Roger Clemens (W)

Visiting team listed first, home team second

ally tied the Braves at 5–5, and the contest went into extra innings. In the last of the tenth, Curtis bopped his second round-tripper of the game, and the Yankees won, 6–5. Mariano Rivera picked up the victory in relief, and the Braves were down 3 games to 0.

Roger Clemens started Game 4 for New York. The right-hander had had only a mediocre regular season, but the five-time winner of the Cy Young Award was in 1999 named one of the greatest baseball players of the 20th century. In Game 4, he showed why, allowing Atlanta only one run and four hits in 7⅔ innings. Jim Leyritz pinch-hit an eighth-inning homer for the Yanks, Rivera notched another save, and New York won, 4–1. For his two saves and one pitching victory, Rivera received the World Series MVP award.

The AL regular-season MVP was catcher Ivan Rodriguez of the Texas Rangers; he won his eighth Gold Glove Award, hit 35 homers, batted .332, and had 113 runs batted in (RBIs) and 116 runs scored. Atlanta's Chipper Jones was named NL MVP; he hit .319 and had 45 home runs and 110 RBIs.

Few pitchers have ever been so dominant as Pedro Martinez was in 1999; in winning the AL Cy Young Award, the Boston right-hander compiled 23 wins against only 4 losses, a 2.07 earned run average (ERA), and 313 strikeouts in 213 innings pitched. The NL honoree was Arizona southpaw Randy Johnson, who won 17 games, struck out 364, and posted a 2.48 ERA. Martinez and Johnson thus became only the second and third pitchers in history to win Cy Young Awards in both leagues.

Rookie-of-the-Year Awards went, in the NL, to Cincinnati Red pitcher Scott Williamson, who won 12 games, saved 19, and recorded a 2.41 ERA; and in the AL, to Kansas City Royal outfielder Carlos Beltran, who batted .293 with 108 RBIs.

Also during the regular season:

● Mark McGwire of the St. Louis Cardinals clubbed 65 home runs, and Sammy Sosa of the Chicago Cubs belted 63; they are the only players in history to have twice exceeded 60 in one season (in 1998, McGwire totaled 70, and Sosa 66). McGwire also hit his 500th career homer in 1999.

● Tony Gwynn of the San Diego Padres and Wade Boggs of the Tampa Bay Devil Rays both collected the 3,000th hits of their illustrious careers.

● Yankee David Cone pitched a perfect game against the Montreal Expos on July 18 in Yankee Stadium, facing the minimum 27 batters and retiring every one.

Atlanta Braves slugger Chipper Jones was named 1999 National League MVP. During the season, he hit .319, knocked in 45 home runs, and had 110 runs batted in.

MAJOR LEAGUE BASEBALL FINAL STANDINGS

AMERICAN LEAGUE

Eastern Division

	W	L	Pct.	GB
*New York	98	64	.605	—
Boston	94	68	.580	4
Toronto	84	78	.519	14
Baltimore	78	84	.481	20
Tampa Bay	69	93	.426	29

Central Division

	W	L	Pct.	GB
Cleveland	97	65	.599	—
Chicago	75	86	.466	21½
Detroit	69	92	.429	27½
Kansas City	64	97	.398	32½
Minnesota	63	97	.394	33

Western Division

	W	L	Pct.	GB
Texas	95	67	.586	—
Oakland	87	75	.537	8
Seattle	79	83	.488	16
Anaheim	70	92	.432	25

*League Championship Series winners

NATIONAL LEAGUE

Eastern Division

	W	L	Pct.	GB
*Atlanta	103	59	.636	—
New York	97	66	.595	6½
Philadelphia	77	85	.475	26
Montreal	68	94	.420	35
Florida	64	98	.395	39

Central Division

	W	L	Pct.	GB
Houston	97	65	.599	—
Cincinnati	96	67	.589	1½
Pittsburgh	78	83	.484	18½
St. Louis	75	86	.466	21½
Milwaukee	74	87	.460	22½
Chicago	67	95	.414	30

Western Division

	W	L	Pct.	GB
Arizona	100	62	.617	—
San Francisco	86	76	.531	14
Los Angeles	77	85	.475	23
San Diego	74	88	.457	26
Colorado	72	90	.444	28

MAJOR LEAGUE LEADERS

AMERICAN LEAGUE

Batting
(top 10 qualifiers)

	AB	H	Avg.
N. Garciaparra, Boston	532	190	.357
D. Jeter, New York	627	219	.349
B. Williams, New York	591	202	.342
E. Martinez, Seattle	502	169	.337
M. Ramirez, Cleveland	522	174	.333
O. Vizquel, Cleveland	574	191	.333
I. Rodriguez, Texas	600	199	.332
T. Fernandez, Toronto	485	159	.328
J. Gonzalez, Texas	562	183	.326
R. Palmeiro, Texas	565	183	.324

Home Runs

	HR
K. Griffey, Seattle	48
R. Palmeiro, Texas	47
C. Delgado, Toronto	44
M. Ramirez, Cleveland	44
A. Rodriguez, Seattle	42
S. Green, Toronto	42

Pitching
(top qualifiers, based on number of wins)

	W	L	ERA
P. Martinez, Boston	23	4	2.07
B. Colon, Cleveland	18	5	3.95
M. Mussina, Baltimore	18	7	3.50
A. Sele, Texas	18	9	4.79

NATIONAL LEAGUE

Batting
(top 10 qualifiers)

	AB	H	Avg.
L. Walker, Colorado	438	166	.379
L. Gonzalez, Arizona	614	206	.336
B. Abreu, Philadelphia	546	183	.335
S. Casey, Cincinnati	594	197	.332
J. Cirillo, Milwaukee	607	198	.326
M. Grudzielanek, L.A.	488	159	.326
C. Everett, Houston	464	151	.325
D. Glanville, Philadelphia	628	204	.325
T. Helton, Colorado	578	185	.320
C. Jones, Atlanta	567	181	.319

Home Runs

	HR
M. McGwire, St. Louis	65
S. Sosa, Chicago	63
C. Jones, Atlanta	45
G. Vaughn, Cincinnati	45
J. Bagwell, Houston	42
V. Guerrero, Montreal	42

Pitching
(top qualifiers, based on number of wins)

	W	L	ERA
M. Hampton, Houston	22	4	2.90
J. Lima, Houston	21	10	3.58
G. Maddux, Atlanta	19	9	3.57

A Little League team from Osaka, Japan, won the 1999 World Series, defeating the U.S. champs, 5–0.

LITTLE LEAGUE BASEBALL

Powered by the strong arm of 12-year-old pitcher Kazuki Sumiyama, a team from Osaka, Japan, won the Little League World Series on August 28, 1999. They defeated the United States champions, from Phenix City, Alabama, by a score of 5–0 in the title game, as Sumiyama allowed only two hits and struck out nine batters. Some 42,000 spectators attended the contest.

Kazutoshi Adachi scored Japan's first run in the second inning, bolting home from third base when the U.S. catcher, Cory Rasmus, committed a throwing error on an attempted steal. Then, sparked by back-to-back doubles by Kazunori Morishita and Kazuya Yamasaki, Japan picked up two more runs in the fourth inning. In the fifth, Yamasaki singled in one of Japan's two final tallies. Team captain Takashi Sakurai also had two hits for the winners. The U.S. team, overmatched by pitcher Sumiyama's fastballs, could manage only two singles, by Rasmus and Zack Martin, in the whole game.

The Japanese squad was made up of players from the Hirakata Little League of Osaka. Rep-resenting the Far East, they reached the championship game of the Little League World Series by winning the International Division of the annual tournament. The other teams in the International group were the Latin American champs, from Yabucoa, Puerto Rico; the Canadian titlists, from Victoria, British Columbia; and Europe's representatives, from Ramstein Air Force Base, Germany.

Phenix City, Alabama, reached the World Series final by defeating Toms River, New Jersey, the previous year's Little League world champs, by the score of 3–2 in the United States title game. That game took two days to play; rain caused it to be suspended after one inning on the first day. Earlier in the tournament, Toms River had defeated Phenix City, 6–0. The other teams in the U.S. group hailed from Boise, Idaho, and Brownsburg, Indiana.

Japan's victory was the fourth Little League title captured by a team from that country, but its first since 1976. The Little League World Series is held each year at Howard J. Lamade Stadium in Williamsport, Pennsylvania.

Forward Tim Duncan (#21) led the San Antonio Spurs to their first-ever NBA title in 1999. He won the Most Valuable Player award for the playoffs.

BASKETBALL

Delayed by a dispute between players and management, the 1998–99 season of the National Basketball Association (NBA) started late. But not even a shortened schedule could dim the luster of the San Antonio Spurs. Led by the "Twin Towers," center David Robinson and power forward Tim Duncan—both 7 feet (2 meters) tall—the Spurs captured the league championship by defeating the New York Knicks, four games to one, in the playoff finals in June. Also in 1999, Michael Jordan retired from basketball, marking the close of one of the finest careers in any sport.

The season was nearly never played at all, as the team owners and the athletes fought over how to divide the huge amounts of money the NBA earns each year. Unable to agree with the players' demands, the owners instituted a "lockout," preventing their employees—the players—from competing in any games. Luckily for hoops fans, the league and the players finally reached an agreement, and the season began on February 5, 1999. Each team would play only 50 regular-season games, instead of the usual 82; but the full playoff schedule would be followed.

In addition to Robinson and Duncan, San Antonio's lineup included guards Mario Elie and Avery Johnson, and forward Sean Elliott. Coach Gregg Popovich also relied on reserve forwards Jerome Kersey and Malik Rose, and reserve guards Jaren Jackson and Steve Kerr.

The Spurs tied the Utah Jazz for the best regular-season records; both teams compete in the Midwest Division of the Western Conference. The two other playoff teams from that division were the Houston Rockets and the Minnesota Timberwolves. Qualifying for post-season play from the Pacific Division of the Western Conference were the Portland Trail Blazers, the Los Angeles Lakers, the Sacramento Kings, and the Phoenix Suns.

In the best-of-five first-round series of the playoffs, San Antonio ousted Minnesota in four games. The later playoff rounds were all best-of-seven; but the Spurs dispatched the Lakers in a four-game sweep in round two, and followed up with another four-game sweep over Portland in the Western Conference finals.

The New York Knicks finished fourth in the Atlantic Division of the Eastern Conference, barely making the playoffs. In that division, the Miami Heat and the Orlando Magic tied for the best regular-season records, and the Philadelphia 76ers also qualified for post-season competition. In the Eastern Conference's Central Division, the Indiana Pacers finished first; they were joined in the playoffs by the Atlanta

NBA FINAL STANDINGS

EASTERN CONFERENCE

Atlantic Division

	W	L	Pct.
Miami	33	17	.660
Orlando	33	17	.660
Philadelphia	28	22	.560
N.Y. Knicks	27	23	.540
Boston	19	31	.380
Washington	18	32	.360
New Jersey	16	34	.320

Central Division

	W	L	Pct.
Indiana	33	17	.660
Atlanta	31	19	.620
Detroit	29	21	.580
Milwaukee	28	22	.560
Charlotte	26	24	.520
Toronto	23	27	.460
Cleveland	22	28	.440
Chicago	13	37	.260

WESTERN CONFERENCE

Midwest Division

	W	L	Pct.
San Antonio	37	13	.740
Utah	37	13	.740
Houston	31	19	.620
Minnesota	25	25	.500
Dallas	19	31	.380
Denver	14	36	.280
Vancouver	8	42	.160

Pacific Division

	W	L	Pct.
Portland	35	15	.700
L.A. Lakers	31	19	.620
Sacramento	27	23	.540
Phoenix	27	23	.540
Seattle	25	25	.500
Golden State	21	29	.420
L.A. Clippers	9	41	.180

NBA Championship: San Antonio Spurs

COLLEGE BASKETBALL

Conference	Winner
Atlantic Coast	Duke (regular season and tournament)
Atlantic Ten	Temple; George Washington (tied, regular season) Rhode Island (tournament)
Big East	Connecticut (regular season and tournament)
Big Ten	Michigan State (regular season and tournament)
Big Twelve	Texas (regular season) Kansas (tournament)
Big West	Boise State; UC Santa Barbara (regular season) New Mexico State (tournament)
Ivy League	Pennsylvania
Missouri Valley	Evansville (regular season) Creighton (tournament)
Pacific-10	Stanford
Southeastern	Tennessee; Auburn (tied, regular season) Kentucky (tournament)
Southwestern Athletic	Alcorn State (regular season and tournament)
Western Athletic	Utah; UNLV; Tulsa (tied; regular season) Utah (tournament)

NCAA, men: Connecticut
women: Purdue

NIT: California

two. And in the Eastern Conference finals, the New York Knicks eliminated Indiana in six.

Games 1 and 2 of the NBA finals were contested at the Alamodome in San Antonio. Tim Duncan dominated Game 1, totaling 33 points and 16 rebounds, as the Spurs won, 89–77. The Knicks, playing the finals without their injured center Patrick Ewing, were unable to match up against either Duncan or Robinson. Jaren Jackson added 17 points for San Antonio; Latrell Sprewell and Allan Houston each had 19 for New York.

The Spurs' defense slammed the door on the Knicks in Game 2. The "Twin Towers" combined to block nine New York shots. Duncan collected 25 points and 15 rebounds; Robinson's respective totals were 16 and 11. In taking a two-games-to-none lead over the Knicks, San Antonio also won its 12th consecutive playoff contest, a league record. Final score: 80–67.

New York's Madison Square Garden was the site of the last three games of the finals. In Game 3, the Knicks gained their only victory

Hawks, the Detroit Pistons, and the Milwaukee Bucks.

Though ranked last among the Eastern Conference playoff teams because of their regular-season record, the Knicks proved that postseason play is "a different ball game." They upset Miami, three games to two, in round one, and then swept Atlanta in four games in round

of the series, 89–81. Houston poured in 34 points, and Sprewell added 24 for New York. Robinson led San Antonio with 25. The Spurs got back in the saddle in Game 4, riding to a 96–89 triumph, and a three-games-to-one lead. Duncan led the way with 28 points and 17 rebounds. Robinson contributed 14 points and 17 rebounds, while Mario Elie scored 18 points, and Sean Elliott and Avery Johnson each had 14.

New York didn't go quietly in Game 5, fighting San Antonio to the final buzzer. But the Spurs dug in their heels and won by one point, 78–77. Tim Duncan was the main man, netting 31 points. The San Antonio Spurs thus won their first-ever NBA crown. It was also the first NBA title by a team that had originally played in the American Basketball Association (ABA)—four ABA teams joined the NBA when the ABA folded in 1976.

Hailed as one of the NBA's new young superstars, Duncan was named Most Valuable Player (MVP) of the playoffs. In the finals, he averaged 27.4 points and 14 rebounds

per game. The 1999 season was only Duncan's second in the NBA; in 1998, he was regular-season Rookie of the Year.

For the 1999 NBA regular season, Utah power forward Karl Malone won his second MVP award; he averaged 23.8 points and 9.4 rebounds per game. Vince Carter of the Toronto Raptors averaged 18.3 points and was named the league's top rookie.

Michael Jordan officially announced his retirement on January 13, 1999. The incomparable "Mike" is regarded by many as the sport's greatest player. He recorded the NBA's highest all-time career scoring average—31.5 points per game.

Women's Pro Leagues. For the third consecutive year, the champions of the Women's National Basketball Association (WNBA) were the Houston Comets, who defeated the New York Liberty, two games to one, in the best-of-three playoff finals. Also for the third straight year, Comet Cynthia Cooper was the playoff MVP. Regular season MVP honors went to Yolanda Griffith of the Sacramento Monarchs, and Chamique Holdsclaw of the Washington Mystics was named the league's top rookie.

The other women's pro circuit, the American Basketball League went bankrupt and folded in late 1998.

College Play. The Huskies of the University of Connecticut, coached by Jim Calhoun, won their first National Collegiate Athletic Association (NCAA) men's basketball championship. They defeated Duke, 77–74, in the final game of the NCAA tournament, as UConn's Richard Hamilton scored 27 points. He was named the tourney's most outstanding player.

Purdue won its first women's NCAA title, and Duke was again the victim in the final game of the tournament. Coach Carolyn Peck's Boilermakers topped the Blue Devils by the score of 62–45, as tourney MVP Ukari Figgs led the victors with 18 points.

FOOTBALL

The year 1999 saw the Denver Broncos repeat as National Football League (NFL) champs, winning their second straight Super Bowl. And Denver's great quarterback John Elway, having accomplished nearly all a pro player could aspire to, retired when the season was over. In the Canadian Football League, the Hamilton Tiger-Cats captured the Grey Cup, symbol of the league's championship. Among college teams, the Seminoles of Florida State University were ranked number one at the end of the regular season; and a superb running back from the University of Wisconsin won the race for the Heisman Trophy.

THE NFL PLAYOFFS AND SUPER BOWL XXXIII

Denver entered the playoffs by finishing first in the Western Division of the NFL's American Conference (AFC) in the 1998–99 regular season. The other AFC titlists were the Jacksonville Jaguars and the New York Jets; the New England Patriots, the Miami Dolphins, and the Buffalo Bills claimed wild-card spots.

In the first round of the playoffs, Miami bested Buffalo, 24–17, while Jacksonville knocked off New England, 25–10. In round two, the Jets skinned the Jaguars, 34–24, and the Broncos ousted the Dolphins, 38–3.

In the AFC title game, Denver fell behind New York by 10–0, but then Bronco running back Terrell Davis took over. The NFL's Most Valuable Player during the 1998–99 regular season, Davis rushed for 167 yards and one touchdown as Denver held the Jets scoreless the rest of the way. The final score was 23–10, and the Broncos were headed back to the Super Bowl.

The Atlanta Falcons, the Minnesota Vikings, and the Dallas Cowboys topped their divisions in the National Conference (NFC); wild-card berths went to the San Francisco 49ers, the Green Bay Packers, and the Arizona Cardinals.

In the first round of the playoffs, Arizona eliminated Dallas by a score of 20–7; while San Francisco dropped Green Bay by 30–27. A week later, in the second round, the Vikings routed the Cardinals, 41–21, and the Falcons nipped the 49ers, 20–18.

The NFC title game was supposed to be a "walk in the park" for Minnesota; the team had

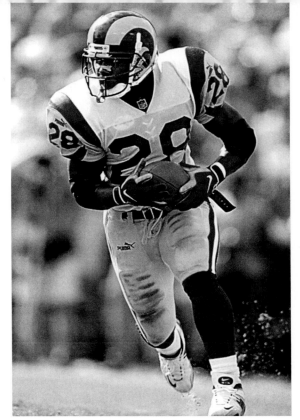

Versatile St. Louis Ram back Marshall Faulk is superb as both a rusher and receiver. He is among the National Conference leaders in both categories.

finished the 1998 regular season with a record of 15–1, and they seemed unbeatable. In fact, the Vikings took a 20–7 lead in the second quarter. But Atlanta rallied, tied the game in regulation time, and stunned Minnesota with a 30–27 overtime victory. Thus coach Mike Shanahan's Broncos would face coach Dan Reeves's Falcons in the Super Bowl.

Super Bowl XXXIII was played in Miami, Florida, on January 31, 1999, before nearly 75,000 people. Denver quarterback John Elway became the first signal-caller ever to start in five Super Bowls, and, at 38, the oldest ever to start in the NFL championship game. It would also be the last game of his distinguished career.

Atlanta took a 3–0 lead five minutes into the game on a 32-yard field goal by Morten Andersen. But Denver scored the next 17 points—on a one-yard touchdown by fullback Howard Griffith, a 26-yard field goal by Jason Elam, and an 80-yard touchdown pass from Elway to Rod Smith. Atlanta's Andersen kicked another three-pointer, and the Broncos held a 17–6 lead at halftime.

The third period was scoreless. But Denver recorded 17 points in the fourth quarter—on a one-yard score by Griffith, a three-yard rushing touchdown by Elway, and two extra points and another field goal by Elam, this one for 37 yards. Atlanta scored two touchdowns, but to no avail. The final score was 34–19.

John Elway was voted the Super Bowl's Most Valuable Player (MVP). In addition to his touchdown pass and run, he completed 18 of 29 passes for 336 yards. Bronco running back Terrell Davis gained 102 yards, receiver Rod Smith collected 152 yards on receptions, and cornerback Darrien Gordon snared two interceptions, returning them for a total of 108 yards.

THE 1999 REGULAR SEASON

Elway retired, and Denver collapsed in the 1999 regular season. The AFC division leaders were the Indianapolis Colts, Jacksonville, and the Seattle Seahawks. Earning wild-card spots were the Tennessee Titans, the Buffalo Bills, and the Miami Dolphins.

In the NFC, the St. Louis Rams, the Washington Redskins, and the Tampa Bay Buccaneers led their divisions, while Minnesota, the Detroit Lions, and Dallas qualified for the playoffs as wild-card teams.

THE CANADIAN FOOTBALL LEAGUE

The Hamilton Tiger-Cats won the championship of the Canadian Football League (CFL), defeating the Calgary Stampeders, 32–21, in the Grey Cup Game, played in Vancouver, British Columbia, on November 28, 1999. The previous year, Calgary had bested Hamilton for the Grey Cup. Tiger-Cat quarterback Danny McManus completed 22 of 34 passes for a total of 347 yards and was named the game's MVP. Six of McManus's strikes went to Darren Flutie (brother of the NFL quarterback Doug Flutie, himself a former CFL star).

Darren Flutie took two of McManus's passes into the end zone, and Tiger-Cat placekicker Paul Osbaldiston contributed 14 points, as Hamilton celebrated its first CFL title since 1986.

COLLEGE FOOTBALL

Florida State was ranked number one in college football at the end of the regular season with an 11–0 record. Rated number two with an identical record was Virginia Tech. The "Seminoles" met the "Hokies" in the Sugar Bowl, and Florida State emerged the victor.

Number-three Nebraska (11–1) toppled Tennessee (9–2) in the Fiesta Bowl; Michigan (9–2) nipped Alabama (10–2) in the Orange Bowl; Arkansas (7–4) trounced Texas (9–4) in the Cotton Bowl; and Wisconsin (9–2) whipped Stanford (8–3) in the Rose Bowl.

Ron Dayne, a senior at Wisconsin, won the Heisman Trophy as the best college player in the nation. The 254-pound (115-kilogram) running back, a bruising rusher, gained 1,834 yards on 303 carries in the 1999 season and set an all-time NCAA Division 1-A career rushing record with 6,397 yards. He thereby broke the career record of 6,279 yards set the previous year by 1998 Heisman winner Ricky Williams.

Second-year quarterback Peyton Manning guided the Indianapolis Colts to the American Conference East Division title in 1999.

University of Wisconsin running back Ron Dayne (shown here with his daughter, Jada) won the 1999 Heisman Trophy as the best college player.

COLLEGE FOOTBALL

Conference	Winner
Atlantic Coast	Florida State
Big Ten	Wisconsin
Big Twelve	Nebraska
Big West	Boise State
Pacific-10	Stanford
Southeastern	Alabama
Western Athletic	Fresno State, Hawaii, Texas Christian University (tied)

Citrus Bowl: Michigan State 37, Florida 34
Cotton Bowl: Arkansas 27, Texas 6
Fiesta Bowl: Nebraska 31, Tennessee 21
Gator Bowl: Miami 28, Georgia Tech 13
Orange Bowl: Michigan 35, Alabama 34
Rose Bowl: Wisconsin 17, Stanford 9
Sugar Bowl: Florida State 46, Virginia Tech 29

Heisman Trophy: Ron Dayne, Wisconsin

1999 NFL FINAL STANDINGS

AMERICAN CONFERENCE

Eastern Division

	W	L	T	Pct.	PF	PA
Indianapolis	13	3	0	.813	423	333
Buffalo	11	5	0	.688	320	229
Miami	9	7	0	.563	326	336
N.Y. Jets	8	8	0	.500	308	309
New England	8	8	0	.500	299	284

Central Division

	W	L	T	Pct.	PF	PA
Jacksonville	14	2	0	.875	396	217
Tennessee	13	3	0	.813	392	324
Baltimore	8	8	0	.500	324	277
Pittsburgh	6	10	0	.375	317	320
Cincinnati	4	12	0	.250	283	460
Cleveland	2	14	0	.125	217	437

Western Division

	W	L	T	Pct.	PF	PA
Seattle	9	7	0	.563	338	298
Kansas City	9	7	0	.563	390	322
San Diego	8	8	0	.500	269	316
Oakland	8	8	0	.500	390	329
Denver	6	10	0	.375	314	318

NATIONAL CONFERENCE

Eastern Division

	W	L	T	Pct.	PF	PA
Washington	10	6	0	.625	443	377
Dallas	8	8	0	.500	352	276
N.Y. Giants	7	9	0	.438	299	358
Arizona	6	10	0	.375	245	382
Philadelphia	5	11	0	.313	272	357

Central Division

	W	L	T	Pct.	PF	PA
Tampa Bay	11	5	0	.688	270	235
Minnesota	10	6	0	.625	399	335
Detroit	8	8	0	.500	322	323
Green Bay	8	8	0	.500	357	341
Chicago	6	10	0	.375	272	341

Western Division

	W	L	T	Pct.	PF	PA
St. Louis	13	3	0	.813	526	242
Carolina	8	8	0	.500	421	381
Atlanta	5	11	0	.313	285	380
San Francisco	4	12	0	.250	295	453
New Orleans	3	13	0	.188	260	434

The U.S. Recaptures the Ryder Cup

The United States and Western Europe are great allies. But not when it comes to the Ryder Cup! In this tournament, played every other year, teams of the best American and European golfers battle to the death— or at least to the 18th hole. The Europeans have won six of the last nine cups. And in 1999, it looked like they would do it again. They were up 6 points to 2 at the end of day one, and 10 points to 6 at the end of day two. But on the final day, the Americans came from behind to win in spectacular fashion. The clincher came at the 17th hole, when Justin Leonard sank an incredible 45-foot putt. The Americans went on to defeat the Europeans 14½ to 13½.

GOLF

PROFESSIONAL		AMATEUR	
	Individual		**Individual**
Masters	José Maria Olazabal	**U.S. Amateur**	David Gossett
U.S. Open	Payne Stewart	**U.S. Women's Amateur**	Dorothy Delasin
Canadian Open	Hal Sutton	**British Amateur**	Graeme Storm
British Open	Paul Lawrie	**British Ladies Amateur**	Marine Monnet
PGA	Tiger Woods	**Canadian Amateur**	Han Lee
World Golf Championships	Tiger Woods	**Canadian Ladies Amateur**	Mary Ann Lepointe
U.S. Women's Open	Juli Inkster		
Ladies PGA	Juli Inkster		**Team**
		Curtis Cup	Britain/Ireland
	Team		
Ryder Cup	United States		

Dallas Stars center Joe Nieuwendyk was named the Most Valuable Player of the NHL playoffs. Nieuwendyk led the Stars to their first Stanley Cup as they defeated the Buffalo Sabres, four games to two.

HOCKEY

In 1999, the Dallas Stars captured the Stanley Cup, symbol of the championship of the National Hockey League (NHL). They outdueled the Buffalo Sabres, four games to two, in the playoff finals. The other big story in hockey in 1999 was the retirement of Wayne Gretzky. At the end of the regular season in April, the "Great One" hung up his skates forever, and two months later he was elected to the Hockey Hall of Fame.

Coach Ken Hitchcock's Stars were the NHL's top defensive team during the 1998–99 regular season, and for the second consecutive year they compiled the league's best record. Finishing first in the Pacific Division, Dallas won 51 games, lost 19, and tied 12, for a total of 114 points.

Buffalo, coached by Lindy Ruff, was fourth in the Northeast Division, with 91 points, behind the Ottawa Senators (103 points), the Toronto Maple Leafs (97 points), and the Boston Bruins (also 91 points, but with two more victories than Buffalo). The Atlantic Division champs were the New Jersey Devils (105 points); leading the Southeast Division were the Carolina Hurricanes (86 points); the defending NHL champion Detroit Red Wings topped the Central Division (93 points); and the Colorado Avalanche (98 points) headed the Northwest Division.

In the first round of the playoffs, the Stars swept the Edmonton Oilers, four games to none. Dallas then ousted the St. Louis Blues in six games in round two. In the Western Conference finals, Dallas was taken to the seven-game limit by Colorado; though down by a game after five contests, the Stars ultimately prevailed, four games to three.

Buffalo advanced through the postseason competition by upsetting Ottawa in a stunning four-game sweep in the first round and beating Boston in six games in round two. In the Eastern Conference finals, the Sabres slashed Toronto, four games to one.

Jaromir Jagr of the Pittsburgh Penguins was the NHL's top scorer and was voted the MVP of the regular season.

The Stanley Cup finals were hard fought—and marred by frequent roughness. Both defenses were stingy, and the teams combined to set a record by allowing the fewest total goals in a six-game final series: only 22. Goaltenders Ed Belfour of the Stars and Dominik Hasek of the Sabres sparkled in the nets.

Games 1 and 2 of the finals took place at Reunion Arena in Dallas. Game 1 went into overtime. After 15:30 of the extra period, Sabre defenseman Jason Woolley smacked a slap shot past Dallas goalie Belfour for the sudden-death victory. Final score: 3–2, and Buffalo led the series, one game to none.

Dallas evened the series in Game 2 with a 4–2 triumph. With the score tied 2–2 and only 2:50 remaining in the third period, the Stars'

hard-shooting right wing, Brett Hull, ripped the puck past Sabre goalie Hasek for the winning tally. Dallas captain Derian Hatcher, a defenseman, added another goal with less than a minute left on the clock.

The series shifted to Buffalo's Marine Midland Arena for the next two contests. Brett Hull sat out Game 3 with an injury, but his Dallas teammates were undeterred. Clamping an airtight defense around Buffalo, the Stars permitted only 12 Sabre shots in the entire game, an all-time record low for the Stanley Cup finals. On the offensive end, Dallas center Joe Nieuwendyk scored twice, and the Stars won, 2–1.

Buffalo turned the tables in Game 4, winning by the same 2–1 tally to tie the series at two victories apiece. Both Sabre goals—by Dixon Ward and Geoff Sanderson—came as a result of turnovers by the Stars. Dallas's Hull was still on the bench nursing his injury.

Back at home for Game 5, the Stars shut out the Sabres, 2–0. Dallas defenseman Darryl Sydor netted the first goal in the second period, and right wing Pat Verbeek put the contest away by scoring late in the third. Center Mike Modano assisted on both goals. Dallas was up, three games to two, and the opponents returned to Buffalo for Game 6.

Beginning on the evening of June 19, and ending in the early morning the next day, it would be the longest final game in a championship series in NHL history—and also one of the most controversial. The score was tied, 1–1, at the end of regulation play, on goals by Dallas's Jere Lehtinen and Buffalo's Stu Barnes. The teams fought on through almost three full overtime periods. After 54:51 of overtime, Dallas's Brett Hull, back in action though still hurting, slapped a rebound past Hasek for the deciding score. But Hull's left skate was in the goalie's crease at the moment he shot—a violation that could have discounted the goal. The Sabres protested heatedly. But they were overruled by NHL officials, who declared that the goal was legal because Hull had had the puck under control before he had encroached upon the crease.

The Stars thus won the first Stanley Cup in the history of their franchise. Dallas center

NHL FINAL STANDINGS

EASTERN CONFERENCE

Atlantic Division

	W	L	T	Pts.
New Jersey	47	24	11	105
Philadelphia	37	26	19	93
Pittsburgh	38	30	14	90
N.Y. Rangers	33	38	11	77
N.Y. Islanders	24	48	10	58

Northeast Division

	W	L	T	Pts.
Ottawa	44	23	15	103
Toronto	45	30	7	97
Boston	39	30	13	91
Buffalo	37	28	17	91
Montreal	32	39	11	75

Southeast Division

	W	L	T	Pts.
Carolina	34	30	18	86
Florida	30	34	18	78
Washington	31	45	6	68
Tampa Bay	19	54	9	47

WESTERN CONFERENCE

Central Division

	W	L	T	Pts.
Detroit	43	32	7	93
St. Louis	37	32	13	87
Chicago	29	41	12	70
Nashville	28	47	7	63

Northwest Division

	W	L	T	Pts.
Colorado	44	28	10	98
Edmonton	33	37	12	78
Calgary	30	40	12	72
Vancouver	23	47	12	58

Pacific Division

	W	L	T	Pts.
Dallas	51	19	12	114
Phoenix	39	31	12	90
Anaheim	35	34	13	83
San Jose	31	33	18	80
Los Angeles	32	45	5	69

Stanley Cup: Dallas Stars

OUTSTANDING PLAYERS

Hart Trophy (most valuable player)	Jaromir Jagr, Pittsburgh
Ross Trophy (scorer)	Jaromir Jagr, Pittsburgh
Vezina Trophy (goalie)	Dominik Hasek, Buffalo
Norris Trophy (defenseman)	Al MacInnis, St. Louis
Selke Trophy (defensive forward)	Jere Lehtinen, Dallas
Calder Trophy (rookie)	Chris Drury, Colorado
Lady Byng Trophy (sportsmanship)	Wayne Gretzky, N.Y. Rangers
Conn Smythe Trophy (Stanley Cup play)	Joe Nieuwendyk, Dallas

For the regular season, Jaromir Jagr of the Pittsburgh Penguins was named MVP; he led the NHL in scoring (127 total points) and assists (83).

Wayne Gretzky's retirement marked the end of an era in the NHL. He played 20 years, set a slew of records, and was generally considered the finest player in the history of the sport. The NHL announced that Gretzky's number, 99, would never be worn by another player. And the Hall of Fame bypassed the normal three-year waiting period to welcome the "Great One" to its ranks; he was elected in June and inducted in November.

Also of note during the 1998–99 season:

The NHL expanded, and increased from four divisions to six.

Toronto played its final game at the fabled Maple Leaf Gardens, the site of much hockey history. Air Canada Centre became the team's new home.

College Play. The University of Maine won the U.S. National Collegiate Athletic Association (NCAA) Division I hockey title, defeating the University of New Hampshire, 3–2, in overtime, in the final game of the NCAA tournament. The Black Bears' goalie, Alfie Michaud, was named MVP of the "Frozen Four" tourney. New Hampshire senior center Jason Krog, who led the nation in scoring, won the Hobey Baker Memorial Award as the U.S.'s top college player.

Nieuwendyk, who had a total of 11 goals in 23 playoff games, won the Conn Smythe Trophy as the most valuable player (MVP) of the playoffs.

A Clean Sweep for the Russians

A figure-skating "first" occurred in March, in Helsinki, Finland. For the first time, competitors from one country—Russia—won all four events at the World Figure Skating Championships.

Maria Butyrskaya (shown at left) won the women's event, beating 1998 world champion Michelle Kwan. Alexei Yagudin won the men's event for the second year in a row. Yelena Berezhnaya and Anton Sikharulidze won the pairs gold medal, also for the second straight year. And in the dance event, Anjelika Krylova and Oleg Ovsyannikov repeated their 1998 victory, too.

Almost 27 years old, Butyrskaya was the oldest woman ever to capture a gold medal in the women's event at the world championships. She easily outpointed 18-year-old Kwan—who entered the competition with a severe cold and fell during the short program. But Kwan did skate away with the silver medal.

ICE SKATING

FIGURE SKATING

World Championships

Men	Alexei Yagudin, Russia
Women	Maria Butyrskaya, Russia
Pairs	Yelena Berezhnaya/Anton Sikharulidze, Russia
Dance	Anjelika Krylova/Oleg Ovsyannikov, Russia

United States Championships

Men	Michael Weiss
Women	Michelle Kwan
Pairs	Danielle Hartsell/Steve Hartsell
Dance	Naomi Lang/Peter Tchernyshev

SPEED SKATING

World Championships

Men	Rintje Ritsma, Netherlands
Women	Gunda Niemann-Stirnemann, Germany

SKIING

WORLD CUP CHAMPIONSHIPS

Men	Lasse Kjus, Norway
Women	Alexandra Meissnitzer, Austria

WORLD ALPINE CHAMPIONSHIPS

Men

Downhill	Hermann Maier, Austria
Slalom	Kalle Palander, Finland
Giant Slalom	Lasse Kjus, Norway
Super Giant Slalom	Lasse Kjus, Norway/Hermann Maier, Austria (tied)
Combined	Kjetil Andre Aamodt, Norway

Women

Downhill	Renate Goetschl, Austria
Slalom	Zali Stegall, Australia
Giant Slalom	Alexandra Meissnitzer, Austria
Super Giant Slalom	Alexandra Meissnitzer, Austria
Combined	Pernilla Wiberg, Sweden

TRACK AND FIELD

World Records Tumble

"Swifter, Higher, Stronger" is the Olympic motto. There were no Olympic games in 1999. But track stars took the "Swifter" part of the motto to heart at other meets during the year and broke four world records.

● In June, 24-year-old **Maurice Greene** of the United States (shown in photo) ran the 100-meter dash in 9.79 seconds. He broke the record of 9.84 seconds set in the 1996 Olympics by Canada's Donovan Bailey.

● In July, 24-year-old **Hicham el-Guerrouj** of Morocco ran the mile in 3 minutes, 43.13 seconds. He bettered the record of 3 minutes, 44.39 seconds set by Noureddine Morceli of Algeria in 1993 by 1.26 seconds.

● In August, at the World Track and Field Championships in Seville, Spain, 31-year-old American speedster **Michael Johnson** shattered the 400-meter record with a time of 43.18 seconds. The previous record, Butch Reynold's 43.39 seconds, had stood since 1988. Johnson also holds the 200-meter record.

● In October, **Khalid Khannouchi,** a 27-year-old Moroccan living in the United States, ran the Chicago marathon in 2 hours, 5 minutes, 42 seconds. He bettered the previous world marathon record, set by Ronaldo da Costa of Brazil in 1988, by 23 seconds.

Andre Agassi, singles champ at the French and U.S. Opens, recaptured the top spot in tennis.

TENNIS

Teenagers and "mature" athletes—those approaching 30—shared the spotlight in tennis in 1999. Eighteen-year-old Martina Hingis held the number-one woman's ranking, although narrowly. Serena Williams, almost 18, won her first Grand Slam singles event, and Steffi Graf, 30, won her last. On the men's side, 29-year-old Andre Agassi regained the top spot after several years in decline, exciting fans with his verve and athleticism.

Hingis, a citizen of Switzerland, was triumphant in the first Grand Slam tournament of the year, the **Australian Open,** played in Melbourne in January. She outmatched her opponent in the finals, the hard-hitting 19-year-old Amelie Mauresmo of France, by scores of 6–2, 6–3. The victory was Hingis's third consecutive Australian crown; and although she would play in two more Grand Slam finals in 1999, she would win neither.

Russia's Yevgeny Kafelnikov, 24, defeated Sweden's Thomas Enqvist, 24, by scores of 4–6, 6–0, 6–3, 7–6 (7–1), in the men's Australian final. Playing a solid, though unspectacular, baseline game, the Russian took advantage of numerous Enqvist errors. Kafelnikov thus won his second Grand Slam title—his first was the 1996 French Open. In accepting the winner's trophy, he modestly suggested that his victory at Melbourne was made possible by the absence of American Pete Sampras—one of the sport's all-time greats—from the competition.

Another all-time great, Graf of Germany, rebounded from a first-set loss to overcome Hingis in the **French Open** final, played in Paris in June, by 4–6, 7–5, 6–2. The victory was Graf's 22nd Grand Slam singles title, and her sixth French Open crown in sixteen tries. Only

TOURNAMENT TENNIS

	Australian Open	French Open	Wimbledon	U.S. Open
Men's Singles	Yevgeny Kafelnikov, Russia	Andre Agassi, U.S.	Pete Sampras, U.S.	Andre Agassi, U.S.
Women's Singles	Martina Hingis, Switzerland	Steffi Graf, Germany	Lindsay Davenport, U.S.	Serena Williams, U.S.
Men's Doubles	Jonas Bjorkman, Sweden/ Patrick Rafter, Australia	Mahesh Bhupathi, India/ Leander Paes, India	Mahesh Bhupathi, India/ Leander Paes, India	Sebastien Lareau, Canada/ Alex O'Brien, U.S.
Women's Doubles	Martina Hingis, Switzerland/ Anna Kournikova, Russia	Venus Williams, U.S./ Serena Williams, U.S.	Lindsay Davenport, U.S./ Corina Morariu, U.S.	Venus Williams, U.S./ Serena Williams, U.S.

Davis Cup Winner: Australia

Tennis Hall-of-Famer Chris Evert, with seven, has won more.

American Andre Agassi came back from a two-set deficit in the finals to capture the men's French championship, outlasting Andrei Medvedev, 24, of Ukraine, 1–6, 2–6, 6–4, 6–3, 6–4. Fans marveled at the resurgence of Agassi, and the revival of his career. His last major title had been the 1995 Australian Open, in the same year that he was last ranked number-one in the world. In the interim, he had dropped as low as number 141, in 1997. Perhaps more important, in winning the French crown, Agassi became only the fifth man in history to win singles titles in all four Grand Slam events—following Hall-of-Famers Don Budge, Roy Emerson, Rod Laver, and Fred Perry.

But a month later, Sampras, 27, upended Agassi in straight sets, 6–3, 6–4, 7–5, in the men's final at the All-England Tennis Championship, held in **Wimbledon.** Sampras collected his 12th Grand Slam singles title, tying him with Emerson for the most in all-time men's competition.

American Lindsay Davenport, 23, won the All-England women's crown, defeating Graf by 6–4, 7–5. After the match, Graf announced her retirement from the sport.

For Davenport, the victory enabled her to temporarily replace Hingis as the number-one-ranked woman player.

Americans also took both singles titles at the **U.S. Open,** held in August and September in New York City. Two weeks before her 18th birthday, Serena Williams downed Hingis in the women's final, 6–3, 7–6 (7–4); it was a match between power and style, and power won. Nevertheless, Hingis retrieved her top overall ranking, supplanting Davenport.

Agassi was the men's U.S. Open champ. Down two sets to one in the finals against fellow American Todd Martin, 29, Agassi recovered to win by 6–4, 6–7 (5–7), 6–7 (2–7), 6–3, 6–2. Sampras and defending U.S. Open champion Patrick Rafter withdrew from the tournament because of injuries. When it was all over, Andre Agassi was once again the number-one-rated men's tennis player.

Venus and Serena Williams teamed up to win the women's doubles title at the U.S. Open. Their dogs Vai and Pete sit in the trophy cup.

Sister Act

Tennis stardom was predicted for them early. And by 1999, the teenaged Williams sisters—Venus, 19, and Serena, 18—had indeed become stars. With their superb conditioning, extraordinary athleticism, and fine court sense, they are also helping to change the women's game from one of style to one of power.

Coached by their father, Richard Williams, Venus and Serena have been playing tennis since they were toddlers. Venus now stands nearly 6 ft., 2 inches tall (188 centimeters), and her scorching serves seem to come from the top of the tennis stadium. Serena, who is shorter and more muscular, has a hard, two-fisted backhand.

Each sister won two Grand Slam mixed-doubles titles in 1998: Venus at the Australian and French Opens, and Serena at Wimbledon and the U.S. Open. And in 1999, they teamed up to win the women's doubles titles at the French and U.S. Opens.

Serena won the first Grand Slam singles crown for either sister when she defeated Martina Hingis at the 1999 U.S. Open. Then, in October 1999, Serena faced her sister at the singles finals of the Grand Slam Cup in Munich, Germany. Serena beat Venus by scores of 6–1, 3–6, 6–3. This was her first victory over her sister in their pro careers.

American Lance Armstrong cycles down the Avenue Champs-Élysées in Paris on his way to winning the Tour de France. Armstrong overcame cancer and beat 180 other cyclists to win this grueling event.

SPORTS BRIEFS

A number of exciting sports stories received special attention during 1999. The U.S. Women's National Soccer Team defeated the Chinese team to win their second Women's World Cup. American cyclist Lance Armstrong overcame cancer and then went on to win the Tour de France, the world's most important bicycle race. And athletes from the United States, Canada, and Cuba dominated the Pan American Games. But sports fans were saddened by the retirement of four of the world's greatest athletes—basketball's Michael Jordan, hockey's Wayne Gretzky, football's John Elway, and tennis's Steffi Graf.

TOUR DE FRANCE

On July 25, 1999, half a million cheering French people lined Paris's beautiful Avenue Champs-Élysées. They were there to watch the finish of the Tour de France, the world's greatest bicycle race.

The winner of that race was 27-year-old Lance Armstrong. He defeated 180 other cyclists to become only the second American to win this race in its 86-year history. But there was something even more amazing about Armstrong: Just three years earlier he had been diagnosed with cancer. And he had been given less than a 50-50 chance of surviving.

After undergoing very difficult treatment, Armstrong was declared cancer-free. But he was so weakened that many people thought he would never bicycle race again. Armstrong thought differently. With great determination he began training, and he was back racing in 1998.

But ordinary races are one thing. The Tour de France is another. This grueling event is

2,287 miles (3,681 kilometers) long. And some of the course runs up and down the steep slopes of the Alps and the Pyrenees Mountains.

Would Armstrong have the strength and stamina to do this? He did! And he not only won, with a time of 91 hours, 32 minutes, 16 seconds, but he beat his nearest competitor by 7 minutes, 37 seconds. In addition, his average speed of 25 miles (40 kilometers) per hour broke the 24.8-miles-per-hour (39.9-kilometers-per-hour) record set in 1998.

THE PAN AMERICAN GAMES

Every four years, athletes from North America, South America, Central America, and the Caribbean compete in the Olympics-style competition called the Pan American Games. In 1999, the Games were held from July 23 to August 8 in Winnipeg, Manitoba, Canada. There, some 5,000 athletes from 42 countries and territories competed in 41 competitions, from archery to wrestling and fencing to volleyball. Following are some of the highlights:

A U.S. Medal Sweep. Athletes from the United States won a total of 296 medals, including 106 gold, 110 silver, and 80 bronze. Among the gold-medal winners were Johnny Gray in

the 800-meter run, Patrick Manson in the pole vault, and Chris Huffins in the decathlon. Once again, U.S. teams failed in their efforts to capture the baseball and basketball golds. But U.S. women's teams emerged victorious in soccer and softball, and the men's team won the water polo championship.

Canadians Swim to the Gold. Canadian athletes came in second in total number of medals won (196), 64 gold, 52 silver, and 80 bronze. They were especially strong in swimming events, with two women—Jessica Deglau and Joanne Malar—swimming away with a total of seven gold medals. Deglau won

Highlights from the 1999 Pan American Games: Canada's Joanne Malar (*above*) swims to a gold medal. Chris Huffins of the United States (*left*) captures a gold in the decathlon.

193

the 200-meter butterfly and freestyle races and was on the winning 400-meter and 800-meter freestyle relay teams. Malar won the 200-meter and 400-meter individual medley races; and she, too, was on the 800-meter freestyle relay team. Out of the water, Yvonne Tousek was outstanding in gymnastics, winning gold medals in the floor competition and the uneven bars, and sharing the gold in the team competition.

Baseball Cuban Style. Cuba was third in the medal standings—69 gold, 40 silver, and 47 bronze, for a total of 156. And for the eighth time in a row, Cubans ran away with the Pan Am baseball title, defeating the U.S. team 5–1. Canada defeated the Mexican team to win the bronze medal. Cuban teams also won the men's volleyball, women's basketball, and men's team handball competitions.

U.S. goalie Briana Scurry blocks a penalty kick during overtime in the final match of the Women's World Cup tournament. The United States defeated China, 5–4.

U.S. Women Win the Soccer World Cup

An international tournament kept America in a sports fever for three weeks during the summer of 1999. The sport wasn't baseball or tennis or any of the other sports Americans usually follow. It was women's soccer, and Americans had good reason to be excited. On July 10, in the tournament's final match, the U.S. team defeated China to capture the Women's World Cup.

Before this, few Americans followed women's soccer—even though the U.S. Women's National Soccer Team was considered the best in the world. (It had won the first World Cup, in 1991, and the gold medal at the 1996 Olympics.) But now enthusiasm spread as the U.S. team advanced through the 1999 tournament, which began June 19.

Sixteen countries played in matches held in seven locations around the United States. By the time the remarkable U.S. women defeated Brazil in the semifinals, they had millions of fans. Everyone knew the U.S. players—especially stars like Mia Hamm, Michelle Akers, Brandi Chastain, Julie Foudy, Kristine Lilly, Carla Overbeck, and goalie Briana Scurry.

More than 90,000 fans, including President Bill Clinton, packed the Rose Bowl in Pasadena, California, for the final game. It was the largest crowd ever for a women's sporting event in the United States. The game also drew the biggest television audience for a women's sporting event.

And the game showed just how closely the United States and China were matched. The two teams played intensely. But neither team could score through 90 minutes of regular play or 30 minutes of overtime. So the game was decided by penalty kicks. The result: An American victory, 5–4, with Chastain scoring the final goal.

In the weeks after the victory, the new world champions toured the country and appeared on television. They were cheered and greeted as heroes wherever they went. They sparked so much excitement that there was talk of starting a professional women's soccer league. But before the U.S. women consider turning pro, they'll tackle their next big challenge: the 2000 Olympics, in Sydney, Australia.

Michael Jordan

John Elway

Wayne Gretzky

FAREWELL TO FOUR GREAT ONES

In 1999, four superstar athletes—basketball's Michael Jordan, hockey's Wayne Gretzky, football's John Elway, and tennis's Steffi Graf—retired from sport. While Wayne Gretzky is the star who is nicknamed "The Great One," there's no doubt that all these outstanding athletes will be remembered as "great ones."

Michael Jordan, 35, announced his retirement on January 13. With an average of 31.5 points per game, Jordan was the top scorer of the National Basketball Association (NBA). Jordan was named Most Valuable Player five times, including in his 13th and final season with the Chicago Bulls. And his last shot in professional basketball clinched the 1998 NBA championship for the Bulls—the sixth NBA championship Jordan helped the team win.

Wayne Gretzky, 38, announced his retirement from hockey on April 16. "The Great One" played twenty seasons in the National Hockey League (NHL), for the Edmonton Oilers, the Los Angeles Kings, the St. Louis Blues, and the New York Rangers. He set 61 records, including most regular-season points (2,857), goals (894), and assists (1,963). During the 1980's, he led the Edmonton Oilers to four Stanley Cup championships.

John Elway, 38, announced his retirement on May 2, after sixteen seasons in pro football. As starting quarterback for the Denver Broncos, Elway had notched a second consecutive Super Bowl win in January 1999. He retired as the leader of the National Football League (NFL) in victories by a quarterback, with a record of 148–82–1. And he ranked second in the NFL for passing yards (51,475), pass completions (4,123), and most 3,000-yard seasons (12).

Steffi Graf

Steffi Graf, 30, retired from tennis on August 3, ending a seventeen-year career that saw her win 107 Women's Tennis Association (WTA) singles titles. These included 22 Grand Slam titles—seven Wimbledon titles, six French Opens, five U.S. Opens, and four Australian Opens. In 1988, she won all four Grand Slams—and also the gold medal at the Olympic Games.

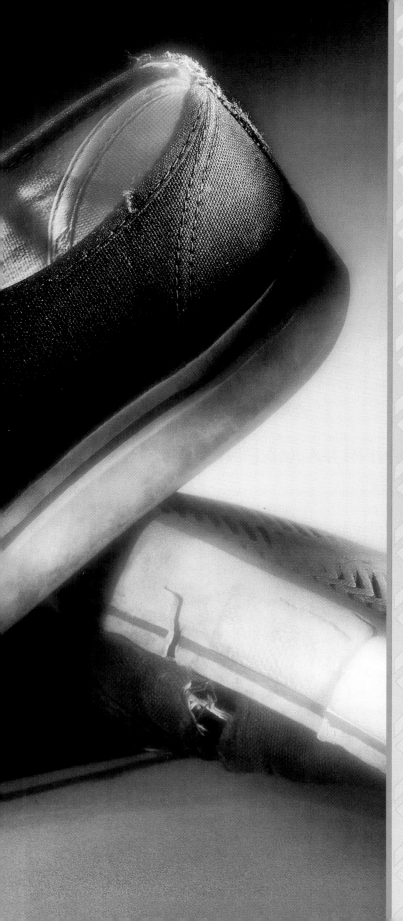

LIVING HISTORY

These ratty old sneakers are history! Sneakers have been around for more than 100 years, but that's a short time when it comes to shoe styles. People have been wearing shoes of one kind or another since ancient times. And what people put on their feet in days gone by tells a lot about how they lived—and their sense of fashion. Today sneakers are the most popular shoes of all, and the reason is comfort. There are sneakers designed for tennis, running, walking, basketball, soccer, and aerobic exercise. But most people use their sneakers for casual wear rather than sports.

MILLENNIUM MADNESS

On New Year's Eve 1999, millennium madness swept the world. Millions of people cheered the arrival of the year 2000. This year marks a milestone in history: the end of one millennium—a thousand-year period—and the start of the next.

It's an exciting, almost magical time. People everywhere are taking the opportunity to look back at the past, celebrate the present, and look ahead to the future.

JUMPING THE GUN?

People who cheered the start of the next millennium at midnight on January 1, 2000, were celebrating early. The new millennium doesn't officially begin until January 1, 2001. That's because the Christian calendar, on which our calendar is based, begins with the year 1.

This system was worked out almost 1,500 years ago by a monk, Denys le Petit, also known as Dionysus Exiguus or Denis the

Small. He started with the calendars used by the ancient Romans, which numbered years from the founding of Rome. Denys figured out that Jesus was born on December 25 in the Roman year 754, so that marked the start of the Christian era.

Denys designated the first year of the Christian Era as Anno Domini (Year of Our Lord) 1—A.D. 1. There was no 0 A.D., so the first millennium ended a thousand years later—at the stroke of midnight on January 1, 1001. And the second millennium will end when the year 2001 arrives.

To most people, though, the year 2000 marks the big change. That big round number seems to signal that a new era has arrived. The new millennium may not really begin until 2001—but the party has already started.

SUPER CELEBRATIONS

Where were you when the year 2000 arrived? One cool place to be was Britain.

expected to visit the Millennium Dome in 2000.

Another great place to welcome the year 2000 was the meridian known as the International Date Line, which runs through the Pacific Ocean. The International Date Line is on the opposite side of the globe from Greenwich, twelve time zones away. Travelers who cross this imaginary line must flip their calendars ahead or back a day, depending on which way they're going. If it's Monday, and you cross the date line from west to east, you go from Monday to Sunday. If you cross from east to west, you go from Monday to Tuesday.

The International Date Line thus was the place where

Greenwich, a borough of London, has historically had a big role in the system that's used worldwide to keep time. The system divides the globe into 24 time zones. The zones run north-south along meridians, imaginary lines drawn from the North Pole to the South Pole. And the first, or prime, meridian runs right through Greenwich. The time kept at the Royal Greenwich Observatory sets the standard for the rest of the world. If you travel east from Greenwich into the next time zone, the time is one hour later in the day. If you travel west, the time is one hour earlier.

Britain takes its timekeeping role seriously, so it planned huge celebrations for the year 2000. The centerpiece of the events was the Millennium Dome, a grand construction that sits astride the prime meridian, on the banks of the Thames River. This is the biggest building of its kind in the world. It's packed with exhibits and attractions, grouped in fourteen theme pavilions. And in an arena that seats 12,000 people, 60 performers put on a glittery show about—what else?—time travel. Some 12 million people are

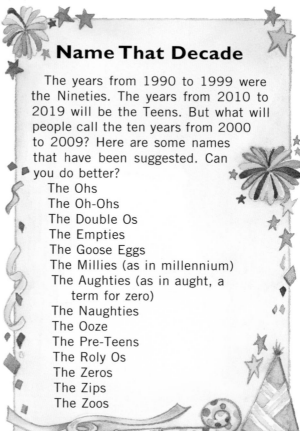

Name That Decade

The years from 1990 to 1999 were the Nineties. The years from 2010 to 2019 will be the Teens. But what will people call the ten years from 2000 to 2009? Here are some names that have been suggested. Can you do better?

The Ohs
The Oh-Ohs
The Double Os
The Empties
The Goose Eggs
The Millies (as in millennium)
The Aughties (as in aught, a
    term for zero)
The Naughties
The Ooze
The Pre-Teens
The Roly Os
The Zeros
The Zips
The Zoos

the year 2000 arrived first. Since the line passes through nothing but water for most of its length, people who wanted to be the first to greet the year didn't have many places to go. One spot was the island of Taveuni, in Fiji, which sits astride the International Date Line. Cruise ships planned special millennium cruises, bringing passengers to the date line just in time to ring in the new year.

Some people didn't celebrate the arrival of 2000, though. They were too worried about the future.

GLOOM AND DOOM

Will the world end in the year 2000? It's pretty safe to say no. But that hasn't stopped some people from worrying. As the year 2000 approached, a flurry of books and articles announced that the end of the world was near. Such doomsday predictions aren't new. Many are rooted in the Christian religion, which holds that the world as we know it will end with a huge battle between good and evil and the return of Christ. But even Christian scholars don't agree about when this is supposed to happen.

Doomsday predictions were thick at the end of the first millennium, too—around the year 1000. There were no widespread celebrations then. Lots of people couldn't read or write and probably weren't even aware of the date. But many educated people, and especially people in the Church, thought the world was certain to end.

Strange events seemed to confirm their fears. A solar eclipse, the appearance of Halley's Comet in 989, a new star (actually a supernova, or exploding star) sighted in 1006, earthquakes, and famines were all taken as signs that the end was nigh. The end never came. But worry over the doomsday predictions prompted a wave of religious pilgrimages, peace councils, and reforms.

Doomsday predictions took a new twist this time around. Some people worried about the end of the world. Many more people worried about something called the Y2K bug—a glitch that would cause computers to crash when their internal clocks rolled over to 1/1/00. Businesses and governments rushed to reprogram their computers and get rid of the bug.

Thanks to these efforts, many people hoped there would be little trouble when 2000 arrived. Others predicted disaster, with power failures, airplane crashes, food shortages, even street violence. Who was right? By the time you read this book, you'll know the answer.

PAST AND FUTURE

If you had lived around the year 1000, your life would have been very different from what it is today. Most children didn't go to school. Unless they were born into a noble family, boys could expect to be farmers or, perhaps, craftsmen such as weavers or blacksmiths. Girls could expect to marry a husband chosen by their parents.

People back then had no electricity or indoor plumbing. They traveled by foot or horseback. Medical care consisted of herbs, charms, and prayers. Books were written out by hand and treasured by the few people who could read. Most people were born, grew up, and died in the same little village. They had few if any of the rights Americans take for granted today, such as freedom of speech and the right to vote.

How will life be different in the next millennium? Futurists, who are experts at spotting trends, say that most people will probably live in cities. By 2025, there are expected to be 650 cities with populations of more than 1 million. It's safe to say that computers and other technology will continue to change the way people live. Other predictions are anyone's guess. Will people set up colonies on Mars? Make contact with space aliens?

Whatever happens, young people will have a lot to say about it. There are about a billion teenagers worldwide. They and their younger brothers and sisters will help shape the world of the third millennium.

Time in a Bottle

Would you like to send a message to the future? A time capsule is one way to do that. And the new millennium has created a boom in time capsules. Everywhere, individuals and groups are stuffing containers with items they think are important, and storing the containers for future generations to find.

Most of these time capsules are meant to be sealed for hundreds or thousands of years. But a time capsule doesn't have to be sealed for that long. You can make a personal time capsule that you can open in five years, ten years, or whatever amount of time you choose. Here's how:

● Decide where you'll hide the time capsule. It should be stored in a place where it won't be disturbed. Many capsules are buried, but that's not always a good idea. The International Time Capsule Society, which registers time capsules, says that most buried capsules are lost!

● Pick a container that will keep the contents cool, dry, and dark. If you bury your capsule, you'll need a waterproof container. If you store it indoors, a simple cardboard box will do.

● Decide what to put in. Here are some ideas: Pictures of you and your family and friends, a handwritten note telling about yourself, a tracing of your hand, a lock of your hair, a copy of a newspaper from the day you seal the capsule, a list of your favorite songs, TV shows, and books.

● Mark the spot where you hide the time capsule. Make a note to remind yourself what you put in it, where you put it, and what day you plan to open it. When that day comes, you'll have a message from your own past.

Y6B: THE YEAR OF 6 BILLION

You've probably heard people talking about Y2K, short for "Year 2000." Did you know that 1999 had a nickname, too? It was Y6B—"the Year of 6 Billion." On October 12, 1999, the world's population officially reached 6 billion, according to United Nations estimates. That's a lot of people!

What makes the 6 billion milestone even more amazing is how quickly it arrived. It took all of human history for the world population to reach the 1 billion mark around 1800. Population grew to 2 billion just 130 years later. Then population began to increase with incredible speed—to 3 billion in 30 years, 4 billion in 14 years, 5 billion in 13 years, and 6 billion in a mere 12 years.

THE POPULATION PROBLEM

What's behind this population explosion? Several factors are at work. Thanks to better health care and nutrition, for example, people worldwide are living longer—on average, 20 years longer than they did in 1950. At the same time, people in many parts of the world continue to raise big families. The United Nations expects that world population will reach 7 billion in 2013. And sometime around the year 2200, it's believed, there will be just under 10 billion people in the world.

However, some population experts doubt that there will ever be 10 billion people. They believe that one of two things will happen first. Family planning efforts may succeed in slowing birth rates to "replacement level" (about two children per couple) worldwide. Or overcrowding will bring on water shortages, famine, and disease—causing death rates to soar.

These population experts point to parts of Africa, where a severe epidemic of AIDS has cut life expectancy dramatically. And in India, where the population is growing by 18 million people a year, water is a problem. The level of underground water that's tapped by wells is dropping more than 3 feet (1 meter) every year. That could mean less water for irrigating crops—and smaller grain harvests.

The population explosion is behind environmental problems, too. As cities and suburbs grow, plants and animals are being pushed out. Pollution and other environmental problems also increase as the number of people grows.

SLOWING THE GROWTH

Family planning has helped reduce birth rates. In the 1950's, women had an average of six children each. That average has been cut in half worldwide, but the figures vary from one part of the world to another. African women, for example, have an average of five children each. In the United States the average is about two. In Europe and Japan, it's 1.4.

And as birth rates have dropped, the rate of population growth has slowed—but growth hasn't stopped. Most of the population growth in years to come will be in the less developed countries of Africa, Asia, and Latin America. Africa, which has 13 percent of the world's people today, is expected to account for about 35 percent of the worldwide population increase in the next 50 years. China and India, the world's two most populous countries, will see about 25 percent of the increase.

In these areas more than a third of the population is under age 15. If young people there grow up to have big families as their parents did, world population will continue to grow.

Six Billion and Counting

● How many is 6 billion? Suppose you covered this page with dots. You might fit 5,000 dots on this page. You'd need to cover 1.2 million pages with dots to represent all the 6 billion people in the world. Those pages would fill about 3,000 books like this one. The books would make a stack almost 250 feet (76 meters) tall.

● The world population is growing by 78 million people a year. That's like adding a city the size of San Francisco, California, every three days.

● There are more than 1 billion people ages 15 to 24 in the world, and nearly 2 billion under age 15.

● The population of India reached 1 billion in August 1999. That made it the second most populous country—behind China, with a population of 1.25 billion. But India's birthrate is almost double China's, and its population is expected to soar past China's by the year 2040.

● With 272 million people, the United States is the world's third most populous country. The U.S. population is expected to reach 335 million by 2025. Most of the growth will come from immigration and longer life spans.

The *Breitling Orbiter 3* soars over the Swiss Alps as it begins its round-the-world journey. Right: Record-setting balloonists Bertrand Piccard and Brian Jones (inside cabin).

UP, UP, AND AWAY!

In 1873, the French author Jules Verne wrote an adventure novel called *Around the World in Eighty Days.* The book's daring hero, Phileas Fogg, bets that he can circle the globe in eighty days, an amazing feat back in the 1800's. He makes part of the trip in a hot-air balloon—and wins the bet.

In 1999, two daring men put Phileas Fogg to shame. They circled the globe in just twenty days, making the *entire* trip by balloon. But what made their trip amazing was the fact that they did it without ever landing. Brian Jones and Bertrand Piccard soared into the record books on March 21, when their *Breitling Orbiter 3* completed the first nonstop balloon flight around the world. The difficult, dangerous flight was one of the great landmarks of aviation history, and it was one that had taken more than 200 years to reach.

FIRST FLIGHT

Long before the start of written history, people probably watched birds fly and wished they could follow. But their wishes remained wishes until 1783. In that year Jacques Étienne and Joseph Michel Montgolfier, two French brothers, developed the first successful flying machine—a hot-air balloon.

Joseph was an amateur scientist and a bit of a dreamer. One day he noticed hot smoke rising from a chimney, and he had a flash of insight. He recognized that hot air rises because it's lighter than the surrounding cold air. If hot air could be captured in a balloon, he realized, it might carry people along for the ride.

Joseph took the idea to his brother, Jacques Étienne, a paper manufacturer. Together, they made a big paper-and-cloth balloon. On June 4, 1783, they filled it with hot smoke from a fire and watched it rise in the sky over Annonay, France.

A few weeks later, the Montgolfiers sent the first balloon passengers into the air—a rooster, a duck, and a lamb. The success of that flight encouraged two men to give flying a try. Jean François Pilâtre de Rozier, a scientist, and François Laurent, a French army officer, soared over Paris in a Montgolfier balloon on November 21. They were the first humans to fly.

The Montgolfiers' success started a ballooning craze. Others improved on their design and built balloons that were filled with hydrogen, a gas that's lighter than air. These balloons could stay aloft longer, and since hydrogen didn't have to be heated they were less likely to catch on fire.

HIGHER AND FARTHER

People continued to experiment with other types of flying machines, such as gliders. But for the next 120 years—until the Wright brothers flew their plane at Kitty Hawk, North Carolina, in 1903—balloons were the only real form of air travel. Just two years after the first flight, two balloonists—Jean Pierre Blanchard of France and John Jeffries of the United States—crossed the English Channel in a gas balloon. In 1859, John Wise, an American balloonist, set a world distance record of

1,150 miles (1,850 kilometers) by flying from St. Louis, Missouri, to Henderson, New York.

The military was quick to find uses for this new invention. The French army used captive, or tethered, balloons as early as 1794. Scouts stationed in the captive balloons could report enemy troop movements. Balloons were used in the same way during the U.S. Civil War and in later wars. And balloons delivered the first aerial bombardment in history. In 1849, Austria used unmanned balloons to bomb the city of Venice.

But as bombers and even as peaceful passenger craft, balloons have a serious drawback: They can't be steered. A hot-air or gas balloon has no power of its own, so it must go where the wind takes it. The most a balloon pilot can do is take the balloon higher or lower in the air, in the hope of finding a breeze headed in the right direction. It isn't surprising that as soon as powered aircraft came on the scene, they replaced balloons for most uses.

Balloons, however, have continued to play an important role in scientific research. Balloons can rise high and stay aloft for a long time, so from the beginning they were used to investigate the upper levels of the atmosphere. This was quite dangerous at first. Several balloonists died because they reached altitudes where the air was too thin to breathe. Auguste

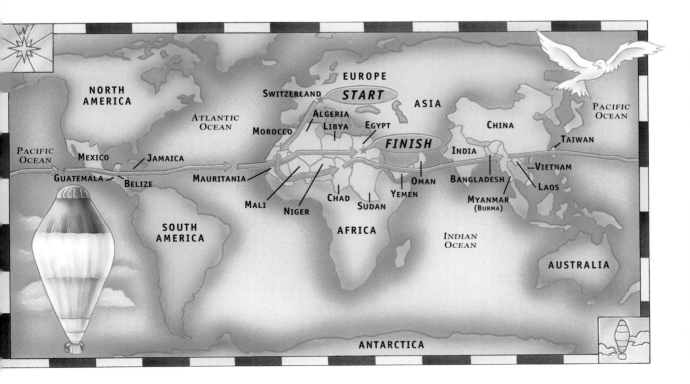

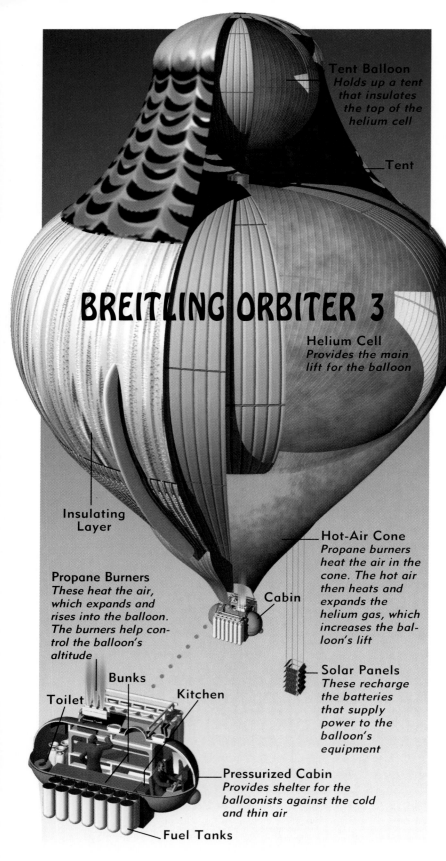

BREITLING ORBITER 3

Tent Balloon
Holds up a tent that insulates the top of the helium cell

Tent

Helium Cell
Provides the main lift for the balloon

Insulating Layer

Propane Burners
These heat the air, which expands and rises into the balloon. The burners help control the balloon's altitude

Cabin

Hot-Air Cone
Propane burners heat the air in the cone. The hot air then heats and expands the helium gas, which increases the balloon's lift

Solar Panels
These recharge the batteries that supply power to the balloon's equipment

Bunks

Kitchen

Toilet

Pressurized Cabin
Provides shelter for the balloonists against the cold and thin air

Fuel Tanks

Piccard, a Swiss scientist, solved the problem. He invented a pressurized balloon cabin, or gondola. In 1931, he used it to make the first flight into the part of the upper atmosphere called the stratosphere.

Ballooning also continued to be popular as a sport. And daring balloon pilots continued to compete for new records. The first balloon crossing of the Atlantic Ocean was made in 1978 by U.S. balloonists Maxie Anderson, Larry Newman, and Ben Abruzzo. Fred Gorell and John Shucraft made the first nonstop balloon flight across the continental United States in 1981. That same year, Abruzzo, Larry Newman, Ron Clark, and Rocky Aoki crossed the Pacific by balloon, traveling about 6,000 miles (9,650 kilometers) from Japan to California.

But a nonstop round-the-world flight remained an elusive goal. Many balloon teams tried, in balloons that were ever more complex and expensive. Something always went wrong.

AROUND THE WORLD
Brian Jones and Bertrand Piccard were well qualified to take up the challenge. Jones was an experienced balloon pilot from Britain. Piccard, a Swiss doctor, was also an experienced balloonist—and he was the grandson of Auguste Piccard, who invented the pressurized gondola for high-altitude flights! The flight was Piccard's third attempt to circle the globe. Breitling, a Swiss manufacturer of watches, backed the efforts.

The *Breitling Orbiter 3*

Piccard and Jones made their record-setting round-the-world flight in a sophisticated craft that cost about $2 million to build. The *Breitling Orbiter 3* used both hot air and helium gas (which is less explosive than hydrogen). An inner cell of helium made up most of the balloon and provided most of the lift. Below it was a cone of hot air, which warmed the helium and increased the lift. The entire balloon was wrapped in a silvery insulating layer. It was 180 feet (55 meters) high—as high as the famous Leaning Tower of Pisa.

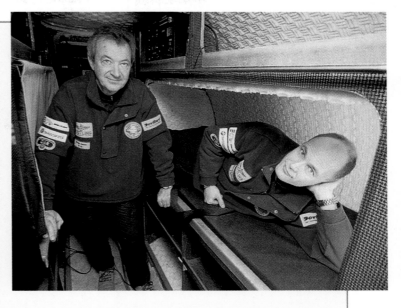

The balloonists operated propane burners to control the balloon's altitude—the hotter the air, the higher they went. Their tiny cabin (*above*) was equipped with bunk beds, freeze-dried food, oxygen, high-tech navigation equipment—and parachutes and inflatable dinghies, in case of a mishap.

After being exhibited in Switzerland and Britain, the cabin and most of the balloon were presented to the Smithsonian Institution. The *Breitling Orbiter 3* will be displayed at the Smithsonian's Air and Space Museum in Washington, D.C., alongside other record-setting craft.

Piccard and Jones took off in their huge, silvery balloon on March 1. They started in the Swiss Alps and flew to North Africa, to catch a strong eastbound jet stream—a high-altitude air current. Jet streams flow at speeds up to 200 miles (320 kilometers) an hour, mostly west to east around the globe. Piccard and Jones planned to ride these "rivers of air" on a course that would take them over Africa, Asia, the Pacific Ocean, Central America, and the Atlantic Ocean.

But jet streams can change direction with little warning, taking a balloon off course. The balloonists also had to find their way around storms, mountains, and hostile countries. There was help, however. A thirteen-member ground crew used computerized weather forecasting methods to help the *Breitling Orbiter 3* catch the most favorable winds. Global positioning satellites helped pinpoint the balloon's exact location at all times.

The balloon traveled high in the atmosphere—more than 30,000 feet—for much of the trip. The balloonists rode in an enclosed, pressurized cabin just 10 feet by 16½ feet (3 meters by 5 meters). It was so cold in the cabin that all their water froze at night.

Finally, after traveling more than 26,000 miles around the Earth, their goal was in sight. Just before 5 A.M. on March 20, the balloon swept across the invisible finish line over Mauritania, in Africa.

The craft continued on to Egypt, where it landed in the desert the next day. In all, the flight covered 29,055 miles in 19 days, 21 hours, and 55 minutes. Piccard and Jones were exhausted but elated. "I am with the angels and just completely happy!" said Piccard.

The success of the *Breitling Orbiter 3* brought the balloonists a $1 million check and a trophy, offered by the Anheuser-Busch brewing company. Most important, they earned a place in history. They had won the race to make the first nonstop balloon flight around the world!

Washington, D.C., for many years. Now a three-year, $18-million project is under way to preserve the flag for future generations.

BY THE DAWN'S EARLY LIGHT. . .

The original "star-spangled banner" flew over Fort McHenry, in Baltimore Harbor, during the War of 1812. British warships attacked the fort on September 13, 1814. From a ship near the harbor, an American lawyer named Francis Scott Key watched the assault. Key had been negotiating with the British for the release of an American prisoner, and he was held on board a British ship when the attack began.

British cannons bombarded the fort all night. But in the morning, "by the dawn's early light," Key saw the Stars and Stripes flying over the fort. The British attack had failed! Key was so inspired that he quickly wrote a poem. Later, his words were set to music. And that song, "The Star-Spangled Banner," became the national anthem.

The tattered flag that survived that night became more tattered over the years that followed. Bits of it were given away as souvenirs. A big piece was used as a burial robe for an American soldier. One of the flag's stars disappeared, perhaps given as a special gift to a notable person. Someone sewed an upside down red "V" onto the flag. (This may have been the start of the letter "A," for Armistead, the last name of Fort McHenry's commander and of the family that owned the flag for many years.) And over the years dirt, dampness, light, and insects damaged the fibers.

Since 1907, the flag has been displayed at the Smithsonian Institution. In 1964 it was placed in Flag Hall, in the Smithsonian's National Museum of American History. There, it was draped over a custom-made replica that filled in 8 feet (2.4 meters) of material missing from the bottom of the original (see photo above). But despite the care taken by the museum, the flag continued to deteriorate.

NEW LIFE FOR THE STAR-SPANGLED BANNER

"The Star-Spangled Banner"—the national anthem of the United States—has inspired generations of Americans. And now the actual flag that inspired the song is being restored to its full glory. This famous flag was made and flown during the War of 1812. It has been a top attraction at the Smithsonian Institution in

Star-Spangled Facts

★ The flag that inspired "The Star-Spangled Banner" was made in 1813 by Mary Pickersgill of Philadelphia and her 13-year-old daughter, Caroline. It cost $405.90.

★ Lieutenant Colonel George Armistead commissioned the flag to fly over Fort McHenry. The Armistead family owned the flag for nearly 100 years. They lent it to the Smithsonian Institution in 1907 and donated it to the museum's collection in 1914.

★ The flag measured 30 by 42 feet (9 by 12.8 meters) when it was new. In those days, that huge size was standard for military forts, where flags flew from 90-foot (27-meter) flagpoles. Today the U.S. flag measures 30 by 34 feet (9 by 10.4 meters).

★ The "star-spangled banner" has 15 stripes and 15 stars—one stripe and one star for each state, as ordered by Congress in 1794. (Later, Congress set the number of stripes on the national flag at 13, for the original 13 states, and added new stars for each state that joined the Union.)

THE FLAG GETS A FACE-LIFT

In 1999, visitors to the Smithsonian Institution couldn't see the "star-spangled banner" in Flag Hall. The flag had been taken down for a full-scale conservation project. Work started in late 1998 with a thorough examination of the damage. Museum experts then covered the fragile, faded flag in a protective wrapping and gently removed it from the wall.

Next, the flag was carefully rolled onto a huge cardboard tube and moved into a pressurized, climate-controlled laboratory. Then the flag was unrolled carefully, a few feet at a time, as experts examined it (see photo below).

From a special observation room, visitors can watch as the flag is cleaned and treated. The flag is stretched out on a huge table. Workers reach it by sitting or lying on a movable platform that's suspended above it. When the historic flag goes back on view, it will be enclosed in a special climate-controlled case. And it will be ready to inspire Americans for generations to come.

SHOES THROUGH THE CENTURIES

What kind of shoes are you wearing? Your oldest, rattiest sneakers? The latest thing in running shoes? No matter what style of shoes you have on, you're walking around on a bit of history. People have been wearing shoes for thousands of years. And over the years, they've put some pretty amazing things on their feet.

Shoes have a very practical purpose. Most animals have fur, thick pads, hooves, or some other form of protection on their feet. You don't. Instead, your shoes protect your feet from rough ground, hot pavement, rain, and cold temperatures.

This prehistoric sandal, discovered in a cave near the Missouri River, is more than 8,000 years old. It was made from a plant called rattlesnake master.

Shoes are much more than protection, though. Consider this: Americans buy more than 850 million pairs of shoes a year. And manufacturers introduce about 100,000 new shoe styles each year. Why? To keep up with the latest fashion trends. There's nothing new about that, either. Right from the start, shoes have been fashion items.

ANCIENT SHOES

It's obviously more comfortable to walk on soft grass or leaves than on sharp rocks. Long ago— no one knows exactly where or when—someone had a brilliant idea: By strapping dried leaves or something else soft to their feet, people could be more comfortable wherever they had to walk. With that idea, shoes were born.

The rulers of ancient Egypt wore richly decorated sandals made from both leather and papyrus.

Some of the earliest shoes known are sandals and simple moccasins. Archeologists recently uncovered an incredible collection of prehistoric shoes from a cave near the Missouri River. For thousands of years, people who lived there made shoes, wore them, and discarded them. Some of the ancient sandals are more than 8,000 years old!

Many of the shoes were woven from the leaves of a yuccalike plant called rattlesnake master, which still grows in parts of the United States. A few were made from leather. Some had double-thick soles or grass linings, for comfort. And the shoes show that fashions changed over the centuries. Sandals from various times had different weaving styles, strap styles, toe styles, and heel styles. Early sandals found in other North American sites even have treaded soles, woven to provide grip like the soles of today's hiking boots.

Sandals were a fashion item in ancient Egypt, too. The Egyptians wove sandals from papyrus, a reed that grows in the Nile River. Sandals made of fine leather have been found in the tombs of Egyptian rulers. Sandal-making was a profession in Egypt, and both leather and papyrus sandals were often richly decorated.

The ancient Romans were very particular about who could wear what on their feet. The emperor—and only the emperor—wore purple sandals and fur trimmed, open-toed boots that glittered with pearls, gold, and jewels. Members of the aristocracy favored red sandals until Emperor Aurelian (A.D. 212–275) claimed that color for himself and his family. Senators wore black sandals. And soldiers had thick-soled sandals that were practical for marching.

In the centuries that followed, shoes continued to be an emblem of status. Common people, meanwhile, were happy to have *anything* to put on their feet. That didn't change for hundreds of years. Even simple shoes were expensive because they had to be made by hand. So poor people went barefoot or strapped on cloth, leather, bark, or leaves. In parts of Europe, peasants wore clogs, shoes carved from wood.

In later centuries, European peasants wore clogs—shoes carved from wood.

Shoes have long been worn to make a fashion statement rather than for comfort. In the 1300's, for example, men wore crackows—shoes with long, pointed toes (*right*). By the 1600's, gentlemen swaggered about in boots with wide, flared tops (*below*).

FASHION FIRST

Fashionable shoes have rarely been practical. In Europe during the 1300's, for example, men took to wearing cloth or leather shoes with long, pointed toes. The style originated in Kracow, Poland, so the shoes were called crackows. As the fad spread, the toes became longer and longer and longer. Men added bells to the toes and stuffed them with packing to keep them stiff. To keep from tripping, they fastened the toes to their knees with gold chains. In England, King Edward III set rules limiting toe length—24 inches (60 centimeters) for nobles, 12 inches (30 centimeters) for gentlemen, 6 inches (15 centimeters) for everyone else.

Pointed toes didn't suit the English King Henry VIII, who ruled in the 1500's. He suffered from gout, a condition that made his toes swell painfully. Henry favored wide, floppy-toed shoes—and since he was the king, everyone copied his style. Wide toes soon became as extreme as pointy toes had been. Some shoes spread as wide as 10 inches (25 centimeters) at the toe. Finally a royal decree limited the width to 6 inches (15 centimeters).

Tall boots started out as practical footwear. Men wore them for horseback riding because they protected the legs. But in the 1600's, fashion overruled practicality once again. Courtiers and other fashion followers swaggered around in boots with wide, flared tops. The flared tops were decorated with lace and other trimmings. They weren't much use for riding, but they made a good place to carry a pistol or a love note.

That style was followed by another impractical fad. Well-dressed men took to wearing tall boots that were so tight they needed the help of servants to get them on and off.

This red velvet chopine (platform sandal) was worn by a wealthy Italian woman in the 1580's.

King Louis XIV of France, who ruled in the 1600's, favored high-heeled shoes because they made him look taller. His courtiers then adopted high heels, too.

GOING UP

Women's platform shoes are "in" today, but they're not a new style. More than 500 years ago, Turkish women were wearing platform sandals called chopines that raised them as much as 8 inches (20 centimeters) above the ground. Originally, the shoes may

Embroidered flowers decorate this stylish pair of women's shoes from the 1880's.

have been designed to keep their long skirts out of the mud. Similar stiltlike sandals have been worn in Japan and other Asian countries for that purpose. But like many other shoe styles, chopines soon became

Buckles, Buttons, and Laces

Shoes aren't much good if they won't stay on your feet. And over the years, people have thought up lots of different ways to keep their shoes on.

Straps were the first method. Early sandals were tied on with straps that circled the feet and sometimes the lower leg. As shoes grew to cover more of the foot, straps shrank into laces.

Buckles were fashionable in the 1700's. In England and America, silver buckles were everywhere. In France, members of the aristocracy wore diamond-studded buckles on their high-heeled shoes. Buckles went out with a bang in the late 1780's, though. During the French Revolution, aristocrats were hauled off to the guillotine and beheaded. Smart people switched from aristocratic buckles to the shoelaces favored by common folk.

Thomas Jefferson introduced the shoelace fashion to America. Jefferson was America's ambassador to France in the late 1780's. He probably liked shoelaces for their "democratic" association. But when he wore laced shoes back in the United States, he was criticized for following a French fashion fad.

During the 1800's, high-button shoes were the height of fashion for women. These shoes had as many as 20 tiny buttons each. Even using a special little tool called a buttonhook, fastening them all took forever. Today's shoes are much easier to put on. Besides laces, shoes and boots have such modern inventions as zippers and hook-and-loop fasteners (Velcro).

Sneaking Around

In the thousands of years that people have been wearing shoes, feet have never had it so good as they do today. That's because today's most popular shoes are sneakers—and sneakers are designed for pure comfort.

The ancestors of today's sneakers were "croquet sandals" introduced in 1868.

These shoes had rubber soles, canvas tops, and laces. They were intended for playing the game of croquet, but before long they had been renamed "sneakers" and were being worn for tennis and other sports.

The sneakers of the 1890's cost less than a dollar, and they were basic by today's standards. White canvas was the only choice in color and materials. Right and left shoes were identical—people wore them until they molded to their feet. New colors (and right and left shoes) came later, but sneakers didn't change much until the 1970's. That's when nylon uppers and molded polyurethane soles appeared. Molded soles were supposedly invented by a University of Oregon track coach, who wanted to develop athletic shoes with good traction. He poured urethane into a waffle iron and came up with a grippy, lightweight sole. It was the basis for the first running shoes.

Today sneakers come in a huge range of styles and types. There are models specifically designed for tennis, running, walking, basketball, soccer, and aerobic exercise. But nine out of every ten pairs of sneakers sold are used for casual wear, not for sports.

fashion items. Many were decorated with silver and mother of pearl.

The style traveled to Europe, where it became really extreme. During the 1500's, wealthy women in Venice and other places tottered around on chopines that were 18 inches (46 centimeters) tall. It was impossible to walk in these shoes. The women had to lean on their servants' shoulders for support. An Italian shoemaker came to their rescue by inventing the high heel. Four-inch (10-centimeter) heels of cork or wood gave women a lift but still allowed them to walk—with difficulty.

High heels spread from Italy to France in the mid-1500's, and they were worn by men as well as women. The French King Louis XIV, who ruled in the 1600's, was especially fond of high heels. At 5 feet, 3 inches (160 centimeters), Louis wasn't especially tall for a monarch of his magnificence. The cork heels on his shoes added an additional 5 inches (13 centimeters) to his height. The king's shoes were trimmed with lace, bows, and jewels. The heels were usually covered with leather in red, a color that symbolized nobility. For special occasions, Louis had the heels of his shoes decorated with scenes of famous French battles. Naturally, when the king adopted high heels, all his courtiers followed suit.

PETITE FEET

Even when women's shoes lacked platforms and high heels, they were seldom designed for serious walking. In fact, fashionable shoes were often meant to be impractical. They showed that the wearer was so wealthy that she didn't have to walk, work, or do much of anything except ring for her

For hundreds of years, lily-foot slippers were worn by upper-class women in China who, as children, had had their feet bound to make them tiny and delicate.

servants. For hundreds of years, wealthy women's shoes were made of delicate fabrics, covered with embroidery, and trimmed with ribbons and lace. Often, they were painfully tight—to show that the wearer had tiny, delicate feet.

In China, the idea that small feet were beautiful caused generations of women to suffer crippling pain. The feet of upper-class girls were bound tightly in cloth bandages, beginning when they were about 5 years old. The

Many of today's shoes are plainer—but much more comfortable—than those of the past. Even today, however, comfort hasn't ended shoe fashion. Men and women, it seems, will always wear shoes that keep pace with the latest fashion trends.

tight bandages caused the bones in the feet to stop growing. As adults, these women had disfigured, child-size feet, and they were barely able to walk. They covered their feet with soft embroidered cloth shoes, called lotus or lily-foot slippers. Foot binding may have begun in China as early as A.D. 1100. It continued until the early 1900's, when the Chinese government outlawed the practice.

SHOES FOR ALL

The 1800's and 1900's brought lots of changes to footwear. One of the most important was the arrival of factory-made shoes, made possible by the invention of the sewing machine in the mid-1800's. Factory-made shoes weren't as elegant as those painstakingly crafted by hand, but many more people could afford them. Decent, stylish shoes were no longer only for the wealthy.

Shoes also became plainer and more practical. In part, this was a sort of fashion backlash against the ridiculously fancy shoes of earlier times. But practical shoes also suited modern life. Men and women alike wanted to walk, ride bicycles and horses, drive carriages or, later, cars, and play sports. And they wanted to do all those things in comfortable shoes. The desire for comfort brought a revolutionary idea to shoe design: right and left. Until this time, both shoes in a pair were identical; people could wear either shoe on either foot!

Practicality and comfort didn't end shoe fashion, of course. Dozens of styles have come in and gone out in modern times—and some have been in and out a few times. Toes have been round, square, or pointed. Women's shoes have had block heels, spike heels, flat heels, and everything in between. Platform soles reappeared in the 1930's, 1970's, and 1990's. What will be next? Whatever styles catch on, new shoes will help you put your best foot forward.

HISTORICAL HOAXES

Have you heard that you can get free computer software, free clothes, thousands of dollars, or maybe a trip to Disneyland—just by forwarding an electronic-mail message to everyone you know? Were you notified about Internet "cleanup day," when all Web servers are shut down for cleaning? How about the death-ray virus, which can cause your home computer to explode? And did you hear that the U.S. Postal Service wants to charge a five-cent fee for every e-mail message sent over the Internet?

Many people who use computers and the Internet have heard at least one of those tales. And many have believed the stories. But you won't pay postage or get free goodies for sending e-mail, and there's no Internet "clean-up day" or death-ray virus. These are just some of the many hoaxes that have popped up and spread like wildfire over the Internet. Some of the hoaxes have even been picked up and reported in the news media.

Internet hoaxes are the latest installment in a long tradition of such foolery. It seems there have always been people who have cooked up unbelievable tales—and other people willing to believe them. Here are some famous hoaxes of the past.

TURNING MANHATTAN AROUND

In New York City in the early 1800's, the lower end of Manhattan Island was a bustling business center. New buildings were going up everywhere. In 1824, a man named Lozier caught everyone's attention with an alarming announcement: The weight of all the new buildings was causing the lower end of the island to sink into the ocean! If something wasn't done quickly, it would break off and be lost.

The solution, Lozier proposed, was to saw Manhattan free from the mainland, tow it out to sea, and turn it around. Then the island could be towed back, and its heavy end attached to land. Lozier convinced hundreds of people to help with this project. Equipment was gathered, and workers signed up. Then, on the day work was to start, he disappeared. Only then did New Yorkers recognize the plan for what it was—a gigantic hoax!

THE MOON PEOPLE

That wasn't the last time New Yorkers were duped by a hoax. During the 1800's the city's competing newspapers tried to win readers with exciting, exclusive stories. They didn't always worry whether the stories were true.

In August 1835, the *New York Sun* ran a series of articles reporting amazing "celestial discoveries." The stories claimed that Sir John Herschel, a noted British astronomer, had used a powerful new telescope to observe the moon. He had seen oceans, land, plants, and animals, including goats and pelicans. Most amazing of all, he had seen furry bat-winged moon people!

The stories had everyone talking in New York and beyond, and sales of the *Sun* soared. Other newspapers, desperate to win back their readers, ran their own versions of the reports. And even after the *Sun* admitted the hoax, some people continued to believe the stories. A Massachusetts missionary society even hatched a plan to send missionaries to the moon, to convert the bat people to Christianity.

THE BALLOON HOAX

In 1844, the *New York Sun* itself was the victim of a hoax cooked up by the famous author Edgar Allan Poe. At the time, Poe wasn't famous. In fact, he was broke, and he desperately needed money. To earn it, he wrote a story claiming that a daring team of aviators had made the first balloon crossing of the Atlantic Ocean. Poe named a well-known balloonist as the pilot and claimed that the balloon had made the crossing in three days, landing near Charleston, South Carolina.

Poe sold the story to the *Sun,* which put out an extra edition just to be first with the news. But a few days later, the newspaper was forced to admit that the story was a complete fake. In fact, the first balloon crossing of the Atlantic wouldn't be made until 1978.

TURNED TO STONE!

Some hoaxes have appeared again and again over the years, each time with a new twist. Among these old favorites were tales of petrified men—men whose bodies had turned to stone. Many such stories circulated through the boomtowns and mining camps of the Old West. In fact, so many of these stories appeared in newspapers of the time that in 1862 another famous American writer, Mark Twain, decided to spoof them.

Twain was working as a reporter in Virginia City, Nevada, at the time. He wrote that a petrified man had been found near Virginia City, perfectly preserved right down to a wooden leg. The man was sitting on a rock, and limestone sediment had glued him to it, the story claimed.

Twain hoped his spoof would help put an end to these turned-to-stone tales once and for all. But to his dismay, many readers believed the story. Tales about petrified people continued to turn up right into the 1920's. Even today, people researching old newspapers sometimes come across one of these stories and are fooled by it.

THE CARDIFF GIANT

The most famous "turned to stone" hoax of all was much more than a newspaper story. In 1869, two laborers digging a new well on a farm in Cardiff, New York, made an astounding discovery. They uncovered what seemed to be the body of a giant that had turned to stone! In fact, it was a fake—part of an elaborate scheme cooked up by George Hull, of Binghamton, New York, and his cousin William Newell, who owned the Cardiff farm.

Hull had secretly hired a stonecutter to carve the massive form of a giant from a block of gypsum. Then he and Newell buried the carving on the farm. A year later, Newell called in the laborers and instructed them to dig a well—right where the carving was buried. News of the discovery brought swarms of people to the farm, and they were willing to pay admission to see the giant.

Hull eventually sold the Cardiff Giant to a group of investors for $30,000. The famous showman P. T. Barnum tried to buy it from them, but they turned him down. At that point, the hoax became a double hoax. Barnum had his own giant carved and then put it on display, claiming it was the real Cardiff Giant. The owners of the first carving took him to court, and the truth came out—both giants were fakes!

THE COTTINGLEY FAIRIES

One famous hoax was carried out by children. It began in 1917 with a little lie told by two girls in the English village of Cottingley. Elsie Wright, 16, and her cousin Frances Griffiths, 10, were late to lunch at Elsie's house one day. Worse, Frances was soaking wet. To explain, the girls said they had been playing with fairies near a stream, and Frances had fallen in. The Wrights didn't believe that for a minute. But the girls insisted the story was true, and they asked to borrow a camera to prove it. To everyone's surprise, the girls produced pictures that showed them surrounded by tiny fairies and gnomes.

Word of the pictures slowly spread. One of those who heard about them was Sir Arthur Conan Doyle, author of the Sherlock Holmes detective stories. Doyle believed in spirits, fairies, and other strange beings. He was convinced that the photos were genuine and that they proved the existence of fairies. In 1920, Doyle arranged for the girls to take more pictures of their fairy friends, which they did.

Elsie and Frances became famous, and they were much too embarrassed to admit that the fairy affair had started with a lie. They didn't tell their secret until 1983. Then they admitted that the fairies in the pictures were paper cutouts, propped up with long pins. (In 1997, the story of the Cottingley fairies was the basis for a feature film, *Fairytale: A True Story*.)

Why was Doyle fooled so easily? Photography wasn't as refined as it is today, so perhaps it was easier at that time to pass off the faked pictures. And because Doyle believed in fairies, he badly wanted the pictures to be real. His fictional detective, Sherlock Holmes, would have known better!

THE MAN WHO INVENTED SANTA CLAUS

St. Nicholas of Myra is a patron saint of Russia. He has also been one of the patron saints of children for centuries. Legend has it that St. Nicholas brings gifts to good children on his feast day, December 6. There are many other legends about him too.

But Santa Claus, as most North Americans have come to know St. Nicholas, was born on December 24, 1822. It was on that frosty Christmas Eve that Dr. Clement Clarke Moore, a scholar and part-time poet, penned the lines of the immortal poem "A Visit from St. Nicholas." Moore turned St. Nicholas into "jolly St. Nick," a plump, happy-go-lucky elf with a sleigh full of toys and eight prancing reindeer, and sent him flying over hill and dale to keep alive the spirit of giving. And so a new St. Nicholas legend came to be.

Here is a fictionalized account of how Dr. Moore created Santa Claus.

It was a cold evening, and the ground was covered with snow. Dr. Moore was on his way home to his estate in what is now the Chelsea section of New York City. He had just delivered Christmas presents to friends in Greenwich Village. Driving his sleigh was an old handyman named Peter, whose weather-beaten face seemed to always wear a smile, and who could be counted upon for a cheerful remark when the world seemed gloomiest.

Suddenly, the 43-year-old professor remembered that he had promised his children a poem as an extra Christmas present. For although he was a scholar, he often wrote light verse for his family's amusement.

"By heaven, I'd nearly forgotten about that," Dr. Moore muttered to himself as old Peter, silhouetted in the moonlight, flicked his whip to spur on the horses. Dr. Moore racked his brain for an idea, turning over in his mind many possible lines of verse. But none seemed just right. Suddenly his eye fell on Peter's face, illuminated by the soft beams of the moon. The handyman's cherubic features, the pipe clenched firmly between his teeth, and the stocking cap pulled tightly over his head gave Dr. Moore an inspiration.

When they arrived home, the professor hurried to his study. "But dinner will be ready shortly," his wife protested. "Yes, yes, I know," Dr. Moore replied. "Just give me a few minutes. I have something important to do."

Alone at his desk, he began to write. The words flowed easily as his quill pen made scratchy sounds on the yellow manuscript paper. " 'Twas the night before Christmas," he began, "when all through the house, not a creature was stirring, not even a mouse . . ."

"Ah, yes, that's exactly right," the professor announced to himself, pleased with his efforts. Quickly, he continued:

The stockings were hung by the
chimney with care
In hopes that St. Nicholas soon
would be there;
The children were nestled all snug in
their beds,
While visions of sugar-plums danced in
their heads;

By the time the family was seated at the dinner table, Dr. Moore had completed all 58 lines of his poem. After dinner he and his wife and children gathered around the fireplace for their traditional singing of Christmas carols. But the children hadn't forgotten their father's promise. "You said you would give us a Christmas poem," they chorused.

At first, Dr. Moore pretended to have forgotten. "A poem? Was I supposed to write a poem?" he asked, a smile on his face. Then, as his children looked on with obvious disappointment, he began to search through his pockets. "Aha, here's something," he said. And with a flourish, he pulled out the sheets containing the newly written verses. While his children sat at his feet, Dr. Moore began to read. From the moment he spoke, the youngsters were captivated. They listened attentively as he continued:

"The moon, on the breast of
the new-fallen snow,
gave the lustre of mid-day to
objects below.
When what to my wondering eyes
should appear,
but a miniature sleigh, and eight
tiny reindeer.
With a little old driver, so lively
and quick,
I knew in a moment it must be
St. Nick."

While the children beamed, Dr. Moore continued, describing how Santa drove his sleigh over the roofs of the buildings and called his reindeer by name: "Now, *Dasher!* now, *Dancer!* now, *Prancer!* and *Vixen!* On, *Comet!* on, *Cupid!* on, *Donder* and *Blitzen!*"

He had a broad face and a round little
 belly
That shook, when he laughed, like a
 bowl full of jelly.
He was chubby and plump, a right jolly
 old elf,
And I laughed when I saw him, in spite
 of myself;

Dr. Moore's children loved the poem so much that they immediately began to memorize the lines. But the professor himself thought little of it; to him it was just a funny story in verse. Never dreaming of its future popularity, or even of having it published, he shoved it into a desk drawer and forgot all about it.

Some months later, a family acquaintance, Harriet Butler of Troy, New York, visited the Moores. Dr. Moore read the poem aloud while they were having tea. Miss Butler was very much taken by the verses and asked permission to make copies. Later she sent one of them to her local newspaper, the Troy *Sentinel*, but failed to mention the author's name.

The Troy newspaper happily published the "anonymous" poem just before Christmas in 1823, noting in its columns: "We know not to whom we are indebted for the following description of the unwearied patron of children . . . but from whomsoever it may come, we give thanks for it."

For years afterward, the poem was often published by newspapers and magazines during the Yuletide season—but without any credit being given to Dr. Moore. In 1830, a wood engraver named Myron King produced the first illustration of St. Nick and his eight reindeer—just as they were described in "A Visit from St. Nicholas." (Santa remained a tiny elf for nearly 40 years. Only in the 1860's did he take his present-day shape of a plump gentleman of normal height, dressed in a red, fur-trimmed suit.)

As for Dr. Moore, he finally got the credit due him when a collection of verse entitled *The New York Book of Poetry* carried the poem with his name on it in 1837. In 1844, the professor included it in one of his own books, but made it a point to note that he considered it of no more significance than "a good, honest, hearty laugh."

But it was when the professor read the lines describing the old fellow in detail, and telling how he came down the chimney "with a bound," that the eyes of his children widened in rapture:

He was dressed all in fur, from his
 head to his foot,
And his clothes were all tarnished with
 ashes and soot;
A bundle of toys he had flung on his
 back,
And he looked like a peddler just
 opening his pack.
His eyes—how they twinkled!
 his dimples, how merry!
His cheeks were like roses, his nose
 like a cherry!
His droll little mouth was drawn up
 like a bow,
And the beard on his chin was as
 white as the snow;
The stump of a pipe he held tight in
 his teeth,
And the smoke, it encircled his head
 like a wreath;

Santa's Secret Village

According to legend, Santa Claus lives at the North Pole. That's a trek—even if you have a reindeer sleigh. But if you have a computer, it's just a click away! Go to **www.northpole.com**, and you will soon be surfing some sensational scenes at Santa's Secret Village.

Here you can see Santa's elves making toys. . .Mrs. Claus baking cookies. . .Santa relaxing in his Den. You can meet Raymond, Santa's newest reindeer, and learn all about Bonnie, Bud, Bif, Burt, Will, and Santa's other eager elves.

At Santa's Secret Village, you can also read Christmas stories and even send a friend an animated Christmas card. So hop on the Web—and make your own "Visit *to* St. Nicholas."

Certainly Dr. Moore never imagined that this little verse would eclipse all his scholarly writings on the Bible and Classical literature. And yet this is exactly what happened. Today not even the most serious scholars are more than vaguely acquainted with Dr. Moore's academic works; but millions of people throughout the world have read and been delighted by "A Visit from St. Nicholas."

The poem has now been reprinted many thousands of times, in dozens of languages. And each year at Columbia University there is a Christmas event known as the Lighting of the Yule Log. It is traditional at this ceremony to read the poem by Dr. Moore, who graduated from Columbia in 1798 at the head of his class and later became a member of its Board of Trustees.

Despite the immense popularity of his poem, Dr. Moore never earned a single penny from it. He probably would have refused the money anyway, for he was a man of independent means who preferred giving to receiving. In fact, Clement Clarke Moore was very much like the Santa Claus he wrote about—a man who quietly went about the job of bringing joy to others, and who was amply rewarded by the happiness he left in his wake. So Professor Moore might well have been describing himself in the closing lines of his time-honored poem:

He spoke not a word, but went straight to his work,
And he filled all the stockings; then turned with a jerk,
And laying a finger aside of his nose,
And giving a nod, up the chimney he rose.
He sprang to his sleigh, to his team gave a whistle,
And away they all flew like the down of a thistle;
But I heard him exclaim, ere he drove out of sight,
"HAPPY CHRISTMAS TO ALL,
AND TO ALL A GOOD-NIGHT!"

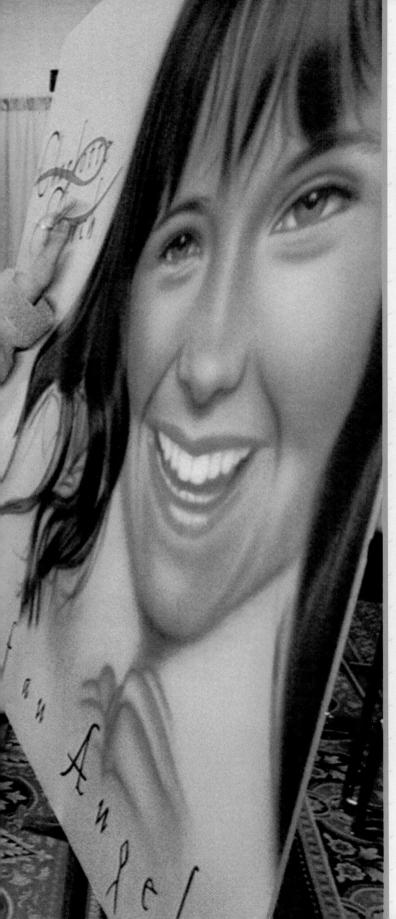

SPOTLIGHT ON YOUTH

With a hit album called Voice of an Angel, *Charlotte Church was one of the fastest rising stars of the classical music world in 1999. And everyone who heard this 13-year-old singer agreed that the album title fit her perfectly. Charlotte, who is from Llandaff, Wales, started singing at age 3 and taking voice lessons at age 8. In 1998 a record company executive heard her sweet soprano voice and signed her up. She became an overnight sensation and the youngest person ever to have a top-selling classical record. Voice of an Angel topped the British classical charts and reached Number 40 on the pop charts. Charlotte was even invited to sing at the Vatican and for Prince Charles of Britain! In 1999, Charlotte's album was released in the United States to rave reviews, and the young singer traveled to America. There she made her acting debut, in an episode of the TV series* Touched by an Angel. *Later in the year, she released a second album. Charlotte took her amazing success in stride. She attends secondary school in Wales when she isn't on tour, likes pop as well as classical music, and enjoys shopping with her friends.*

WWW.COOLSITES

Want to learn about buggy behavior? Check out great yo-yo tricks? Find out how you can make your money grow? Share a story you've written with kids around the world? You can do all this on the Internet's World Wide Web—one of the coolest places to be these days. The Web is a huge community in cyberspace filled with thousands of sites that contain information on every subject imaginable. If your computer is connected to an online service, you can visit the four fun Web sites on these pages. Each site has an address that begins with the letters http. Type in the address exactly as shown, and in seconds you'll be at the site.

Bug-Wonderful!
http://insect-world.earthlife.net/main/six.html

Everything you ever wanted to know about bugs is waiting for you at The Wonderful World of Insects. Find out which insect is the biggest, the smallest, or the fastest flyer. Learn cool facts to amaze your friends. Did you know that one of every four animals on Earth is a beetle? Or that a swarm of desert locusts may contain 28 billion of them? Discover, too, which insects can live in saltwater, which lay the most eggs, and why people don't like Africanized honeybees. If spiders and scorpions are more your thing, click to the Arachnid page and learn about these eight-legged relatives of insects.

Yo-Yo Magic
http://www.smartypantsyo-yo.com

The yo-yo is a simple device—a double disk with a string attached to its center—but you can do magical things with it. Whether you're a yo-yo beginner or master, you'll find this animated site a winner. It offers clear, step-by-step instructions on lots of tricks, from basics such as Rock the Baby and the Forward Pass to advanced moves such as Lunar Loop and Around the World. Check out the News & Events section for information on yo-yo demonstrations and competitions. And enter the chat room, where you can talk about your favorite yo-yos and tricks. If you're lucky, you may even talk with Smarty Pants himself!

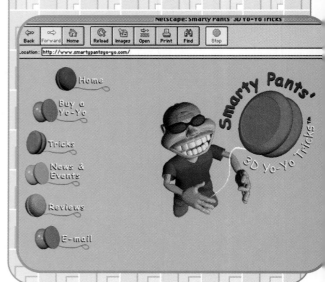

... a fun place for children to learn about money and banking.

Java Version   Non-Java Version

Parents: Please visit our introduction and download pages.

Kids Bank.Com™ is brought to you by:

Sovereign Bank

"Success is Confidence. We can help you get there."

Copyright 1999 Sovereign Bank - Success is Confidence. We can help you get there.
An MJM Website. All rights reserved. Call 1-877-SOV-BANK

Let's Talk Cent$
http://www.kidsbank.com

Wonder what interest is and how you get it? How money moves around the world? Where pennies came from and how they are made? Head for Kids Bank and learn from Mr. EFT, Dollar Bill, Checks the puppy, and other characters. If you want to know more, visit Mr. Money's bulletin board, ask a question, and you'll soon receive an answer. Then use the three calculators. They'll show you how much and how long you need to save to make sure you can afford a car when it's time to get your driver's license, and how your pennies can add up to spending cash for the holidays.

Publish Your Stories
http://www.cs.bilkent.edu.tr/~david/derya/ywc.html

Join The Young Writers Club and meet kids from all over the world. This jam-packed site has a monthly Web magazine called *Global Wave*, produced entirely by kids and featuring kids' work. If you want to send in an article you've written, use the handy submission form. The club also has an archive of stories and poems written by members. In another section you can see what kids think of the books they have read. The club even has its own members-only live chat room, where you can meet members, learn more about the world, and, of course, discuss writing.

This club aims to encourage children of all ages to enjoy writing as a creative pasttime by getting them to share their work and help each other improve their writing abilities. If you want to be a member of "THE YOUNG WRITERS CLUB" get your paper and pencils (keyboards and fingers) ready. If you like writing, we think you are going to love this club!

If you love animals, you might consider making them your career. You might, for example, enjoy being a veterinarian and treating sick and injured pets.

CAREERS WITH ANIMALS

Do you melt at the sight of a playful puppy? Love having a purring cat in your lap? Thrill at the thought of a galloping horse? Are the moos of a cow music to your ears?

If you are someone who has a special concern and affection for animals, you may want to consider making these creatures your career. Careers that involve animals cover a wide range. Perhaps you would like to work with dogs, cats, and other pets. Maybe horses or livestock animals are more your style. Or you may want to work with wildlife, helping to save endangered species.

Animal specialists work in many different settings—parks, zoos, veterinary clinics, and animal welfare shelters, to name just a few. The amount of education and the other qualifications that are needed for various animal-related careers also vary widely.

Following is a sampling of careers that involve animals. Each has its own requirements and rewards. Before you set your sights on one of them, however, a few words of caution are in order. In most of these jobs, you can expect long hours and hard work. And animals aren't always cute, cuddly, and sweet. They may be dirty, and they may bite, scratch, or kick—especially if they are injured or wild. But if you can accept these drawbacks and are still enthusiastic about working with animals, you can choose from a group of careers that provide exceptional enjoyment and satisfaction.

VETERINARY MEDICINE

A **veterinarian** is an animal doctor. Just like medical doctors, veterinarians are concerned with curing disease and ensuring the good health of their patients. And like medical doctors, veterinarians are highly trained.

Many veterinarians work in large clinics or operate their own private practices. They treat sick and injured animals, give vaccinations and general health check-ups, and advise owners on how to care for their animals. Some veterinarians have mixed practices—they see all kinds of animals. Many concentrate on small animals such as dogs, cats, and other household pets. Other veterinarians focus on large animals, such as cows and horses. Large-animal specialists often take their skills on the road, traveling to see their patients at farms, ranches, and stables.

Some veterinarians concentrate on just one type of animal. There are veterinarians who treat only race horses, only dairy cattle, or only pet birds. A few veterinarians specialize in treating the exotic animals kept at zoos. And besides concentrating on certain kinds of animals, a veterinarian may specialize in a certain area of animal health care. For example, there are veterinary ophthalmologists—animal eye doctors.

Other veterinarians operate emergency clinics, which help injured animals in the same way that hospital emergency rooms help injured people. But most practicing veterinarians can expect to get some emergency calls—to rush to a farm in the middle of the night to help deliver a foal, or to open the clinic after hours to treat an injured cat.

Not all veterinarians are in practice, however. Many are involved in research projects that are sponsored by veterinary schools, the government, private groups, and companies that produce animal medicines and livestock feed. Most of these projects focus on finding better ways to treat and prevent animal diseases and on improving animal care and nutrition. Veterinary research can sometimes even lead to important breakthroughs in human medicine.

Some veterinarians work for government agencies. They may direct efforts to wipe out diseases or parasites that could spread from animals to people or cause harm to valuable livestock. Veterinarians who work for the U.S. Cooperative Extension Service and similar agencies provide the public

Veterinarians who specialize in large animals often travel to farms and ranches to see their patients.

A marine biologist studies ocean life. This scientist is jotting down her observations of a young manatee.

with information on animal care.

In private practice, research, and the other areas where they work, veterinarians make use of many of the same sophisticated techniques that have become common in human medicine. And veterinary training is just as rigorous as medical training.

People who want to be veterinarians must complete four years of college and then continue their education for four more years at a veterinary school. There they have a chance to actually work with animals as they learn about the science of animal health care. There are about 30 veterinary schools in the United States and Canada, and competition to enter them is keen. Students who apply to a veterinary school should have good grades, especially in biology and other areas of science.

Veterinarians aren't the only workers in the field of animal health care. In recent years, many people have chosen careers as **veterinary** (or **animal health**) **technicians.** Technicians work alongside veterinarians— giving medication, helping to restrain the animals, monitoring heart and breathing rates, and performing many laboratory procedures. A technician may assist a veterinarian in a surgical operation. But technicians don't perform surgery, prescribe drugs, or diagnose illnesses.

Most veterinary technicians are graduates of two-year college-level programs that provide both practical and scientific training. Some states require veterinary technicians to be licensed, and they may set specific educational requirements for this career.

WORKING WITH WILDLIFE

As the population of the world continues to grow, people need more and more land to live on. And many kinds of animals are in danger of dying out because of this. Endangered species range from tiny insects to such huge creatures as the elephant. People have become increasingly aware of the need to protect these animals. And, at the same time, people have become more aware of how much can be learned by studying all wild animals, even those species that aren't at risk.

If you're interested in working with wildlife, many careers are open to you. As a **biologist** (a scientist who specializes in life sciences) or **zoologist** (a scientist who specializes in animals), you might conduct research into various wild species.

Like veterinarians, biologists and zoologists often concentrate on specific areas. There are **mammalogists,** who specialize in mammals; **ornithologists,** who specialize in birds; **entomologists,** who specialize in insects; and **herpetologists,** who specialize in reptiles. **Marine biologists** study ocean life, while **ichthyologists** concentrate on fish. **Ecologists** are concerned with how animals live together in a common environment.

Some wildlife research is done in the lab. But often, wildlife researchers spend much of their time in the field, studying animals in their natural surroundings. Such studies often produce new information about the animals— their food sources, breeding habits, migration routes. And through the research, people learn how to better protect the animals and their habitats.

Biologists and zoologists are also involved in programs to help endangered species survive. For example, a number of such programs have sought to breed threatened species in captivity and then release the young into the wild. This strategy has allowed scientists to reintroduce caribou in Maine, where they had been wiped out by hunters and disease in the early 1900's. Scientists hope that similar efforts will help save the rare California condor and other creatures that are in danger of dying out.

Wildlife research projects may be sponsored by the government, by a university, by a zoo, or by private groups. The scientists who direct these projects generally have advanced degrees (usually a doctorate) in their fields. They are helped by **research assistants,** who may have a four-year college degree or a master's degree in zoology, biology, or a related field.

Some wildlife specialists work in state and national parks, where they oversee large numbers of wild animals. A **conservation officer,** for example, may help count the animals in a park, rescue injured or stranded animals, relocate groups of animals to areas where they will find better grazing, and educate the public about the animals in the park. Patrolling for poachers and enforcing regulations designed to protect wildlife are important parts of the job. Many conservation officers have four-year degrees in biology, wildlife management, or a similar field.

Other park jobs that involve working with wildlife include those of **park rangers** and

James Herriot: Veterinarian and Author

You've probably never heard of James Alfred Wight. He was a veterinarian who spent his entire career in a remote British village. But you may have heard of James Herriot—the pen name Wight used to write stories based on his experiences. *All Creatures Great and Small,* a collection of those stories published in 1972, became an international best-seller and made James Herriot famous. Along with seventeen other Herriot books that followed, it inspired many people to take up veterinary medicine as a career.

Wight was born in 1916 in Glasgow, Scotland, and grew up there. He planned to be a city veterinarian. But when he graduated from school, he couldn't find a city job. The only position available was in the country town of Thirsk, in Yorkshire, England. He took it, and he lived there until his death in 1995.

By all accounts, Wight was an excellent veterinarian. In his practice, he treated everything from pet cats to cows. But what really set him apart was his ability to tell stories. The names of people and places are changed—Thirsk is called Darrowby—but he drew from his own experiences to write his tales. His books are filled with wonderful characters, both human and animal.

More than 60 million copies of Herriot's books have been sold, and two movies and a television series have been based on them. Tourists flock to Thirsk, where his former offices have been turned into a museum. But Wight always thought of himself as a veterinarian first. "If a farmer has a sick cow," he once said, "they don't want Charles Dickens turning up; they want a good vet. And that's what I've tried to be."

park naturalists. Range managers help maintain the balance between wild and domestic animals on tracts of public land that are open for livestock grazing. They make sure that the land isn't overgrazed by helping to decide the kinds of livestock and the numbers of animals that will be allowed on the range.

A CAREER AT THE ZOO

Some of the most exciting animal-related careers involve working at zoos. A zoo provides an opportunity to work with all sorts of exotic animals—from aardvarks to zebras—that few people are familiar with.

Zookeepers are responsible for the daily care of animals. This often involves a lot of hard work—pens must be cleaned, the animals must be fed. But zookeepers must also be keen observers of animal behavior, and they must be thoroughly familiar with the animals in their care. An important part of the job is to be on the lookout for the first signs of illness or injury. If an animal is sick, the keeper contacts the zoo veterinarian. Later, the keeper may be assigned the job of giving the animal medicine that the veterinarian has prescribed.

Zookeepers are responsible for the daily care of zoo animals. They must be keen observers of animal behavior—an important part of the job is to look for any signs of illness or injury. Left: A zookeeper examines a day-old hartebeest. Below: A zookeeper weighs a baby alligator.

Animals Now!

If you're thinking about an animal-related career, you can begin working with animals right now. You'll find out if this type of career is right for you, and you'll begin to develop the skills you'll need.

Caring for pets is one way to get started. Having a pet—whether it's a hamster or a hound dog—is a big responsibility because your pet depends on you for everything. After you've gained experience caring for your pets, you might want to start a pet-sitting service. Taking care of other people's pets is a great way to gain experience and earn some spending money after school and on weekends.

Some youth groups offer opportunities to work with animals. Kids in 4-H, for example, often raise and train animals as a project. In rural areas, they may work with farm animals, such as cows and sheep. In cities and suburbs, they are more likely to work with small animals.

If you're looking for a part-time job, check with local veterinarians, pet stores, kennels, and riding stables. These businesses often need part-time animal caretakers. You might also contact animal shelters and animal welfare groups in your town, to find out if there are opportunities for young people to volunteer. Most of these agencies depend on volunteers to run day-to-day operations as well as special programs, such as "adoption fairs" for abandoned pets.

If there's a zoo or an aquarium near you, see what they have to offer. Some zoos have

special programs for volunteers (sometimes called docents or interns). There may also be opportunities for part-time work, although the job might be working in a snack bar or gift shop rather than directly with animals. Some of these facilities also have summer programs that give kids a chance to see what goes on behind the scenes, and learn how to care for the animals. For example, the SeaWorld and Busch Gardens parks in California, Texas, and Florida have week-long summer camp programs for kids.

Curators are in charge of the zoo's various groups, or collections, of animals. A zoo might have a curator of reptiles, a curator of mammals, and a curator of birds. These people supervise the work of the zookeepers, making sure that all the animals in their section are properly cared for. They also help decide what animals the zoo will obtain and exhibit. Zoos today get most of their animals by buying from and trading with other zoos. They also breed many animals, and curators may be in charge of the breeding programs.

A **zoo designer** (or **curator of exhibits**) creates the settings in which the animals live and are displayed. This job has become an important one in recent years as many zoos have built exhibits that duplicate the animals' natural habitats. A good zoo exhibit provides the animals with a comfortable home. Thus the designer needs to know a great deal about each animal—its habits and the kind of climate and surroundings it prefers. In addition, the exhibit should make it easy for zoo visitors to see the animals while providing the animals with a place to hide when they have had enough. And the exhibits must be escape-proof and safe—for animals and zoo workers alike.

Many zoos also employ veterinarians and veterinary technicians, as well as researchers and people who run educational programs for the public. The **zoo director** oversees the entire institution and is responsible for seeing that all the programs and activities run smoothly. The director also plans any major expansions and renovations. And the director has another important job: raising money for the zoo.

The qualifications needed for zoo jobs vary. Many zoos hire keepers who have had a year or two of college-level study in zoology or a related field. There are also a few two-year college programs designed specifically to train zookeepers. Students in these programs get practical experience in caring for animals as they study animal nutrition, breeding, and other aspects of animal care.

In some cases, keepers have a chance to advance to higher positions. Most higher-level zoo jobs require at least a four-year college degree. And often the people who serve as zoo curators and directors have advanced degrees and many years of experience in working with animals.

OTHER CAREERS WITH ANIMALS

Many other careers involve work with animals. For example, you might want to work in the field of **animal welfare**—preventing cruelty to animals, educating people about the proper care of their pets, and rescuing injured and abandoned animals. Both government agencies and private groups are involved in this field. Many towns and cities employ animal control officers. Their job includes investigating reports of cruelty and enforcing licensing and other regulations. **Humane agents,** who usually work for private animal welfare groups, do similar work.

Other people find enjoyment and satisfaction in **breeding and raising animals.** You might choose a career in horse breeding, cat-

Zoo designers create exhibits that duplicate the natural habitats in which animals live in the wild. This rhinoceros feels perfectly comfortable in this zoo replica of its native homeland.

Some animal trainers specialize in teaching dogs to help people who have physical disabilities.

tle ranching, or another area of livestock production. Or you might want to raise dogs, cats, or other pets. Some people make a career out of **grooming** animals such as dogs or horses.

Animal training is another field to consider. Like many other animal-related jobs, training includes a wide range of specialties. There are people who train dogs in basic obedience or for special jobs, such as guiding the blind or rescuing victims of avalanches and earthquakes. Horse trainers may work with racehorses, pleasure horses, or show jumpers. Other specialists train the dolphins and other marine animals that perform at many aquariums and ocean parks.

A few daring trainers work with the lions, tigers, and other exotic animals that appear in circuses. And there are trainers who prepare animals for roles in Hollywood films. The key requirements for any training career are a thorough understanding of the animals you work with and a great deal of patience.

Finally, nearly every facility that keeps animals—dog kennels, pet shops, stables, farms, veterinary clinics, animal shelters—needs **animal caretakers**. These are people who help with daily care, feeding, and cleaning. Often the pay is low and the work is hard and dirty. But working as an animal caretaker is one way to find out if a career with animals is really for you. If so, you can look forward to the special satisfaction that comes from working in a field you love.

Getting Started

There are many ways to begin a career with animals. Discuss the idea with school guidance counselors, and read books about animal-related careers. Maybe you can work part-time with a local veterinarian or in a pet store. For more information about careers with animals, contact the following organizations:

The American Veterinary Medical Association—1931 North Meacham Road, Schaumburg, IL 60196

Canadian Veterinary Medical Association—339 Booth Street, Ottawa, Ontario K1R 7K1

Canadian Wildlife Federation—2740 Queensview Drive, Ottawa, Ontario K2B 1A2

Society for Integrative and Comparative Biology—401 N. Michigan Avenue, Chicago, IL 60611

The Wildlife Society—5410 Grosvenor Lane, Bethesda, MD 20814

The American Association of Zoological Parks and Aquariums—Oglebay Park, Wheeling, WV 26003

The Humane Society of the United States—2100 L Street, N.W., Washington, DC 20037

Canadian Federation of Humane Societies—102-30 Concourse Gate, Nepean, Ontario K2E 7V7

Monsters from Japan invaded North America in 1999.
They were **Pokémon**—short for "pocket monster." And Pokémon video
games and cards turned out to be one of the biggest crazes ever.

There are 150 monsters in all, most more cute than scary. Wartortle, for
example, looks like a scrappy little tortoise. Pikachu looks like a yellow
mouse. But each Pokémon has certain powers, and they use weapons such
as water, fire, and electricity. In the video games, the goal is to capture and
"train" as many Pokémon as possible. Capture them all, and you're a "Pokémon master."

As the Pokémon craze spread, the cards became collector's items, like baseball cards. There were spinoffs, too—including a television cartoon show, a
movie, action figures, and lots of Pokémon merchandise. Some schools
banned Pokémon trading cards and hand-held video games, so they would-
n't distract students. But Pokémon fans weren't ready to stop playing!

A desert sheik? No. It's 15-year-old **Max Highley** of Collinsville, Illinois. Max has been riding since he was 10 years old. His favorite horses are Arabians, a breed that originated in the deserts of the Arabian Peninsula. He has won more than 200 first-place ribbons. And he has twice won the native costume division at the U.S. National Arabian Horse Show.

Whipping up a meal for 75 people is no problem for **Ashlee Vann** of Springfield, Missouri. In 1999, Ashlee, 11, was coordinator of Kids Cafe, a meal service for needy children. She prepared food, set tables, supervised volunteers, and helped serve meals. It was a big job, and good training. Someday, Ashlee hopes to run her own restaurant.

Natalia Toro won first place and a $50,000 college scholarship in the 1999 Intel Science Talent Search. Previously known as the Westinghouse Science Talent Search, this competition is America's most important pre-college science contest. Natalia was one of 1,470 students from 49 states who entered the 1999 contest. And she was only 14 years old when she picked up the first-place award in March—the youngest person ever to win this competition. But because she skipped several grades, she was a senior at Fairview High School in Boulder, Colorado.

Swimming and tennis are Natalia's favorite sports, and she's fluent in Spanish. But her love of math and science was evident very early in her life. She even took college-level math courses when she was in 6th grade. Natalia needed lots of math for her prize-winning science project, which involved tiny subatomic particles called neutrinos. Scientists say that Natalia's work is an important contribution to the field of high-energy physics. Keep your eye on this high-energy girl!

Youth Technology Consultant to the Minister of Commerce and Technology—that's a big title for someone who's just 14. But **Makonnen David Blake Hannah** of Kingston, Jamaica, proved up to it in 1999. Makonnen has been using computers since he was 4 years old. He has written programs and designed his own Web page. And as a government consultant, he keeps Jamaica's Minister of Commerce and Technology up to date on the latest computer and Internet news. When he's not surfing the 'Net, Makonnen can often be found surfing the waves—on the beaches of his Caribbean island-nation.

Elizabeth Chapman has struggled with cerebral palsy since birth. It affects her muscles and coordination—but not her imagination or her talents. And one of her best talents is writing. In 1999, Elizabeth, 14, won first place in an international letter-writing contest, for an essay on living with cerebral palsy.

Star Wars Episode I: The Phantom Menace was the big film of 1999. And kids were the big stars! **Natalie Portman,** 18, played Queen Amidala, ruler of the planet Naboo. She has been acting in films since age 11. In 1999, she also appeared in the film Anywhere But Here. But neither acting nor the publicity over The Phantom Menace kept her from finishing her senior year at Syosset High School in Long Island, New York. A top student, she was accepted at several Ivy League universities.

Jake Lloyd played Anakin Skywalker—the character who grows up to be the evil Darth Vader in later chapters of the Star Wars saga. In The Phantom Menace, Anakin is a boy who begins training as a Jedi knight—a defender of good. Jake, 10 in 1999, lives in Los Angeles. He set his sights on an acting career as soon as he was old enough to go to the movies. He was just 8 when he canceled his birthday party to audition for The Phantom Menace—and won it over about 2,500 other candidates!

The bell rings, and the school day ends—but your schoolwork isn't over. At home, there's just enough time for a quick snack before you tackle your assignments. You have a bunch of math problems to get through. You have to review material for tomorrow's science test. Your social studies report is due Friday. You'll be lucky to finish by dinnertime.

If your teachers are piling on **homework assignments,** you're part of a national trend. According to one study, kids aged 9 to 11 spend more than three-and-a-half hours a week on homework. Back in 1981, two hours and 49 minutes was the average for that age group. And homework has increased for all ages. Even first and second graders spend two hours a week on assignments. Not that long ago, they rarely had homework at all.

Teachers aren't trying to torment kids with homework. The goal is to help kids learn more. Research shows that homework can help raise test scores, especially in grades 7 and up. And American students still spend less time on their studies than kids in many other countries.

Nupur Lala, an eighth-grader from Tampa, Florida, became the latest U.S. spelling bee champ on June 3, 1999. Nupur spelled "logorrhea" (a word that means "excessive, often incoherent talkativeness") to take top honors in the Scripps Howard National Spelling Bee. Her win brought her a $10,000 first prize, encyclopedias, two airline tickets, and other goodies.

This wasn't Nupur's first try for the title. In 1998 she reached the third round of the finals, which are held each year in Washington, D.C. In 1999, she lasted all the way through 12 rounds, beating 248 other contestants.

Competitors in the spelling-bee finals, all aged 9 to 15, qualify by winning regional contests. They are sponsored by local newspapers. Nupur, 14, drilled two hours a day to prepare for the spelling bee. But she still found time to swim, play the violin, and surf the Internet. Her hard work allowed her to correctly spell such puzzlers as "nociceptor," "trianon," and "bouchon" on her way to victory.

Is **Tahj Mowry** a genius? No—but he plays one on television. In 1999 this 12-year-old had the starring role in *Smart Guy,* a television comedy series about a super-smart kid. In real life, Tahj is super busy. When he's filming episodes of his show, he's tutored on set so he won't fall behind in his schoolwork. He juggles acting and school with football, track, and lessons in karate, hip-hop, and tap. And he earns his allowance by cleaning his room. Besides *Smart Guy,* Tahj has appeared in commercials and a Michael Jackson music video. His sisters, Tia and Tamera, are actors, too—on the television show *Sister, Sister.*

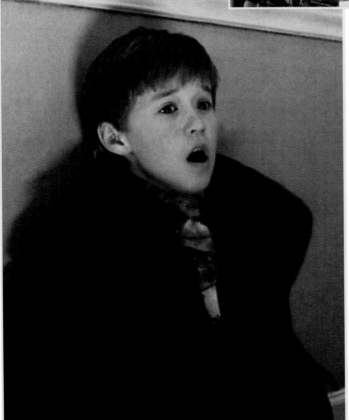

Young actor **Haley Joel Osment** had nightmares after he read the script for the 1999 film *The Sixth Sense*—a creepy, scary ghost story that was a summer blockbuster. But that didn't stop him from giving the performance of his life, playing a boy who sees ghosts. Critics raved about his performance.

Haley, 11, has been acting since he was 5 years old. He played the son of Tom Hanks in the film *Forrest Gump.* And he had roles on TV shows and in a Pizza Hut commercial.

CREATIVITY

Princess Mononoke, *raised by a wolf, is the title character in one of 1999's most beautiful and unusual animated films. Designed to appeal to adults and older children, this film was created by Hayao Miyazaki, a Japanese master of animation. The story, set in 15th-century Japan, is about a fight for the future of a magical unspoiled forest. On one side are animals and forest spirits who want to protect the wilderness. On the other are the people of Iron Town, who want to cut down trees to get iron ore. Good guys and bad guys aren't clearly separated in this film—there's good and evil on both sides.*

John Singer Sargent's portrait *Madame X* is one of his most famous paintings today. But when it was painted in 1884, it was considered shocking and outlandish.

JOHN SINGER SARGENT

John Singer Sargent made his reputation as a painter with dashing, sometimes daring portraits. He specialized in painting members of the elegant society of the Gilded Age, in the late 1800's. But portraits were only one aspect of this remarkable artist's work. An American

who lived in Europe for much of his life, he painted landscapes, street scenes, figure studies—more than a thousand oils and watercolors in all.

In 1999, Americans had a chance to see many of Sargent's most beautiful works. A major exhibition with 115 of his oils and watercolors was on view at the National Gallery of Art in Washington, D.C., from February through May 1999. The exhibition then moved to the Museum of Fine Arts in Boston. It was the first time since the 1920's that so many of Sargent's paintings had been assembled for one show. And together, the works provided a window into the artist's life and times.

EARLY YEARS ABROAD

Sargent's childhood was anything but conventional. His parents were from Philadelphia, but they moved to Europe before he was born to take advantage of the art and culture there. Sargent was born in Florence, Italy, on January 12, 1856. He spent his youth there and in other cities of Europe—Rome, Vienna, Geneva, London, Madrid. He had little formal education. But his parents recognized his artistic talent and encouraged it.

In 1874 the family moved to Paris. Sargent went to study at the studio of Carolus-Duran, a fashionable portrait painter. There, he learned to paint realistically but with a free style that emphasized the effects of light on his subjects. He also traveled to Spain and Holland, to study the works of masters, and to Morocco. He was determined to be more than a portrait painter, and he did a number of paintings based on his travels.

During his years in Paris, Sargent became friendly with the group of painters who became known as the Impressionists. The Impressionists believed that paintings should portray nature and everyday scenes. They sought to capture passing moments in dabs and strokes of pure color. Sargent adopted many of their ideas and techniques, but he developed his own style.

In his portraits, Sargent liked to pose people in natural but unconventional ways, as if they had just been interrupted. He was praised for his compositions, rich tones, and use of light and shadow. He began to be known as a promising young artist. But that changed in 1884, when he turned the Paris art world upside down with a painting called *Madame X*. A portrait of a society woman, this painting offended the standards of the day. People were shocked by the subject's proud pose, pale skin, and low-cut dress.

Sargent moved to Britain and set up a studio in London. London would be his base for the rest of his career. But at first, he had little success as a portrait painter there, either. With time on his hands, he painted landscapes and other subjects. And in 1887 one of those paintings helped build his reputation. The painting was *Carnation, Lily, Lily, Rose,* a gentle scene of two children lighting paper lanterns in a garden. It was a great success when it was shown at the London Royal

Sargent was especially close to the French Impressionist painter Claude Monet. In this picture, *Claude Monet Painting by the Edge of a Wood,* Sargent showed his friend working outdoors and painting a scene from nature—something Monet and other Impressionist painters often did.

After that, fewer people came to Sargent's Paris studio for portraits. And that was a problem, because portraits were an artist's bread-and-butter—the best way to make a living through art.

Academy, and that helped make his name in England.

Later that year, Sargent crossed the Atlantic to paint a portrait of a wealthy New York banker's wife. An American citizen, Sargent

already had many friends in the United States, including the noted author Henry James. They greeted his arrival with delight. More important, they brought him commissions for more portraits. Within months of arriving in the United States, Sargent had his first one-man show, in Boston.

Americans were taken with Sargent's modern style and deft brushwork. He also had a way of making his subjects seem more elegant than they were in real life. But his paintings didn't always flatter the subjects. He was a keen observer and sometimes revealed more about his subjects' characters than they might have liked. "It's positively dangerous to sit to Sargent," one portrait subject said. Dangerous or not, the wealthy families and society figures of New York and Boston all but lined up to have him paint their portraits. On a second trip, in 1890, he painted more than 40 portraits in nine months.

Success in America led, finally, to success in England. Sargent became a fashionable portrait painter on both sides of the Atlantic. He never married, and he devoted himself to his work. He divided his time between Boston, New York, and London, painting up to 20 portraits a year. He also made regular summer trips to the European continent. Venice, with its canals and troves of great art, was one of his favorites.

A PAINTER FIRST

Sargent was elected to the Royal Academy in 1897. It was a mark of the success he had achieved. But despite the popularity of his portraits, Sargent saw

Sargent completed this self-portrait in 1906, at the request of the famous Uffizi Gallery in Florence, Italy. The request was a great honor for the painter, and a mark of his success.

himself as a painter first, and a portraitist only second. He continued to paint landscapes and other subjects. And in his view, his most important works were murals.

In 1890, Sargent began work on a series of murals for the Boston Public Library. Their subject was the history of religion, and he traveled to Egypt and the Middle East to do research. After 1907, he gave up portrait paint-

the spot, with free brush strokes. They are filled with a sense of light.

In 1918, Sargent took up a darker subject—World War I. He was sent by the British government to the Western Front to sketch scenes for a mural commemorating the war. His wartime watercolors and the finished mural, *Gassed,* portrayed the horrors of war. In the years after the war, he completed a

Sargent painted *Cashmere* around 1908, late in his career. His 11-year-old niece was the model for all seven of the mysterious shawl-wrapped figures. The figures stand out sharply against a flat background, in a way that would have suited the murals Sargent was also painting at the time.

ing almost entirely to concentrate on the library murals. Later, he did murals for Widener Library at Harvard University and for the Museum of Fine Arts in Boston.

Sargent also turned increasingly to watercolor in his later years. His watercolors include travel sketches showing scenes in Venice, the Alps, Italy, Spain, and the Rocky Mountains. He also made watercolor sketches of fruit, plants, and people, often as studies for his murals. These works were painted quickly, on

series of murals for the Boston Museum of Fine Arts. These paintings, showing figures from Greek mythology, were his last works. He died in 1925 in London.

Sargent's reputation suffered after his death. Because he had been a fashionable portrait painter and didn't follow the modern art trends that developed after 1900, some people dismissed his paintings as superficial. But today his brilliance is recognized, and his wide-ranging talent is once again admired.

Gwyneth Paltrow (best actress) and Joseph Fiennes in *Shakespeare in Love* (best motion picture).

ACADEMY

CATEGORY	WINNER
Motion Picture	*Shakespeare in Love*
Actor	Roberto Benigni (*Life Is Beautiful*)
Actress	Gwyneth Paltrow (*Shakespeare in Love*)
Supporting Actor	James Coburn (*Affliction*)
Supporting Actress	Judi Dench (*Shakespeare in Love*)
Director	Steven Spielberg (*Saving Private Ryan*)
Cinematography	*Saving Private Ryan*
Visual Effects	*What Dreams May Come*
Song	"When You Believe" (*The Prince of Eygpt*)
Foreign–Language Film	*Life Is Beautiful* (Italy)
Documentary Feature	*The Last Days*
Documentary Short	*The Personals: Improvisations on Romance in the Golden Years*

Awards

1999

Left: Roberto Benigni (best actor) and Giorgio Cantarini in *Life Is Beautiful* (best foreign-language film). Above: Tom Hanks in *Saving Private Ryan* (best director, Steven Spielberg; and best cinematography). Below: *The Prince of Egypt* (best song).

Mazes have delighted—and confounded—people since ancient times. One of the most well-known is Britain's hedge maze at Hampton Court, planted in the late 1600's. This cartoon shows a harassed schoolteacher looking on as her students get thoroughly lost in the Hampton Court maze.

GET LOST!

You've lost your way, and you're completely confused. Should you turn right or left. . .or continue straight ahead? All the paths look the same. So you take a guess, stride forward, and turn right—into a dead end. Are you worried? Not at all. Wrong turns and dead ends are just part of the fun of mazes.

You might wonder how getting lost could be fun. But getting lost—and finding your way again—is the whole idea behind a maze. A maze is an intricate pattern of passages. It can be a drawing or something you actually walk through. The idea is to find your way through the passages to a goal in the center, and then come out again. Don't expect it to be easy— mazes are designed to confuse and fool you every step of the way. People have been fascinated by mazes since ancient times. And today these intricate puzzles are enjoying a burst of popularity. Mazes are in!

CENTURIES OF CONFUSION

There are actually two kinds of mazes. One kind is a puzzle maze, with lots of dead ends that force you to make decisions about where to go. The other kind, called a labyrinth, has no dead ends or wrong turns. It's just one long, twisting path that winds its way around and around to the center.

Mazes have been around for at least 3,000 years. The ancient Egyptians and Greeks built underground mazes that may have been used to store treasure (and befuddle would-be thieves) or as prisons. Native Americans carved maze designs on rock walls.

Mazes also played an important part in the myths and beliefs of the ancient world. To the Hopi, the labyrinth was a symbol of the Earth. But the most famous mythological maze was the labyrinth of Crete. Legend says that Daedalus, the master craftsman, built the labyrinth for King Minos of Crete. In the labyrinth Minos confined the Minotaur, a half-man, half-bull monster that devoured anyone who entered. And no one who entered ever came out—until Theseus, the legendary hero of Athens, arrived. Theseus unrolled a spool of thread behind him as he went deep into the labyrinth. Then he killed the Minotaur and followed the thread to find his way out.

In Europe during the Middle Ages, maze patterns were built into the tiled floors of some churches and cathedrals. The patterns symbolized the difficult path of Christian pilgrimage, or perhaps the journey of life. Walking this pavement labyrinth was an opportunity for prayer and reflection.

Similar mazes were cut into the turf of village greens in England, just for fun. The most famous of these turf mazes can still be seen in the village of Saffron Walden. Its winding path is a mile long! In the 1700's, young people of the village used the maze for games.

Mazes were a favorite amusement of European royalty and nobility, too. Nobles often planted hedges in the form of mazes in their gardens. Many hedge gardens were planted in geometric patterns that weren't hard to walk through. But others were puzzle mazes, filled with detours and dead ends. They were truly confusing.

One of the best-known of these puzzle mazes was planted in the late 1600's at Hampton Court, near London, by the English King William III. There, the members of the court held races to see who could find the way to the center of the maze and back in the fastest time. This maze still confuses and delights the thousands of people who visit Hampton Court each year. But the maze is easy to solve for those who know the key: Keep one hand (right or left, but always the same hand) in contact with the hedge at all times. If you do this, you'll eventually come to the center and find your way back out—because the maze is one long connected hedge.

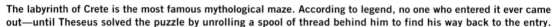

The labyrinth of Crete is the most famous mythological maze. According to legend, no one who entered it ever came out—until Theseus solved the puzzle by unrolling a spool of thread behind him to find his way back to the entry.

Such simple tactics won't get you through another famous English hedge maze. The Chevening maze, which was planted in the early 1800's, is made of a series of hedges, with dozens of confusing right-angle turns. If you try keeping a hand on the hedge, you'll just go around and around the same section, or pop back out the entrance—because the Chevening maze is a series of *unconnected* hedges. The designer of this bewildering and perplexing puzzle was the second Earl of Stanhope, a mathematician.

MODERN MAZES

Today people are just as fascinated by mazes as they were in the Earl of Stanhope's day. Lots of people love to solve the puzzle mazes that are printed in books and magazines. And there are plenty of new walk-through mazes, including some that are more challenging than the most famous mazes of old.

One of the most complicated mazes anywhere opened in 1978 at Longleat, a famous estate in Britain. More than 16,000 waist-high yew trees were planted to form it. They've grown into an impenetrable hedge that borders looping, swirling paths. Adding to the confusion are half a dozen bridges that link unconnected sections of the maze. Visitors who tire while trying to reach the goal—a viewing platform at the center—can stop at any of four resting spots. But all four spots look alike. Coming on one, you're certain you've passed that way before. . .or have you?

Longleat has become a center for maze lovers, with several other puzzlers on the grounds. One of the most exciting is King

Left: During the 1700's, the winding paths of the turf maze at Saffron Walden in Britain were used by young people to play games. Below: Britain's Longleat maze, which opened in 1978, may be the most complicated hedge maze in the world.

254

Maize Mazes

Cornfield mazes are the latest version of these ancient puzzles. Farmers plant their corn, and then cut or remove plants to form the winding paths of the maze. As the corn plants grow, they form dense walls as tall as any hedge. Cornfield mazes are sometimes called maize mazes—"maize" is the British term for corn.

Some cornfield mazes are designed by professionals. For example, Adrian Fisher, who has created many walk-through mazes and written books about mazes, designed 24 cornfield mazes in seven countries in 1999. Some of these mazes are very challenging and very long. People may wander around for hours! But there's always a way to get help. Sometimes the maze operators give visitors flags that they can raise above the corn. A maze master, standing on a platform that overlooks the maze, sees the flag and shouts directions.

The maze trend is spreading, and cornfield mazes are turning up on farms everywhere.

Farmers like the mazes because they bring visitors who pay to try their luck and may also buy fruit, pumpkins, and other farm products. And for the visitors, the mazes are a great opportunity for a fun day in the country. The mazes stand from late summer through fall, when the dried cornstalks are finally cut down. Next year, a new maze, and a new challenge, appears in the field.

Arthur's Mirror Maze, which opened in 1998. It's an indoor maze, housed in a former coach house. Visitors pretend they are knights and set out on a quest to find the Holy Grail, wandering through a spooky forest to a ruined chapel. At every turn, mirrors reflect the passageways and add to the confusion. There are even special effects, including a frightening thunderstorm.

You don't have to travel to Britain to find a walk-through maze. In North America, mazes are popular attractions at amusement parks, museums, and other sites. And new ones are being built all the time. Some are traditional. For example, at the Governor's Palace in Colonial Williamsburg, Virginia, there's a maze made of holly hedges. It's based on the Hampton Court maze design. What may be the world's largest permanent hedge maze opened in Hawaii in 1997. It covers 100,000 square feet (329,000 square meters). In West Palm Beach, Florida, the Norton Museum of Art has a

brick pavement maze. At the center is a picture of Theseus slaying the Minotaur. "Robin Hood's Race" is a new version of a medieval turf maze. It's at Lebanon Valley College, in Annville, Pennsylvania.

But mazes have changed with the times, and you'll find many made of modern materals—plastic sheeting and mirrors, for example. Mazes made of wood fencing are especially popular. They can be built quickly—no waiting for a hedge to grow—and they're solid. Typical is the Brekenridge Maze, in Brekenridge, Colorado. It's made of wooden fencing and has a mile of twisting paths. Visitors race against the clock, trying to complete it in the fastest time. Many wooden mazes have bridges and towers, making them three-dimensional puzzles.

Maybe you'll visit one of these a-mazing attractions. Or maybe there's a maze near where you live. Either way, next time you're looking for fun, just get lost!

In 1499, the Italian artist and inventor Leonardo da Vinci planned a magnificent bronze statue for his patron, the Duke of Milan. It would show the Duke's father mounted on a horse—**the largest statue of a horse in the world.** Leonardo got as far as making a full-size clay model of the horse. But then French troops invaded Milan. They destroyed the model, and that was the end of the project.

In 1999, 500 years later, Leonardo's dream horse became a reality. A prancing, snorting stallion, 24 feet (7 meters) tall, was created as a gift from the American people to the Italian people. Based on Leonardo's design, it took shape thanks to a 20-year, $6-million project. The bronze statue was cast in seven sections at a foundry in New York. Then the sections, weighing 15 tons, were flown to Milan, Italy. The horse was assembled there and unveiled on September 10—the 500th anniversary of the day the French soldiers destroyed Leonardo's model. *Il Cavallo* (Italian for "The Horse") may not be exactly as Leonardo would have made it. But it's a tribute to his work and his dream.

Actress **Sarah Michelle Gellar** was one of 1999's top TV stars, thanks to her hit series *Buffy the Vampire Slayer*. Gellar, 22, has been acting since she was 4 years old. She landed her first regular TV role on the soap opera *All My Children* in 1993. Between shooting her show and guest appearances on other shows, she also finds time for charity work.

Italian comedian **Roberto Benigni** had lots to smile about at the 1999 Academy Awards. He was named best actor for his role in the film *Life Is Beautiful*. And the movie, which he also directed, was named best foreign film. Benigni, 47, is loved in Italy for his slapstick comedy. But *Life Is Beautiful* had a serious theme: It was set in a concentration camp during World War II. Benigni played an Italian Jew who shelters his son from the truth about the camp by pretending that it's a game.

Chicago was turned into a big outdoor art moo-seum in 1999. Some 300 life-size cow sculptures grazed downtown streets and sidewalks. A "cowch potato" relaxed in front of a TV set in a city park. There were cows in building lobbies, climbing buildings, and flying overhead! They all were part of an exhibit called **"Cows on Parade."** Fiberglass cow sculptures were painted and posed by Chicago artists. Each was one of a kind. There were cows wearing everything from sneakers to evening gowns. When the exhibit ended on October 31, the herd was rounded up and sold at a "cattle auction" to raise money for charities.

Whimsical sculptures turned up on the National Mall in Washington, D.C, too. *Typewriter Eraser, Scale X,* by Claes Oldenburg and Coosje van Bruggen, was one of 18 works featured in the new **National Gallery of Art Sculpture Garden** there. The garden, which was in the works since the 1960's, opened to the public in May 1999. The artworks on display were all created after World War II, mostly by leading American artists. They reflect the many different movements of modern art. The sculptures are scattered among shrubs and plants and are linked by winding paths.

ACCEPTING THE AWARD, WILLIAM SHAKESPEARE

... FIRST, I'D LIKE TO THANK EVERYBODY IN STRATFORD-UPON-AVON... MY WIFE ANNIE, MY MUM AND DAD AND OF COURSE, GRAMPS... ALL MY PALS FROM STRATFORD GRAMMAR SCHOOL: PUDGY, BOOPS AND WOOGIE—THIS IS FOR YOU!...THE CAST AND CREW DOWN AT THE GLOBE THEATER—YOU KNOW WHO YOU ARE... HER MAJESTY ELIZABETH I, EVERYONE DOWN AT THE BOAR'S SNOUT... MY PET HAMSTER "PINKY"...

One of the biggest names in show business in 1999 was also one of the oldest: **William Shakespeare.**

Shakespeare's plays—*Romeo and Juliet, Hamlet,* and at least 35 others—have been delighting theatergoers for 400 years. The Bard, as Shakespeare is sometimes called, has long been considered one of the world's finest dramatists and poets. And in 1999 the Bard was bigger than ever.

Shakespeare in Love, a clever and mostly fictional comedy set in 1593, turned into a huge hit. It starred Joseph Fiennes (top) as the young playwright. The movie wowed audiences and was nominated for thirteen Academy Awards. It won seven of them, including Best Picture, Best Actress (Gwyneth Paltrow), and Best Supporting Actress (Judi Dench). There was more Shakespeare during the year, too. A movie of his play *A Midsummer Night's Dream* was released in May, and new film versions of other Shakespeare plays—including *Hamlet* and *Love's Labour's Lost*—were in the works.

It's rare for a children's book to top national bestseller lists. But British author **J. K. Rowling** (above) has done it with three wildly popular fantasies about **Harry Potter,** a boy with a knack for magic. The third book in the series arrived in U.S. bookstores in September 1999, and eager fans snapped it up.

In the first book, *Harry Potter and the Sorcerer's Stone,* Harry discovers his talents. An 11-year-old orphan, he gets a mysterious letter inviting him to Hogwart's School for Witchcraft and Wizardry—a school unlike any other. Before long Harry is learning to fly on a broom, hatch dragon eggs, and cast spells. He also tangles with Lord Voldemort, a terrifying villain who holds the secret to Harry's destiny.

In the second book, *Harry Potter and the Chamber of Secrets,* the young wizard is back at Hogwart's for a second term. But new horrors interrupt his classes in Herbology, Potions, and other magical musts. The third book, *Harry Potter and the Prisoner of Azkaban,* finds him dealing with flying Hippogriffs and a fiendish villain named Sirius Black. The sales figures of all three books show that Harry has clearly cast a spell over readers. Luckily for them, Rowling plans to continue the series with four more books.

Jazz fans everywhere marked April 29, 1999—the 100th anniversary of the birth of **Duke Ellington.** Ellington, who died in 1974, was one of the greatest jazz composers, pianists, and bandleaders ever. In his 60-year career, he wrote thousands of songs and compositions. Among them were classics such as "Mood Indigo," "Take the 'A' Train," and "Sophisticated Lady."

While jazz lovers were celebrating Duke Ellington's anniversary, they were also taking note of a new star. Jazz singer and pianist **Diana Krall,** 34, released her latest hit album, *When I Look in Your Eyes,* in 1999. Krall, who is from British Columbia, Canada, has also landed some film and television roles.

Haley Joel Osment (with Bruce Willis) played a boy who sees dead people in the spooky chiller *The Sixth Sense*.

MOVIE TIME!

Comedy, drama, thrillers—the top movies of 1999 offered something for everyone. After waiting sixteen years, fans of the movie *Star Wars* and its two sequels finally got to see a new chapter in this classic science-fiction saga. But the year brought lots of other exciting new films, including some unusual animated features.

THRILLS AND CHILLS

New versions of some Hollywood horror-film classics hit theaters in 1999. Back in 1932, *The Mummy* had audiences screaming in terror. The 1999 version produced some screams, too—but also lots of laughs. The new *Mummy* was a parody of horror films. In the story, two young adventurers (Brendan Fraser and Rachel Weisz) stumble into an ancient Egyptian crypt and come face to face with a walking mummy and an evil priest. Before long, mummies and other creepy horrors are popping up all over the place.

Mighty Joe Young was a remake of a 1949 film about a 15-foot (5-meter) gorilla. At the start of the film, the hulking Joe lives in the jungles of Central Africa with his protector—a young woman named Jill (Charlize Theron). They've been together for twelve years, ever since both their mothers were killed by poachers. Then a zoologist (Bill Paxton) finds them and convinces Jill to move Joe to Los Angeles, where he can be protected in a wildlife preserve. But, thanks to those evil poachers, the move doesn't go as planned. Before long, Joe is running amok in the streets of the city.

Serious chills were offered in the spooky film *The Sixth Sense*. The main character in this movie, 8-year-old Cole Sear (Haley Joel Osment), has a problem: He claims that he can see the dead. A child psychologist, Malcolm Crowe (Bruce Willis), is called in to help. Some scary scenes unfold as the mystery slowly builds to a surprise ending.

Breathtaking special effects helped make *The Matrix* a hit with science-fiction fans. This film had an unusual premise: What if the "real" world is just a computer simulation, created and controlled by evil machines? A computer hacker named Neo (Keanu Reeves) is tipped off to the illusion by a mysterious figure named Morpheus (Laurence Fishburne), and he sets out to free humanity from virtual slavery. This film's fight scenes took martial arts to new levels. Filmmakers used state-of-the-art special-effects techniques to show actors making gravity-defying leaps and other impossible stunts.

There were no special effects at all in what was probably the year's scariest film, however. *The Blair Witch Project* was a low-key, low-budget movie, made by and starring unknowns. It started with an off-beat idea: Three film students go into the Maryland woods to shoot a documentary about a local legend, the Blair Witch. They never return. The movie is supposed to be their film, discovered in the woods a year later. Shot entirely with hand-held cameras, *The Blair Witch Project* scared audiences out of their seats.

ROMANCE

Comedy mixed with romance in *Drive Me Crazy,* a film aimed squarely at teenagers. This film starred Melissa Joan Hart and Adrian Grenier as Nicole Maris and Chase

The Force Returns

Star Wars: Episode I—The Phantom Menace was 1999's most eagerly awaited movie. Weeks before the film opened on May 19, fans were camped out outside theaters, waiting for tickets to go on sale.

But why "Episode I," when this was the fourth *Star Wars* film? Filmmaker George Lucas, the creator of the film, called it a "prequel" because it covered events leading up to the action in the other movies.

Like the other *Star Wars* films, *Phantom Menace* is set in a galaxy far away. And like those films, it's about a battle between good and evil. On the side of good are the Jedi knights and their allies. Their enemies are the evil characters who embrace the "dark side."

Star Wars fans found plenty of familiar names. Obi-Wan Kenobi, a Jedi master in *Star Wars,* is a young man in *Phantom Menace,* played by Ewan McGregor. Anakin Skywalker, who becomes the evil Darth Vader of *Star Wars*, is a boy, played by 9-year-old Jake Lloyd. The gnomelike Jedi master Yoda is on hand. And no *Star Wars* movie would be complete without those two clever "droids," R2-D2 and C-3PO!

Phantom Menace featured plenty of new characters as well. Among them were Queen Amidala, played by Natalie Portman; Jedi elder Mace Windu, played by Samuel L. Jackson; and Jedi knight Qui-Gon Jinn, played by Liam Neeson. There were 140 new, weird aliens and plenty of stunning special effects—underwater cities, new star fighters, light-saber duels, even a battle between frog-faced aliens and droids!

Lucas plans to make two more *Star Wars* "prequels" to complete his science-fiction saga. And fans can't wait!

Ben Affleck and Sandra Bullock teamed up in *Forces of Nature*—a romantic comedy about a groom desperately trying to get from New York to Savannah, Georgia, in time for his wedding.

Hammond, next-door neighbors and child-hood pals. Nicole and Chase have taken separate paths in high school—she's popular with the sports and social crowd, while he's a rebellious intellectual. Then Nicole is dropped by her boyfriend, and Chase is dropped by his girlfriend. They team up in a plot to get their sweethearts back—but the outcome isn't what they expect.

Top stars were paired in several other romantic comedies. In *Forces of Nature*, Ben (Ben Affleck) is determined to get from New York to Savannah, Georgia, for his wedding. But he's stalled by one disaster after another—everything from a crippled airplane to a hurricane gets in his way. Not the least of his troubles is Sarah (Sandra Bullock), a free-spirited woman who becomes his traveling companion. Plot twists kept audiences guessing: Would Ben get to Savannah on time? And if he did, would he still want to get married?

Julia Roberts starred with Hugh Grant in *Notting Hill*, a film about an unlikely romance between a famous actress and a shy London bookstore owner. And Roberts played opposite Richard Gere in another romantic comedy, *Runaway Bride*. This time, she was a woman whose wedding-day jitters cause her to bolt from one fiancé after another. Grant, meanwhile, teamed up with Jeanne Tripplehorn in *Mickey Blue Eyes*. In that film, he played a mild-mannered art auctioneer who discovers that his fiancée is the daughter of a Mafia boss.

JUST FOR LAUGHS

Several TV cartoon characters came to the screen in live-action comedies in 1999. *Inspector Gadget* featured the bumbling bionic policeman familiar to cartoon audiences. Matthew Broderick played the title role and two other parts. In *Dudley Do-Right*, Brendan Fraser starred in the title role as a Canadian Mountie who is handsome, good, and really dumb. Like the cartoon, which was popular in the 1960's, the film was a spoof of old-fashioned melodramas. Dudley is so dim-witted that he mounts his horse backward. All the same, he thwarts the schemes of the mustachioed villain Snidely Whiplash, played by Alfred Molina, and wins the heart of Nell Fenwick, played by Sarah Jessica Parker.

High school was the setting for *Never Been Kissed*. In this film, a 25-year-old newspaper reporter (Josie Geller, played by Drew Barrymore) poses as a student to get the scoop on teenagers. Josie was mercilessly picked on during her own high-school days, so she jumps at the chance to try again. This time around, she's part of the popular crowd. But she also has a different perspective on the school social scene, and she learns that high-school popularity isn't all it's cracked up to be.

Organized crime was played for laughs in *Analyze This!* Robert De Niro, famous for playing tough guys, spoofed his own past roles by playing Paul Vitti, a mob boss who decides he needs psychiatric help. Billy Crystal played Ben Sobel, the unlucky psychiatrist Vitti insists on seeing. The mobster's problems draw Sobel deep into the crime world and mess up his wedding plans, with hilarious results.

In a sequel to his popular 1997 spy spoof *Austin Powers: International Man of Mystery,* Mike Myers returned to the screen in 1999 with *Austin Powers: The Spy Who Shagged Me.* The film featured Myers in multiple roles, including the crooked-toothed secret agent of the title and Dr. Evil, his archenemy. Dr. Evil's goal is world domination, and he plans to reach it by zapping Washington, D.C., with a laser beam. Powers has the job of stopping him. The story involves time travel (to 1960's London), a Dr. Evil clone named Mini-Me, and a nonstop stream of puns and low-comedy routines.

ANIMATED HITS

Animated films are always popular with kids, partly because it lets filmmakers create effects that would be difficult or impossible to produce in live action. And in 1999, several interesting and unusual films took animation in new directions.

The DreamWorks studio chose an unusual subject for its first full-length animated feature—a bible story. *The Prince of Egypt* retold

October Sky

In 1957, the Soviet Union amazed the world by launching *Sputnik,* the first satellite. *Sputnik* opened the space age. And it opened a world of new possibilities for Homer Hickam, Jr., a teenage boy in the drab mining town of Coalwood, West Virginia.

Homer Hickam's true story was the basis for one of 1999's most praised films, *October Sky.* Instead of following his father to work in the coal mines, Homer (played in the film by Jake Gyllenhaal) set his eyes on the skies. He and his friends had no background in science or math, but they decided to build a rocket. And with the help of teachers and townspeople, they succeeded. In fact, they built several rockets, and entered them in a national science fair. Homer grew up to become an engineer with the National Aeronautics and Space Administration (NASA). The movie was based on his memoir, *Rocket Boys.*

Tarzan

Tarzan, the English orphan raised by African apes, is no stranger to movie audiences. This character's jungle yells and vine-swinging feats entertained the parents and grandparents of today's kids. And in 1999, with a new animated version, Tarzan showed he was ready to swing into the next century.

Tarzan first appeared in an adventure novel written by Edgar Rice Burroughs in 1914.

That book was followed by 23 more, as well as a comic strip, TV shows, and nearly 50 Tarzan movies. In 1999, Walt Disney Pictures came out with the latest *Tarzan* film—a full-length animated feature that retold the original story with a few twists.

Tarzan (voiced by Tony Goldwyn) is orphaned as a baby when his parents are killed by a leopard. He's adopted by apes and grows up wondering why he looks different. Then he comes face to face with the first humans he's ever seen. And one of them is Jane Porter (Minnie Driver), who'll be the love of his life. Tarzan and Jane team up to defeat a group of bad guys who plan to capture Tarzan's ape family. Songs, comedy, and lots of vine-swinging acrobatics helped make this animated version lively. Animators studied skateboarders to draw some of Tarzan's moves!

the story of the Book of Exodus in the Bible. The film follows the life of Moses from infancy, when he is set adrift in a basket in the Nile River and adopted by a princess, to leadership of the Hebrews in their flight from slavery in Egypt. The movie won high praise for bringing this biblical epic to life.

The Iron Giant was another unusual animated film—a science-fiction tale with lots to say. Based on the book *The Iron Man*, by the British poet Ted Hughes, the story was set in 1957, in a Maine village. A boy named Hogarth Hughes finds something strange in the woods—a 50-foot (15-meter) robot from outer space that has fallen to Earth accidentally. The monster robot eats metal (he wolfs down cars like cookies), but he turns out to have a gentle soul. Hogarth befriends him and tries to hide him from the townspeople. But rumors spread. Before long, a government agent is snooping around. Then the military gets involved. Suspicion gets out of control, and the result is nearly a disaster for the once-quiet village. Most of the animation for this film was done in the traditional way— drawn by hand. But the filmmakers used computer animation to create the giant, to make the character stand out and underscore the idea that he came from a different world.

The Pokémon craze, which swept America in 1999, reached the big screen when *Pokémon: The First Movie* opened in November. Fans of Pokémon games and trading cards made it one of the biggest children's films of the year. This animated movie was made in Japan, where Pokémon began. It featured dozens of "pocket monsters" like Pikachu and Charizard. Fans of Pokémon TV cartoons recognized the human characters—three kids named Ash, Misty, and Brock, and their archenemies Jessie and James. The movie also had evil scientists,

Pokémon clones, and plenty of action. Hordes of kids rushed to see it. Theaters were jammed on opening day, when special-edition Pokémon trading cards were given away to ticket buyers.

Another animated film from Japan drew notice in 1999. *Princess Mononoke* was a beautiful and unusual film designed to appeal to teens and adults. It was created by Hayao Miyazaki, a Japanese master of animation. The story, set in 15th-century Japan, is about a fight for the future of a magical unspoiled forest. On one side are animals and forest spirits who want to protect the wilderness. On the other are the people of Iron Town, who want to cut down trees to get iron ore. A young prince, Ashitaka, comes to the forest hoping to free himself from a curse placed on him by a demon. To do that, he must find a way to bring peace to the warring sides. In the forest, he sees and falls in love with Princess Mononoke, a girl who has been raised by wolves and is known as San.

Princess Mononoke was the most popular film in Japan when it was released there in 1997. The Disney company brought it to America, dubbed into English. But it was very different from most Disney animated films. There were no song-and-dance numbers or tie-in toys, and the animals weren't cute. There were many battles and other scenes of violence. Good guys and bad guys weren't clearly separated in this film—there was good and evil on both sides. And the film didn't have a storybook happy ending.

AND MORE. . .

Robin Williams brought his comic talents to two films, each of which carried a serious message. In *Jakob the Liar,* Williams played a Polish Jew trapped in a ghetto during World War II. The future is grim for the people of the ghetto—the Nazis who have occupied their homeland plan to destroy them. But Jakob pretends to have heard good news: Russian troops are advancing, and soon the Germans will be driven out. He keeps everyone's spirits up by inventing reports of the Russians' progress.

In *Patch Adams*, Williams took on the role of a former mental patient who discovers the healing powers of laughter. He sets his sights on medical school, planning to bring warmth and humor to a career as a doctor. The medical establishment frowns on his clowning antics, but patients love him. The movie was based on a real-life story.

"Real life" television shows such as MTV's "Real World" provided the inspiration for *EDtv*. In this movie, Matthew McConaughey starred as Ed Pekurny, a video-store clerk who agrees to let television cameras follow him around 24 hours a day. "The Ed Show" presents all the details of his daily life, no matter how personal, and it turns out to be a huge hit. Suddenly Ed's famous—and that creates problems for everyone in his life. Stardom, it turns out, definitely has drawbacks.

Courtney Thorne-Smith, Gil Bellows, Calista Flockhart, Jane Krakowski, Peter MacNicol, Greg Germann, and Lisa Nicole Carson in *Ally McBeal* (best comedy series).

EMMY

Awards

CATEGORY	WINNER
Comedy Series	*Ally McBeal*
Actor—comedy series	John Lithgow (*3rd Rock From the Sun*)
Actress—comedy series	Helen Hunt (*Mad About You*)
Supporting actor—comedy series	David Hyde Pierce (*Frasier*)
Supporting actress—comedy series	Kristen Johnston (*3rd Rock From the Sun*)
Drama Series	*The Practice*
Actor—drama series	Dennis Franz (*NYPD Blue*)
Actress—drama series	Edie Falco (*The Sopranos*)
Supporting actor—drama series	Michael Badalucco (*The Practice*)
Supporting actress—drama series	Holland Taylor (*The Practice*)
Miniseries	*Horatio Hornblower*
Variety, Music, or Comedy Series	*Late Show With David Letterman*

1999

Top Left: Michael Badalucco (best supporting actor, drama series) in *The Practice* (best drama series). Above: John Lithgow (best actor, comedy series) and Kristen Johnston (best supporting actress, comedy series) in *3rd Rock From the Sun*. Left: Edie Falco (best actress, drama series) in *The Sopranos*.

Christina Aguilera was one of the many talented teen performers who emerged on the music scene in 1999.

THE MUSIC SCENE

For nearly all of 1999, teens dictated which artists would dominate the charts. Boy bands and teen queens followed the 1998 success of the Spice Girls, catering to the musical tastes of those under twenty.

The trend seemed to mimic the early days of rock and roll, when groups were groomed and packaged for teen appeal. Some people wondered if it was a response to the gloomy grunge music of the early '90s. But others credited an end-of-the-century need for "lite" fun. Whatever the cause, the result was lots of young talent stealing the spotlight from the old guard.

WHAT'S NEW?

In January, 17-year-old Britney Spears stormed the charts with a song, ". . .Baby One More Time," and a debut album of the same name. Both hit the Number 1 spot, and suddenly the young singer was a national phenomenon. The next teen sensation was Christina Aguilera, 18, who sprinkled some magic onto the pop charts with her smash hit, "Genie in a Bottle."

A cavalcade of talented teenage singers followed, including Mandy Moore, whose sweet "Candy" was a pop hit; Tatyana Ali, formerly of the TV series *Fresh Prince of Bel-Air,* who showcased her singing talents on *Kiss the Sky;* and 13-year-old Charlotte Church, who introduced opera to a new generation with *Voice of an Angel.* Meanwhile, "old-timers" Brandy and Monica retained their strong presence in the R&B arena. It was a year of Girl Power.

Also targeting teens were guy groups. The Backstreet Boys seemed unstoppable with the release of their third album, *Millennium.* By year's end they had sold a total of nearly 40 million albums worldwide and appeared ready to break every sales record in existence. Hot on their heels were 'N Sync and 98 Degrees, both of whom had released their major-label debuts in 1998.

Countless other guy groups emerged in the wake of these three. They included LFO, who had a hit with "Summer Girls," and Ideal, whose smooth R&B break-up song, "Get Gone," caught on with listeners.

Many of the year's other new acts were female. Irish singers B*Witched released *Awake and Breathe,* and had young girls copying their denim outfits and Northern accents. Destiny's Child gave the world "Bills, Bills, Bills," which held onto the Number 1 spot for weeks. Urban trio 702 hit the big time with their second album, *702,* and a single, "Where My Girls At?" Newcomers Blaque, who duetted with 'N Sync on their song, "Bring It All to Me," worked their way up the charts.

RETURNING FAVORITES

Joining the new young artists on the charts were a number of established performers. Jewel released *Spirit,* the follow-up to her 1996 debut. Sarah McLachlan delivered *Mir-*

rorball, and Tori Amos gave us *To Venus and Back.* Alanis Morissette's latest effort was *Supposed Former Infatuation Junkie,* while Fiona Apple's was *When the Pawn....* Mariah Carey showcased her five-octave vocal range on *Rainbow.*

British rockers Bush unveiled *The Science of Things.* Alt-country faves Wilco released *Summer Teeth.* Puff Daddy released *Forever,* which broke into the Top 20, and R&B diva Mary J. Blige gave us *Mary.* Nine Inch Nails unloaded their weighty double album, *The Fragile,* and Beck turned over *Midnite Vultures.* Live released *The Distance to Here,* which quietly climbed the charts.

TLC released their first album in almost five years, *FanMail.* It debuted at Number 1 and had already spawned two major singles by year's end. Other albums that left a mark in 1999 included Ani DiFranco's *Up, Up, Up, Up, Up, Up* and the Black Crowes' *By Your Side.*

Several former members of the Spice Girls went solo in '99. Geri Halliwell (Ginger Spice) released *Schizophonic.* Melanie Brown (Scary Spice) contributed to the soundtrack of the new *Austin Powers* movie, while Melanie Chisholm (Sporty Spice) released her solo album just as the holidays rolled around.

Meanwhile, a number of musicians from the generation that discovered rock and roll reappeared with some of 1999's biggest hits. Cher took over the radio waves with her infectious electro-pop ditty, "Believe." Eric Clapton, Barbra Streisand, Melissa Etheridge, Paul McCartney, Jimmy Buffett, David Bowie, Sting, and Whitney Houston all released popular albums. Eurythmics reunited for *Peace,* their first album in many years. The Artist Formerly Known As Prince had a new album with a new single, "The Greatest Romance Ever Sold."

Songs that saturated the airwaves included "Steal My Sunshine," by Len; "My Own Worst

SPOTLIGHT ON...
Britney Spears

Britney Spears is pop music's newest sensation. In 1999, she became the first new solo singer ever to top the charts with a debut album and single at the same time. And Britney was just 17!

Britney hails from Kentwood, Louisiana. She's always had her sights set on a show-business career. She started dancing lessons at age 4 and appeared in commercials and plays while she was still in grade school. When she was 11, she won a regular spot on the *Mickey Mouse Club* television show.

After the show was canceled in 1994, Britney turned to singing. Even before her album, *...Baby One More Time,* was released, she was winning fans as the opening act for the pop group 'N Sync.

Britney doesn't write her own music, but her fans love her sweet voice and terrific dance moves. All that—plus her fresh good looks and winning smile—has helped propel her to the top of the teen-pop world.

Hard rockers Korn (*above*) won two MTV Video Music Awards and late in the year released a new album, *Issues*. TLC (*left*) had a hit album, *Fanmail*.

and "Beautiful Stranger," by Madonna, from the *Austin Powers* movie soundtrack.

Balancing out all the sugary pop was a more hard-driving rock sound. Pioneered by Korn and Limp Bizkit, it gave a voice to the pent-up frustration of young men.

HIP HOP AND YOU DON'T STOP

Rivaling teen pop in the mainstream in 1999 was urban music. Artists like Lauryn Hill (whose solo debut, *The Miseducation of Lauryn Hill,* was released in 1998) and TLC maintained their reign on the charts, as did rappers like Jay-Z, DMX, and Master P.

Underground hip-hop got an above-ground charge with the growing popularity of groups like OutKast, Black Star member Mos Def, and hip hip-hopper Timbaland. Q-Tip, former member of A Tribe Called Quest, went solo with *Amplified*. Will Smith, whose clever pop/hip-hop has become a favorite of adults and teens alike, released *Willenium*.

Younger rappers brought some fresh attitude into the mix. The ambitious 20-year-old Nas released *I Am. . .The Autobiography* and the hit single *Nastradamus*. Mase, another rapper barely in his twenties, released his

Enemy" by Lit; "Kiss Me," by Sixpence None the Richer; "All Star," by Smash Mouth; "No Scrubs," by TLC; "Every Morning," by Sugar Ray; "(You Drive Me) Crazy," by Britney Spears; "She's So High," by Tal Bachman; "Everything Is Everything," by Lauryn Hill;

WHAT IS. . .
The Latin Explosion?

The rhythms of Latin music could be heard everywhere in 1999. Ricky Martin (right), a former member of the teen group Menudo, began the trend after winning the 1998 Grammy for Best Latin Pop Album. His high-voltage performance at the Grammy awards show wowed millions of viewers, and he released his first English-language album soon after, in May 1999.

Actress-turned-singer Jennifer Lopez (below) was the next to reach the top of the pop charts. Her debut album, *On the 6,* had songs in both English and Spanish, including "If You Had My Love," a smash hit single and video. Fans believed that Lopez, who had por-trayed Latina pop queen Selena in a TV movie, could be the crossover star that the slain Selena never became.

Among the year's other breakthrough Latin artists were Marc Anthony, who also enjoyed a successful acting career, and Enrique Igle-

sias, son of Spanish crooner Julio. And veteran guitarist Carlos Santana, who pioneered the Latin sound of the '70s, released a new album, *Supernatural,* which included a hit song, "Smooth," with vocals by Matchbox 20's Rob Thomas.

What's called "Latin music" is actually a fusion of many different sounds. It originated in Latin America and the Caribbean, a cultural crossroads where African rhythms merged with European and native Indian traditions to produce salsa, mambo, merengue, and other musical forms. More recently, these have blended with pop sounds as Latin music entered mainstream American culture.

Latin sounds have long been a part of American popular music. Salsa king Tito Puente, '50s rocker Ritchie Valens, Carlos Santana, and more recently, Ruben Blades and Gloria Estefan all made their mark on the music scene. But the widespread appeal of this new generation of dynamic young artists, combined with a growing U.S. Hispanic population, just might make Latin music the wave of the future.

273

second solo album but then left the music industry to devote himself to God. Foxy Brown handed over *Chyna Doll,* though it didn't make too many waves.

Stealing the limelight from them all was Missy "Misdemeanor" Elliott. Most agreed that Elliott, who got her start writing songs for Whitney Houston, Janet Jackson, and Mariah Carey, was one of the most innovative and influential music producers of the '90s. More recently, she began to record her own songs and appear in visually creative music videos.

Among the phenomena of 1999 were a number of "blue-eyed" rappers. Kid Rock hit the big time with *Devil Without a Cause,* his 1998 release. Eminem, a protégé of Public Enemy's Dr. Dre, stormed radio and MTV with the song, "My Name Is," from his debut album, *The Slim Shady LP.* Former House of Pain rapper Everlast put out his solo album, *Whitey Ford Sings the Blues,* in late 1998, and it remained on the charts until well into 1999.

COUNTRY

Two words could describe country in 1999: Dixie Chicks. With their debut album, *Wide Open Spaces,* still on the charts, the three sassy lasses—Natalie Maines, Martie Seidel, and her sister Emily Erwin—released their second album, *Fly.* It was an instant hit, with songs like "Ready to Run" and "Cowboy Take Me Away."

Other young artists making a mark in country music in 1999 were Mandy Barnett, who was revered as the next Patsy Cline, and SHeDAISY, another girl group, which was the best-selling new act in country in 1999. Also

British dance-music master Fatboy Slim won three MTV Video Music Awards during the year.

riding high were Shania Twain, whose 1997 album *Come On Over* was still going strong, and Garth Brooks, whose *Double Live* album broke sales records.

ELECTRONIC BOOGALOO

Electronic music finally broke into the mainstream of popular culture in 1999, led by Fatboy Slim. With the release of his second album, *You've Come A Long Way, Baby,* he dominated the airwaves, even providing music for five TV commercials. The video for his single "Praise You" won three MTV Video Music Awards. The Chemical Brothers released their third album, *Surrender.* Moby, the great-great-grand-nephew of novelist Herman Melville, released *Play,* which merged African-American folk songs into electronic tunes.

ON THE ROAD

Two of the most important events in the music sphere in 1999 involved concerts. In July, more than 350,000 fans descended on the former Grifiss Air Force Base in Rome, New York, for Woodstock '99. Concert-goers paid $150 per ticket and endured mud and heat to catch dozens of acts, including the Dave Matthews Band, the Offspring, Metallica, and Alanis Morissette.

But as the three-day concert drew to a close, the crowd rioted, lighting fires and trashing vending stalls. The concert's promoters stood behind the event, vowing to continue the Woodstock tradition in years to come.

For many young women, the end of the Lilith Fair was a disappointing moment in music. The event's organizer, Sarah McLachlan, did as she had planned and called it quits after just three years. The summer's tour, however, was a huge success, featuring such top female artists as Monica, the Pretenders, the Dixie Chicks, and Beth Orton.

MUSIC NOTES

Inductees into the Rock and Roll Hall of Fame were tried and true bearers of the rock and roll torch. Included were perfomers Bruce Springsteen, Billy Joel, Del Shannon, Paul McCartney, Curtis Mayfield, and the Staple Singers and producer George Martin.

HEIDI SHERMAN
Music Editor, *Seventeen* magazine

Hip-hop singer Lauryn Hill walked off with five Grammy Awards—the most ever won in one year by a female performer.

1999 Grammy Awards

Record of the Year	"My Heart Will Go On"	Celine Dion, artist
Album of the Year	*The Miseducation of Lauryn Hill*	Lauryn Hill, artist
Song of the Year	"My Heart Will Go On"	James Horner, Will Jennings, songwriters
New Artist of the Year		Lauryn Hill
Pop Song, Female	"My Heart Will Go On"	Celine Dion, artist
Pop Song, Male	"My Father's Eyes"	Eric Clapton, artist
Pop Song, Group	"Jump Jive An' Wail"	The Brian Setzer Orchestra, artists
Rock Song, Female	"Uninvited"	Alanis Morissette, artist
Rock Song, Male	"Fly Away"	Lenny Kravitz, artist
Rock Song, Group	"Pink"	Aerosmith, artists
Rhythm and Blues Song, Female	"Doo Wop"	Lauryn Hill, artist
Rhythm and Blues Song, Male	"St. Louis Blues"	Stevie Wonder, artist
Rhythm and Blues Song, Group	"The Boy Is Mine"	Brandy & Monica, artists
Rap Album	*Vol. 2...Hard Knock Life*	Jay-Z, artist
Rap Song	"Gettin' Jiggy Wit It"	Will Smith, artist
Rap Song, Group	"Intergalactic"	Beastie Boys, artists
Music Video Performance	"Ray of LIght"	Madonna, artist
Alternative Music Performance	*Hello Nasty*	Beastie Boys, artists
Score for a Motion Picture	*Saving Private Ryan*	John Williams, composer
Musical Show Album	*The Lion King*	Mark Mancina, producer
Classical Album	*Barber: Prayers of Kierkegaard/ Vaughn Williams: Dona Nobis Pacem/Bartok: Cantata Profana*	Robert Shaw conducting the Atlanta Symphony Orchestra

FUN TO READ

When night comes, kids in the city go to bed and fall asleep—just like children everywhere. But the city is wide awake. Boats chug up and down the river. Trucks carry fruits and vegetables to market. And workers of all kinds are busy all through the night. Night City, a colorful picture book by Monica Wellington, reveals everything that goes on when the sun goes down behind the skyscrapers.

Robert Louis Stevenson's Treasure Island *is one of the most famous adventure stories of all time—a rousing tale of a boy who gets involved with pirates and a hunt for buried treasure. It has been delighting readers for more than 100 years.*

As a boy, Stevenson himself loved adventure and the sea. But poor health often kept him home, and thus his adventures were limited to reading and his imagination.

Poor health continued to plague Stevenson for most of his life. But even as an adult, he loved adventure—and he conveyed all that love in the many stories that he wrote.

the story on a visit to Switzerland, and it was published in Young Folks, *a magazine for young people. In 1883, it appeared in book form.* Treasure Island *soon became a classic. It has been translated into many languages and filmed several times.*

The hero and narrator of Treasure Island *is young Jim Hawkins, the son of an innkeeper. His chilling adventure begins when Billy Bones, a pirate, comes to stay at the inn and dies in frightening circumstances. Jim and his mother search the dead pirate's seachest for money that he owed them and find a map— a treasure map,*

Treasure Island *was Stevenson's first novel. It was begun in 1881, while the writer and his family were staying in Scotland. It rained every day, and Stevenson passed some of the time drawing and painting with his young stepson, Lloyd Osbourne. One day Stevenson drew a watercolor map of an imaginary island, complete with places named after pirates and clues to buried treasure. He then began to make up a story to go along with the map. Each morning Stevenson wrote; after lunch, he read what he had written to the family.*

A friend who heard the tale urged Stevenson to publish it. The author later finished

showing the burial place of the treasure of the notorious pirate Captain Flint. Jim narrowly escapes a group of Flint's men who are after the map, and he takes it to the leading men of the district, Squire Trelawney and Dr. Livesey. They decide to seek the treasure. They charter the schooner Hispaniola, *and Jim is to go along as cabin boy. The excerpt that follows begins as the* Hispaniola *is about to set sail. Captain Smollett has doubts about some of the crew—with good reason, as it turns out. But no one suspects the jovial, peg-legged ship's cook, Long John Silver. (If you come across terms you don't know, check the glossary on the last page.)*

Treasure Island

THE VOYAGE OF THE HISPANIOLA

All night we were in a great bustle getting things stowed in their place, and boatfuls of the squire's friends came to wish him a good voyage and a safe return.

We never had a night at the "Admiral Benbow Inn" when I had half the work; and I was dog-tired when, a little before dawn, the boatswain sounded his pipe, and the crew began to man the capstan-bars. I might have been twice as weary, yet I could not have left the deck; all was so new and interesting to me—the brief commands, the shrill note of the whistle, the men bustling to their places in the glimmer of the ship's lanterns.

Long John, who was standing by, with his crutch under his arm, at once broke out in the air and words I knew so well:

"Fifteen men on the Dead Man's Chest—"

And then the whole crew bore chorus:

"Yo-ho-ho and a bottle of rum!"

Even at that exciting moment it carried me back to the old "Admiral Benbow" in a second; and I seemed to hear the voice of the captain piping in the chorus. But soon the anchor was short up; soon it was hanging dripping at the bows; soon the sails began to draw, and the land and shipping to flit by on either side. And before I could lie down to snatch an hour of slumber the *Hispaniola* had begun her voyage to the Isle of Treasure.

I am not going to relate that voyage in detail. It was fairly prosperous. The ship proved to be a good ship, the crew were capable seamen, and the captain thoroughly understood his business. But before we came the length of Treasure Island, two or three things had happened which require to be known.

Mr. Arrow, the mate, turned out even worse than the captain had feared. He had no command among the men, and people did what they pleased with him. But that was by no means the worst of it; for after a day or two at sea he began to appear on deck with hazy eye, red cheeks, stuttering tongue, and other marks of drunkenness. Time after time he was ordered below in disgrace. Sometimes he fell and cut himself; sometimes he lay all day long in his little bunk at one side of the companion; sometimes for a day or two he could be almost sober and attend to his work at least passably.

In the meantime we could never make out where he got the drink. That was the ship's mystery. Watch him as we pleased, we could do nothing to solve it; and when we asked him to his face, he would only laugh, if he were drunk, and if he were sober, deny solemnly that he ever tasted anything but water.

He was not only useless as an officer and a bad influence amongst the men, but it was plain at this rate he would soon kill himself outright; so nobody was much surprised, nor very sorry, when one dark night, with a head sea, he disappeared entirely and was seen no more.

"Overboard!" said the captain. "Well, gentlemen, that saves the trouble of putting him in irons."

But there we were, without a mate; and it was necessary, of course, to advance one of the men. The boatswain, Job Anderson, was the likeliest man aboard, and, though he kept his old title, he served in a way as mate. Mr. Trelawney had followed the sea, and his knowledge made him very useful, for he often took a watch himself in easy weather. And the coxswain, Israel Hands, was a careful, wily, old, experienced seaman who could be trusted at a pinch with almost anything.

He was a great confidant of Long John Silver, and so the mention of his name leads me on to speak of our ship's cook, Barbecue, as the men called him.

Aboard ship he carried his crutch by a lanyard round his neck, to have both hands as free as possible. It was something to see him wedge the foot of the crutch against a bulkhead, and, propped against it, yielding to every movement of the ship, get on with his cooking like some one safe ashore. Still more strange was it to see him in the heaviest of weather cross the deck. He had a line or two rigged up to help him across the widest spaces—Long John's earrings, they were called; and he would hand himself from one place to another, now using the crutch, now trailing it alongside by the lanyard, as quickly as another man could walk. Yet some of the men who had sailed with him before expressed their pity to see him so reduced.

"He's no common man, Barbecue," said the coxswain, to me. "He had good schooling in his young days and can speak like a book when so minded; and brave—a lion's nothing alongside of Long John! I seen him grapple four, and knock their heads together—him unarmed."

All the crew respected and even obeyed him. He had a way of talking to each, and doing everybody some particular service. To me he was unweariedly kind; and always glad to see me in the galley, which he kept as clean as a new pin: the dishes hanging up burnished, and his parrot in a cage in one corner.

"Come away, Hawkins," he would say, "come and have a yarn with John. Nobody more welcome than yourself, my son. Sit you down and hear the news. Here's Cap'n Flint—I calls my parrot Cap'n Flint, after the famous buccaneer—here's Cap'n Flint predicting success to our voyage. Wasn't you, Cap'n?"

And the parrot would say, with great rapidity, "Pieces of eight! pieces of eight! pieces of eight!" till you wondered that it was not out of breath, or till John threw his handkerchief over the cage.

"Now, that bird," he would say, "is maybe two hundred years old, Hawkins—they lives forever mostly; and if anybody's seen more wickedness it must be the devil himself. She's sailed with great Cap'n England, the pirate. She's been at Madagascar, and at Malabar, and Surinam, and Providence, and Portobello. She was at the fishing up of the wrecked plate ships. It's there she learned 'Pieces of eight,' and little wonder; three hundred and fifty thousand of 'em, Hawkins!

She was at the boarding of the *Viceroy of the Indies* out of Goa, she was; and to look at her you would think she was a babby. But you smelt powder—didn't you, Cap'n?"

"Stand by to go about," the parrot would scream.

"Ah, she's a handsome craft, she is," the cook would say, and give her sugar from his pocket, and then the bird would peck at the bars and swear straight on, passing belief for wickedness.

"There," John would add, "you can't touch pitch and not be mucked, lad. Here's this poor old innocent bird o'mine swearing blue fire, and none the wiser, you may lay to that. She would swear the same, in a manner of speaking, before chaplain." And John would touch his forelock with a solemn way he had, that made me think he was the best of men.

In the meantime, the squire and Captain Smollett were still on pretty distant terms with one another. The squire made no bones about the matter; he despised the captain. The captain, on his part, never spoke but when he was spoken to, and then sharp and short and dry, and not a word wasted. He owned, when driven into a corner, that he seemed to have been wrong about the crew, that some of them were as brisk as he wanted to see, and all had behaved fairly well. As for the ship, he had taken a downright fancy to her. "She'll lie a point nearer the wind than a man has a right to expect of his own married wife, sir. But," he would add, "all I say is we're not home again, and I don't like the cruise."

The squire, at this, would turn away and march up and down the deck, chin in air.

"A trifle more of that man," he would say, "and I shall explode."

We had some heavy weather, which only proved the qualities of the *Hispaniola.* Every man on board seemed well content, and they must have been hard to please if they had been otherwise; for it was my belief there was never a ship's company so spoiled since Noah put to sea. Double grog was going on the least excuse; there was duff on odd days, as, for instance, if the squire heard it was any man's birthday; and always a barrel of apples for any one to help himself that had a fancy.

"Never knew good come of it yet," the captain said to Dr. Livesey. "Spoil fo'c'sle hands, make devils. That's my belief."

But good did come of the apple barrel, as you shall hear; for if it had not been for that, we should have had no note of warning, and might all have perished by the hand of treachery.

This was how it came about:

We had run up the trades to get the wind of the island we were after—I am not allowed to be more plain—and now we were running down for it with a bright lookout day and night. It was about the last day of our outward voyage, by the largest computation. Some time that night, or, at latest, before noon of the morrow, we should sight the Treasure Island. We were heading S.S.W., and had a steady breeze abeam and a quiet sea. The *Hispaniola* rolled steadily, dipping her bowsprit now and then with a whiff of spray. All was drawing alow and aloft; everyone was in the bravest spirits, because we were now so near an end of the first part of our adventure.

Now, just after sundown, when all my work was over and I was on my way to my berth, it occurred to me that I should like an apple. I ran on deck. The watch was all forward looking out for the island. The man at the helm was watching the luff of the sail, and whistling away gently to himself; and that was the only sound excepting the swish of the sea against the bows and around the sides of the ship.

I got bodily into the apple barrel, and found there was scarce an apple left; but, sitting down there in the dark, what with the sound of the waters and the rocking movement of the ship, I had either fallen asleep, or was on the point of doing so when a heavy man sat down with rather a clash close by. The barrel shook as he leaned his shoulders against it, and I was about to jump up when the man began to speak. It was Silver's voice, and, before I had heard a dozen words, I would not have shown myself for all the world, but lay there, trembling and listening, in the extreme of fear and curiosity; for from these dozen words I understood that the lives of all the honest men aboard depended upon me alone.

WHAT I HEARD IN THE APPLE BARREL

"No, not I," said Silver. "Flint was cap'n; I was quartermaster, along of my timber leg. The same broadside I lost my leg, old Pew lost his deadlights. It was a master surgeon, him that ampytated me—out of college and all—Latin by the bucket, and what not; but he was hanged like a dog, and sun-dried like the rest, at Corso Castle. That was Robert's men, that was, and comed of changing names to their ships—*Royal Fortune* and so on. Now, what a ship was christened, so let her stay, I says. So it was with the *Cassandra*, as brought us all safe home from Malabar, after England took the *Viceroy of the Indies*; so it was with the old *Walrus,* Flint's old ship, as I've seen-a-muck with the red blood and fit to sink with gold."

"Ah!" cried another voice, that of the youngest hand on board, and evidently full of admiration, "for he was the flower of the flock, was Flint!"

"Davis was a man, too, by all accounts," said Silver. "I never sailed along of him; first with England, then with Flint, that's my story; and now here on my own account, in a manner of speaking. I laid by nine hundred safe from England, and two thousand after Flint. That ain't bad for a man before the mast—all safe in bank. 'Tain't earning now, it's saving does it, you may lay to that. Where's all England's men now? I dunno. Where's Flint's? Why, most on 'em aboard here. Old Pew, as has lost his sight, spends twelve hundred pound in a year, like a lord in Parliament. Where is he now? Well, he's dead now and under hatches; but for two years before that, shiver my timbers! the man was starving. He begged, and he stole, and he cut throats, and starved at that, by the powers!"

"Well, it ain't much use, after all," said the young seaman.

" 'Tain't much use for fools, you may lay to it—that, nor nothing," cried Silver. "But now, you look here; you're young you are, but you're as smart as paint. I see that when I set my eyes on you, and I'll talk to you like a man."

You may imagine how I felt when I heard this abominable old rogue addressing another in the very same words of flattery as he had used

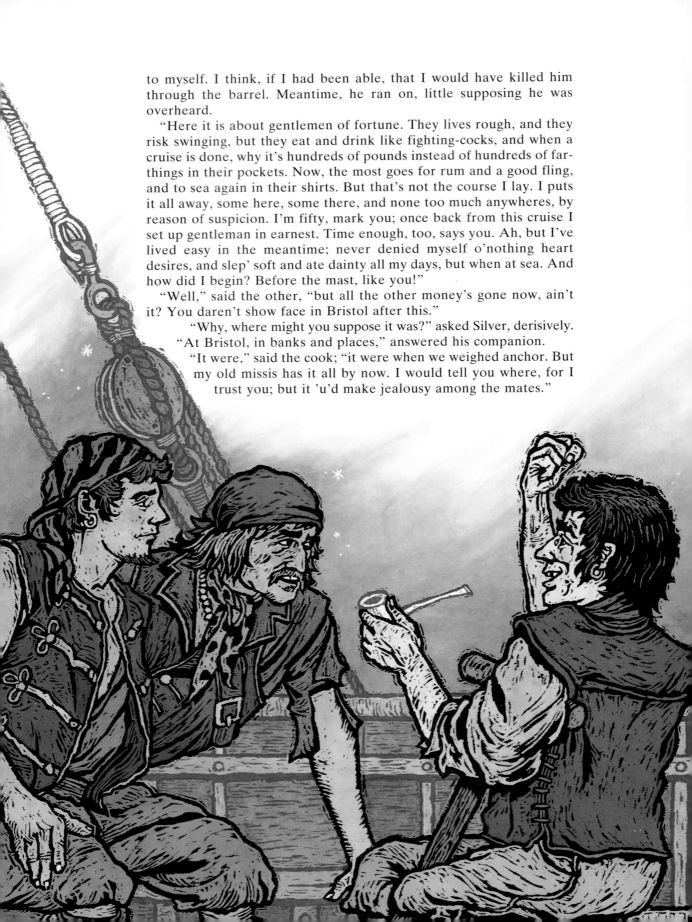

to myself. I think, if I had been able, that I would have killed him through the barrel. Meantime, he ran on, little supposing he was overheard.

"Here it is about gentlemen of fortune. They lives rough, and they risk swinging, but they eat and drink like fighting-cocks, and when a cruise is done, why it's hundreds of pounds instead of hundreds of farthings in their pockets. Now, the most goes for rum and a good fling, and to sea again in their shirts. But that's not the course I lay. I puts it all away, some here, some there, and none too much anywheres, by reason of suspicion. I'm fifty, mark you; once back from this cruise I set up gentleman in earnest. Time enough, too, says you. Ah, but I've lived easy in the meantime; never denied myself o'nothing heart desires, and slep' soft and ate dainty all my days, but when at sea. And how did I begin? Before the mast, like you!"

"Well," said the other, "but all the other money's gone now, ain't it? You daren't show face in Bristol after this."

"Why, where might you suppose it was?" asked Silver, derisively.

"At Bristol, in banks and places," answered his companion.

"It were," said the cook; "it were when we weighed anchor. But my old missis has it all by now. I would tell you where, for I trust you; but it 'u'd make jealousy among the mates."

"And can you trust your missis?" asked the other.

"Gentlemen of fortune," returned the cook, "usually trusts little among themselves, and right they are, you may lay to it. But I have a way with me, I have. When a mate brings a slip on his cable—one as knows me, I mean—it won't be in the same world with Old John. There was some that was feared of Pew, and some that was feared of Flint; but Flint his own self was feared of me. Feared he was, and proud. They was the roughest crew afloat, was Flint's; the devil himself would have been feared to go to sea with them. Well, now, I tell you, I'm not a boasting man, and you seen yourself how easy I keep company; but when I was quartermaster, *lambs* wasn't the word for Flint's old buccaneers. Ah, you may be sure of yourself in old John's ship."

"Well, I tell you now," replied the lad, "I didn't half a quarter like the job till I had this talk with you, John; but there's my hand on it now."

"And a brave lad you are, and smart, too," answered Silver shaking hands so heartily that the barrel shook, "and a finer figurehead for a gentleman of fortune I never clapped my eyes on."

By this time I had begun to understand the meaning of their terms. By a "gentleman of fortune" they plainly meant neither more nor less than a common pirate, and the little scene that I had overheard was the last act in the corruption of one of the honest hands—perhaps of the last one left aboard. But on this point I was soon to be relieved, for, Silver giving a little whistle, a third man strolled up and sat down by the party.

"Dick's square," said Silver.

"Oh, I know'd Dick was square," returned the voice of the coxswain, Israel Hands. "He's no fool, is Dick." And he turned his quid and spat. "But look here," he went on, "here's what I want to know, Barbecue: how long are we a-going to stand off and on? I've had a'most enough o' Cap'n Smollett; he's hazed me long enough, by thunder! I want to go into that cabin, I do. I want their pickles and wines, and that."

"Israel, " said Silver, "your head ain't much account, nor ever was. But you're able to hear, I reckon; leastways, your ears is big enough. Now, here's what I say: you'll berth forward, and you'll live hard, and you'll speak soft, and you'll keep sober, till I give the word; and you may lay to that, my son."

"Well, I don't say no, do I?" growled the coxswain. "What I say is, when? That's all I say."

"When! by the powers!" cried Silver. "Well, now if you want to know, I'll tell you when. The last moment I can manage; and that's when. Here's a first-rate seaman, Cap'n Smollett, sails the blessed ship for us. Here's this squire and doctor with a map and such—I don't know where it is, do I? No more do you, says you. Well then, I mean this squire and doctor shall find the stuff, and help us to get it aboard, by the powers! Then we'll see. If I was sure of you all, sons of double Dutchmen, I'd have Cap'n Smollett navigate us half-way back again before I struck."

"Why, we're all seamen aboard here, I should think!" said the lad Dick.

"We're all fo'c'sle hands, you mean," snapped Silver. "We can steer a course, but who's to set one? That's what all you gentlemen split on, first and last. If I had my way I'd have Cap'n Smollett work us back into the trades at least; then we'd have no blessed miscalculations and a spoonful of water a day. But I know the sort you are. I'll finish with 'em at the island, as soon's the blunt's on board, and a pity it is. But you're never happy till you're drunk. Slit my sides, I've a sick heart to sail with the likes of you!"

"Easy all, Long John," cried Israel. "Who's a-crossin' of you?"

"Why, how many tall ships, think ye, have I seen laid aboard? and how many brisk lads drying in the sun at Execution Dock?" cried Silver, "and all for this same hurry and hurry and hurry. You hear me? I seen a thing or two at sea, I have. If you would on'y lay your course, and a p'int to windward, you would ride in carriages, you would. But not you! I know you. You'll have your mouthful of rum tomorrow, and go hang."

"Everybody know'd you was a kind of chapling, John; but there's others as could hand and steer as well as you," said Israel. "They liked a bit o' fun, they did. They wasn't so high and dry, nohow, but took their fling, like jolly companions every one."

"So?" says Silver. "Well, and where are they now? Pew was that sort, and he died a beggar-man. Flint was, and he died of rum at Savannah. Ah, they was a sweet crew, they was! on'y where are they?"

"But," asked Dick, "when we do lay 'em athwart, what are we to do with 'em, anyhow?"

"There's the man for me!" cried the cook, admiringly. "That's what I call business. Well, what would you think? Put 'em ashore like maroons? Or cut 'em down like that much pork?"

"Billy Bones was the man for that," said Israel. " 'Dead men don't bite,' says he. Well he's dead now hisself; he know the long and short on it now; and if ever a rough hand come to port, it was Billy."

"Right you are," said Silver, "rough and ready. But mark you here: I'm an easy man—I'm quite the gentleman, says you; but this time it's serious. Dooty is dooty, mates. I give my vote—death. When I'm in Parlyment, and riding in my coach, I don't want none of these sealawyers in the cabin a-coming home, unlooked for, like the devil at prayers. Wait is what I say; but when the time comes, why, let her rip!"

"John," cries the coxswain, "you're a man!"

"You'll say so, Israel, when you see," said Silver. "Only one thing I claim—I claim Trelawney. I'll wring his calf's head off his body with these hands. Dick!" he added, breaking off, "you just jump up, like a sweet lad, and get me an apple, to wet my pipe like."

You may fancy the terror I was in! I should have leaped out and run for it, if I had found the strength; but my limbs and heart alike misgave me. I heard Dick begin to rise, and then some one seemingly stopped him, and the voice of Hands exclaimed:

"Oh, stow that! Don't you get sucking of that bilge, John. Let's have a go of the rum."

"Dick," said Silver, "I trust you. I've a gauge on the keg, mind. There's the key; you fill a pannikin and bring it up."

Terrified as I was, I could not help thinking to myself that this must have been how Mr. Arrow got the strong waters that destroyed him.

Dick was gone but a little while, and during his absence Israel spoke in the cook's ear. It was but a word or two that I could catch, and yet I gathered some important news, for, besides other scraps that tended to the same purpose, this whole clause was audible: "Not another man of them 'll jine." Hence there were still faithful men on board.

When Dick returned, one after another of the trio took the pannikin and drank—one "To luck"; another with a "Here's to old Flint"; and Silver himself saying, in a kind of song, "Here's to ourselves!"

Just then a sort of brightness fell upon me in the barrel and, looking up, I found the moon had risen, and was silvering the mizzen-top and shining white on the luff of the foresail; and almost at the same time the voice of the outlook shouted "Land ho!"

COUNCIL OF WAR

There was a great rush of feet across the deck. I could hear people tumbling up from the cabin and the fo'c'sle; and, slipping in an instant outside my barrel, I dived behind the foresail, made a double toward the stern, and came out upon the open deck in time to join Hunter and Dr. Livesey in the rush for the weather bow.

There all hands were already congregated. A belt of fog had lifted almost simultaneously with the appearance of the moon. Away to the southwest of us we saw two low hills, about a couple of miles apart, and rising behind one of them a third and higher hill, whose peak was still buried in the fog. All three seemed sharp and conical in figure.

So much I saw, almost in a dream, for I had not yet recovered from my horrid fear of a minute or two before, and then I heard the voice of Captain Smollett issuing orders. The *Hispaniola* was laid a couple of points nearer the wind, and now sailed a course that would just clear the island on the east.

"And now, men," said the captain, when all was sheeted home, "has any one of you ever seen that land ahead?"

"I have, sir," said Silver. "I've watered there with a trader I was cook in."

"The anchorage is on the south, behind an islet, I fancy?" asked the captain.

"Yes, sir; Skeleton Island they calls it. It were a main place for pirates once, and a hand we had on board knowed all their names for it. That hill to the nor'ard they calls the Fore-mast Hill; there are three hills in a row running south'ard—fore, main, and mizzen, sir. But the main—that's the big 'un with the cloud on it—they usually calls the Spy-glass, by reason of a lookout they kept when they was in the anchorage cleaning; for it's there they cleaned their ships, sir, asking your pardon."

"I have a chart here," says Captain Smollett. "See if that's the place."

Long John's eyes burned in his head as he took the chart; but, by the fresh look of the paper, I knew he was doomed to disappointment. This was not the map we had found in Billy Bones's chest, but an accurate copy, complete in all things—names and heights and soundings—with the single exception of the red crosses and the written notes. Sharp as must have been his annoyance, Silver had the strength of mind to hide it.

"Yes sir," said he, "this is the spot, to be sure; and very prettily drawn out. Who might have done that, I wonder? The pirates were too ignorant, I reckon. Ay, here it is: 'Capt. Kidd's Anchorage'—just the name my shipmate called it. There's a strong current runs along the south, and then away nor'ard up the west coast. Right you was, sir," says he, "to haul your wind and keep the weather of the island. Leastways, if such was your intention as to enter and careen, and there ain't no better place for that in these waters."

"Thank you, my man," says Captain Smollett. "I'll ask you, later on, to give us a help. You may go."

I was surprised at the coolness with which John avowed his knowledge of the island; and I own I was half frightened when I saw him drawing nearer to myself. He did not know, to be sure, that I had overheard his council from the apple barrel, and yet I had, by this time, taken such a horror of his cruelty, duplicity, and power, that I could scarce conceal a shudder when he laid his hand upon my arm.

"Ah," says he, "this here is a sweet spot, this island—a sweet spot for a lad to get ashore on. You'll bathe, and you'll climb trees, and you'll hunt goats, you will; and you'll get aloft on them hills like a goat yourself. Why, it makes me young again. I was going to forget my timber leg, I was. It's a pleasant thing to be young, and have ten toes, and you may lay to that. When you want to go a bit of exploring, you just ask old John, and he'll put up a snack for you to take along."

And clapping me in the friendliest way upon the shoulder, he hobbled off forward, and went below.

Captain Smollett, the squire, and Dr. Livesey were talking together on the quarter-deck, and, anxious as I was to tell them my story, I dared not interrupt them openly. While I was still casting about in my thoughts to find some probable excuse, Dr. Livesey called me to his side. He had left his pipe below, and being a slave to tobacco, had meant that I should fetch it; but as soon as I was near enough to speak and not be overheard, I broke out immediately:—"Doctor, let me speak. Get the captain and squire down to the cabin, and then make some pretense to send for me. I have terrible news."

The doctor changed countenance a little, but next moment he was master of himself.

"Thank you, Jim," said he, quite loudly, "that was all I wanted to know," as if he had asked me a question.

And with that he turned on his heel and rejoined the other two. They spoke together for a little, and though none of them started, or raised his voice, or so much as whistled, it was plain enough that Dr. Livesey had communicated my request; for the next thing that I heard was the captain giving an order to Job Anderson, and all hands were piped on deck.

"My lads," said Captain Smollett, "I've a word to say to you. This land that we have sighted is the place we have been sailing for. Mr. Trelawney, being a very open-handed gentleman, as we all know, has just asked me a word or two, and as I was able to tell him that every man on board had done his duty, alow and aloft, as I never ask to see it done better, why, he and I and the doctor are going below to the cabin to drink your health and luck, and you'll have grog served out for you to drink our health and luck. I'll tell you what I think of this: I think it handsome. And if you think as I do, you'll give a good sea cheer for the gentleman that does it."

The cheer followed—that was a matter of course; but it rang out so full and hearty that I confess I could hardly believe these same men were plotting for our blood.

"One more cheer for Cap'n Smollett," cried Long John, when the first had subsided.

And this also was given with a will.

On the top of that the three gentlemen went below, and not long after, word was sent forward that Jim Hawkins was wanted in the cabin.

I found them all three seated round the table, the doctor smoking away, with his wig on his lap, and that I knew was a sign that he was agitated. The stern window was open, for it was a warm night, and you could see the moon shining behind on the ship's wake.

"Now, Hawkins," said the squire, "you have something to say. Speak up."

I did as I was bid, and as short as I could make it, told the whole details of Silver's conversation. Nobody interrupted me till I was done, nor did any one of the three of them make so much as a movement, but they kept their eyes on my face from first to last.

"Jim," said Dr. Livesey, "take a seat." And they made me sit down at the table beside them, and all three, one after the other, and each with a bow, drank to my good health, and their service to me, for my luck and courage.

"Now, captain," said the squire, "you were right, and I was wrong. I own myself an ass, and I awaits your orders."

"No more an ass than I, sir," returned the captain. "I never heard of a crew that meant to mutiny but what showed signs before, for any man that had an eye in his head to see the mischief and take steps according. But this crew," he added, "beats me."

"Captain," said the doctor, "with your permission, that's Silver. A very remarkable man."

"He'd look remarkably well from a yard-arm sir," returned the captain. "But this is talk; this don't lead to anything. I see three or four points, and with Mr. Trelawney's permission, I'll name them."

"You sir, are the captain. It is for you to speak," says Mr. Trelawney, grandly.

"First point," began Mr. Smollett. "We must go on, because we can't turn back. If I gave the word to go about, they would rise at once. Second point, we have time before us—at least, until this treasure's found. Third point, there are faithful hands. Now sir, it's got to come to blows sooner or later; and what I propose is, to take time by the forelocks, as the saying is, and come to blows some fine day when they least expect it."

"Jim, here," said the doctor, "can help us more than anyone. The men are not shy with him, and Jim is a noticing lad."

"Hawkins, I put prodigious faith in you," added the squire.

I began to feel pretty desperate at this, for I felt altogether helpless; and yet, by an odd train of circumstances, it was indeed through me that safety came. In the meantime, talk as we pleased, there were only seven out of the twenty-six on whom we knew we could rely; and out of these seven one was a boy, so that the grown men on our side were six to their nineteen.

GLOSSARY

abeam—at right angles to a ship's keel. The keel runs from the front to the back and forms a sort of backbone for the ship.

bilge—water that collects in the lowest part of a ship.

boatswain—a low-ranking officer on a ship.

bowsprit—a spar, or pole, extending forward from the front of the ship.

broadside—a burst of fire from all the guns along the side of a warship.

bulkhead—a partition separating compartments aboard ship.

capstan-bars—the handles of a device used to raise a ship's anchor.

careen—to lean a ship to the side, so that the hull can be cleaned and repaired.

coxswain—a sailor who is in charge of a ship's boat and its crew.

deadlights—a ship's windows. Silver uses the term to refer to Pew's sight.

duff—a pudding.

fo'c'sle—a ship's forecastle, the area in the front, or bow, where sailors bunked.

haul—to change course and sail closer to the direction from which the wind blows.

lanyard—a cord or rope.

luff—the forward side of a sail.

mizzen-top—the top sail on the mizzen-mast, which is the third mast from the front on ships with three or more masts.

pannikin—a small saucepan or cup.

pieces of eight—old Spanish silver coins.

quartermaster—on a ship, a low-ranking officer responsible for navigation.

sheet—one of the ropes attached to the corners of sails and used to position them.

trades—the trade winds, which are winds that blow in the tropics and were used by sailing vessels on long trading voyages.

You will have to read the rest of the book to find out what happens!

POETRY

THE KITE

My kite is three feet broad, and six feet long;
The standard straight, the bender tough and strong,
And to its milk-white breast five painted stars belong.

Grand and majestic soars my paper kite,
Through trackless skies it takes its lofty flight:
Nor lark nor eagle flies to such a noble height.

As in the field I stand and hold the twine,
Swift to unwind, to give it length of line,
Yet swifter it ascends, nor will to earth incline.

Like a small speck, so high I see it sail,
I hear its pinions flutter in the gale,
And, like a flock of wild geese, sweeps its flowing tail.

ADELAIDE O'KEEFE (1776–1855)

DEEP REFLECTION

Patiently fishing in the lake, the crane's
Long red legs have shortened since the rains.

BASHÔ (1644–1695)

THE TEAPOT DRAGON

There's a dragon on our teapot,
  With a long and crinkly tail,
His claws are like a pincer-bug,
  His wings are like a sail;

His tongue is always sticking out,
  And so I used to think
He must be very hungry, or
  He wanted tea to drink.

But once when Mother wasn't round
  I dipped my fingers in,
And when I pulled them out I found
  I'd blistered all the skin.

Now when I see the dragon crawl
  Around our china pot,
I know he's burned his tongue because
  The water is so hot.

RUPERT SARGENT HOLLAND (1878-1952)

A GUINEA-PIG SONG

There was a little guinea-pig,
Who, being little, was not big;
He always walked upon his feet,
And never fasted when he eat.

When from a place he run away
He never at the place did stay;
And while he run, as I am told,
He ne'er stood still for young or old.

He often squeaked, and sometimes violent,
And when he squeaked he ne'er was silent.
Though ne'er instructed by a cat,
He knew a mouse was not a rat.

One day as I am certified,
He took a whim and fairly died;
And as I am told by men of sense,
He never has been living since.

ANONYMOUS (1773)

SUNSET

The summer sun is sinking low;
   Only the tree-tops redden and glow;
Only the weather-cock on the spire
   Of the village church is a flame of fire;
All is in shadow below.

HENRY WADSWORTH LONGFELLOW (1807–1882)

HOW TO WRITE A LETTER

Maria intended a letter to write,
But could not begin (as she thought) to indite;
So went to her mother with pencil and slate,
Containing "Dear Sister," and also a date,

"With nothing to say, my dear girl, do not think
Of wasting your time over paper and ink;
But certainly this is an excellent way,
To try with your slate to find something to say.

"I will give you a rule," said her mother, "my dear,
Just think for a moment your sister is here,
And what would you tell her? Consider, and then,
Though silent your tongue, you can speak with your pen."

ELIZABETH TURNER (1775?-1846)

cinated by snow—something Vermont has plenty of. And when he was 17, he got a camera with its own microscope and began to photograph snowflakes. The project became his life's work, and he became world famous as an expert on snow. It was Bentley who discovered that no two snowflakes are exactly alike. Azarian, a Vermont artist, used woodcuts to bring his little-known story to life. The book won the 1999 Caldecott Medal, awarded each year to the best American picture book for children.

A wild mixture of fantasy, real life, humor, and adventure made Louis Sachar's novel *Holes* a hit with older readers. The hero of this tale is Stanley Yelnats (that's Stanley spelled backward), a boy who's convicted of a crime he didn't commit. He's packed off to a detention center with an unlikely name—Camp Green Lake. There's nothing green at this dismal place, and the lake dried up years

LOOKING AT BOOKS

From nursery rhymes to a novel set in a village in Peru, young readers had plenty to choose from in 1999.

AWARD-WINNING BOOKS

You've probably heard that no two snowflakes are the same, but do you know how that fact became known? Find out in *Snowflake Bentley,* an unusual and beautiful picture book written by Jacqueline Briggs Martin and illustrated by Mary Azarian. Set in Vermont in the late 1800's, the book tells the true story of Wilson Bentley. Even as a boy, Bentley was fas-

before. The camp's evil warden, who paints her nails with rattlesnake venom, puts the inmates to work digging holes all over the dry lake bed. When Stanley sets out to find out why, he unlocks secrets of his family's past. The book won the 1999 Newbery Medal as the most distinguished work of American literature for young people.

Everyone has a favorite nursery rhyme, and lots of those favorites are included in Kady MacDonald Denton's *A Child's Treasury of Nursery Rhymes*. Along with familiar rhymes, there are less well-known rhymes from the Caribbean region, Africa, and other parts of the world. There are songs, poems, and riddles, too—100 selections in all. Denton's colorful pictures brought the book Canada's Governor General's Literary Award for best illustration in an English-language children's book.

During the American Revolution, many Loyalists—British colonists who remained loyal to the King of England—headed north into Canada. *The Hollow Tree,* by Janet Lunn, is set in that exciting time. The heroine is 15-year-old Phoebe Olcott, who sets off into the wilderness to carry a message to Canada. This historical novel won Canada's Governor General's Literary Award for English-language text.

PICTURE BOOKS

The year 2000 marks the end of a millennium—a thousand years. In *Turn of the Century,* Ellen Jackson takes readers on a whirlwind tour of the millennium, stopping off at the start of each century from the year 1000 to today. Illustrations by Jan Davey Ellis show how children lived in each century, peering into their homes to show them at work and play.

All kids dream about the things they'll do when they grow up. George Ella Lyon, the author of *A Sign,* was no exception. In this clever book, she recalls her dreams—to make neon signs, thrill crowds as a circus tightrope walker, travel through space to the moon. Instead, she grew up to be a writer. But somehow, each of those dreams stayed alive, help-

A Sign

ing her in her work. Chris K. Soentpiet's watercolor illustrations re-create the small town where Lyon grew up in the 1950's and 1960's.

A chimp can dream, too. At least, that's the idea behind *Willy the Dreamer,* a picture book by Anthony Browne. Willy, a young chimpanzee, dozes off in a comfortable chair. His wild and wonderful dreams fill the pages of the book. He's a film star, a singer, a sumo wrestler, a ballet dancer. He tries to run, but his feet are stuck to the ground. He's as big as a giant, and as small as a mouse. In Browne's clever illustrations, bananas turn up in the most unlikely places. And many of the pictures are filled with comic references to famous works of art and literature.

Turtle Spring, by Deborah Turney Zagwÿn, links nature and the seasons to changes in family life. When a new baby brother enters her family, Clee feels left out. Then her uncle gives her a gift—a turtle. She keeps her pet in a sandbox in her yard, but when fall's cold weather comes she finds her turtle cold and still. Believing that the turtle is dead, she sadly buries it in the compost pile. Winter passes slowly. By the time spring rolls around, Clee has learned to love her baby brother. Then, to her surprise and delight, her turtle crawls out of the compost pile. It wasn't dead after all—just hibernating.

Willy the Dreamer

"Once upon a time there was an old woman who lived under a wave." That's the beginning of *The Old Woman and the Wave,* a picture book by Shelley Jackson. A huge wave hangs curled over the old woman's cottage for years, never falling. She sees it as a huge, wet pest, and she covers her house with umbrellas to ward off its constant dripping. Then Bones, her dog, swims to the top of the giant wave and won't come back. The old woman jumps into a washbasin boat and paddles after him— and discovers the wave's true

Turtle Spring

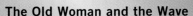
purpose. Jackson's collage illustrations are filled with details that add extra meaning to the story.

The photographs in Walter Wick's *Optical Tricks* show old-fashioned toys and other objects, and at first glance many of them seem ordinary. But look again—there's something weird about each picture. For example, the "optical trick" shown below looks like a bunch of puzzle pieces. But if you turn the picture

upside down, what do you see? The game in this book is to figure out how the photographer created the optical illusions.

MIDDLE AND OLDER READERS

Three Harry Potter books *(Harry Potter and the Sorcerer's Stone, Harry Potter and the Chamber of Secrets,* and *Harry Potter and the Prisoner of Azkaban)* were some of the most popular children's books in years—so popular that they appeared on adult best-seller lists! Harry Potter, the hero of these fantasies by J. K. Rowling, is an orphan raised by a vile aunt and uncle. But when he is accepted at Hogwart's School of Witchcraft and Wizardry, Harry learns that he has magical powers. And soon he's up to his chin in a mystery that involves his parents' death and an evil wizard named Voldemort.

Legendary adventure is at the heart of Nancy Springer's *I Am Mordred: A Tale from Camelot.* This novel retells the story of King Arthur from an unusual viewpoint. The narrator is Mordred, the son of Arthur who, it's prophesied, will kill the king. In most versions of the legend, Mordred is a complete villain. But in this retelling he seems almost likable as he struggles to avoid fulfilling the dark prophecy.

Joan Abelove's *Go and Come Back* is another novel with an unusual point of view. It's set in a remote village deep in the Amazon jungles of Peru; and the story is narrated by Alicia, a teenager who lives in the village. When two white anthropologists arrive, Alicia and the other villagers are mystified by their strange ways. Abelove, an anthropologist who has worked in this region, uses the story to show the sharp contrast between two cultures.

Optical Tricks

Following the Light

In 1874, a group of struggling young artists organized a joint exhibition in an upstairs studio at 35 Boulevard des Capucines in Paris. The group called itself the Anonymous Society of Artists, Painters, Sculptors, Engravers, Etc. Its 30 members included Claude Monet, Auguste Renoir, Edgar Degas, Paul Cézanne, Camille Pissarro, Alfred Sisley, and other now-famous names.

For the poor, little-known artists of the Anonymous Society, the 1874 exhibition proved to be a major disappointment. Few people attended, and some laughed out loud at what they saw. Only a handful of paintings were sold, and the prices were meager. Worst of all, the most respected art critics of Paris wrote scathing reviews of the show, mocking the paintings and harshly attacking the artists. The members of the Society closed up the exhibit and went back to their easels. Although they organized other shows in subsequent years, they continued to work in relative poverty and obscurity. It would be another decade or more before any of them gained acceptance with the art world or the general public.

Today, Monet, Renoir, Degas, Cézanne, Pissarro, Sisley, and the others stand out as giants in the history of art. Together they are referred to as the Impressionists. And their paintings are as loved, as richly valued, and as familiar as any in the world—scenes of the streets and cafés of 19th-century Paris, sailboats on the Seine, the woods at Fontainebleau, lily ponds and poppy fields, ballet classes and horse races, drinkers, bathers, boaters, and mademoiselles in fancy hats.

The hundreds of canvases painted by the Impressionists in the latter half of the 1800's now hang in the great museums of the world.

Reproductions decorate living rooms everywhere. Fine art books devoted to the group—with magnificent color plates that many people frame—are constantly being published. And when an original canvas from a private collection is auctioned, the bids often reach millions of dollars.

People's great appreciation of the beauty of Impressionist paintings was clearly evident in 1999—the 125th anniversary of the Anonymous Society's 1874 exhibition. At a May sale at Sotheby's, the famous New York City auction house, Cézanne's *Still Life With Curtain, Pitcher and Bowl of Fruit* (1893–94) fetched $60 million—setting a record for the artist. And in July, at another Sotheby's auction, Degas' pastel painting of a ballerina, *Dancer in Repose* (1879), brought $28 million—setting a record for that artist.

The Impressionists of the Anonymous Society would probably never have believed it if they had been told that their paintings would one day be worth millions of dollars. It wasn't that they didn't take their work seriously; it was that nobody else took it seriously. It wasn't that they didn't make enormous sacrifices for their art; it was that their sacrifices never brought the rewards of money or recognition. And it wasn't that their paintings weren't unique or original; it was that the paintings were *too* unique and original. Nobody had seen anything like them before.

In the middle of the 19th-century, the paintings considered "respectable" in French art circles were traditional, highly realistic scenes, often from the Bible or classical mythology. Portraits were always elegant and dignified. Still lifes were precise, detailed, photolike renderings. The works were often skillfully executed, but typically they were heavy, somber, and lacking in imagination and creativity. To preserve the traditional style, the powerful Academy of Fine Arts refused to recognize any artist who didn't conform to established standards. If artists were to be successful, they would have to be selected for official Salon showings—regularly held exhibitions governed by the Academy. Any artist with a different vision was considered unworthy and stood little chance of success.

And so, in the staid, placid world of 19th-century art, the so-called Impressionists were nothing less than revolutionaries. They didn't fight with guns or bombs: Their weapons were paints, brushes, canvases, and a complete commitment to a new, freer style of painting. They found their subject matter in the "open air" of forests, rivers, and village lanes. Turning away from classical themes and formal portraits of the wealthy, they painted ordinary people in everyday settings—mingling in the streets and cafés of Paris, on picnics, in dance halls, at the

Edgar Degas' *Ballerina on Stage*. Impressionist paintings like this one—showing life and nature in an everchanging light—are worth millions of dollars today.

races. They abandoned the dark, dry, timeworn traditions and brought to the canvas a bright, colorful, new *feeling* for the world around them. In swarms of exuberant brushstrokes, each shimmering with color, they depicted life and nature in an everchanging light. They were fascinated by light—how it enhances images, how it creates moods, how it changes from minute to minute. They studied it, they found inspiration in it, and they struggled to recreate its special qualities on canvas. Against all convention and authority, they truly followed their "own light."

Each of the Impressionist painters had his or her own style and technique. Monet's paintings were different from Renoir's, Degas', Pissarro's, and Manet's. Perhaps what they had most in common was their strong friendship, their love of painting, and their struggle against the rules, expectations, and strict formality of the established art community. Ridiculed and rejected for more than two decades, they stuck together and continued to follow the light. At times in the 1860's and 1870's, they had little to eat and not enough money even to buy paints. Renoir took bread from his parents' table to feed a starving Monet. Renoir wasn't much better off, unable to answer letters because he couldn't afford postage.

The story that follows is a fictionalized re-creation of how these artists struggled for recognition and a steady livelihood. It's set in and around Paris in 1873–74. There, the group continued to paint—often together—in such places as Argenteuil, a scenic town on the banks of the Seine. As they had for nearly ten years, they also met frequently at the Café Guerbois, a small café in the Montmartre section of Paris. It was where they gathered to discuss their art and plan their strategies. It was there, most likely, that they first discussed the idea of a joint exhibition. The story tells of how they organized the first show in 1874; of how the public reacted; of how one mocking critic gave them the name "Impressionists," and of how they clung to a brighter vision.

The glassy, gently rippling surface of the river mirrored a cloud-puffy late-afternoon sky and a blaze of orange, red, and yellow foliage from the tree-lined shores. The point where the water ended and the trees began was lost in glimmering splashes of color that spread from both banks, leaving only a slim channel of blue at midstream. Ahead in the distance, through a parting of the trees, the town of Argenteuil rose up from the water and into the sky, a single church spire and the shimmering outlines of airy, whitewashed houses.

On the deck of a small boat, moored to two wooden poles embedded in the river, Claude Monet stepped back from his easel, scanned the view downstream, looked back again at the easel, and pulled on his thick black beard in frustration. The boat was a kind of floating studio, fitted with a small hut to store his painting materials and, if necessary, to sleep in. The boat-studio gave him a wider choice of river views than he could obtain from

the shore. At midstream he could capture a long perspective and the full depth of color reflection. Since he had settled in Argenteuil three months earlier, Monet had indulged his fascination with water in dozens of paintings of the Seine.

"The devil of it is that the light changes so quickly!" he thought.

As he dabbed the canvas with the last touches of magenta, a voice echoed across the water.

"Claude! Claude! Come quickly! Durand-Ruel! A letter!"

At the edge of the river, against the background of trees, stood Auguste Renoir, waving a white envelope high over his head. A thrill shot up Monet's spine as he made out Renoir's words. Paul Durand-Ruel was an art dealer who had set up a gallery in London and had been buying some of the canvases by Monet, Renoir, and the others. In the last two years, Monet had achieved a

modest prosperity and finally could support his wife and young son. Durand-Ruel was a godsend.

Monet quickly packed up his materials, stowed them in the hut, and poled to shore.

"How goes it?" he said cheerily as he secured the boat.

"Not at all bad," said the thin, angular Renoir. "It will prove interesting again to compare how you and I have painted the same scene from our different perspectives. But first," he said, handing Monet the letter, "see what news from Durand-Ruel."

Monet tore open the envelope and began ro read. As his dark, deep-set eyes flitted across the page, his expression of excitement and anticipation changed gradually to one of disappointment. When he came to the bottom of the page, he let out a deep sigh and looked toward the sky. The bright pink-white clouds were rapidly fading to dull steel gray.

"Well," he said finally, pulling on his beard, "already our modest success is proving short-lived. Paul has sold nothing in six weeks. Nothing! Collectors are abandoning him and calling him a crook for passing off our work as art. He is in great debt and plans to close the gallery."

Renoir said nothing. He was stunned. Monet sat on a rock and stared at the ground.

"Well that settles it," said Monet after a long silence. "We cannot go back to the way it was before. We have made too many sacrifices already. Painting is all I know, and I will not do it any other way. We must organize a show. Me, you, Manet, Degas, Cézanne, Sisley, Morisot. Everyone. Forget the Salon! Forget the bourgeois collectors! We will leave it up to the public. And if they don't like it, we will have more shows and more shows until they do!"

"But where will the money come from?" asked Renoir, downcast. "A formal exhibition is very expensive, my friend."

"We will work things out," shot back Monet. "For every painting that is sold, a small percentage will go toward our expenses. Certainly we will sell *some* paintings."

"And if we don't?" replied the gloomy Renoir.

"What's the matter, Auguste? You're the one who always says *I'm* a pessimist! I tell you what. We'll make a bet right now. I'll wager that at least 10,000 people attend the show, and that the sale of paintings will fetch at least 50,000 francs. If neither of those things comes true, I shall take out a full-page ad in the newspaper declaring you the artistic genius of our time. If they do come true, however, you must declare the same of me, in like fashion. A deal?"

"Very well," laughed Renoir. "A deal."

"Very well, then," said Monet, standing up. "Now let's go. My wife is no doubt waiting with a nice supper. Let us at least enjoy our 'riches' while we can. Then tomorrow we can return to Paris and speak with the others."

As the sun dropped slowly behind the trees and the river was cast in shadow, the two artists walked side by side along the water's edge, talking and laughing, toward town.

. . . . .

At 11 Grande rue des Batignolles, a narrow cobblestone street on the hill of Montmartre overlooking Paris, a small crowd gathered in the back room of the Café Guerbois. A single gas lamp in the middle of the ceiling bathed the room in a dull yellow light that flickered each time the door opened and closed. The thin wooden floor creaked and sagged as each person entered, the room gradually filled with smoke, and glasses of ale and absinthe soon covered the long wooden tables.

At the head of one of the tables, surrounded by six or seven other men, Édouard Manet was engaged in his usual animated conversation. Like several of the others, he wore a formal waistcoat, a neatly tied silk cravat, and a full beard. Yet a receding hairline and flecks of gray, along with a supremely self-assured manner, distinguished Manet as the senior figure in the group.

"I still insist open air painting is a mistake," he said. "I share your fascination with light and color, but we must not abandon the masters altogether. Form and composition should always be the key elements."

Paul Cézanne, who was a little stoop-shouldered and had a slight nervous shudder, was the first to respond. Monet had wanted to jump in, but he let Cézanne say his piece.

"Pictures painted in the studio will never be as good as ones done outside," he argued. "Natural light creates contrasts and shadows that *define* form and composition."

Edgar Degas, whose arched eyebrows and high forehead gave him an air of shrewdness, was about to enter the discussion when Monet finally interrupted.

"Excuse me, gentlemen," he said firmly, "but this is a point we have been arguing over for many years. I think we know where everybody stands on the question, and there is a more urgent matter to discuss tonight. Gather round everyone."

When the ten or twelve other artists had found places at the table, Monet, wearing his usual smock and white shirt with frilly cuffs, reported the urgent news. He told of the letter from Durand-Ruel and the dire need for a new source of income.

"We can debate about theory and technique until we are blue in the face," he went on. "We can go to Argenteuil or Louveciennes and paint in the open air, or we can retire to the studio and paint magnificent portraits. As long as we paint in our own way and follow our best instincts, that is what counts. What we can no longer do is cower to the Salon. What we can no longer do is rely on a handful of enlightened dealers. It's high time we take matters into our own hands and appeal directly to the public with a formal group exhibition. This is something we have discussed at various times in the past, but tonight I propose that we give it *serious* consideration. We can collect dues from each artist. We can charge an admission fee from the public. We can each donate a percentage of the paintings we sell. The details can be worked out, but we must make our plans . . . and at once!"

After a brief silence, Camille Pissarro, one of the most respected and best-liked members of the group, spoke up in favor of Monet's proposal. Alfred Sisley, the son of a wealthy English businessman but a longtime member of the Paris circle, also favored a group show separate from the Salon. Berthe Morisot, the most prominent woman artist in the group, agreed enthusiastically. So did Renoir, of course, along with Degas and most of the others.

Only Manet disagreed. Although he had had several paintings accepted by the Salon, he had become a celebrity with the avant-garde for the scandalous subject matter of his work. Later, when some of his paintings were rejected for another official exhibition, Manet defiantly set up his own pavilion. That made him an instant hero with the group of young artists. He became the acknowledged leader of the group and something of a father figure to the younger painters. Now, however, to the shock of everyone, he refused to take part in the group show.

"The Salon is still the only proper place in which to exhibit," he insisted. "We must not abandon the battle. If we are to vindicate ourselves, we must do it through official channels. If we can do that, we will really have won."

Even as he spoke, Manet could see the disappointment in the eyes of his fellow artists. They felt he was abandoning them—and their cause—for personal glory. In that one brief moment, he suffered a loss of respect that would never be fully recovered. In the weeks and months that followed, it was Monet who emerged as the central figure in the group.

There was total silence as Manet got up from the table and put on his overcoat. The floor creaked as he walked across the room, and the gaslight flickered as the door closed behind him.

The meeting continued. Pissarro, who had some experience as an organizer, made several concrete proposals on how the show should be run. The artists would form a kind of joint stock company, with each member buying a share in small monthly installments. It would be like a society of artists with monthly dues. In addition, one franc would be charged for admission to the show. One-tenth of the income from all art sales would go into the common fund. And a catalog of the exhibit would be sold for 50 centimes per copy.

Most of the group was in accord with Pissarro's proposals, and the details were hammered out over the next several weeks. A formal charter was signed in late December and, after considerable debate, the group agreed to call itself the Anonymous Society of Artists, Painters, Sculptors, Engravers, Etc. All that was left was to find a suitable location for the show, recruit as many participants as possible, and mount the exhibit.

The problem of location was quickly solved when the photographer and balloonist Felix Nadar, a longtime friend of the group, offered to lend his studios. The apartment was located on the second and third floors of a building on the Boulevard des Capucines, right in the heart of Paris. It was a series of large, airy rooms with red-brown walls that got plenty of light. It was perfect for the show.

. . . . .

The opening took place on April 15, 1874, just a few days before the official Salon exhibition. The show was to last one month, with hours from ten to six and—as something new—in the evening from eight to ten. A total of 165 works by 30 artists were on display. Among them were twelve Monets, ten Degas, nine Morisots, six Renoirs, five Pissarros, five Sisleys, and three Cézannes.

On the morning of the opening, Monet and Renoir lingered around the fringes of the studio to count heads and listen to the reactions of the viewers. Several other artists wandered through the gallery posing as ordinary visitors. Still others loitered on the sidewalk below to see who entered.

By noon only 47 tickets had been sold. Things picked up in the afternoon, but a deep disappointment gradually etched itself in the face of each artist.

"I don't understand," whispered Monet to Renoir. "We put up posters all over Paris. The newspapers carried announcements. Why is nobody coming? I've hardly even seen any critics."

Their conversation was suddenly interrupted by a burst of laughter from the next room. The two artists looked at each other and closed their eyes. Monet pulled on his long, thick beard. Then came another burst of laughter.

Monet and Renoir walked slowly into the next room, and they merged into the small group of visitors. On the wall in front of them hung three paintings—Pissarro's *Ploughed Field;* Renoir's *Harvesters;* and Monet's *Boulevard des Capucines,* a street scene painted right from Nadar's window. It was hard to tell which one they were laughing at; maybe it was all three. The women covered their mouths with handkerchiefs. The men held their bellies. They all shook their heads and laughed.

"I think I've figured it out!" shouted one well-dressed gentleman, pounding his cane in mirth. "What they do is load a pistol with tubes of paint and fire at the canvas. Then they sign their names and *voilà,* a masterpiece!"

Monet and Renoir both joined in the laughter to look like part of the group. Like the others, they laughed so hard that tears came to their eyes.

By closing time that night, 175 people had attended the show. The first day was always the heaviest, they all knew, and the numbers were certain to dwindle.

"At this rate," sighed Pissarro, "we shall not even draw 5,000."

"Let's not jump to conclusions," said Monet. "One never knows. Let's see what tomorrow brings. Let's see what the critics say. This is only the beginning!"

Despite his outward optimism, Monet knew full well that the show would be a disaster. So did all the others. It wasn't so much the attendance. That could always pick up if a good word got around. It was the laughter. It was the jokes. And what they dreaded most was the reviews.

The first one appeared in *La Presse* a few days later. Monet read it aloud to the group before the doors opened that morning. "The artists fall into a senseless confusion, completely mad, grotesque, and, fortunately, without precedent in the annals of painting. The excesses indulged in by this school are revolting."

Another one appeared in *La Patrie* a week later. "Looking at the first rough works," it read, "you simply shrug your shoulders. Seeing the second set, you burst out laughing. But with the last ones you finally get angry. And you are sorry you did not give the franc you paid to get in to some poor beggar. You wonder if you are not the victim of some hoax."

Of all the reviews, the most damaging in the minds of Monet and Renoir was a piece in the magazine *Le Charivari* by the critic Louis Leroy. The article was called "Exhibition of the Impressionists," and it was a biting satire based on a visit to the show in the company of an artistic master.

"It was a sorry day when I took it upon myself to go to the first exhibition in the Boulevard des Capucines, accompanied by Monsieur Joseph Vincent," the story began.

As the two men proceed through the gallery, the great master is bewildered, then unnerved, and finally rendered delirious by the "smears," "dribbles," and "swish-swash" of the paintings.

Faced with an especially troublesome work by Monet—a red sun seen through the mist over the water at Le Havre—Vincent asks: "What does the canvas depict? Look at the catalog."

" *Impression, Sunrise*', it is called."

"*Impression*—I was certain of it. I was just telling myself that, since I was impressed, there had to be some impression in it . . . and what freedom, what ease of workmanship! Wallpaper in its embryonic state is more finished than that seascape!"

Monet was deeply hurt by the review, but he said nothing. Renoir, upon finishing it, threw down the magazine and let loose a torrent of anger.

"If they don't like our work, that's one thing," he exploded, "but these critics are mean and vicious. Better they say nothing than take the food out of our mouths! We have been painting the best way we know how and in good faith. Now we have mounted

a show with our last centimes, and the only thing we get out of it is a label! Impressionists! How dare he! Now *everyone* will be calling us Impressionists!''

"That is the least of our problems," ventured Degas, and several others nodded in agreement.

On the night the show closed, May 15, the artists gathered in Nadar's studio to hear the final accounting. Pissarro had been in charge of the bookkeeping, and he read through a brief financial statement. General expenses for the exhibition came to a total of 9,272 francs. Exactly 3,511 francs had been collected in entrance fees. The sale of paintings totaled 3,600 francs, of which 360 francs (10%) was commission. Along with membership dues, catalog sales, and small gifts, the total receipts added up to 10,221 francs. To the amazement of everyone, they had actually come out ahead by 949 francs!

"Perhaps we should think about another show," suggested Monet.

"Perhaps," said Berthe Morisot, "but not right away. I think we all have a desire to get back to our 'impressions.' "

. . . . .

On a bright summer morning near Argenteuil, four tiny sailboats set off from the grassy banks of the Seine. Their gently billowing sails rose up against a cloudless azure sky, and creamy white silhouettes were cast along the placid blue water. A soft, cool breeze wafted across the surface of the river, rippling the reflections of green grass, creamy canvas, and burnt-red boathouses along the shore.

On the opposite bank of the river, under a shady cluster of elms, the three friends stood side by side in front of three easels, working desperately to capture the moment. They painted in quick, short strokes, adding color and detail with deft rapidity, trying to keep up with the shifts in light.

"What sublime agony!" declared Monet, finally setting down his brush. "It is wonderful to be painting again, but the devil of it is that the light changes so quickly!"

"Ah, yes, sublime," said Renoir, admiring his friend's work. "Yet I, for one, do not agonize. It is a magnificent scene, and I take sheer joy in painting. What say you, Édouard?"

Manet was still painting furiously, but he paused a moment to look over at Renoir's easel.

"Perhaps you should agonize a little more, my friend," he said with good-natured humor. "Your work might finally begin to improve!"

Renoir couldn't resist a little jab of his own. "But Édouard," he said, "you speak like someone with great experience in painting outdoors. Surely it is nothing the *Salon* has demanded of you."

Manet took no offense, but he put down his brush and answered in a serious tone. "You are quite right, my friend. I must admit there is much to be learned from painting in the open air. I find it a great challenge and, like you, a great joy. I do not know how you persuaded me, but I am glad you did. As for the Salon, I just hope you realize that my motives in not joining your show were honest and heartfelt. I believed then and I believe now that our final vindication must come through official channels, no matter how hard the fight.''

''Well,'' interjected Monet, ''we may disagree about the Salon, but we hold no grudges about your decision. We know your motives are the same as ours. We know you were in good faith, and our friendship is not shaken in the least.''

Renoir nodded in agreement.

''The most important thing,'' Monet went on, ''is that we continue to paint in our own fashion and not give up. Sooner or later we will be taken seriously. The show was a failure and we are no better off than ten years ago, but none of us has any regrets. I got a letter from Pissarro yesterday. He is flat broke, you know, and living with relatives in Brittany. Let me read part of it to you.''

Monet reached into his knapsack and took out the letter.

''What I suffer at the actual moment is terrible,'' wrote Pissarro, ''much more than when I was young, full of enthusiasm and ardor, convinced as I am now of being lost for the future. Nevertheless, it seems to me that I should not hesitate, if I had to start over again, to follow the same path.''

The thought of their friend, so devoted and so talented, in such destitution saddened the three artists—even though they faced similar circumstances.

''A lamp unto his feet and a light unto his path,'' said Manet.

A few moments passed before Monet finally spoke. ''One last thing,'' he said cheerfully, breaking the mood. ''If I were you, Édouard, I would not criticize Renoir so severely. It appears he has a grand future.''

''What on earth do you mean?'' said Manet. Renoir himself looked puzzled.

Monet went to his bag again, this time pulling out a copy of *La Presse*.

''Oh no!'' exclaimed Renoir. ''Not more reviews! Will they never let us alone?''

''A review of sorts,'' said Monet cryptically, thumbing through the paper.

Finally he reached the page. He folded back the paper and held it up for the others to see. In heavy bold letters, covering the entire page, were the words ''AUGUSTE RENOIR, ARTISTIC GENIUS OF OUR TIME.''

Monet winked at Renoir, and Renoir grinned as he remembered their bet.

''So you see,'' said Monet to Manet, ''you should be careful about criticizing our great friend.''

''Perhaps you are right,'' laughed Manet, ''but he is still just an *Impressionist!*''

JEFFREY H. HACKER
Author, *Carl Sandburg*

309

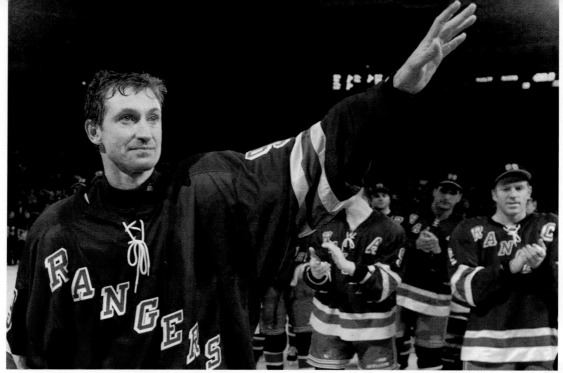

Wayne Gretzky ("The Great One") waves good-bye to hockey fans after playing in his last game on April 18, 1999.

READ ALL ABOUT. . .WAYNE GRETZKY

On April 18, 1999, thousands of hockey fans jammed Madison Square Garden in New York City. The game they watched was between the New York Rangers and the Pittsburgh Penguins, and the Penguins won by a score of 2–1. But that didn't bother the fans at the Garden, or the millions more who watched the game on television. They were there to say good-bye to 38-year-old Ranger hockey star Wayne Gretzky as he played his last game. To them, Gretzky is—and always will be—"The Great One."

And no wonder. In 20 seasons in the National Hockey League (NHL), Gretzky set 61 scoring records, including most regular season points (2,857), goals (894), and assists (1,963). He was voted Most Valuable Player nine times, won the NHL scoring title ten times, and played in eighteen All-Star Games. During the 1980's, he led the Edmonton Oilers to four Stanley Cup championships. And during the 1998–99 season, he scored the 1,072nd goal of his career, including those made in the regular season, in playoff games,

and in one season in the World Hockey Association (WHA). That put him one goal ahead of hockey legend Gordie Howe, Gretzky's boyhood idol.

But The Great One did more than score goals. When he left the Edmonton Oilers and moved to the United States to join the Los Angeles Kings for the 1988–89 season, he single-handedly created an interest in hockey in the southern United States. He showed great artistry—not muscle—on the rink. And he was always humble, always a gentleman, always the perfect role model for young people.

When Gretzky retired, the NHL honored him by retiring his No. 99 sweater. And just two months later, he was voted into the Hockey Hall of Fame, capping a love affair with ice hockey that had begun when he was just a child.

BORN TO THE ICE

About an hour's ride southwest of Toronto, Canada, is the city of Brantford. It was named for the great Mohawk chief Joseph Brant, who settled there in the late 1700's. And a hundred years after that, it was the site of Alexander Graham Bell's first long-distance telephone call. The city has a rich history, indeed. And on January 26, 1961, it was made even richer, when Walter and Phyllis Gretzky welcomed the first of their five children into the world. They named him Wayne.

Wayne Gretzky was only two years old when he first put on ice skates. He learned to skate on a frozen-over river that ran through his grandparents' nearby farm. And when his father built a makeshift hockey rink behind the family house, Wayne skated there. "He couldn't get enough of it," said his father. A

goals in 68 games. It's no wonder that a Canadian sportswriter nicknamed young Wayne "The Great One."

But all wasn't great with The Great One. He scored so easily and so often that some of his teammates—and their parents—accused Gretzky of hogging the puck. This charge upset Gretzky because he was an exceptional passer whose assists were as impressive as his goals. But because of the charges, Gretzky and his father decided it was time for him to move on.

At age 14, Gretzky went to Toronto, where he played with another youth team. After two years in Toronto, he joined the Sault Sainte Marie Greyhounds, where he donned

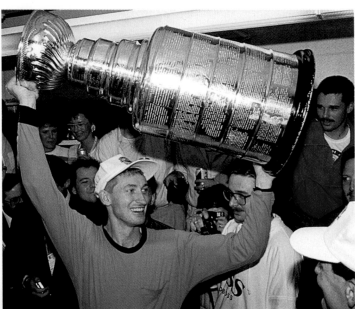

Gretzky was already an impressive hockey player before he was 10 years old. His exceptional skills on the ice helped lead the Edmonton Oilers to four Stanley Cup championships during the 1980's.

former minor-league hockey player, Walter Gretzky began teaching his son the fine points of the sport. He taught him how to handle the stick and how to shoot. And he impressed upon him the need for concentration.

By the time Wayne was 5 years old, he was good enough to compete in organized leagues with kids twice his age. In just his third year in the Peewee leagues, he scored 104 goals in 62 games. And when he was 10, he scored 378

the No. 99 sweater for the first time. The Greyhounds were in the Ontario Junior A Major Hockey Association, a steppingstone for young players like Gretzky who dreamed of playing in the NHL.

TURNING PRO

Gretzky, now 17, didn't make it to the NHL right away. But he did make it to the WHA, as a member of the Indianapolis Racers. That stint

311

After his retirement, Gretzky was honored by the Edmonton Oilers at a ceremony before the start of the NHL's 1999–2000 season. With him are his wife Janet and his children, Trevor, Paulina, and Ty.

lasted just three games before the Racers dealt him to the Edmonton Oilers. And what a first year he had with them! "A player like Gretzky comes along only once every ten years," said Oiler coach Glen Sather. And Gretzky proved him right by winning the WHA Rookie of the Year award, as well as a spot on the WHA All-Star team that took on the famed Russian National Team.

Gretzky continued to astonish fans and players alike during the 1979–80 season, when the Oilers were absorbed into the NHL. In his first NHL season Gretzky, now 18, led the league in assists. He became the youngest NHL player ever to score 50 goals in a season. And he tied for the league lead in points with 137. His heroics on the ice won him the Hart Trophy, as the league's most valuable player, and the Lady Byng Trophy, as the league's most gentlemanly player.

But this was just the beginning for Gretzky—and the Oilers. In 1981–82, he scored 92 goals, shattering the previous season record of 76. And in 1984 he led the Oilers to their first-ever Stanley Cup. The Oilers repeated in 1985, 1987, and 1988. But despite winning four cups in five years, the Oilers were in financial trou-

ble. Gretzky was in great demand by the wealthier American teams, so the owner of the Oilers traded him to the Los Angeles Kings for several younger players and $15 million.

While with the Kings, Gretzky chalked up his tenth Art Ross Trophy, as the NHL's leading scorer. But he was never able to lead them to a Stanley Cup. Nor was he able to do that for the St. Louis Blues, when he played for them in 1996, or for the New York Rangers from 1997 to 1999.

When Gretzky announced his retirement in 1999, he was still averaging almost a point a game. But a neck injury was causing him pain, and his skills weren't what they had been. "I'm done," he said, "It's just time. Of course I'm sad. I've played hockey for 35 years, since I was 3 years old. I'm going to miss it."

And hockey fans will miss him. Who else can score five goals in one game? Who else can score 200 points in a season—no less four seasons? What other hockey player seems to have eyes in the back of his head? The fans surely agree with New York Islander coach Mike Milbury, when he said, "By far Gretzky is the most talented player ever. Every time he gets the puck something exciting happens."

THE NEW BOOK OF KNOWLEDGE
2000

The following articles are from the 2000 edition of
The New Book of Knowledge. They are included
here to help you keep your encyclopedia up to date.

A teacher shares his knowledge with students using both an ancient form of direct communication—speech—and a modern, computer-based form of communication—the Internet.

COMMUNICATION

Communication means sending and receiving information. Every time you wave your hand at someone you recognize in a crowd, talk to a friend on the telephone, mail a picture you have drawn to your grandmother, or send a message to a classmate using a computer, you are communicating. Communication lets people share ideas expressed in gestures, words, images, and other forms.

The word "communicate" comes from the Latin *communicare*, which means "to share" or "to make common." Any kind of communication requires a sender, a recipient, a message (the idea one wants to communicate), and a medium (the method of carrying the message).

For most of human history, the sender and recipient were both people. People sent and received messages that could be directly sensed, or perceived, using their eyes and ears—by speech or by gesture. Such direct communication could take place only at one time and over a short distance.

When people began writing their ideas in words and pictures, messages could be seen at a later time and in a different place from when and where they were first written. As a result, knowledge was no longer limited to what a person could observe directly or find out about from others.

Today, modern communication systems can carry messages over long distances. These systems turn messages that can be directly perceived, such as spoken words, into signals that can be easily sent, such as the electrical signals of telephones. These signals are then turned back into messages that can be perceived at the receiving end.

Humans perceive information mainly through the senses of seeing and hearing. But they may use other senses, too. People who cannot see or hear can learn to communicate by the sense of touch. Sightless people read by touching raised letters with their fingertips. Deaf people communicate in sign language using their hands and fingers.

It is now often the case that the sender or recipient of communication is not a person at all. Computer systems collect weather information, for example, and can "speak" a forecast to someone who calls on a telephone. Scientists on Earth send commands to control space probes exploring distant planets.

Animals are able to communicate, too. However, animals do not use what we would call a language. They communicate by chirping, barking, and making other noises or movements. They can warn each other of danger, call their mates, or express pain and joy. Some animals can communicate by emitting chemicals that can be smelled.

▶ SPEECH AND SONG

We have no way of finding out how speech began. In prehistoric societies, people did not know how to write, so they could not keep records. Somehow they learned to make others understand what their vocal sounds meant, and they learned to put the sounds together into language.

Ancient tribes preserved their history in the form of spoken words and songs. People told stories over and over, so listeners would remember them and tell them to their children. The stories changed in the telling as people forgot some details and exaggerated others. After many retellings, these stories became legends and myths.

For thousands of years, only storytellers and singers preserved these legends. In Europe during the Middle Ages (A.D. 500 to 1500), minstrels did the job that books and newspapers do today. They wandered from one area to another, giving listeners stories and news in the form of songs called ballads.

▶ PICTURES AND WRITING

Stone Age people knew how to make a picture represent an object. Cave dwellers painted pictures of animals on the walls of their caves. So thousands of years later, these people still communicate with us. Their pictures tell us what animals they hunted.

Progressing from drawing to writing as we now know it took several steps. At first, people communicated using simple **pictograms**—drawings of objects that represent the objects themselves. Gradually, the drawings no longer represented the objects but rather ideas associated with the objects. A picture of the sun, for example, might mean "day." These **ideograms**, as they are called, made it

Above: A tribal elder from Africa uses gestures and spoken words to tell a story. In this way, traditional tales have been passed down through generations.

possible to express more complicated messages. An example of early ideogram communication is Egyptian hieroglyphics.

The next step was to invent a written language in which each symbol stood for a single sound instead of a whole word. We call this system an **alphabet**. The word "alphabet" comes from the names of the first two letters of the Greek alphabet, *alpha* and *beta*. The Hebrews and the Phoenicians were the first to use an alphabet. Since the Phoenicians were great sea traders, they needed a simple way of writing to keep their business records. So about 3,000 years ago, they developed a system of 22 symbols, or letters, that stood for the sounds of the consonants in their language. This was much better than using a different picture to mean each word, because they could make any word they wanted from their 22 letters.

The Greeks, Etruscans, and Romans all based their writing on the Hebrew and Phoenician alphabets. The Greeks added symbols that meant vowel sounds. More than 2,000 years ago, the Romans developed the alphabet that we still use in the Western world.

Among the few people in medieval Europe who knew how to read and write were monks living in monasteries. They made copies of books by writing on parchment with pens made from quills (large feathers). These were **manuscript books**. (The word "manuscript" comes from the Latin for "written by hand.") Each book was a work of art. Only the monastery libraries and very rich people could afford these books.

Even after writing had developed, pictures still remained an important means of communication. Because many people were illiterate (unable to read or write), paintings and stained-glass windows in churches told stories from the Bible, while murals and tapestries commemorated battles and other events.

One of the reasons manuscript books were so rare was that it took so much time and skill to make them. Another reason was that there was no inexpensive, lightweight material on which people could write. As early as the A.D. 100's, the Chinese knew how to make paper from silk and from a mixture of tree bark, cloths, and rope fibers. But there was little communication between the Far East and Europe. It took another 600 years for the Arabs to begin making paper. Not until the 1100's was papermaking introduced to Europe, when the Muslims conquered Spain.

▶ PRINTING

By the 700's, the Chinese and Koreans knew how to make copies by **block printing**. Artisans carved pictures or words on blocks of wood. They carved them backward (like

A newspaper rolls off a modern printing press, some 600 years after Johann Gutenberg's invention revolutionized communication and education.

the page you see if you hold a book up to a mirror) so that they would print the right way on pages. Then they coated the surface of the wood with ink, placed sheets of paper over the block, and rubbed it. The Chinese printed entire books that way.

Between 1041 and 1048, Pi Sheng in China invented **movable type**, in which individual letters were assembled to form a page of type for printing. These letters could later be rearranged and reused. However, because the Chinese did not have a small alphabet like that of Western countries, the invention was not the huge success it would become in Europe 400 years later.

In the 1400's, Johann Gutenberg of Germany perfected a practical printing press using movable type and a technique called **letterpress**. He used a wooden handpress, similar to a winepress, to push the type against the paper. He invented molds for casting metal type, special metal alloys for type, and a new kind of oil-based ink. The famous two-volume Gutenberg Bible published in 1456 was his masterpiece. Gutenberg's press signaled the beginning of the age of printing.

Printing revolutionized communication and education. Movable type and letterpress made it possible to print books in large numbers. Many people could own copies of the same book. Ideas began to spread more rapidly. In the late 1800's and early 1900's, powered printing presses and a technique called offset printing allowed books, newspapers, and magazines to be printed faster and less expensively.

In 1938, American Chester Carlson developed another technique, called **xerography** or **photocopying**. His invention allowed anyone to make copies of printed or written documents quickly and easily using machines designed for offices. Today, it is difficult to imagine how modern offices could operate without photocopiers, which have become a handy way to copy printed pages for small groups of people.

In the 1970's, publishers began using computer-controlled **typesetting systems** to print large amounts of information for many people quickly and efficiently. These systems enabled text, and later images, to be entered into computers. Printing plates could then be produced directly without any actual type like Gutenberg's. In the 1980's and 1990's, much smaller and cheaper personal computers and printers became widely available. These systems allow individuals to print professional-looking documents that rival those printed by large publishing companies.

▶ POSTAL SERVICE

In various parts of the ancient world, relay runners carried written or spoken messages over long distances. After people learned to tame horses, post riders were used. Early Persians had developed a relay system of post riders. These riders were stationed at certain places. One would pick up the message and ride off with it to the next.

As long ago as 1000 B.C., King Solomon and the Queen of Sheba exchanged messages attached to carrier pigeons. This kind of pigeon finds its way home after being released. During the French Revolution (1789–99), pigeons carried war news to outlying districts.

Postal service in ancient times was only for very rich or important people. But in the 1500's, English rulers began to see that ordinary people needed to send messages, too. By 1683, the London penny post would deliver a letter anywhere in London for a penny.

Ships began delivering mail across oceans about this time. However, such communication was very slow. When the American colonies began to quarrel with England in the 1760's, it took weeks or months for each side to know how the other side answered the latest argument. Poor communication across the Atlantic Ocean was one of the reasons that the English and Americans could not understand each other's point of view.

After the Revolutionary War (1775–83), American leaders realized the vital importance of communication. Separate states and scattered frontier settlements had to be tied together into a single country. At first, travelers, peddlers, and circuit riders brought news from the East only occasionally to pioneers in the West. Riverboats carried letters and newspapers between towns that sprang up along rivers.

In 1860, Pony Express riders carried messages across the continent in nine to twelve days. They used a relay system not unlike that of the ancient Persians. But the Pony Express lasted only 18 months. In 1861, telegraph wires connected New York and California, enabling a message to be flashed across the country in seconds.

Horse-drawn wagons and early motorized vehicles were used 100 years ago to deliver the mail; mail can now be sent around the world by airplane.

Today, government postal services and private courier companies use trucks and airplanes to carry letters and packages long distances. It is now possible to send a letter to most parts of the world in a day or two.

▶ **SIGNS AND SIGNALS**

Modern means of communication have not entirely replaced a very simple kind: communication by sign or signal. People often communicate without words—by a smile, a shake of the head, a wave of the hand. A driver signals for a turn. The colors of a traffic light tell drivers to slow down, stop, or go. Many signs use shape, color, or symbols rather than words. Ships use signal flags to spell out messages.

Thousands of years before the telegraph was invented, people sent messages by beating out codes on drums or hollow logs. Each beat had a particular meaning. Far away on a hilltop, the next drummer would hear the message, answer it, and pass it on.

In pioneer days, Americans on the frontier some-

Signal flags such as these are a traditional means of nautical communication. Ships use them to spell out messages.

Photography has progressed from this mid-1800's daguerreotype (the first taken in North America) to three-dimensional holograms on today's credit cards.

sender waved a blanket over a fire, making puffs of smoke go up in a certain way to form a message. Someone watching far away could read the puffs and understand the message. The ancient Chinese, Egyptians, Greeks, and Persians all signaled by smoke or fire.

Visual signals can also be sent by light beams. As early as the 400's B.C., the Greeks signaled by reflecting sunlight in a metal mirror. Until recently, ships used blinking lights to send messages to other ships or to shore.

▶ PHOTOGRAPHY

As early as the A.D. 800's, the Chinese and the Arabs had invented ways of forming an image of a scene on a screen. This enabled easier drawing of pictures. In the 1880's, several inventors experimented with ways of recording camera images chemically. The first practical photographic system was developed by a French painter, Louis Daguerre, in 1839. His pictures were called **daguerreotypes**. Early pictures were taken on metal or glass plates coated with chemicals. The photographer had to carry a huge, heavy camera, and much equipment was needed to process these pictures.

In 1889, American George Eastman produced a simple, lightweight camera. Roll film soon replaced glass plates. Photographs could be taken and reproduced in minutes. It became possible to see pictures of people and places all over the world, and eventually pictures from space showing how Earth looks. Rare old manuscripts and paintings could also be photographed so that many people could study and enjoy them.

During the 1890's, American inventor Thomas Edison and others found that by making many photographs in a rapid sequence, they could record moving images. The **motion picture camera** was born. Motion pictures quickly became a major source of entertainment and news (until the 1950's, when television news broadcasts replaced newsreels shown in theaters).

Photographs can also be taken so that each of the viewer's eyes sees a slightly different image. Such photographs create the impression of three dimensions—that is, flat two-

times used guns for signal communication. In a small town, several revolver shots meant a fire alarm. People sent messages by horn blasts, gunshots, or ringing bells.

For centuries, people have used bells to ring out important news. Bells were used to ring the curfew hour (time to be indoors, off the streets) or to announce that the town crier in the city square had something important to tell. Bells still ring in the new year and call people to church or to school. Doorbells signal that someone is at your door.

The sound of a siren tells that a fire truck or an ambulance is coming. In cities, cars stop when they hear the fire siren. During wartime, sirens signal air raids.

Sound signals are fast because sound travels at about 1,100 feet (335 meters) a second. Signals that you see rather than hear are even faster because they travel by light waves. Light moves at about 186,000 miles (300,000 kilometers) a second.

Visual signals can be sent by smoke, as Native Americans once communicated. The

dimensional pictures appear to have the added dimension of depth. In the 1960's, scientists discovered how to use lasers to make three-dimensional images called **holograms**. These are now commonly used on credit cards to make forgeries more difficult.

In the 1990's, small **digital cameras** became available, equipped with devices that convert light into electronic signals. These cameras record images not on film, but on magnetic disks and computer memory cards. Instead of using chemicals to develop film and make prints in a darkroom, a person with a digital camera can simply transfer the images to a computer and make copies of them on a printer. The computer can also be used to change the image in many ways. Colors can be brightened and special visual effects can be added.

▶ AUDIO AND VIDEO RECORDINGS

For over a century we have been able to record the spoken word and other sounds. Thomas Edison invented the first practical phonograph in 1877. The first sounds Edison recorded on a grooved cylinder were the verses of "Mary Had a Little Lamb."

In the 1920's, scientists began to record sounds magnetically on a roll of wire instead of mechanically on disks with grooves. Later they found that **audiotape**—a thin, narrow strip of magnetic tape wound on a reel—worked better. By the 1940's, the first practical tape recorders were developed.

The invention of **videotape** in the 1950's made it possible to record pictures as well as sounds. In the 1980's, the videocassette recorder (VCR) enabled people to record and play back television shows. It also let people rent or buy videocassette versions of movies and watch them at home instead of in theaters. With an added video camera, people could even make their own movies.

In the 1980's, **compact discs**, or CD's, became a popular way of recording music. Compact disc players use lasers to play back the music recorded on the plastic CD's, which are coated with a reflective metal film and protected by an outer plastic layer. In the 1990's, similar devices called **digital video**

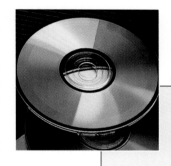

discs, or **digital versatile discs** (DVD's), were developed to play back recorded movies.

▶ TELEGRAPH

The age of electrical communication began when American inventor Samuel Morse demonstrated the first practical telegraph in 1837. In early systems, a telegraph operator would tap on a key to produce short and long buzzer signals (dots and dashes). These signals traveled as "on" and "off" electrical pulses over wires from one place to another. Messages were sent in Morse code, in which combinations of dots and dashes spell out individual letters and numbers. At the receiving end, a telegraph operator would translate the dots and dashes back into the original message.

Electrical impulses move as fast as light waves and travel as far as power and equipment permit. Thus, the telegraph enabled people to communicate over long distances almost instantly. In the 1850's and 1860's, Cyrus Field and other engineers

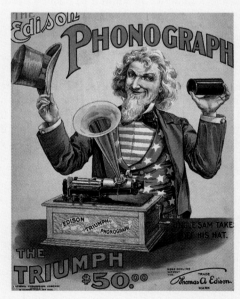

The quality of music played from a modern compact disc is much superior to the crackling sounds from an early phonograph cylinder, pictured below.

laid several underwater telegraph cables between North America and Europe. After many setbacks, they managed to connect the two continents by telegraph. Later, telegraph cables connected other parts of the world. This created a global communication system for the first time in human history.

By the 1920's, telegraph messages could be easily typed on machines with keyboards called **teletypewriters**. These teletype systems would automatically translate the message into telegraph code. The message was then sent via wire or radio to another teletypewriter, which would print out the message in typed letters.

The telegraph was the forerunner of modern **digital communications**. The word "digital" refers to any system that uses simple digits to represent information. Computers are digital because they use combinations of the digits 0 and 1 to stand for numbers, letters, and bits of data that make up pictures and sounds. In digital communications, information is converted into on-off electrical pulses, similar to the dots and dashes used in old-fashioned telegraph code.

▶ TELEPHONE

Another outgrowth of the telegraph was the telephone. In the 1870's, American inventor Alexander Graham Bell and an electrician friend, Thomas Watson, experimented to see if a telegraph wire could transmit the sound of the human voice. Bell sent the first telephone message by accident. Just as he was about to try out his transmitter, he spilled acid on his clothes. He cried out, "Mr. Watson, come here. I want you." Through the receiver in another room, Watson heard Bell's voice. The telephone worked.

Gradually, as telephones became common in most homes and businesses, telephone companies had to develop ways of handling large numbers of calls. They also had to connect calls reliably, switching automatically to a different route if a cable or other connection failed to work. Such needs led to the invention of automated switching and routing devices that could do the work of human switchboard operators much more efficiently.

In 1881, Bell transmitted voice signals over a light ray. He developed a way of converting an electrical telephone signal to a variation in the brightness of a light. The signal was then converted back to sound with a special receiver. In the 1920's, a similar method was invented to convert sound to an optical signal that could be recorded at the edge of a film, adding sound to movies. Eventually, laser light was used to send large numbers of telephone calls and other kinds of information over **optical fibers**— thin glass or plastic strands that carry light long distances.

Today, many types of devices are connected to telephone lines. **Fax machines** are used to transmit images, drawings, and text from one place to another in seconds or minutes. **Answering machines** record calls and supply recorded information to callers when phones are unattended. When the messages are stored on a central system instead of a telephone, the system is called voice mail. **Videoconferencing systems** send television-like images over telephone lines, allowing people to see as well as hear one another.

Cellular phones do not require any wires and allow people to carry telephones with them all the time. Arrays of radio transmitter-receiver towers covering overlapping areas, or cells, provide a continuous connection between cellular phones and regular telephone network wires. Other devices, called **pagers**, also receive radio signals, telling someone to return a phone call. The signals are converted into audible beeps and brief text messages that appear on a small screen.

Above: Early telephones transmitted voices over electrical wires. Modern optical fibers can now carry greater numbers of conversations.

RADIO

Traveling at the speed of light, radio waves can carry sounds, pictures, and digital information. Italian inventor Guglielmo Marconi first sent radio waves through the air in 1895. By 1901, Marconi was able to send his "wireless telegraph" signals, using something similar to Morse code, across the Atlantic Ocean.

Because radio needs no wires, it is of tremendous help on ships, planes, spacecraft, and other vehicles. Radios in the control towers of airfields are used to direct the airplane pilot so that the craft is landed safely. Some airplanes can now use radio signals to locate runways even in dense fog and land automatically. Police cars, delivery trucks, and taxis all use radios to find out where to go and to report their status.

Radio broadcasting began in 1920, when station KDKA in Pittsburgh, Pennsylvania, broadcast the presidential election returns: "Harding elected President." Radio then rapidly became a favorite form of entertainment and information.

Radio waves are now used for connecting many new communications devices in addition to mobile telephones and pagers. Some computer networks are now wireless. They can provide information about suspects to police officers in their cruisers, for example, or timely information such as stock quotes to traveling businesspeople.

TELEVISION

By the 1920's, radio engineers had developed the first televisions, which transmitted pictures, as well as sounds, over radio waves. But technical problems and the disruptions of World War II (1939–45) slowed television's progress. TV broadcasting did not begin on a large scale until the late 1940's. Then it quickly became one of the most popular forms of communication and entertainment.

Cable television started in remote areas where over-the-air reception was difficult and required large, expensive antennas. One large receiving antenna would be connected to many homes by a cable. Gradually cable systems were installed in cities and suburbs, too, since they were convenient and provided a large number of channels. The number of channels available on cable systems gave rise to specialized programming, such as 24-hour news, sports, and weather channels.

The invention of radio in the early 1900's made wireless communication possible. It became essential for people on the move, such as soldiers on the battlefield.

In the 1990's, television began to merge with computers and computer networks. Some cable television and satellite systems allow people direct connections to such networks through their televisions. By the end of the 1990's, television broadcasting began converting to a new transmission method based on the digital language of computers. **Digital TV** provides clearer pictures, better sound, more channels, and special interactive services. These services allow viewers to shop, for example, using their TV sets and handheld remote-control units.

COMMUNICATIONS SATELLITES

In the 1950's and 1960's, rockets began lifting devices with radio transmitters and receivers into space. These devices, called communications satellites, orbit high above Earth. Many of them relay radio messages across distances that are too great for signals from ground-based antennas to reach. In 1962, the first important U.S. communications satellite, *Telstar I*, was placed in orbit. For the first time, people sat at home in New York City and watched something happening in London or Paris at the moment it took place.

Many communications satellites connect just two locations. For example, satellites are used to carry video from a reporter in one place to a television station in another. But recently it has become possible for television viewers to own their own satellite receivers. Millions of viewers now receive television signals directly from satellites. Mobile phones

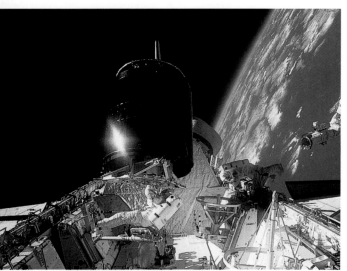

Satellites, such as this one being released from an orbiting space shuttle, now enable people virtually anywhere on Earth to communicate with one another.

can also communicate through networks of many satellites. These phones can be used to place calls from virtually anywhere on Earth, since there is almost always a satellite overhead that can connect the calls.

Satellites that generate signals rather than simply retransmitting them have become very important. Equipped with cameras or other sensors, they can collect astronomical information, help predict the weather, or gather surveillance information for military use. A group of 24 satellites called the Global Positioning System (GPS) transmits signals that people use to pinpoint their exact position. Devices called GPS receivers can be installed in vehicles as navigation aids, while some are small enough to be carried by hikers.

▶ **COMPUTERS**

Although computers were originally designed mainly to store and process data, they are now increasingly serving as communications devices. Even before computers could be connected to one another by networks, they were useful in communications in many ways. People could use a computer for entering and editing text. Or they could access information that had been stored by others in collections of records called databases.

After the first computer networks were developed in the late 1960's, computers could also exchange information among themselves. They became much more of a communications medium.

Computers can communicate with other computers through telephone wires, cables, fiber optics, satellites, or radio. In many places, computers connect to networks using a device called a **modem**, which sends digital data over regular telephone lines. Even devices other than computers can now connect to networks. Handheld devices can receive information from computers, such as music, text, and pictures. Some household appliances, such as microwave ovens, are being developed to transmit or receive information as well.

When a message is sent over a computer network, the network breaks it up into smaller amounts of information, called packets. Each packet contains the address of the computer that is to receive it. At the receiving end, the packets are reassembled into the complete message.

In the 1970's and 1980's, thousands of computers scattered across North America began connecting to a "network of networks." This eventually became what is known as the Internet. By the end of the 1990's, the Internet had grown rapidly, connecting many millions of computers around the world and becoming one of the most important methods of communication in history.

Today, the Internet and other so-called online networks connect computers in homes, schools, businesses, and governments. Internet users can exchange text, sounds, and pictures with people all over the globe through **electronic mail**, or **e-mail**. A particular method of exchanging and displaying information, called the **World Wide Web**, has become a publishing medium. Using computer programs called browsers, people can view "pages" on the Web that resemble those in print, with not only text and images but also sound and video.

The Internet has also created some concerns. It can be difficult to know whether information on the Internet is reliable, or whether a person using the Internet is trustworthy. Computer networks also make it easy to copy and distribute information. Some sources, such as online magazines, are protected by copyright laws. Copying from these sources without their permission is illegal.

In addition, computer networks make it easy to exchange and combine personal information about individual people. This means that personal information provided to one place (such as a merchant or a government agency) might end up being accessible to others. Such access deprives people of their right to privacy.

Computers have greatly expanded everyone's ability to access information and communicate with others. Some systems can even be designed to help people with disabilities communicate.

▶ **MASS COMMUNICATION**

The tools for mass communication are sometimes called **mass media**. Printing was the first such tool, allowing many people to share information. Over the past century or so, a great number of public libraries have grown up, letting people borrow and read more books than they could afford to buy.

Magazines reach even more people than books do. Because they appear regularly and are printed more rapidly than books, magazines can publish news and opinions on public affairs more quickly. Newspapers move even faster than magazines to print news and opinions. American and Canadian newspapers reach many millions of readers a day. Now newspapers and magazines may be read on the World Wide Web. Some of these are electronic versions of existing paper publications, and others exist only in electronic form.

The writers of the United States Constitution realized the importance of the public press. So the First Amendment to the Constitution guaranteed **freedom of the press**. That means that the government cannot decide what the news media—newspapers, magazines, radio, and television—should say. This is one of the most precious freedoms Americans have. It protects every person's right to disagree with the government or with any other authority, in public and in print.

Because of this freedom, the news media have an unwritten obligation to the public. They must print news—that is, facts—as well as opinion. The opinion part of the paper is the editorial section, where editors present various points of view. But editors are not supposed to distort or slant the news so that people are reading opinion when they think they are reading facts. Radio and television have the same obligation, too.

Mass media have a huge responsibility. They must keep people informed. They must decide which news is most important. They must be sure it is accurate. And they must make wise use of their power to influence people's thoughts and attitudes.

Only a few laws regulate mass media. It is illegal to harm people by publishing false information about them. In the United States and many other countries, laws protect the public from false or misleading statements that are considered libelous, or harmful.

The mass media of communication have enriched our lives in many ways. Television, radio, newspapers, books, magazines, and the Internet bring the world of news, ideas, and entertainment into our homes. All of this adds to the variety of our lives and to our education about the world around us.

V. MICHAEL BOVE, JR.
Principal Research Scientist, MIT Media Laboratory
Massachusetts Institute of Technology

SCIENCE FAIRS

Have you ever wondered what type of soap is best for killing bacteria, which materials are the best insulators, or how different pesticides affect tomato plants? If you wonder about interesting questions such as these, you may be well on your way to designing an excellent project for a science fair.

Science fairs are events that allow students to present their own scientific research to teachers, scientists, and the general public, as

At science fairs, students can share their discoveries and make new friends. Participants create exhibits that explain the results of their research.

well as to make new friends who share similar science interests. These activities give students a chance to improve their research and communication skills while having fun.

Planning a Project. The key to preparing a good science project is selecting an interesting topic. Be curious—pose questions about the world around you. Ask yourself, "Do I care about the answers to these questions?" If you say yes, that means other people will probably be interested in what you discover.

To help find ideas for an interesting topic, visit a library, where you can browse science magazines and books and search for information using computer networks such as the Internet. Find out what scientists already know about the topic, and what they have yet to discover. Talk to other young people, teach-

ers, and scientists. If possible, join science clubs at your school or local museum. You may want to work on your project individually or with a team of other students.

After choosing a topic, think of some specific questions that you would like to try to answer. Keep in mind that your project should be unique—that is, it should not repeat what someone else has already done. Try to build upon the research that you read about by asking your own questions.

Before starting your project, it may be helpful to find a **mentor**—a teacher, scientist, or experienced student who can give you useful advice. This person can help you out when you are stuck and need some guidance. Your mentor should carefully go over the rules of the science fair with you before you begin.

Conducting an Experiment. A good science fair project follows the **scientific method**, a process that scientists use to gain knowledge through the results of experiments. The first step in this process is forming a **hypothesis**, an educated prediction about what you think will be the answer to a question. To figure out what kind of experiment you could carry out to test your hypothesis, you will probably have to do some more research. Find out how others have performed similar experiments and why they were successful or unsuccessful. This will give you valuable clues about designing your own experiment.

Next, write a list of the materials and apparatus (equipment) that you will need to carry out the experiment. Also, describe how to conduct the experiment by writing a **procedure**, a clear set of instructions. Before beginning, go over the materials and procedure with your mentor. Also, check with your mentor to make sure that the materials you need are not dangerous and that the experiment you plan to carry out will be done safely.

When you perform your experiment, keep careful records of your **observations**—what you see and measure—in a lab notebook. Take precise measurements using reliable rulers, stopwatches, and other instruments you may need. Document both expected and unexpected results. Usually, you will need to repeat your experiment a number of times in order to be sure of your results, which may be somewhat different each time. These differences can tell you how accurate your results are. They can also reveal possible sources of error in your experimental set-up.

Once you have enough results, you may begin your **analysis**—organizing your observations and measurements in ways that will let you see trends or patterns. You may wish to make graphs of your measurements, so

---

CHECKLIST AND TIPS FOR A SUCCESSFUL EXHIBIT

Before you begin to work on your exhibit, you should have certain information about the science fair and the types of exhibits it will include. The following checklist will be helpful:

✓ Where and when will the science fair be held? In what size and type of room will the exhibits be shown? At what times and on what days are you permitted in the room?

✓ How much space will you be allowed for your exhibit? Will you have a table on which you can place things? Where can you set up posters and signs?

✓ How will you get your exhibit to the science fair? Will you have anyone to help you carry and set up your exhibit? Will you have someone to help you watch your exhibit to prevent damage?

✓ What safety regulations must you follow? Are you permitted to use 110-volt electricity? What kinds of chemicals may you use? Are living things allowed to be part of your exhibit? If so, what kinds may you have, and how must you care for them?

Your exhibit should be eye-catching, and it should explain itself. Here are some tips to help you accomplish these goals:

✓ If you will have a table, you might make a large poster by fastening three sheets of poster board together with strong plastic tape, forming hinges. Such a poster can stand upright on the table, in front of which other parts of your display can be set. If you will not have a table, you can mount your poster and any light objects that can be fastened to it on a wall or standing bulletin board.

✓ Choose easy-to-read colors and sizes of type for your display. You might have the title in one color and large letters, the headings in a different color and medium-sized letters, and text under the headings in a third color and smaller letters. All text should be printed neatly and large enough so that visitors can read it from a distance of up to a yard (roughly a meter).

✓ Make the title, headings, and other text as brief as you can. Remember that visitors might not stay at your exhibit very long, so they should be able to understand the story of your project quickly. Do not try to cram too much into the exhibit—it will look cluttered, and the most important aspect of your project might not be clear.

✓ Models, photographs, drawings, and graphs attract attention. They may also give visitors a clearer understanding of your activity. If possible, display some of the actual equipment and materials you used in your project. You might want to show the activity actually taking place. Visitors always enjoy taking part in the activity themselves.

✓ What you yourself do during the science fair can be very important in attracting attention to your exhibit. You should be obviously interested in your project and in the entire science fair. You should offer to answer any questions that visitors might want to ask.

that you can see mathematical relationships between variables such as distance, volume, and time. Again, your mentor can serve as a helpful guide, offering suggestions that might clarify your results.

From the results and analysis of your experiment, you will be able to make appropriate **conclusions**. Your conclusions should state whether your experiment supported or disproved your hypothesis. You should also point out any errors that may have affected your results. This information is important for others who may try to improve upon your experiment in the future.

Communicating Your Findings. When professional scientists discover something new, they share their findings by publishing them in journals and discussing them at conferences. Science fairs give young people a similar chance to share their discoveries. In order to communicate your results, it is important to put together an effective written report and exhibit of your project. Keep your audience in mind. Your exhibit may be visited by people who know little about your area of research, so make sure that what you present is easy for the general public to understand.

Your report should begin with an **abstract**, a brief overview of your project stating your hypothesis and summarizing your findings. The report should also describe the materials and procedure you used, explaining how and why your experiment was conducted. And the report should contain an analysis of your results and the conclusions you reached.

Your exhibit should consist of a poster display that is organized so that others can quickly understand the important steps of your project. Make your poster as creative as you can to catch people's attention, but do not make it so flashy that it distracts people from your research. In addition to written text, use graphs, charts, and other images to explain your work. Remember, a picture is worth a thousand words.

Participating in Competitions. Now that you have finished the hard work of putting together your exhibit, you are ready for the fun part: competing in a science fair. There are many science fair competitions that take place every year on various levels across North America. If you are an elementary or middle school student, ask your teachers about local and city-wide competitions that you can enter. High school students can take part in regional and state or provincial competitions. If your exhibit is successful, you may be selected to participate in the International Science and Engineering Fair (ISEF), which brings together students from around the world.

Top high school students compete in the International Science and Engineering Fair (ISEF). Author Karen Mendelson is a two-time ISEF winner.

At these competitions, you will set up your exhibit, including your written report, lab notebook, poster, and other parts of your display, such as your apparatus. You will be asked to explain your project to judges, who typically include teachers and often scientists, as well as to students and other members of the general public. Explain your project in a logical manner and leave plenty of time for people to ask you questions. Teachers and other professionals can offer you suggestions on how to improve your work.

Entering science fair competitions will give you a lot of self-confidence. And by talking to fellow participants, you can get an idea of the type of work that other students your age are doing. Have fun sharing your science interest with others. You may also have the chance to interact with adult scientists and learn about their interesting careers. You may even be inspired to become a successful scientist in the future. So what are you waiting for? Let the science begin. Good luck!

KAREN MENDELSON
1997 Recipient, Intel Young Scientist Scholarship
1998 Recipient, Glenn Seaborg Nobel Visit Award
International Science and Engineering Fair

GENETICS

Why do people look different from each other? Why are cats different from dogs? The answer lies in **genes**—biological instructions that control how every living creature generally appears, how it functions, how it reproduces, and even partly how it behaves.

Genes are found inside the cells of the body and are passed down, or **inherited**, from one generation to the next. You may inherit dimples from your mother or the ability to roll your tongue from your father. These features, or **traits**, are determined by combinations of genes that are different for every child.

While each individual is unique, most genes are common to every person on Earth. In fact, humans share many of the same genes with other kinds, or **species**, of animals, too—from the simple fruit fly to our close cousin, the chimpanzee.

The study of genes is a branch of biology called **genetics**, and the scientists who study how genes are inherited and how they control traits are called **geneticists**. Although the field of genetics dates back to the mid-1800's, most of what we know about genes has been learned in only the last few decades.

New technologies developed to study genes are helping scientists understand the rich diversity of life on our planet. These genetic tools are also letting doctors diagnose and treat previously incurable diseases, aiding police in the investigation of crimes, and giving researchers the ability to design better agricultural crops.

▶ THE GENETIC CODE

All organisms, from the tiniest virus to the largest whale, have genes. The complete collection of genes for each organism is called its **genome**. Each species has its own unique genome.

Every genome is like a giant cookbook, with each gene being a single recipe. This cookbook is passed down from generation to

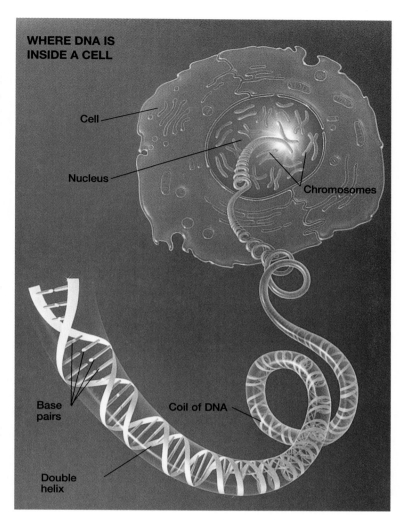

WHERE DNA IS INSIDE A CELL

Cell

Nucleus

Chromosomes

Base pairs

Coil of DNA

Double helix

generation, just like family recipes. And like recipes, genes are step-by-step instructions. They tell how to make the various parts of cells and control the work they do. Genes tell a new cell to become a blood cell or a muscle cell. During pregnancy, genes guide the development of a fully formed human child from the union of a single egg and sperm.

Genes are "written" in a language called the **genetic code**. The code is based on a molecule called *d*eoxyribo*n*ucleic *a*cid, or **DNA**. This molecule is shaped like a twisting ladder, often called a double helix. It consists of two strands that spiral around one another. The rungs of the ladder are made up of pairs of chemical units, called **bases**, that connect the two strands.

There are four bases: adenine (A), cytosine (C), guanine (G), and thymine (T). Their let-

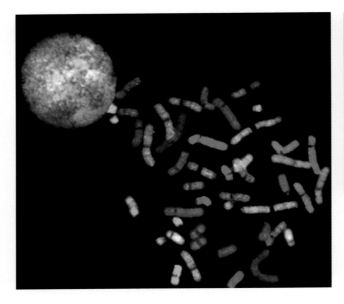

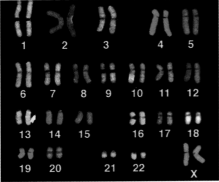

Left: This microscope image (magnified 63 times) shows a human cell nucleus and its chromosomes, which have been artificially colored. *Above:* To analyze the chromosomes, geneticists arrange and number them in pairs from largest to smallest. The last pair is an exception: It is made up of two X chromosomes in females (as shown here) and an X and a Y chromosome in males.

ters are the "alphabet" of the genetic code. Adenine always pairs up with thymine, and cytosine always pairs up with guanine. Sequences of these interlocking base pairs spell out individual genes.

Where Genes Are

One DNA molecule can contain thousands of genes. The molecule forms a long, threadlike part of the cell called a **chromosome** (from Latin words meaning "colored body"). When a cell is stained with certain colored dyes, its chromosomes can be easily seen under a microscope. When a cell divides, chromosomes become especially noticeable: their strands coil up, becoming short and thick. In primitive single-celled organisms such as bacteria, the genes may be located on a single circular chromosome and also on rings of DNA called **plasmids**. In more advanced organisms, from amoebas to human beings, the genes are located on a number of chromosomes in a part of the cell called the **nucleus** (plural: nuclei).

In humans and other animals, chromosomes are found in every cell in the body, except red blood cells (the only type of cell that lacks a nucleus). In most cells of the body, called **somatic cells**, chromosomes come in pairs, like shoes, the members of which are similar in both size and shape. Half of the chromosomes come from the individual's mother, and the other half from the father.

Different species can have different numbers of chromosomes in their cells. The fruit fly has only 4 pairs. Corn has 10 pairs. Humans have 23 pairs of chromosomes, or a total of 46, in most of our body's roughly 100 trillion cells. The exceptions are the **germ cells** (sperm and eggs), which have just 23 chromosomes each. When a sperm and egg combine, the resulting cell (called an embryo) contains a full set of 46 chromosomes. As the cell divides into more cells, each new cell of the embryo contains a copy of those original 46 chromosomes.

What Genes Do

Genes can be thought of as the sentences spelled out by the sequences of letters that stand for the bases. These sequences are divided into shorter "words," or instructions for assembling molecules called **amino acids**. Amino acids are the building blocks of important molecules called **proteins**. Some of these proteins, in turn, go on to become part of larger structures in the cell, while others (called enzymes) control various functions in the cell. Other parts of the genetic sequence act as punctuation marks, indicating where genes start and stop.

Different genes are "turned on," or activated, at different times during an organism's life, and in different parts of its body. Some genes are needed only during the growth of the embryo, while others may be needed only during adolescence. Also, different cells use different sets of genes. For example, muscle cells do not use the genes that produce color in hair cells, even though muscle cells contain those genes in their chromosomes.

To activate genes, various parts of the cell come into play. First, the DNA is unraveled and separated into its two strands. These strands act as patterns, or templates. Another long molecule, called *ribonucleic acid* (or **RNA**), is then formed from these templates. The RNA acts as a messenger, carrying the genetic information encoded on the chromosomes to other parts of the cell called **ribosomes**. The ribosomes "read" the messenger RNA molecules and construct proteins out of the amino-acid building blocks in the cell.

▶ **HEREDITY AND VARIATION**

Genes can be thought of as the basic units of **heredity**—the inheritance of traits from one generation to the next. Genes determine a variety of physical features, including your gender, height, and hair and eye colors. To find out how genes control such traits, geneticists study the patterns of **variation**, or change, in traits passed along from parents to their offspring.

When an individual exhibits a trait, geneticists say that the **phenotype** for that trait is expressed. Phenotypes are determined by combinations of different versions of a gene. Just as chromosomes come in pairs, so do most genes. These similar genes are called **alleles**. Alleles are located at the same site on each member of a chromosome pair and contain the genetic code for alternate forms of the same gene. The combination of alleles is called a **genotype**.

Genetic variation can happen when germ cells (sperm and eggs) are formed. In this process, called **meiosis**, cells will divide twice to produce four germ cells. During the first division, genes can be reshuffled between chromosomes. This reshuffling, or **genetic recombination**, varies the traits we see in individuals, even within the same family.

Dominant and Recessive Genes

Despite this variety, many members of a family can have similar features. These traits are often examples of phenotypes that are said to be **dominant**. Other characteristics in a family may be seen in only some members. These traits are often examples of **recessive** phenotypes.

For example, suppose two parents had both the dominant and recessive alleles for a certain trait—say, the ability to roll the tongue. Let us label the dominant allele (for the tongue rolling trait) with a capital T, and the recessive allele (for no tongue rolling ability) with a lowercase t. Each parent's genotype, or combination of alleles, is Tt. (See the diagram below.)

Each of the parents' children would inherit one allele from the mother (either T or t) and one from the father (again, either T or t). So,

INHERITANCE EXAMPLE

Parents with both types, or alleles, of the tongue-rolling gene can produce children with four possible combinations of alleles, or genotypes. All three children carrying the dominant allele T can roll their tongues. Only the child with both copies of the recessive allele t is unable to do so.

each child could have one of four possible genotypes: TT, Tt, tT (the same as Tt), or tt. Because T is dominant, both parents can roll their tongues, and any child with that allele will be able to do so as well. Only a child with the genotype tt will lack the ability.

Family members with either the genotypes TT or tt are called **homozygous**. Members with the genotype Tt are called **heterozygous**. They are often referred to as carriers of the recessive allele—that is, they do not exhibit the recessive trait but they still carry the gene for it.

How Traits Are Inherited

Can you roll your tongue or bend your thumb backward? If you have these abilities, you probably inherited them from your parents. Other such hereditary traits, as they are called, include freckles on the skin, dimples in the cheeks or chin, and a "widow's peak" in the hairline on the forehead, as shown in the photographs here.

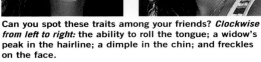

Can you spot these traits among your friends? *Clockwise from left to right:* the ability to roll the tongue; a widow's peak in the hairline; a dimple in the chin; and freckles on the face.

As these traits are passed down from one generation to the next, they can be seen in many, but not all, members of the same family. Some of these traits are seen more often and are said to be dominant. Others are seen less often and are said to be recessive.

Take a look at members of your own family—brothers, sisters, parents, grandparents, aunts, uncles, and cousins. Perhaps you also have pictures of great-grandparents and great-great-grandparents, too. Draw a family tree, starting with the oldest generation of your family, and draw lines connecting parents to children to children's children, and so on. (See the article GENEALOGY in this volume for an example of a family tree.)

Under the names of each family member, list some physical traits that you can notice. Are there certain traits that appear to be dominant or recessive? If you can notice these inheritance patterns, you are on your way to becoming a geneticist!

Gene Interactions

Not all phenotypes are simply dominant or recessive. Geneticists believe that many traits involve several genes that interact with one another in complex ways. These interacting genes, called **polygenes**, can produce a continuous variation in a trait that ranges from one extreme to another. In humans, characteristics such as height, weight, and skin color are all the result of polygenes.

Even some aspects of human intelligence and behavior appear to be influenced by multiple genes. For many years, scientists have debated whether intelligence and behavior are determined by genetics or shaped by how we are raised. Today, most scientists believe that genes, upbringing, and the interaction between the two are responsible.

▶ GENETIC DISORDERS

When variations in genes are harmful, they result in what are called genetic disorders. Such diseases are inherited by offspring from their parents, just as normal traits are. Genetic disorders are caused by **mutations**, which can be thought of as misspellings in the genetic code. Mutations may cause cells to make a protein incorrectly, or to make too much or too little of the right protein.

Sometimes the mutation is as small as a change in a single base in the chemical structure of DNA. An example is sickle cell anemia, in which an improper protein makes some red blood cells malfunction and take on the shape of a sickle, instead of a red blood cell's proper circular shape. In other cases, an entire chromosome can be affected, as in the case of children with Down syndrome, who have an extra copy of the 21st chromosome.

Causes of Mutations

Some mutations may be caused by exposure to chemicals in the environment, ultraviolet radiation from the sun, or even invisible particles given off by radioactive materials. However, most mutations occur naturally in a random and spontaneous way. This usually happens when mistakes are made inside cells during routine processes, such as cell division.

Most mutations are harmful to cells, causing them to malfunction or die. In many cases, cells can correct genetic mistakes on their own. However, some errors may become a permanent part of an individual's genes and may be passed on to future generations. This can happen when the mutation occurs in parts of the body that produce germ cells.

Hereditary Diseases

There are approximately 4,000 known types of inherited, or hereditary, diseases. Some, like Huntington's disease, are caused by a dominant allele that is an abnormal version of a gene. This, in turn, produces an abnormal protein that leads to a progressive breakdown in the parts of the brain that control movement. Other hereditary diseases, like cystic fibrosis, are caused by a recessive allele. In this case, the abnormal protein produced by the gene mutation leads to the buildup of thick mucus in the body that prevents normal breathing and digestion.

A special type of hereditary disease is called **sex-linked**, because it is associated with one of the sex chromosomes. At conception, when a sperm fertilizes an egg, the resulting embryo contains two sets of chromosomes, one from the mother and the other from the father. The embryo has 22 pairs of chromosomes plus one pair of sex chromosomes, which come in two varieties. One is the female, or X, chromosome, and the other is the male, or Y, chromosome. The egg always carries an X. If the sperm carries another X, the embryo has two X's and will develop into a

girl. If the sperm carries a Y, the embryo has an X and a Y and will become a boy.

Hemophilia is an example of a sex-linked hereditary disease. It affects the blood's ability to clot properly and can lead to uncontrolled bleeding. The abnormal gene responsible for hemophilia is recessive and found on the X chromosome.

Genes and Environment

We have already learned that many normal physical traits, such as a person's height, are controlled not by a single gene but by several genes. The same is true for many human diseases. Cancer, heart disease, and diabetes are all examples of genetic disorders for which geneticists have found a number of related genes, sometimes scattered over more than one chromosome.

However, not every person who has these genes will necessarily become ill. That is because many genetic disorders depend on various **environmental factors**. Examples of these include what kinds of food a person eats, what chemicals or other hazardous materials the person may have been exposed to, and even what kind of lifestyle the person leads.

Such environmental factors may affect a person's risk of developing a disease or the severity of the disease, depending on what genes that person has. Even if a gene is harmless by itself, it may increase a person's risk of developing a certain disease.

▶ GENETICS AND EVOLUTION

While most genetic mutations are harmful to organisms, some may give an organism an advantage over other members of its species. The organism is said to be "selected" for survival. If beneficial mutations are passed on to the generations that follow, those organisms may start to look different from their ancestors. The organisms may eventually become, or evolve into, a new species. This process is called **evolution**.

Scientists believe evolution of life on Earth has occurred chiefly through such **natural selection** in response to gradual or sudden changes in the environment. Natural selection in turn depends on the variations of genes in a population.

In nature, evolution usually takes place over many thousands of years. However, much more rapid instances of natural selec-

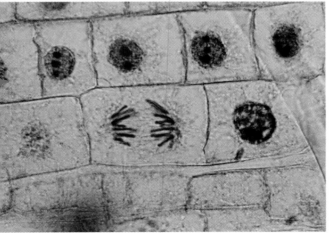

This microscope image shows a dividing plant cell (center). It copies its chromosomes, which separate to form the nuclei of two new cells. Mistakes during this copying are one way in which mutations can happen.

tion have happened because of changes brought about by human activity. One example is the change in peppered moths outside Manchester, England. In the mid-1800's, the area was covered with fields and woods. As factories were built, their smoke settled on the trees as dark soot. As a result, moths with dark-colored wings had a better chance of surviving than moths with light-colored wings. It was harder for birds to see the dark-winged moths against the sooty bark. Fewer were eaten, and their numbers multiplied. By the mid-1900's, the peppered-moth population near Manchester was almost entirely dark-winged.

▶ GENETIC ENGINEERING

Long before the principles of genetics were known, early people began to domesticate wild animals and plants and selected those that could be used for food or for doing work. This selective breeding was an early kind of genetic engineering—a deliberate effort to develop types, or **strains**, of organisms that would benefit human beings.

In time, many new strains of plants and animals were developed. Among these were new strains of cattle, horses, dogs, cats, wheat, rice, and corn. For example, people developed breeds of horses to meet specific needs. Some

of these were fast, sleek racehorses. Others were large, strong workhorses.

During the 1900's, genetic engineering became a much more accurate science. Scientists learned to breed pure strains of plants and animals. These **purebred** strains are genetically constant—that is, all their offspring are exactly like the parents. The purebred strains did not always show desirable qualities. But when different purebreds were bred with one another, some of the offspring showed unusual vigor or higher yields. These strains were called **hybrids**. They had genes from two or more different strains.

Making Mutations

At first, scientists depended on natural mutations to produce the kinds of genes that could be used in developing new strains. Later they learned to cause mutations by exposing organisms to radiation such as X rays. Offspring with useful mutations were developed into new and valuable strains.

Millions of lives have been saved by one product of genetic engineering that was developed in this way. In 1928, Scottish scientist Alexander Fleming discovered that *Penicillium* molds make a bacteria-fighting substance, called penicillin. It was first used during World War II (1939–45) to treat infections in soldiers' wounds. However, the molds did not produce enough penicillin to meet the demand. In the laboratory, some strains of *Penicillium* were x-rayed to cause mutations. In time, high-yielding strains of the mold were developed and large amounts of penicillin could be produced.

Splicing Genes

As scientists learned more about genetics, they learned how to remove, purify, and study the genes of simple organisms. Bacteria were of particular interest because of their ability to make enzymes that can cut through strands of DNA at specific places. With these enzymes, bacteria can attack viruses that invade their cells by cutting the DNA from the viruses into harmless fragments.

These enzymes also have made possible a dramatic new kind of genetic engineering called **gene splicing**. Using this method, scientists can take a gene from one organism and

Did you know that...

scientists have made mice glow green using DNA from jellyfish? The DNA contains a gene for producing a chemical called green fluorescent protein, or GFP. The protein makes jellyfish glow, or fluoresce, in visible green light when invisible ultraviolet light is shined on them. Although making mice glow green may seem strange, it has a very practical purpose. The GFP gene serves as a "biomarker": It can be linked to other genes in an animal, such as genes controlling how the animal develops. When those genes are passed on from one generation to another, so is the biomarker gene. Thus, by observing which animals glow green, for example, geneticists can easily tell which animals have inherited certain other genes.

splice it into (make it part of) another organism's genetic material. The resulting new organism is called **transgenic**. Because gene splicing recombines DNA in new ways, this technique is also called recombinant-DNA technology.

Since the bases of DNA are the same for most organisms, pieces of DNA from quite different species can be spliced together. Almost any kind of plant or animal DNA can be inserted into the DNA of bacteria, and vice versa. Even synthetic DNA can be spliced into a cell's genetic material. This is DNA made entirely in the laboratory.

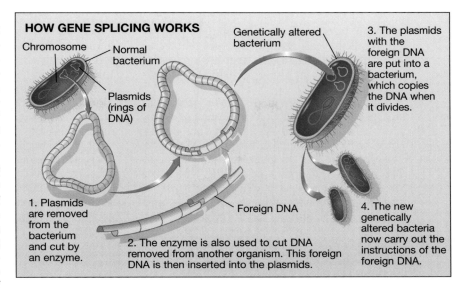

HOW GENE SPLICING WORKS

Chromosome

Normal bacterium

Plasmids (rings of DNA)

Genetically altered bacterium

3. The plasmids with the foreign DNA are put into a bacterium, which copies the DNA when it divides.

1. Plasmids are removed from the bacterium and cut by an enzyme.

Foreign DNA

2. The enzyme is also used to cut DNA removed from another organism. This foreign DNA is then inserted into the plasmids.

4. The new genetically altered bacteria now carry out the instructions of the foreign DNA.

Manufacturing Proteins

Usually, a gene that has been spliced into a bacterium's genetic material will tell the cell to put together a certain protein. Bacteria will manufacture not only their own proteins but also any protein specified by genes that have been spliced into their DNA.

For example, scientists have spliced the insulin-making gene from human cells into bacterial DNA. Insulin is made by the pancreas to control the amount of sugar in the blood. In some people, the pancreas does not make enough insulin, resulting in a form of diabetes. People with this condition must be given insulin from another source, such as cattle. But animal insulin is not exactly the same as human insulin. It can cause undesirable side effects in people who use it.

When the human insulin gene was spliced into the bacterial DNA, the bacteria began to make insulin. The insulin made by the bacteria is exactly like the insulin made by your body. Once the bacteria-made insulin was tested and proven to be safe, it became available for use by people with diabetes.

Safety Concerns

Some people believe that gene splicing could be used to create new kinds of dangerous organisms, either accidentally or on purpose. Government and private research organizations follow guidelines for gene splicing. Some kinds of experiments can be carried out only in laboratories that have special safety features. So far, gene splicing has not caused any outbreaks of serious illnesses or environmental disasters, as critics have feared. However, the possibility exists that gene splicing will not always work as planned. As a result, some people have called for stricter regulations of this technology. (See the accompanying Wonder Question, Are genetically engineered crops safe?)

▶ GENETICS AND BIOTECHNOLOGY

Products obtained by gene splicing and other kinds of genetic technologies have become a common part of our lives. These products are examples of **biotechnology**—the application of genetics and other fields of modern biology to solve practical problems. Scientists have developed powerful new genetic engineering tools since the mid-1970's, which marks the beginning of what is often called the biotechnology revolution.

The two most important uses of biotechnology are in medicine and agriculture. Biotechnology is also used in forensic science (the science of solving crimes), in population studies, and in certain industries.

Medical Biotechnology

We have already seen how genetic engineering can be used to make, or synthesize, artificial human insulin. Techniques such as gene-splicing can also be used to synthesize other beneficial chemicals that are otherwise difficult to obtain. These include the following substances:

Human Growth Hormone. Some people do not produce enough of this chemical, which controls body growth. As a result, they do not grow to normal heights. Children who have this problem can be given growth hormone taken from the bodies of people who have died. But using genetic engineering to make human growth hormone is an easier and cheaper way of making the hormone.

Interferon. This is a protein made by the human body when viruses invade it. The interferon fights, or interferes with, the viruses. Interferon has been shown to be useful in the fight against some kinds of cancer. Huge amounts of blood were once needed to obtain tiny amounts of interferon. But now bacteria and yeast can be genetically engineered to produce much more human interferon.

Tissue-Plasminogen Activator. This natural substance dissolves clumps of blood, called clots. Blood clots that cause heart attacks or strokes in the brain can lead to further damage. Injecting genetically engineered tissue-

WONDER QUESTION

Are genetically engineered crops safe?

Most of the vegetables and fruits we eat today are bigger and more nutritious than the wild varieties from which they were first cultivated. Over many centuries, farmers have carefully chosen desired qualities in plants by selectively breeding the best plants.

In the past few decades, more rapid improvements have been made to many of our foods through modern genetic engineering. Using this technology, scientists can transfer a gene from one organism to another. For example, the gene that instructs certain soil bacteria to produce an insect-killing chemical called Bt can be inserted into corn plants. The result is a variety of corn that can produce its own Bt and resist insect pests.

Many farmers have preferred to grow the new corn because it avoids the need for pesticides, which are costly and can also harm the environment. However, in the late 1990's, researchers discovered a problem with the new corn. Pollen from these corn plants falls on nearby milkweed plants. Milkweed is the main food of monarch caterpillars, which develop into monarch butterflies. However, pollen from the genetically engineered corn was found to harm the caterpillars.

The case of Bt-producing corn shows that genetic engineering can sometimes have unex-

The corn shown above has been genetically engineered to resist insect pests. However, its pollen has been found to harm the caterpillars that turn into monarch butterflies (*left*).

pected effects. Most scientists believe that the dangers posed by Bt-producing varieties of corn and other plants, such as cotton and potatoes, are probably less than the dangers from spraying with pesticides. However, further research will likely be needed to make sure that genetic engineering of crops continues to be as safe or safer than traditional methods.

plasminogen activator into patients who have suffered these attacks eliminates the clots and helps the patients recover better.

In addition to synthesizing useful medical substances, genetic engineering is also being used in medical research. In order to find effective drugs to treat a human disease, researchers must first have a "model" in the form of an animal that has a similar illness. The most widely used model for such research is the mouse. Since it is a mammal, its genes are very similar to those in humans. Also, scientists can study the effects of a drug more easily in mice than in humans.

Many different kinds of mice have been carefully bred and studied over the past 100 years or so. More recently, scientists have developed various strains of transgenic mice, containing inserted genes associated with human diseases, as well as "knock-out" mice, which are genetically engineered to lack certain genes. Mouse models of illnesses such as Lou Gehrig's disease, cystic fibrosis, muscular dystrophy, and obesity are providing clues to treating these life-threatening conditions.

Agricultural Biotechnology

Most of today's foods come from plant and animal varieties that were unknown a century ago. Many of these varieties took many generations to develop, using selective breeding. Today, using advanced genetic technologies, scientists can create plants and animals with new characteristics in a single generation. Some examples of new varieties being developed this way are listed below.

Disease-Resistant Crops and Animals. Plants such as wheat, rice, and cotton are being genetically manipulated to be more resistant to insects and diseases. The new varieties require less use of pesticides, which can harm the environment. Likewise, farm animals are being made more resistant to diseases, thus eliminating the need to feed them antibiotics.

Plants That Make Their Own Fertilizer. Farmers have to add expensive fertilizers containing nitrogen compounds to fields in which they grow corn, wheat, and other crops. But certain so-called nitrogen-fixing bacteria can take nitrogen from the air and change it into the compounds that plants need. Biologists can take the nitrogen-fixing genes from these bacteria and splice them into the genetic material of corn and other plants.

A researcher extracts DNA from the tissue of a plant that resists fungus infection. Studies of the DNA aid in the design of other disease-resistant crops.

Bigger and Faster-Growing Animals. Genes that control growth and development can be inserted into cows, pigs, sheep, and fish to increase the amount of meat they produce and to speed up their development.

Vegetables That Stay Ripe. Tomatoes can be genetically altered to stay ripe and take longer to turn rotten. This avoids the need to pick the tomatoes while they are still green in order to get them from the farm to the store before they spoil.

Crime Investigation

Just as people's fingerprints are unique, so are their genetic codes. Fingerprints are very useful in identifying both suspects and victims of a crime. But not all criminals leave fingerprints at the scene of a crime. Also, fingerprints cannot be taken from badly burned or decomposed bodies of victims.

Using a technique called **DNA fingerprinting**, investigators can identify both suspects and victims from even the smallest traces of skin, hair, blood, saliva, and other bodily fluids and tissues that contain DNA.

Experts called forensic scientists test such samples in machines that produce a pattern of lines resembling a bar code on a grocery store item. If the DNA pattern from a sample matches the pattern from a suspect, there is strong evidence linking the suspect to the crime. If the patterns do not match, then the suspect is likely innocent.

HOW SCIENTISTS DISCOVERED THE "SECRET OF LIFE"

On February 28, 1953, two scientists walked into a pub in Cambridge, England, announcing, "We have discovered the secret of life." Their boast was not far from the truth. James Watson and Francis Crick had just solved one of biology's great mysteries: the structure of life's most important molecule, DNA.

Born on April 6, 1928, in Chicago, Illinois, James Dewey Watson was a bright young student. As a teen, he impressed audiences with his talents on a popular radio show called Quiz Kids. At age 15, he entered the University of Chicago to study zoology. During that time, he read a book entitled *What Is Life?* by the famous Austrian physicist Erwin Schrödinger. The book made Watson interested in finding out the secret of genes—the biological instructions that control all living things.

After getting a Ph.D. degree from Indiana University at the age of 22, Watson

James Watson, Francis Crick, and their model of DNA.

conducted research in Denmark and later England. There, at the Cavendish Laboratory, he met Crick, who was studying the structure of protein molecules.

Born on June 8, 1916, in Northampton, England, Francis Harry Compton Crick was an inquisitive boy, often conducting his own chemistry experiments—some of which ended in failure with an explosion. His scientific studies improved when he entered University College in London, where he studied physics and mathematics. Crick, too, was inspired by Schrödinger's book, which led in part to his later pursuit of biology.

At the Cavendish Laboratory, Crick used a technique called X-ray diffraction to determine the three-dimensional structure of proteins. If X rays are aimed at a sample of molecules, the rays will scatter, or diffract, producing a pattern on a photographic plate. By studying this diffraction pattern, scientists can determine how the molecules are put together in three dimensions.

Population Studies

DNA fingerprinting can also be used to study the diversity and history of various human populations. Scientists can compare DNA patterns from human populations living today and in the past—even those from ancient Egyptian mummies. The same technique also helps scientists determine which animal species are the most closely related, giving clues to the evolution of those species. In addition, DNA fingerprinting of animal populations can provide researchers with signs of whether a rare, threatened species (such as certain whales) may be in danger of becoming extinct.

Uses in Industry

Gene-splicing techniques can be used to develop micro-organisms that act as biological "factories," manufacturing certain chemicals important in industry. For example,

scientists have modified brewer's yeast to convert lactose (a chemical in the whey produced during cheese processing) into alcohol that can be used in medicine and industry. Genetically engineered bacteria have also been developed to "eat" oil spills and decompose many forms of garbage.

▶ THE HUMAN GENOME PROJECT

In 1990, scientists in the United States and several other countries began the largest biology project ever undertaken: to produce a detailed "map" of the entire human genome by finding all of its roughly 100,000 genes encoded on some 3 billion base pairs of DNA.

In the United States, the project was launched with $3 billion in funding from two agencies of the federal government: the National Institutes of Health and the Department of Energy. At first, researchers expected

When Watson and Crick teamed up in 1951, they became interested in work by two biochemists at King's College in London, Maurice Wilkins and Rosalind Franklin. Wilkins and Franklin had produced X-ray diffraction patterns of DNA, the molecule of genes. Using their findings, Watson and Crick began building models of how the chemical units of DNA might fit together. After much trial and error, they finally came up with a structure that explained the findings. DNA, they concluded, was in the shape of a twisting ladder, or double helix.

In 1962, Watson, Crick, and Wilkins were awarded the Nobel Prize in physiology or medicine for their work. (Franklin, who had originally disagreed with their double-helix theory, was left out of the award, despite her contributions.)

Watson went on to become director of the Cold Spring Harbor Laboratory in New York, where he conducted cancer research. In 1990, he helped launch the Human Genome Project—an effort to find all the roughly 100,000 genes in human beings. Crick eventually joined the Salk Institute in California. There, he developed theories to explain a number of great scientific mysteries, including how the brain gives rise to consciousness and whether microbes drifting through space may have seeded life on Earth.

that the project would take 15 years to complete. However, by the end of the 1990's, the project's leaders predicted that the entire human genome would be decoded three years ahead of schedule, thanks to rapid advances in technology.

Mapping the Genome

There are different kinds of genome maps, just as there are different types of geographical maps—from topography maps to road maps. A **genetic map** is based on careful study of inheritance patterns within families. This kind of map tells us which chromosome a gene is located on, which genes are close to it, and which genes are far from it.

To produce a genetic map, geneticists study family trees, called **pedigrees**, and trace the inheritance of a disease-causing gene mutation. They do this by determining whether the mutation is inherited along with some unique segments of DNA, called **DNA markers**. These markers can be easily found in samples of genetic material taken from family members and analyzed in a laboratory. When a disease seems to be inherited in the same pattern as one of these markers, it is said to be "linked" to the marker. Thus, DNA markers are powerful tools in identifying genes involved in disease.

Another kind of map is a **physical map**, based on physical pieces of DNA. It is made by finding pieces that overlap one another in their genetic code and putting them in their proper order. Physical maps vary in the amount of detail, or resolution, they can show. The physical map with the least amount of resolution is one made by staining all the chromosomes from a cell. When the staining is examined closely, a distinct pattern of light and dark bands can be seen across each chromosome. The most detailed physical map is a complete DNA sequence. It is represented by a long sequence of the letters that stand for each of the four bases (A, C, G, and T).

Determining the exact sequence of all the DNA bases in the human genome is the ultimate mapping goal of the Human Genome Project. However, putting the genome's 3 billion base pairs in their proper order is a very complex task. If these sequences were printed out, they would fill 1,000 thousand-page books! The only effective way to handle such a large amount of information is to use computers. Programs have been written to simplify this task and make the information available to researchers anywhere in the world on the Internet computer network.

Gene Testing

One of the first applications of the Human Genome Project has been gene testing. This procedure allows a doctor to determine whether a patient carries a gene that could cause or contribute to a disease.

There are three types of genetic tests: gene-carrier testing, prenatal gene testing, and predictive gene testing. Gene-carrier testing is sometimes used by couples who want to know whether they could pass on a genetic disorder to their children. Prenatal gene testing is done before birth to see whether an embryo has any genetic problems. Predictive gene tests predict the chance that a person will develop

Gene Therapy

Another promising application of the Human Genome Project is gene therapy. In this type of procedure, doctors can correct a mutation in a gene. Such a gene fails to work properly, producing the wrong type or wrong amount of a certain protein. To correct this error, doctors put normal copies of the gene into cells of the patient's body. These altered cells, in turn, properly produce the protein, thus overcoming the effects of the mutation.

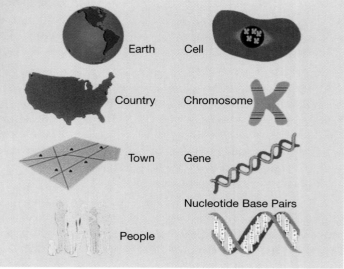

In order to map the human genome, scientists must locate each of the 3 billion DNA base pairs that make up all the roughly 100,000 genes in the chromosomes of our cells. Such a mammoth task is comparable to creating a map of Earth in which every inhabitant of every town in every country is identified. To speed up this task, geneticists use automated mapping machines like the one above to find genes rapidly.

a particular disease later in life. Genetic tests involve the examination of the DNA in cells that are typically taken from a blood sample or from inside a mother's womb.

An important part of gene testing is **genetic counseling**, in which a person, couple, or family meets with a genetic counselor before and after the testing. The counselor provides patients with information about the condition that is being tested for. In doing so, the counselor helps the patients make informed decisions about the kinds of health care they may wish to choose. In some disorders, a genetic mutation is only one factor that affects whether a person will develop an illness. Factors such as lifestyle and environment also play a role in triggering the disease. By explaining the importance of these factors and how they interact, genetic counselors can help patients understand their risks.

In 1990, a 4-year-old girl by the name of Ashanti DeSilva became the first human being to undergo gene therapy. She was suffering from a genetic disorder called severe combined immunodeficiency, or SCID. The mutation responsible for this disease disables a gene that normally produces an enzyme called adenosine deaminase, or ADA. This enzyme is especially important for cells of the immune system. Without this enzyme, the immune system cannot function correctly, making the body susceptible to infections.

At the National Institutes of Health in Bethesda, Maryland, doctors removed some of Ashanti's white blood cells. They then inserted a normal copy of the ADA gene into the cells and put the treated cells back into her body by injecting them into her bloodstream. After eleven such treatments over

338

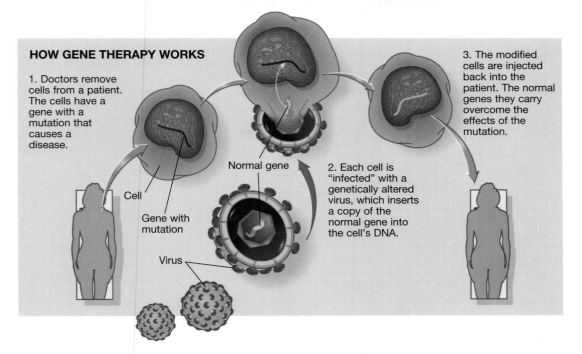

HOW GENE THERAPY WORKS

1. Doctors remove cells from a patient. The cells have a gene with a mutation that causes a disease.

Cell

Gene with mutation

Normal gene

Virus

2. Each cell is "infected" with a genetically altered virus, which inserts a copy of the normal gene into the cell's DNA.

3. The modified cells are injected back into the patient. The normal genes they carry overcome the effects of the mutation.

two years, Ashanti's disabled immune system was repaired. The gene therapy worked, enabling her to lead a normal life.

To deliver genes to just those cells that need them, doctors use what are called **vectors**. Viruses are an example of a vector. They reproduce themselves by inserting their genetic material into the DNA of other cells. Cells infected by a virus make copies of the virus's own genetic material. These copies form new viruses, which then infect other cells.

Using genetic engineering, scientists can alter viruses to make them harmless and carry normal copies of a gene. The altered viruses can then be used to "infect" specific cells with the normal genes. The cells, in turn, produce the right protein.

Several other types of vectors also show potential for gene therapy. These include tiny fat globules, called liposomes, that can surround the

Sequences of light and dark bands on a specially prepared transparency reveal genes in a DNA sample.

DNA to be delivered. Another way to deliver genes is using a "gene gun." In this technique, normal copies of a gene are attached to tiny metal spheres, which are "shot" inside a cell. Scientists have also made artificial chromosomes, which can deliver any number of genes to a cell.

Gene therapy is being developed to treat various genetic disorders, including cystic fibrosis and muscular dystrophy, as well as complex conditions such as cancer and even infectious diseases such as AIDS. However, gene therapy also raises ethical issues about the possible misuse of this technology. For instance, should gene therapy be used to enhance physical traits or abilities? Should gene therapy be used to treat diseases in the fetus? These and other questions pose major challenges for society.

Importance to Society

When completed, the Human Genome Project is expected to usher in a new age of medicine. For example, gene testing will provide more precise diag-

HISTORY OF GENETICS

The field of genetics began in the 1850's when Gregor Mendel, an Austrian monk in what is now the Czech Republic, carried out plant-breeding experiments in the tiny garden of his monastery. He crossed, or bred together, various kinds of pea plants and studied the number and kinds of offspring produced. From his detailed records, Mendel was able to recognize dominant and recessive traits, such as the color of the peas. Mendel concluded that these traits were the result of heredity "factors"—what we now call genes.

Gregor Mendel's studies of how pea plants inherit traits paved the way for modern genetics.

Mendel reported his conclusions in 1866. His work was an entirely new approach to the problems of heredity. But it remained largely forgotten for 34 years, until it was rediscovered in 1900 by several European biologists.

In the early 1900's, other scientists realized that Mendel's laws of heredity did not always apply. William Bateson of England discovered that many cross-breeding results could be explained by the interactions of genes. American scientist Thomas Hunt Morgan found the first sex-linked genetic traits, in his experiments with fruit flies. And fellow American Hermann Muller, in his studies of fruit flies exposed to X rays, observed that radiation can cause genetic mutations.

White-eyed fly

Curly-winged fly

Normal fruit fly

Hermann Muller found that X rays can cause fruit flies to develop mutations, such as white eyes and abnormal wings.

In the 1940's, American geneticist Barbara McClintock discovered "jumping genes" while studying inherited traits of corn. These genes can change their positions on chromosomes and affect neighboring genes.

Also during this period, American researchers Oswald Avery, Colin MacLeod, and Maclyn McCarty proved that DNA is the material in cells responsible for heredity. At that time, little was known about how DNA works. But less than a decade later, in 1953, American biochemist James Watson and British biophysicist Francis Crick solved this mystery when they discovered the double-helix structure of DNA. Their discovery enabled geneticists to "crack" the genetic code and see how genes were put together at the level of molecules. (See the feature about Watson and Crick that accompanies this article.)

By the end of the 1960's, geneticists had figured out the basics of how proteins are assembled from the amino acids encoded on DNA, and how RNA is involved in the process. As the 1970's began, researchers learned how to synthesize DNA in the laboratory. In

noses of diseases and enable doctors to intervene earlier. Ultimately, results from human genome research will shift medical care from primarily treating diseases after they are diagnosed to preventing diseases before they start.

Despite the project's enormous medical benefits, some experts warn that the knowledge gained from it could be misused. For example, using genetic testing, doctors could predict whether a person will develop certain diseases later in life. If an insurance company or employer knew that the person was destined to develop an illness, could the person be denied health coverage or a job?

Because of these concerns, about 5 percent of the funding for the Human Genome Project is devoted to exploring the project's potential consequences on society. This part of the project, called the ethical, legal, and social implications program, is one of the first efforts designed by scientists to address the potential impact of a new area of

1973, American scientists Stanley Cohen and Herbert Boyer successfully inserted genes from a toad into bacteria using recombinant-DNA technology. Their achievement marked the beginning of modern-day genetic engineering.

Within a few years, concern grew over the safety of transferring genes between bacteria and plants and animals. This concern prompted scientists to call for guidelines to make sure that recombinant-DNA research would be carried out under proper controls.

Progress in genetic engineering accelerated. And in 1980, a team led by American geneticist Frank Ruddle created the first transgenic animals—mice that had developed from embryos injected with foreign DNA. In 1982, the U.S. government's Food and Drug Administration approved the first drug produced by genetically modified bacteria. It was a synthetic form of human insulin developed by the biotechnology company Genentech. The first transgenic plants soon followed.

Also in the 1980's, researchers developed several important genetic tools. A technique called polymerase chain reaction, or PCR, was invented by American scientist Kary Mullis to rapidly produce huge quantities of DNA from just a small sample. DNA fingerprinting was invented by British scientist Alec Jeffreys to identify individuals based on their unique genetic code.

In 1990, the U.S. National Institutes of Health (NIH) launched the Human Genome Project to find all the roughly 100,000 genes that control human growth, reproduction, health, and disease. That same year, NIH researchers French Anderson and Michael Blaese performed the first human gene therapy operation.

Meanwhile, other researchers developed more efficient ways of producing transgenic animals. In 1996, a team led by Scottish scientist Ian Wilmut made the first exact copy, or clone, of an animal—a sheep named Dolly— from its adult cells. The new cloning technique opened the door to breeding identical animals that could also be

Modern genetic engineering began when researchers inserted genes from an African clawed toad (*above left*) into bacteria. Today, scientists can clone animals, such as the sheep shown above, that carry genes for producing medicines in their milk.

genetically modified to produce valuable medicines in their milk, for instance. But the breakthrough also worried many political and religious leaders, who called for a ban on human cloning.

research early on so that proper safeguards can be put into place.

▶ **FUTURE OF GENETICS**

As more genes are discovered, researchers are making greater progress toward curing and even preventing many diseases. Genetically modified crops offer hope for feeding an ever-growing world population. However, biotechnology must be used wisely, given its potential for misuse. Society must be careful not to discriminate against individuals based on their genetic makeup. And strict controls must ensure that biotechnology does not endanger our health or the environment.

Discoveries in genetics have shown us how similar we all are to one another, and to our fellow creatures on Earth. As the 21st century begins, genetics will no doubt continue to offer new opportunities for understanding—and changing—both ourselves and the world around us.

PAULA GREGORY
Director of Outreach and Education

341

TELEPHONE

The word "telephone" comes from Greek words meaning "far" and "sound," and it describes what the telephone does: The telephone uses electricity to carry sound over great distances, so that people who are far away can talk to each other.

Alexander Graham Bell developed the first successful telephone in 1876. By the end of the 20th century, more than 800 million telephones were installed in homes, schools, and offices around the world. Today in the United States alone, the average telephone subscriber makes some 3,000 calls a year.

▶ **HOW THE TELEPHONE WORKS**

A telephone has three main parts: the **transmitter** (or microphone), the **receiver** (or speaker), and the connecting **wires**. The transmitter and receiver are both part of the **handset**, the part of the telephone that you hold. You speak into the transmitter, and you hold the receiver next to your ear. A dialing mechanism may be located in the handset or in a base unit.

When you speak into a telephone, the transmitter changes the sound waves of your voice into an electric current. The transmitter accomplishes this using a thin metal sheet, or **diaphragm**. In older telephones, the diaphragm covers a small cup containing carbon granules. Sound waves striking the diaphragm press the granules together, changing the amount of electric current flowing through them. In newer telephones, which have much smaller transmitters, the diaphragm is an electrically charged foil called an **electret**. The foil sits on top of a metal plate with holes. Sound waves make the foil vibrate in the holes and change the strength of an electric field between the foil and the plate. This changing electric field creates changes in the electric current flowing through the transmitter. In both types of transmitters, these changes in current form an electrical "pattern" of your voice.

From the transmitter, the fluctuating (changing) electric current travels over a pair of wires that connect your telephone to a telephone cable. The cable, which may be suspended from a series of telephone poles or buried underground, runs to a central telephone office, where calls are routed automat-

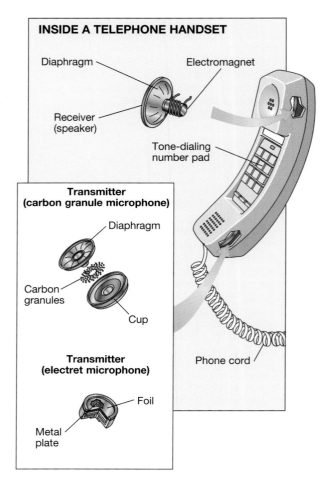

INSIDE A TELEPHONE HANDSET

Diaphragm

Electromagnet

Receiver (speaker)

Tone-dialing number pad

Transmitter (carbon granule microphone)

Diaphragm

Carbon granules

Cup

Transmitter (electret microphone)

Foil

Metal plate

Phone cord

ically through a network of telephone lines to other telephones.

When your call reaches another telephone, its receiver changes the fluctuating current carrying your voice back into sound waves. To do this, the receiver contains a permanent magnet, a diaphragm, and an **electromagnet**. An electromagnet is made of a coil of wire around a soft iron core. When current enters the receiver, it passes through the electromagnet, which creates a magnetic field that moves the diaphragm and makes the air vibrate. These vibrations reproduce the sounds of your voice.

A Telephone Call. When you lift the handset of a telephone to call a friend, you hear a **dial tone**, which tells you that the central telephone office is ready to handle your call. By dialing, you tell the office what phone you wish to reach. Some older phones use **pulse dialing**, in which the electric current is interrupted for each digit—three interruptions, for example, for the number three. Most phones now use a faster method called **tone dialing**, in which each digit is assigned a unique tone. Machines at the telephone office recognize the digits and route the call automatically.

If you are making a local call, automatic switching equipment at the central office connects you to your friend's phone. Besides making the connection, the automatic switching equipment monitors the call. It provides a busy signal if your friend's phone is being used, and it makes records of long-distance calls for billing.

More advanced kinds of connections are needed when calling outside your local area. To make some long-distance calls, you must dial an **area code** before the local number. This tells the equipment at the telephone office what part of the country you wish to reach. From the central switching station near your home, a long-distance call is connected first to a long-distance carrier, which then routes the call to the appropriate town or city. International calls pass through special switching stations. Today, most parts of the world can be dialed directly.

Telephone Lines. A telephone call may travel in a variety of ways. Older long-distance telephone cables consist of thousands of copper wires or of special pipelines called coaxial cables. Each wire or pipeline can handle a number of calls at the same time. The calls do not interfere with each other because each one is transmitted at a slightly different frequency, or rate of vibration. Because the signals fade over distance, they are amplified, or made stronger, by devices called **repeaters** that are spaced along the line.

In many areas, copper and coaxial cables are rapidly being replaced with new **fiber-optic cables**. These are made up of optical fibers—fine, flexible glass strands that carry light in the same way a

pipe carries water. A fiber-optic cable no thicker than your finger can carry some 50,000 phone calls at a time. It would take more than four copper cables, each as thick as your arm, to carry the same number of calls. In addition, fiber-optic cables require fewer repeaters.

In a fiber-optic system, the electrical signal produced by your voice is changed into a code made up of ones and zeros, like the code that operates computers. This **binary** (two-digit) code switches a tiny laser on and off thousands of times a second. Pulses of laser light travel down the optical fiber to their destination, where they are changed back into electrical signals.

Telephone cables may be strung from telephone poles, buried underground, or laid under the ocean. Sometimes, however, running cables is impractical. Long-distance telephone calls may also be transmitted by **microwave radio relay**. The signals are beamed through the air from one relay station to another or to communications satellites, which act as relay stations.

Alexander Graham Bell is shown making the first long-distance telephone call from New York to Chicago in 1892, 16 years after the patent for his telephone was issued.

Radio waves provide a wireless connection to users of portable communications devices such as a doctor's pager, a businesswoman's cellular phone, or a girl's cordless phone at home. In each case, the device provides a link to telephone line networks.

▶ HISTORY

The story of Alexander Graham Bell's invention of the telephone is told in the biography of Bell in Volume B. By 1878 there were 10,755 telephones in service in the United States. And in that year, the first commercial switchboard was built, in New Haven, Connecticut.

Since then, many improvements have been made. For example, in Bell's early telephones, the transmitter was also used as the receiver. That is, the same instrument was held first to the mouth and then to the ear. Later designs had a more convenient separate earpiece, with the mouthpiece and the bulk of the set's equipment mounted on the wall. The handset, which combined the receiver and transmitter, was introduced for general use in 1928.

As telephones improved, so did telephone lines. In the early 1900's, the vacuum tube was invented, and an amplifier making use of it was developed. In 1915, this made it possible to talk across North America from coast to coast. In 1927, commercial radio telephone service spanned the Atlantic Ocean between New York City and London. Undersea telephone cables were first laid in the 1950's, and satellite transmission began in the 1960's.

Many changes have also been made in switching. In early switchboards, connections were made by hand. An operator sat in front of a board that had a **jack** (or socket) for each line served. When a subscriber wanted service, a light would flash at the appropriate jack, and the operator would ask the subscriber what number he or she wished to reach. Then the operator would connect the two lines by plugging the ends of a short wire into the two jacks. In the 1890's, much faster automatic switching devices came into use.

Today most telephone connections are made by electronic switches, which were introduced in the 1960's. These devices, which use transistors to perform switching operations in millionths of a second, can perform much more complicated operations than the older electromechanical switches. For example, by dialing a code, users can transfer calls from their homes to any other place where they may be. Conference calls can be set up between three or more telephones.

▶ NEW TECHNOLOGY

Today telephones are available with many special features. Automatic dialers have tiny magnetic memory banks in which frequently called numbers can be stored. The user can then dial a number with a touch of one or two buttons. Some telephones have built-in answering machines, which record incoming calls and allow them to be played back later.

In **voice-mail** systems, incoming calls are routed to a telephone company's central computer if there is no answer at the number being dialed or if the number is busy. The computer records the calls, which the user can later retrieve from any telephone.

Cordless home telephones are now quite common. A cordless telephone consists of a portable handset, complete with dialing and switch-hook mechanisms, linked to a base unit by a two-way radio connection rather than wires. Calls can be made and received within several hundred feet of the base unit.

Cellular telephones are portable units that can be used away from home. A cellular phone call travels by two-way radio to a tower at a transmitter-receiver base station. These stations are set up in a network, with each one covering a specific cell, or area. As the user moves from one cell to the next, the call is automatically connected to the nearest station, which relays the call to a central switching office. Older cellular networks use **analog** transmission, in which the radio signals travel in waves that are analogous, or similar, to the sound waves of the original call. Analog transmissions are susceptible to a problem called interference, in which other signals combine with the transmissions and create static, like the noise heard between two stations on a radio.

By the mid-1990's, many cellular networks were using **digital** transmission, in which a person's voice is translated into a series of rapid radio pulses, similar to computer binary code. In digital transmission, computers check the signals for errors and automatically correct them. As a result, digital networks are able to provide cellular telephone users with much clearer calls, free of static. Digital networks also offer computer-based services, such as sending text messages that appear on a small screen on the telephone.

In the late 1990's, small mobile **satellite telephones** were introduced. Unlike cellular telephones, which have limited ranges, these new models can send and receive calls from virtually anywhere in the world. The calls are relayed by dozens of communications satellites orbiting Earth.

Other portable devices, called **pagers**, can alert users if someone is trying to reach them by telephone. In older pagers, the user is alerted by a beeping or buzzing sound. In newer models, a short text message from the person trying to reach the user may be displayed on a small screen, or a brief voice message may be heard.

Today, advances in computer technology are opening up a new world for telephone systems. People are now able to place voice and even video calls over computer networks such as the Internet. In these systems, special telephones or computers equipped with microphones, speakers, and video cameras let people both see and talk with each other.

JAMES JESPERSEN
Coauthor, *Mercury's Web: The Story of Telecommunications*

Above: Satellites now let mobile phone users send and receive calls from virtually anywhere in the world.
Below: Camera-equipped computers connected over networks let people place voice and video calls.

LAW AND LAW ENFORCEMENT

Laws are rules that define our rights and responsibilities. Laws regulate the activities of citizens and of governments. They are made official through approval by a legislature, a court, or another governmental agency. Almost every aspect of our lives is affected by law. Criminal law helps keep people safe. Laws that apply to trade and business help our economy thrive. Laws limiting the power of government protect the freedom of citizens to speak openly, practice their chosen religion, and maintain their privacy.

▶ **HISTORICAL BACKGROUND**

Philosophers once believed that prehistoric people lived without laws, in a "state of nature." Back then, the philosophers thought, people obeyed only force. As a result, life became so dangerous that leaders had to create laws to protect people and property.

Scholars no longer believe this. Instead, it is thought, people probably worked out rules for getting along with one another as soon as they began living in groups. Group members came to accept and support the manners, customs, and beliefs that controlled the living habits and behavior of the group. These shared customs and habits of life (sometimes called "folkways") were most likely the real beginnings of laws and of moral codes.

Early Laws

Some of these customs were written down as the earliest recorded laws, or **codes** of law. In Egypt written laws date from about 3400 B.C. Those in Mesopotamia date from 3500 to 2360 B.C., the period of the Sumerians.

The Babylonians developed the Code of Hammurabi, one of the greatest of the ancient codes. Hammurabi was king of Babylonia from 1792 to 1750 B.C. His code was found on three fragments of a stone column at Susa, in what is now Iraq, in 1901. It included laws defining penalties for crime and laws governing the rights of those who were injured, owned property, or made loans. It also specified procedures for enforcing the law.

Among the Hittites, who were an ancient people of Asia Minor and Syria, written law was first recorded around 1300 B.C. Among the ancient Hebrews, written laws appeared around 1200 B.C. In European history, the most famous early written code was the Twelve Tables of Roman law. These rules governed crimes, property, debts, and injuries. They were recorded on bronze and wooden tablets ("tables") in 450 B.C. The complete body of Roman law was codified (written down) about a thousand years later, in A.D. 535, by order of the emperor Justinian. The Justinian Code had a great influence on the development of modern law in Europe and

The Roman emperor Justinian (483–565) and members of his court. Under Justinian, Roman law was codified, or written down. The Justinian Code had a great influence on modern law in Europe and America.

in countries around the world where Europeans exerted their influence.

Law in the Middle Ages

In medieval Europe, laws varied from place to place. Powerful landholders created and followed their own laws. Towns and small cities that were controlled by guilds also made their own laws. Special kinds of laws developed to govern social and economic relationships between localities. **Mercantile law**, for example, was a group of rules and regulations that governed the way merchants and traders across Europe conducted business. These rules were designed to prevent cheating in trade. The Roman Catholic Church had its own set of laws, called **canon law**. It incorporated some aspects of Roman law.

In the late Middle Ages (1300–1500), local laws and specialized laws began to give way to laws that governed entire nations.

Civil Law and Common Law

As new nations arose in continental Europe, many adopted national laws based on principles of ancient Roman law. The law of those countries that developed this way is called **civil law**. These laws were eventually codified in the 1800's. The most famous of the civil codes was the Napoleonic Code, or **Code Civil**, adopted in France in 1804.

A different system of law, called **common law**, evolved at the same time in England. In place of written laws, or **statutes**, common law relied on judicial decisions. That is, to decide a dispute, judges in common law courts would look to prior court decisions in similar cases. In contrast, judges in civil law courts would consult a code for guidance. Common law took form gradually, one case at a time, and established countless rules. Among them was the right of a person accused of a crime to have a jury trial and to be presumed innocent until proved guilty. A famous compilation of these rules is the treatise of Sir William Blackstone, written in the late 1700's.

The English jurist William Blackstone (1723–80). Blackstone's famous treatise codified English common law.

Because it served as the foundation for much of the law in the United States, English common law remains an important source of guidance for American courts today. Blackstone is still cited in decisions of the United States Supreme Court. The law of one state, Louisiana, grew out of the Napoleonic Code and from the civil-law tradition, not the common law, because Louisiana was settled by the French, not the English.

International Law

Just as small communities once banded together to develop national law, nations have developed international law to regulate relations with each other. As early as the 1500's in Europe, legal thinkers such as Hugo Grotius (1583–1645), a Dutch jurist and statesman, and Emerich de Vattel (1714–67), a Swiss jurist, worked out systems of international law. Then as now, the primary goals were to try to prevent war and promote good relations between countries.

International law today consists of treaties—formal agreements between countries—and long-standing customs. International law is enforced in international courts. The most important is the International Court of Justice at The Hague, in the Netherlands.

▶ THE LEGAL SYSTEM IN THE UNITED STATES

In the United States, laws exist at three levels. Federal laws apply to the entire country. State laws apply to activities within the borders of one state. Local laws apply within a city or township.

The supreme law in the United States—the law with which all other law must conform—is set out in the United States Constitution. States have adopted their own constitutions, governing the law in each state. These written documents determine the organization of government as well as the rights of the people. Like the United States Constitution, most state constitutions are quite short. They express rules in general

The Virginia state legislature in session. In the United States, federal, state, and local laws are adopted by legislatures—lawmaking bodies that are elected directly by the people.

Statutes typically may be repealed (canceled) or amended (changed) by a majority of the legislature with the agreement of the executive. Constitutions are not as easy to change. Article V of the U.S. Constitution provides that any amendment must be proposed by two-thirds of both houses of Congress, or two-thirds of the states' legislatures. Then the amendment must be ratified (approved) by "the Legislatures of three-fourths of the several States, or by Conventions in three-fourths thereof."

terms, leaving courts and lawmakers to work out specific applications of the rules.

How Laws Are Made

At federal, state, and local levels, written laws are adopted by a legislature or, in the case of local laws, a council elected by the people. When a legislature approves a new law, it is said to enact legislation. In addition, government agencies are sometimes authorized by a legislature to develop rules in their area of expertise. These "administrative" rules and regulations have the force of law.

Federal laws are adopted by the U.S. Congress. A bill, which is a proposal for a new law, may be introduced in either house of Congress—the Senate or the House of Representatives. The bill is first reviewed by a committee of legislators who may hold hearings to get opinions from experts and others who may be interested in the issues addressed by the bill. The bill must be approved by the committee and then by both the House of Representatives and the Senate. Then, to become law, it must be signed by the president. If the president vetoes, or rejects, a bill, the veto may be overridden by a vote of at least two-thirds of both the House and Senate. Similarly, governors must sign state legislation, and state legislatures have the power to override a veto.

Judges, as well as legislators, make law. Judges adopt rules of court that dictate procedures in the court system. Judges also interpret other sources of law, elaborating on the rules, expanding or narrowing their effects, or applying the rules to new situations. American courts, as the English courts before them, generally look to prior decisions on a legal issue for guidance on how to decide cases that raise a similar issue. By declaring legal rules and interpreting other sources of law such as the Constitution and statutes, courts provide guidance for those who seek to comply with the law and predict its requirements.

Did you know that...

the American Civil Liberties Union (ACLU) was founded in 1920 to protect the constitutional rights and liberties of people in the United States? The ACLU provides legal counsel in cases involving such civil liberties as freedom of speech, separation of church and state, due process of law, and the right to privacy. It also provides legal representation for people whose civil liberties have been violated.

Public Law and Private Law

U.S. law can be divided into two broad categories, **public law** and **private law**. Public law concerns the legal relationship between the government and citizens. It includes constitutional law, criminal law, regulations of administrative agencies such as the Internal Revenue Service and the Environmental Protection Agency, and the law governing court procedures. A violation of a person's civil rights, a theft or murder, and a case of illegal pollution are matters that involve public law.

Private law, often called civil law, regulates the relationships between private individuals and between individuals and nongovernmental entities, such as businesses and other organizations. Private law includes the law of contracts (agreements between people or between people and businesses), torts (wrongful acts that are not crimes but cause harm), and property. Matters such as the purchase of a home, a divorce, inheritance, and the formation of a corporation all involve private law.

▶ **HOW LAWS ARE ENFORCED**

Police, courts, and government agencies all play roles in enforcing the law. The role of the police is to investigate crimes and apprehend those suspected of committing crimes.

In the United States, each town, each county, and each state has its own police force. The federal government has several law enforcement agencies, including the Federal Bureau of Investigation and the Bureau of Alcohol, Tobacco, and Firearms. These various law enforcement agencies have to work together frequently. Sometimes they form task forces to coordinate their efforts to investigate particular types of crime.

The role of the courts is to provide a forum for weighing evidence of crimes and settling disputes fairly. The U.S. Constitution, as well as state and federal laws, sets out the minimum standards for fairness in court proceedings. These include the right of those accused of crimes or involved in disputes to be notified of the proceedings and to be heard by the court before a decision is made. The jury system is very important to the goal of fairness. Jurors are ordinary people who are chosen to hear and decide court cases. Their decisions are seen as fair because they are not associated with the government or with one side or the other in any case. Court pro-

ceedings are open to the public so that people can assess for themselves whether the processes are fair.

Government agencies may also help enforce the law. The Equal Employment Opportunity Commission (EEOC), for example, enforces the law prohibiting employment discrimination by seeking reinstatement or back pay for employees who can show that they have been denied a job or a promotion because of their race, sex, religion, veteran's status, age, or disability. Agencies may act through administrative sanctions or through lawsuits. Administrative sanctions are penalties imposed by an agency for violations of its rules. For example, the Internal Revenue Service may fine citizens who do not pay the taxes they owe.

A highway patrol officer tickets a truck driver for a traffic violation. To protect the community at large, the police must apprehend those who violate the law.

Enforcing Criminal Law

When a crime is committed, police and agents of law enforcement agencies such as the Federal Bureau of Investigation help uncover and collect the evidence. Then attorneys representing the government, called prosecutors or district attorneys, bring charges against the suspected lawbreaker in

A Glossary of Legal Terms

Act of God: A legal term for a natural event of overwhelming force, such as an earthquake or an accident that could not have been prevented by human action. Under the law of negligence, a person cannot be held responsible for damages or injuries caused by such an event.

Blue laws: Legislation that seeks to regulate matters of individual conscience or conduct, such as laws prohibiting drinking or working on Sunday. The term originated during colonial days in New Haven, Connecticut, where such laws were bound in blue paper.

Bylaws: Laws or rules by which a city, corporation, or other organization governs its affairs and members. In the case of a municipality, a bylaw has the force of law; in other private organizations, it is merely an agreement among members. The term also refers to a secondary rule subordinate to a constitution.

Capital punishment: The execution (killing) of a person found guilty of a serious crime.

Class action: A type of lawsuit in which a few persons represent a large group of people with the same legal problem. Class actions are often brought in employment discrimination and consumer rights cases. The outcome of a class action affects all those in the group except those who opt out of the lawsuit.

Contempt of court: A term used in law courts to refer to an act that hinders or obstructs court proceedings or lessens the dignity or authority of the court. The term also refers to failure to comply with a court order. Persons charged with contempt may be imprisoned or fined.

Court martial: A military court responsible for trial of members of armed forces or those civilians who commit offenses against military or naval law in time of war or during military operations.

Double indemnity: Payment of twice the basic amount promised. Double indemnity clauses often appear in life insurance contracts, requiring that the beneficiary be paid double the amount of the policy if death of the insured is accidental.

Double jeopardy: Prosecution twice for the same criminal offense. "Jeopardy" begins when a jury is sworn in, or when evidence is first introduced. The U.S. Constitution prohibits double jeopardy. A second trial may be held, however, if the jury in the first trial could not reach a verdict or if the verdict is appealed on the grounds of procedural errors.

Due process: A term for legal proceedings that follow an established system of law. Due process is guaranteed by the U.S. Constitution. It ensures that a person accused of a crime will be treated fairly. Due process requires that an accused person understand the charges, be informed of his or her legal rights, and be given a fair trial. The concept of due process dates back to the English Magna Carta (1215), which stated that no person may be deprived of life, liberty, or property, except "by the lawful judgment of his peers and by the law of the land."

Estate: Property that a person owns, including all personal possessions. An estate that is held by one person for another is called a trust.

Gentlemen's agreement: An agreement in which the parties involved are bound by honor and not by a legal contract. The term is applied to any such agreement between individuals, groups, or nations. It was used to describe an agreement between Japan and the United States in 1907. Japan agreed to restrict emigration of workers to the United States. In return President Theodore Roosevelt promised that no law would be passed to prevent Japanese from entering the United States.

A court officer swears in a witness. In trials, attorneys (foreground) question witnesses and present evidence. Jurors (at right) weigh evidence to determine guilt or innocence.

Habeas corpus: Latin for "you should have the body." A writ issued by a judge ordering an official to release a prisoner held in custody in violation of the law. It originated in early English law to prevent illegal imprisonment and is considered a cornerstone of civil liberty. According to the U.S. Constitution, the remedy of habeas corpus cannot be suspended unless, in cases of rebellion or invasion, public safety is at stake.

Injunction: A written court order either prohibiting a person or group from performing, or requiring them to perform, a certain act. Injunctions are often used in labor disputes and in instances of restraint of trade.

Inns of Court: The four legal societies that prepare students for the practice of law in England. Founded in London in the late 1200's and early 1300's, they are called Gray's Inn, the Inner Temple, Lincoln's Inn, and the Middle Temple.

Inquest: An inquiry made by a group of people appointed by a court. The term applies either to a jury that conducts a legal investigation of evidence or to the findings of such a jury. A coroner's inquest involves the investigation of the death of a person who may have died of unnatural causes.

Justice of the peace: An official of a town, county, or precinct, with limited judicial and administrative powers. The office may be elective or appointive. Powers and duties differ in different states. A justice of the peace may preside at the trials of small civil suits and crimes involving minor offenses. Among other duties, a justice of the peace may also perform marriage ceremonies. The office, which has existed in the United States since colonial times, began in the 1200's in England.

Kangaroo court: A court in which legal principles are ignored or perverted. The term usually refers to a prison court organized by the inmates to punish newcomers and those who do not conform to their rules or "code." The title is often applied to courts without legal standing set up in frontier territories. The phrase possibly originated in Australia, where kangaroos are found, when it was a British penal colony.

Limitations, Statute of: Law, originated (1623) under James I of England, limiting the period of time during which a person or group may bring claims to court, defend certain rights, or bring action against criminal offenders. It prevents prosecutors from delaying a trial until the evidence needed for defense has been destroyed or witnesses have died. In criminal cases, it supports the principle that the offender or suspect cannot be subject to prosecution forever.

Martial law: Rule by military forces. Martial law is usually declared by the head of a nation or state when danger, emergency, or panic creates a situation that cannot be handled by the local government. Martial law is usually temporary. But some nations have been ruled by martial law for long periods of time.

Miranda rights: Term from *Miranda* v. *Arizona* (1966), in which the U.S. Supreme Court ruled that statements made by suspects during questioning by police may not be used as evidence unless the suspects have been informed of their rights and warned that their statements may be used in court against them. These rights include the right to remain silent and to consult a lawyer.

Next of kin: The term for a person's nearest relative or relatives. It refers to those who may legally share in the estate of a person who died without making a will. The term usually applies only to people who are related by blood. But, in some areas, laws may also include a husband or wife.

Notary public: A public official authorized by a state government to certify official documents by signing them and stamping them with a notary public seal in order to give them credit and authenticity. Notary publics also administer oaths and take acknowledgements of documents.

Old Bailey: The common name for the Central Criminal Court in London, England. An older court that was the scene of many historic trials, it was described by Charles Dickens in *A Tale of Two Cities.* Newgate Prison, demolished in 1902–03, once stood opposite it. Old Bailey was so named because it was in a "bailey" (a space between the inner and outer walls) of early London.

Ombudsman: A public official appointed to receive, investigate, and channel complaints of citizens involving abuses of power by government officials. The ombudsman cannot order or reverse administrative action but can make recommendations for corrective measures. *Ombudsman* is a Swedish word meaning "representative."

Quorum: The number of members of an organization that must be present in order to conduct business legally. In England "quorum" originally referred to certain justices of the peace who were required to be present at court sessions.

Reprieve: From the French word *reprendre,* meaning "to take back." In criminal law, the postponement or suspension of the execution of a sentence. It is declared by a court or officials with pardoning power.

Search warrant: An order issued by a legal authority authorizing a particular officer to search a specific house or other premise for stolen property, unlawful goods, and occasionally persons. Usually the order requires that the goods or persons searched for and found be brought before the magistrate.

Sunset laws: Laws requiring periodic review of boards, commissions, and other agencies of government. These laws provide for automatic termination, or "sunset," of such agencies unless they are re-authorized. Many states of the United States have passed sunset laws in the hope of increasing efficiency in government.

Sunshine laws: Laws designed to keep government proceedings open to the public. These laws forbid or restrict closed sessions of many government boards and councils, except in specified situations.

court. The charges are reviewed by a judge or a grand jury to make sure they have some basis ("probable cause") for bringing the accused to trial. A judge decides whether the accused should be released pending trial or kept in jail. If the judge chooses to release the accused, an amount of money known as **bail** must be placed with the court as a guarantee that the accused will return at an appointed time to stand trial.

To help ensure fairness, defendants in criminal cases are protected by certain guarantees. For example, anyone accused of a serious crime, or felony (a crime carrying a penalty of over one year's imprisonment), has the right to a jury trial. Every person accused of a serious crime is also entitled to a lawyer to help present a defense against the charges. If the defendant (the accused person) cannot afford to pay a lawyer, the court will provide an attorney. People may represent themselves in court if they wish. But people without legal training are rarely skilled enough in the law to say and do the things that are needed to properly represent their own interests in court.

Only a small portion of criminal cases—10 percent or less—actually go to trial. Many criminal charges are dropped before trial or rejected by a judge or jury as unfounded. And most convictions are the result of guilty pleas before trial. Often the accused will plead guilty in exchange for a shorter sentence or the dismissal of another charge. This "plea bargaining" saves the government the cost of having to conduct a trial. It also allows prosecutors to handle more cases than they

could if each case went to trial before a judge or jury.

Criminal law is enforced through punishment, usually imprisonment and fines. Legislatures set limits on the penalties for each crime, and those limits are contained in the statutes defining the crime. While a jury may decide at trial whether or not a person committed the crime charged, it is usually the judge who decides what punishment to impose within the limits set by law.

Private Lawsuits

Laws other than criminal laws are enforced through private lawsuits. A person who claims that another has failed to obey the law may sue that person. The plaintiff (the person bringing the suit) asks the court for a judgment forcing the defendant (the person being sued) to comply or pay a sum of money. For example, a person who thinks another has failed to carry out a written agreement may sue for "breach of contract."

In lawsuits between private parties, the parties and their lawyers investigate the facts and present their sides of the story to the courts in written papers and at trial. The standard of proof required in private lawsuits is not as high as that required in criminal cases. Plaintiffs do not need to prove their claims "beyond a reasonable doubt," the standard in criminal trials. They only need to show that their claims are "probably true." However, most lawsuits are settled out of court. That is, the parties reach an agreement before the case goes to trial.

▶ CAREERS IN LAW

Lawyers help people understand the law and obtain the benefits and protections it provides. In the United States, lawyers (also called attorneys) are college-trained women and men who have completed law school and are licensed to practice law.

Legal Education

In law school, students learn how to analyze and present legal problems. They study the Constitution, treaties, statutes, and regulations of the United States, as well as state laws. Many students study the laws of other countries and international law. Law students also study court decisions and the ways that judges use them to decide new cases. As lawyers, they will be better able to predict how the courts will decide their cases, to advise their clients what actions to take, and to persuade judges why the law supports their clients' interests.

Basic courses cover criminal law, torts, contracts, and property law. Students also take courses in professional responsibility (the ethical standards required of lawyers), civil and criminal procedure (the rules that govern how laws are enforced), and special forms of law, such as tax law, copyright law, or family law. A huge variety of human activity is dis-

It takes hard work to succeed as a law student. Law school courses are demanding and call for excellent writing and research skills.

cussed in law school classes. Lawyers must learn how to study new subjects, spot problems, absorb information quickly, and present information clearly in writing and in speech.

After law school, a lawyer may decide to concentrate on a particular kind of law, such as criminal law, labor law, patent law, or tax law. Some of the special fields require additional training. Those who practice tax law, for example, usually have some training in mathematics and accounting.

Licensing

After students have completed formal law school training, they must secure a license to practice law. They must take and pass a difficult test, known as the bar examination. Usually lawyers must take a bar examination in each state in which they wish to practice, because each state has its own rules about training and licensing lawyers.

Applicants also must show that they are of good character. A committee appointed by the court or bar association investigates the background, training, employment, and past behavior of the applicant. Lawyers are bound by a code of ethics that requires them to maintain the highest standards of fidelity and honesty, and to devote themselves to the cause of their clients. The code requires that as well as being loyal to their clients, lawyers must be fair and honest with judges and other lawyers.

Ethical rules are enforced by the bar association and the courts of each state. Should a lawyer violate these ethical rules, the lawyer can be punished and may even lose his or her license to practice law.

Practicing Law

Much of a lawyer's work is carried on in an office, not in the courtroom. Lawyers advise clients about how to comply with the law, help clients resolve legal problems, and negotiate settlements in disputes. They help people set up and manage businesses and draw up wills and contracts.

When a dispute arises, lawyers may initiate a lawsuit, asking a court to decide whose position is right. For instance, a lawyer may help a person who has been injured by a product bring a lawsuit against the product's manufacturer. The process of preparing, developing, and resolving or trying these lawsuits is called **litigation**. It is usually much less costly to settle disputes out of court, before trial. The only disputes that end up in the courtroom are those that lawyers and clients cannot resolve in other ways.

In criminal cases, lawyers may be prosecutors or defense attorneys. Prosecutors present the evidence against the accused and argue for conviction. They work for the government. A defense attorney represents the defendant and tries to show why the defendant deserves to be released or acquitted, or to receive a less serious penalty. Public defenders are lawyers who are paid by the government to represent people who have been accused of crimes and cannot afford to hire a defense attorney.

Lawyers may work on their own or as members of a law firm. Law firms range in size from a few lawyers to hundreds. The largest firms have offices in several cities. Some lawyers work for only one business or client, as "house counsel," rather than for a

A lawyer explains the terms of a will to his client. The day-to-day work of many lawyers involves counseling individuals on legal issues pertaining to routine matters of life and death.

nity from crime and enforce the law. Police officers investigate crimes, apprehend people suspected of crimes, collect evidence needed to prove crimes, and often testify in court about these activities. Police also work to prevent crime. They help control crowds and protect dignitaries, and they visit schools and other organizations to help teach others about safety and crime prevention. Police officers may specialize in a certain type of police work; for example, canine experts work with police dogs, and arson investigators become experts on fires. The term "police" usually refers to municipal law enforcement agencies. Agencies that perform similar duties include state highway patrols, public safety agencies, and county sheriffs' offices.

A variety of other careers are vital to fair and efficient law enforcement. Counselors and advocates help victims of crime and witnesses to crime. Victims and witnesses may need help coping with the effects of crime and with their responsibilities in a prosecution. Scientists and other experts analyze evidence such as blood, fibers, drugs, and firearms. Government employees maintain arrest records, fingerprint records, even DNA profiles of offenders. Each court is staffed by administrators, secretaries, clerks, bailiffs, and security officers.

Probation officers prepare sentencing recommendations and monitor offenders who are released on probation—that is, on conditions such as maintaining employment or submitting to drug tests. Prisons employ guards, wardens, doctors, psychiatrists, and ministers. Parole boards in many states decide whether prisoners may be released from prison before the end of their sentences. Parole officers are similar to probation officers, keeping track of those who are released from prison and working with them to make sure they meet the conditions of release.

law firm representing many clients. Lawyers are involved in public interest litigation, too, working on cases involving welfare, education, the environment, or the rights of consumers. Some of these lawyers work for legal aid societies, unions, and other organizations that represent people who cannot afford to hire their own lawyers.

The broad and varied training lawyers receive helps many succeed in careers other than law. Lawyers often go into business or government. Some enter politics and run for public office. Of all the presidents of the United States, more than two-thirds were licensed to practice as lawyers. Lawyers also may become judges, either by election or political appointment.

▶ CAREERS IN LAW ENFORCEMENT

Police officers are government employees whose job is to protect their commu-

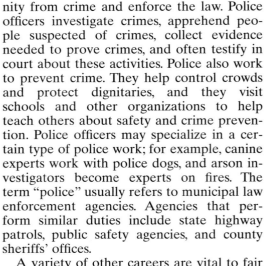

Nancy Jean King
Vanderbilt University
School of Law

Alerted by a broken window, a police officer checks out the scene of a possible break-in. Police work is often dangerous.

Magnificent guildhalls represented the power and wealth of medieval guilds. The Guildhall in the City of London, dating from the 1400's, still stands and now houses the City's government.

GUILDS

Guilds were societies or associations formed during the Middle Ages (500–1500) in Europe by people in the same line of work. A guild protected the economic interests of its members. There were merchant guilds and craft guilds. At their peak, the guilds controlled a town's trade and industry and often exercised political power.

A guild looked after its members. When a member died, the guild might pay for his funeral as well as help his widow and children. Guilds also had their own courts and settled quarrels between members. If a member was thrown into jail in another town, the guild worked to free him.

Guilds were also the center of social life for their members. Members met in guildhalls for grand feasts and other celebrations and festivals, and they would hold parades in honor of the guild's patron saint. Guilds sometimes participated in town projects as well, setting up schools and hospitals, helping pave streets, and establishing water systems.

▶ MERCHANT GUILDS

In the early Middle Ages traders traveling from town to town needed protection from robbers. Even nobles sometimes turned highwaymen and robbed passing merchants. Nobles often collected tolls from traders who journeyed across their land. So merchants banded together to protect their lives and goods.

The merchants of a town also wanted protection against competition from other traders. A guild's main purpose was to hold a monopoly, or exercise complete control, of trade. Each guild received a charter from the local king or lord, and the charter gave the guild this right of monopoly. With the monopoly, the guilds often grew rich and powerful. Each guild also fixed prices and set standards of weights, measures, and quality for its particular business. Only guild members were allowed to conduct business in a town; a visiting trader could only conduct business after he received permission from the town's guild and paid a high fee.

▶ CRAFT GUILDS

Skilled craftsmen made by hand everything medieval people used—saddles, woolen cloth, shoes, furniture. At first craftsmen produced goods mainly for the nobles. As market towns grew, they produced more and more for the general trade. Increased trade demanded more craftsmen. Soon the craftsmen organized guilds of their own.

Like the merchant guilds, each craft guild had a charter granted by the king or noble. Unlike the members of the merchant guilds, however, the craft guild members made one particular product. Only guild members in a town had the right to make certain articles. Each craft—the goldsmith's, arrowsmith's, weaver's, cobbler's—had a separate guild. In fact, a guild might specialize in making a single kind of hat, as the peacock-hatters did.

Also like the merchant guilds, the craft guilds set prices, standards of workmanship, and conditions of sales. They also controlled hours and wages.

Most members took pride in their fine craftsmanship. Occasionally, however, some workers took shortcuts, folding cloth to hide worn spots or using cheaper metal in a pot that later melted when a customer tried to use it on the fire. If a guild caught a member doing such things, it fined him. A member who continued might be banished from the town, which meant that he could no longer sell his goods there.

▶ TRAINING FOR THE CRAFT GUILDS

The craft guild had three ranks: apprentice, journeyman, and master.

Apprentice. A boy in his teens became apprenticed to a master. He served for three to twelve years, depending on how much skill he needed for his craft. Seven years was usual in England. The apprentice lived like a son in his master's house and worked in his master's shop. His master gave him clothing, room, board, and training. The boy received no money, except sometimes during the last years of his service. If he ran away, he was brought back and punished. But the guild also punished masters who were cruel to apprentices. When an apprentice finished his service, he received a sum of money and "graduated" to journeyman.

Journeyman. The journeyman (the French word *journée* means "day") hired out his services by the day to master craftsmen for wages. He improved his skill and saved money to buy his own tools in hopes of setting up his own shop. Sometimes he chose to work for an aging master. When the master died, he might inherit the shop. Usually he had to produce a "masterpiece" as proof of his skill and pay a sum of money. Only then would the guild promote him to master rank and admit him to membership.

Master. A journeyman was usually in his early 20's when he became a master. A master craftsman directed the work in his own workshop and owned the materials and tools used there. On festival days he was entitled to wear a special uniform called livery. Master craftsmen ran the guilds and elected their officers. They also inspected the workshops of guild members.

▶ THE GUILDS WEAKEN

As time passed the guilds became less democratic. A father handed down his membership to his son. Outsiders found it harder and harder to join. Some of them set up their own shops and competed with the guilds. Masters controlled the guilds and made jour-

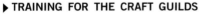
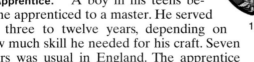

Above: The coats of arms for the Twelve Great Livery Companies of London, the present-day descendants of medieval guilds: (1) Mercers (fabric dealers), (2) Grocers, (3) Drapers, (4) Fishmongers, (5) Goldsmiths, (6) Skinners, (7) Merchant Taylors, (8) Haberdashers (men's clothing merchants), (9) Salters, (10) Ironmongers, (11) Vintners (wine merchants), and (12) Clothworkers.

To become a skilled craftsperson, intensive training and practice are as important today as they were in the Middle Ages. Here, students are learning to become luthiers—makers of stringed musical instruments.

neymen work many years before promoting them to master rank. Many never became masters, remaining journeymen all their lives. After a while journeymen broke away and formed their own associations.

By the 1500's, guilds began to lose their monopolies. Central governments became stronger, and towns were no longer so independent. Independent businessmen hired people living outside the towns to do piecework in their homes. These home, or domestic, workers were not under guild regulations. The introduction of machines during the 1700's further weakened the guilds' control over production.

Home workshops and then factories took over the production of goods, but the guild lingered on as a social club. Guild members still wore their bright costumes for special parades on traditional feast days.

▶ GUILDS TODAY

The term "guild" is used more freely today than it was in the Middle Ages; it can refer to a formal organization as well as to a social club. Modern guilds fall into two basic categories, professional and amateur, and they share some common traits. Both seek to promote a particular hobby, profession, or industry. They usually create guidelines for membership and set standards for conduct and quality of work. These guilds provide an opportunity for people with a common interest to share ideas and learn more about their craft through educational programs or meetings. Some guilds are open to both professional and amateur members and may have national as well as international chapters.

Professional. Professional guilds are similar to labor unions. They act as advocates for their members as well as for the profession, often ensuring fair wages, protecting their legal rights, monitoring working conditions, and offering pensions and health benefits. The guidelines and structures of professional guilds tend to be rather formal because members make their living by their craft. Examples of professional guilds are the Writers Guild of America and the Graphic Artists Guild.

Amateur. These guilds are mainly recreational and social; they usually focus on a particular hobby and do not offer the extensive benefits that professional guilds can. Because members are less likely to make their living from their craft, the guidelines for membership and practice tend to be looser. Guilds of this type include organizations for quilters, embroiderers, glass engravers, knitters, and even operagoers.

Reviewed by KENNETH S. COOPER
George Peabody College

and grandparents of their own, and to learn about how their lives differed from yours.

▶ GENEALOGY AS A HOBBY

By the late 1800's, an increasing number of Americans had become interested in researching their family histories. Many were proud of relatives who had served in the American Revolution or the Civil War. Organizations called lineage societies became popular during this period. Among the best known is the National Society of the Daughters of the American Revolution (DAR), an organization for women. In order to join the DAR, a woman must research her ancestors and prove that she has a direct lineal descent from someone who helped the United States become an independent nation. A direct lineal descent is a direct relationship to an ancestor, rather than a connection through marriage. Other well-known lineage societies include the Sons of Union Veterans of the Civil War, the United Daughters of the Confederacy, and the General Society of Mayflower Descendants.

Interest in genealogy soared in 1976 with the publication of Alex Haley's book *Roots*, a best-seller that later became one of the most popular miniseries in the history of television. The story described Haley's African American heritage and family history, which was deeply influenced by the institution of slavery. Many people were inspired by *Roots* and by Haley's obvious pride in his ancestors.

When personal computers came into use in the early 1980's, genealogy software programs were created, making it much easier to research and keep track of one's family history. More and more people began to pursue genealogy as a hobby. Later the Internet added a new dimension to genealogical research. Now people can network with long-lost family members and friends around the world, right from their own homes. Even a beginning genealogist can use online databases to search for his or her ancestors. For all these reasons, genealogy

Above: A mother shares family stories with her young son while looking at a photo album. *Right:* Old family photographs are excellent sources of genealogical information, particularly ones that are dated and contain the names and relationships of the people pictured.

GENEALOGY

Genealogy is the study of a person's family history. When and where were your parents born? Who were your grandparents? When and where were they born? When did your family move to where you live now? Why did they move, where did they come from, and what did they leave behind? All these questions, and many more, are the things you will need to ask yourself when you first think about beginning your genealogical research.

Some people love history and want to know more about their ancestors and their own place in history. Knowing that a family member lived through a particular historical event or made a mark on the world can be exciting and a great source of pride. Or you may simply be curious about the older members of your family. It can be fun to think of your grandparents as small children, with parents

A FAMILY TREE

has become one of the most popular hobbies in the world today.

▶ A FAMILY TREE

Many types of charts can illustrate how family members are related to one another. Two standard ones are a pedigree chart and a descendant chart. Each shows a series of boxes that contain information about every individual in your family. The boxes are connected to one another with a series of lines that display the lineal descent from each ancestor to a specific individual. As you fill out one of these charts, you create a family tree.

Begin with a box for yourself. Show two "branches" of your tree that point to two new boxes—one for each of your parents. Then do the same for each set of their parents (your grandparents), and keep going. It is easy to see how your family tree branches out, backward in time, to several groups of ancestors.

My Ancestors

Name of Person _____

Relation to Me _____

Birth Date _____ Place _____

Father's Name _____

Mother's Name _____

Brothers' and Sisters' Names _____
_____

Schools Attended _____
_____

Occupations _____
_____

Where He/She Lived _____
_____

Spouse's Name _____

Marriage Date _____ Place _____

Children:
Name _____ Birth Date _____
_____

Death Date _____

Place of Burial _____

▶ BEGINNING YOUR RESEARCH

Genealogical research is not a quick and easy process. It is a lot like a puzzle or a detective story in which your family members are the characters. Be prepared to keep detailed notes and to spend a lot of time organizing all the information you gather. Start with a set of blank questionnaires, one for each individual. Fill these forms out as completely as possible, and keep them together in a three-ring binder for easy access. If you have a computer, you can use one of the many genealogy software programs available to make your record keeping much easier. These programs allow you to enter information and print a variety of reports and forms that can help you organize your research.

Begin with Yourself and Your Family

When researching genealogy, always begin with yourself and go backward in time, working from the known to the unknown. Talk to all the relatives in your family, including your parents, grandparents, aunts, uncles, cousins, and the oldest living members of the family.

Ask them about their lives, the lives of their parents, and any memories they have of their ancestors. As you fill out the forms and charts, you will need to ask for specific facts, such as the dates and locations of your family members' births, marriages, and deaths; where they are buried; and their occupations and religions. Your family probably has other sources that you can explore. Sometimes heirlooms—precious objects that have been passed from one generation to the next—can tell a story. Photographs, family papers, diaries, and other family documents may all reveal information regarding your family history.

The Importance of Records

Genealogy is a process of confirming your own relationship to each person in your ancestry through reliable records. First, obtain a copy of your birth certificate, which will provide information about your own parents. Then get a copy of your parents' marriage certificate and their birth certificates. Try to do the same for your grandparents, and keep going. As you move back in time, you will find that records are a bit harder to find, especially vital records such as birth and death certificates dating back a hundred years or more. So you will need to look through other types of records, such as land records, lists of people in the military, ships' passenger lists, and federal census records. There are four places where you can begin searching for these records: your local LDS Family History Center (FHC), your local library and various genealogical or historical societies, and the Internet.

LDS Family History Centers. Family History Centers (FHC's) are run by the Church of Jesus Christ of Latter-day Saints (LDS), also known as the Mormon Church. There are more than 3,000 FHC's worldwide, and they are open to everyone, not just to LDS Church members. There is no fee to use an FHC, but there are small rental fees to order copies of microfilmed records from the central Family History Library in Salt Lake City, Utah. The LDS Church is dedicated to making records easily accessible to their church members, who do genealogical research to fulfill religious responsibilities, and it shares these same resources with the entire genealogical community. Theirs is the world's largest collection of records, so an FHC is the first place to start your own search for records about your family. Volunteers at the FHC's are very helpful, and they will point beginners in the right direction.

Libraries and Societies. Many city libraries have collections of genealogy and local history books, and a growing number of town libraries have similar collections. Be sure to visit libraries in your area to learn what books are available that might help you.

Similarly, you can find genealogical and historical societies all around the world. Genealogical societies generally have monthly meetings and a regular publication, such as a newsletter or journal. Often they hold classes to help people who are new to genealogy. Some societies are very active in their local community. Often they participate in projects to preserve historical records and encourage others to do the same.

The Internet. The Internet has affected genealogy in many ways. Family historians are having more success now than ever before. There are many educational resources online, including courses, articles by professionals, and electronic newsletters and magazines. The Internet also allows genealogists to share their ideas and the results of their research. People regularly share database files and photographs by e-mail. There are also genealogy mailing lists with the names and e-mail addresses of people interested in hundreds of different topics related to genealogy. These lists allow people to communicate as a group. Some mailing lists are dedicated to specific surnames (a family's last name). Others limit their research to specific counties, states, or countries around the world. There are also mailing lists for certain religious groups, such as the Quakers, and for historical events, such as the Civil War.

In the past, genealogists who wanted to share their family history research with others had to publish a book. This was often an expensive project that took a lot of work and time. Now a family historian can easily publish small portions of his or her research on a personal Web site at almost no expense. And instead of being available on the shelves of a few hundred libraries, that research is available to anyone in the world with access to the Internet.

The Internet also has many databases and text files consisting of transcribed records (copies of originals) or extracted records (excerpts from originals), such as census reports or ships' passenger lists. A genealogist must always keep in mind that such records may contain errors. For the most part, records found on the Internet should be used only as tools to help you find the actual original records.

▶ **OTHER RESOURCES**

There are many other useful resources in addition to those detailed above. The **National Genealogical Society (NGS),** founded in 1903, serves the needs of individuals, families, societies, and libraries across the United States. It offers educational materials, annual genealogy seminars, and an extensive library at its headquarters in Arlington, Virginia. The **National Society of the Daughters of the American Revolution (DAR)** is a lineage society established in 1896. Thousands of members live in many countries around the world. The DAR library, located in Washington, D.C., is open to the public and is one of the largest of its kind. The **Library of Congress** was established in 1800 as an official library for the government. At first, the book collection consisted mainly of Thomas Jefferson's personal library. Today the collection includes more than 100 million items, including a copy of almost every new book published in the United States. The library also has a genealogy room with a unique collection of family histories and other resources. The **National Archives and Records Administration (NARA)** stores important U.S. government records. Genealogists make use of the 13 regional branches in order to look at copies of the U.S. Federal Census for the years 1790 through 1920. Also available from the National Archives are military records, ships' passenger lists, and a large variety of other records. The **New England Historic Genealogical Society (NEHGS),** nicknamed the Hist-Gen, was formed in Boston, Massachusetts, in 1845. It is the oldest genealogical society and is best known for records pertaining to ancestors who lived in the six New England states. The society has a large library collection of nearly 200,000 books, as well as journals, microfilms, and CD-ROM's.

CYNDI HOWELLS
Netting Your Ancestors: Genealogical Research on the Internet

TELEVISION

Can you imagine spending a day without encountering television? It is almost everywhere you turn.

Television is the most popular form of entertainment in the United States and most other countries. More than 98 percent of American homes have at least one television set. About three-quarters of those homes have at least two sets, some so portable they can be put in a pocket. The average family has television on about seven hours a day, about the same number of hours a student spends in school each day.

Television plays many important roles. It is the main source of news as well as entertainment for most Americans. Television is also used as a teaching tool in schools and businesses. At baseball, football, and basketball games, huge television screens help fans enjoy the action through close-ups and replays.

Television has important uses in industry and science, too. It allows workers to watch over radioactive materials or dangerous machinery from a safe distance. Surgeons use tiny television cameras to guide them during delicate operations. TV cameras have been placed aboard satellites to help meteorologists predict the weather, and they have traveled millions of miles into space to bring back scenes of Mars.

The word "television" comes from Greek and Latin words that mean "to see from far off." Television is a way of sending images (and sound) over distances. The images may be sent a short distance to just a few people, such as the workers who use television to watch over dangerous machinery. Or they may be sent over long distances to many people—the audience for an episode of a popular television show may number in the millions. Those images may also be saved and

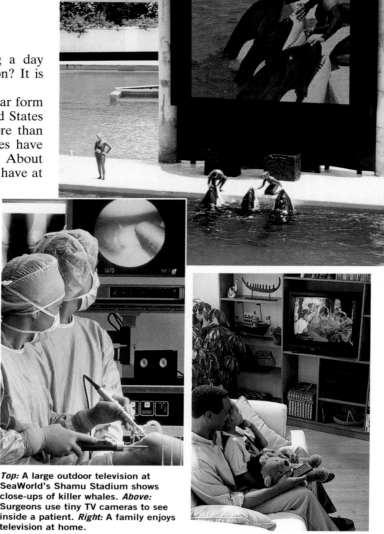

Top: A large outdoor television at SeaWorld's Shamu Stadium shows close-ups of killer whales. *Above:* Surgeons use tiny TV cameras to see inside a patient. *Right:* A family enjoys television at home.

watched later, using video recording systems. And now television is being used to transmit computer information as well as images.

▶ HOW TELEVISION WORKS

In television, images and sound travel electronically—that is, by means of electrical energy. A television camera changes the light that is reflected from a scene into electronic signals. Then a device called a transmitter sends out the signals (along with signals for the accompanying sound, which has been picked up by microphone). Finally, a television receiver (or set) in your home receives the signals and converts them back into images and sound.

Creating Television Signals

A basic television camera consists of a lens, mirrors, image-sensing devices, various electronic circuits, and a viewfinder, through which the camera operator sees what the camera is looking at.

Light reflected from a scene passes through the lens, which focuses the image. In color television cameras, the light is then split into three beams by mirrors that separate the light into three basic, or primary, colors: red, green, and blue. Each colored beam strikes an image-sensing device. In older television cameras, these devices are glass vacuum tubes called **pickup tubes**. At one end, a pickup tube contains a light-sensitive material called a **target**. When incoming light hits the target, this material develops a pattern of positive electrical charges. At the back of the tube is a device called an **electron gun**, which shoots a beam of negatively charged particles called electrons across the target. The beam moves, or scans, much as your eyes do when you read. As it does so, it converts the pattern on the target into an electrical signal that is a "copy" of the original image.

Today, most television cameras detect images using electronic components called **charge-coupled devices** (CCD's), instead of pickup tubes. Developed in the 1970's, CCD's are small chips made of silicon that are divided into a grid of several million tiny squares called pixels, short for "picture elements." As light strikes the pixels, they build up a pattern of electrical charges that vary with the intensity of the light at any given spot. This pattern is then converted into an electrical signal.

Sending the Television Signal

In most cases, television signals are broadcast through the air. The video and audio (sound) signals travel from the camera to a transmitter, which turns the signals into electromagnetic waves. Electromagnetic waves radiate (travel in all directions) from their source, moving at the speed of light. This movement is expressed as **frequency**. Frequency is the number of cycles, or complete waves, transmitted in one second.

Television signals must be broadcast at a high frequency in order to carry the video in-

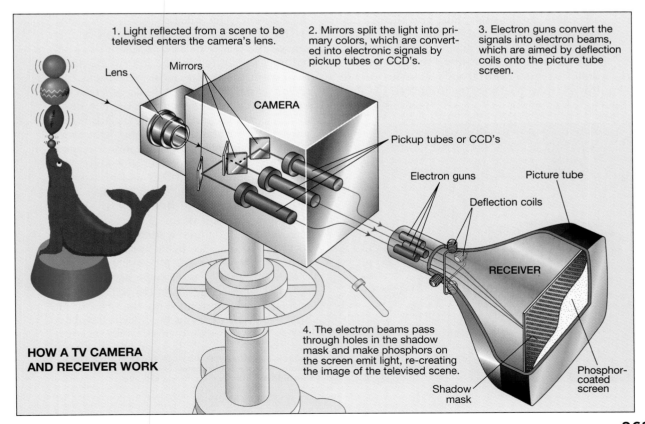

1. Light reflected from a scene to be televised enters the camera's lens.

2. Mirrors split the light into primary colors, which are converted into electronic signals by pickup tubes or CCD's.

3. Electron guns convert the signals into electron beams, which are aimed by deflection coils onto the picture tube screen.

Lens

Mirrors

CAMERA

Pickup tubes or CCD's

Electron guns

Picture tube

Deflection coils

RECEIVER

4. The electron beams pass through holes in the shadow mask and make phosphors on the screen emit light, re-creating the image of the televised scene.

Shadow mask

Phosphor-coated screen

HOW A TV CAMERA AND RECEIVER WORK

formation. The transmitter emits a **carrier wave**, a powerful high-frequency electromagnetic wave. Through a process called modulation, the video and audio signals are combined with the carrier wave.

The signal is sent out by a transmitting antenna, which is usually placed as high as possible because television signals move in a straight line. Hills, high-rise buildings, and even trees can interfere with the television signals. Generally, a clear picture can be received within a 50-mile (80-kilometer) radius of the transmitting antenna.

A group, or band, of frequencies that carries a television transmission is called a **channel**. Broadcast stations located in the same area are assigned separate channels so that their transmissions do not interfere with one another. In the United States, these assignments are made by the Federal Communications Commission (FCC), a government licensing body. For home television broadcasting, a station is assigned to one of twelve Very High Frequency (VHF) channels (channels 2–13) or to one of 56 Ultra High Frequency (UHF) channels (14–69).

Because the electromagnetic waves sent out by a transmitter cannot travel very far, television signals that must travel long distances are sent by other means. They may be carried by coaxial or fiber-optic cable. They may be sent by microwave relay (a system that relays signals through a series of tall towers spaced across the country). Or they

may be transmitted to satellites that orbit Earth. The satellites receive the signals and bounce them down to receiving stations far away from the signal source.

The major U.S. and Canadian television networks use these methods to send signals to local stations, which then broadcast the signals to homes in their areas. Cable television companies also receive their programs via satellite. They then send them to their subscribers over cable.

Receiving the Television Signal

A transmitted television signal can be received through an antenna on the television set itself if the distance to the transmitter is not too great. A roof-mounted antenna helps capture weak or distant signals. Today, television signals reach most North American homes via cable, and many homes now have satellite dishes that receive television signals directly from satellites.

The television receiver has a **tuner**, which picks up the frequency of the channel selected and blocks out other frequencies. As the video and audio signals are received, they are sent to a **demodulator**, a complex electronic circuit that allows the audio and video information to be processed.

The electronic video information is then sent to the receiver's screen, where the original image collected by the television camera is reconstructed. In most televisions, the screen is the front end of a large glass vacuum tube called the **picture tube**. The inside of the screen is coated with thousands of tiny **phosphors**, substances that emit light when struck by electrons. Each phosphor is responsible for reproducing either the color red, blue, or green. At the other end of a typical color picture tube are three electron guns, one for each of these three primary colors. Each gun shoots a beam of electrons at the screen, scanning it line by line.

As the beams race to the screen, they pass through a **shadow mask**, a thin screen pierced with hundreds of thousands of holes. The holes allow the beam from the red gun to hit only the red phosphors on the screen, the blue beam to hit only the blue phosphors,

Portable cameras allow television crews to cover news events wherever they happen. The images can then be transmitted "live" to a studio via satellite.

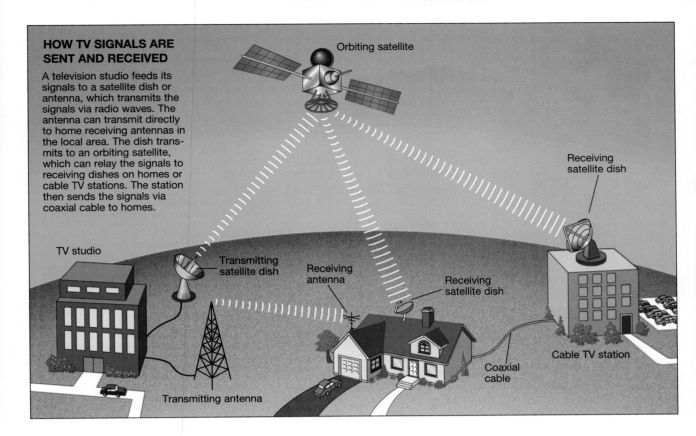

HOW TV SIGNALS ARE SENT AND RECEIVED

A television studio feeds its signals to a satellite dish or antenna, which transmits the signals via radio waves. The antenna can transmit directly to home receiving antennas in the local area. The dish transmits to an orbiting satellite, which can relay the signals to receiving dishes on homes or cable TV stations. The station then sends the signals via coaxial cable to homes.

Orbiting satellite

Receiving satellite dish

TV studio

Transmitting satellite dish

Receiving antenna

Receiving satellite dish

Cable TV station

Coaxial cable

Transmitting antenna

and the green beam to hit only the green phosphors. When each dot is hit, it glows with its respective color. Because the dots are so close together, the viewer's eyes see the mixture of primary colors as the whole range of colors that were in the original scene.

Because picture tubes are almost as deep as they are wide, they can be made only so large before they become too bulky to fit easily in most living rooms. However, some modern television sets, called projection TV's, overcome this problem by projecting images from small picture tubes onto a much larger screen. In this way, projection TV's can have screens as wide as 6 feet (nearly 2 meters) but still be only 2 feet (0.6 meter) deep.

In some new receivers, images are created without a picture tube, using a thin **flat-panel display** instead. Some displays are so thin, they can be hung on a wall like a painting. One type of display, also used in laptop computers, is the liquid crystal display, or LCD. It is made up of hundreds of thousands of cells in which crystal molecules "twist" light from a light source when an electrical charge is applied. The light passes through filters and ap-

pears as a red, green, or blue dot, depending on which direction the light was twisted.

A more advanced type of flat-panel display is the plasma monitor. It is like a honeycomb sandwiched between two sheets of glass. Each cell in the honeycomb represents a pixel and holds a gas mixture (such as neon and xenon) as well as a tiny phosphor in one of the three primary colors. When an electrical charge is applied, the gas mixture becomes a plasma—a hot gas in which the atoms are stripped of their electrons—and begins emitting ultraviolet light. That light, in turn, hits the phosphors, which then glow to create a picture.

▶ **DEVELOPMENT OF TELEVISION TECHNOLOGY**

In the early 1900's, inventors found that electrical signals could be transmitted through the air, as electromagnetic waves. At first, this discovery led to the wireless transmission of sound.

Soon, inventors began searching for ways of transmitting pictures as well. The problem was how to "scan" a scene line by line in order to turn it into electrical signals. The first

Inventor Philo T. Farnsworth demonstrates an early television receiver. Images were displayed on a small round screen.

television sets accomplished this mechanically, using large spinning disks with holes in them. An amateur Scottish inventor, John Logie Baird, was the first to successfully use the disks, making them out of old hatboxes in his apartment. In 1925, at Selfridge's department store in London, England, Baird presented the world's first public demonstration of television. Viewers were able to see only crude outlines of shapes transmitted a few feet away.

Mechanical systems were too bulky to produce a good moving picture. However, electronic systems, which used vacuum tubes and electron beams, could scan many lines very quickly.

Two people were mainly responsible for developing electronic television. One was a self-educated Idaho farm boy named Philo T. Farnsworth, and the other was a successful engineer named Vladimir K. Zworykin, who had immigrated to America from Russia. In 1927, Farnsworth created the world's first all-electronic television system. He was able to transmit a single black line from one end of his lab to the other. Meanwhile, Zworykin was carrying out his own work at the electrical company Westinghouse and later at the Radio Corporation of America (RCA). He soon introduced his own television system.

During the 1930's, many manufacturers began producing television receivers, most based on either the Zworykin or Farnsworth

system. However, these receivers could not process the same television signals. In 1941, the National Television Systems Committee (NTSC) established a national system that combined the best features of Farnsworth's and Zworykin's systems. In the NTSC system, television pictures are made up of 525 lines each, displayed at a speed of 30 pictures, or frames, per second. At that speed, the frames appear to blend smoothly.

Color television broadcasts began in the 1950's, and by 1965 the major U.S. networks were broadcasting nearly all their programs in color. By the late 1990's, 98 percent of American homes had color TV sets.

In 1956 another important breakthrough took place: the development of the videotape recorder (VTR). Before this time, all television programs had to be either broadcast "live" or recorded on motion picture film. Before film could be used for broadcast, it had to be developed. Then it was played back and converted into electronic images. The VTR records programs on videotape, which can be played back immediately.

Meanwhile, closed-circuit television systems were becoming increasingly important in industry, medicine, and other fields. In these systems, television cameras are linked by cable to a limited number of receivers. Closed-circuit television is used in factories, to oversee assembly lines, and in hospitals, to monitor patients. It is an important part of many security systems.

There have been many other technological improvements since the early days of television. Lightweight, portable cameras, developed in the 1970's, allow television crews to travel almost anywhere to cover news or sports events. And many programs are now broadcast in stereo sound.

Alternate Delivery Systems

When television first became widely available in the 1940's and 1950's, it was distributed mostly over the airwaves. Today, new television technologies offer other ways for viewers to receive signals. These methods are referred to as alternate delivery systems.

Cable. One form of cable television, called community antenna television (CATV), was created in the 1940's to deliver broadcast signals to isolated places that could not receive them—in mountain valleys, for example. An antenna on a mountain picked up the broadcast signal and then sent it down a coaxial cable to the homes in the valley. Cable television did not experience rapid growth until some thirty years later. By the late 1990's, more than two-thirds of American households—some 63 million homes—relied on cable as their primary source of television.

Satellites. Television satellites are "parked" in geosynchronous orbit 22,300 miles (35,900 kilometers) above Earth. "Geosynchronous" means that as Earth rotates, the satellites follow and stay in exactly the same place over the ground.

Television stations send a powerful signal to a **transponder** on the satellite. The transponder receives the upcoming signal, amplifies (strengthens) it, and transmits it back down to Earth, where it can be received at the ground stations of cable systems that have dish antennas. Satellite signals can also be received directly by viewers, through home dish antenna systems.

Videocassette Recorders. Videocassette recorders (VCR's) for home use were introduced in the mid-1970's. By the late 1990's, more than 80 percent of American homes had at least one VCR. Viewers use VCR's to record programs for viewing at a later time and for viewing prerecorded tapes. Tapes of feature films—mostly in the video home system (VHS) format—are widely available for sale or rental. Many people also create their own tapes using home video cameras.

VCR's have also made television more useful in other settings. Teachers use VCR's in classrooms, and corporations use VCR's to train employees.

Laser Disk Players. Laser disks offer the highest-quality video and audio for home systems. They first became available in the United States in 1980 in the form of 12-inch plastic-and-metal disks called videodiscs. In the mid-1990's, smaller versions called digital video discs, or digital versatile discs (DVD's), were introduced. About the size of music

Flat-panel televisions, only a few inches deep, can be hung on a wall like a picture. The wide screen is specially designed for high-definition television.

compact discs (CD's), DVD's can store the video and audio of feature-length films as well as other information, such as background notes about a movie. Special players, connected to television sets or built in to some computers, are used to play DVD's.

High-Definition and Digital Television

In the 1990's, the television industry began preparing for high-definition television, or HDTV. This format uses more than twice the conventional number of scanning lines to produce better definition—that is, a sharper, clearer image and better color and brightness. HDTV also features a wider screen and theater-quality stereo sound.

HDTV was first developed in Japan in the 1980's. But the Japanese system was not compatible with U.S. broadcast standards.

By the late 1990's, HDTV became a reality in the United States, when the first stations began broadcasting digital television. Digital TV, or DTV, is a major change in the way television signals are sent and received. In conventional television, pictures and sound are converted into analog signals—electronic signals that are analogous, or similar, to sound and light waves. Digital TV converts pictures and sound into electronic pulses that stand for the digits 1 ("on") and 0 ("off"), like the binary code used by computers.

Televisions using liquid crystal displays can be made small enough to fit in the back of a headrest in a vehicle or even in the palm of your hand.

Digital TV signals can come in several formats. One is the HDTV format, which delivers high-quality video and audio, one program at a time. Other formats, however, allow networks to broadcast five or six programs at once with standard-definition video and audio, like those of conventional television. These formats use computers to compress TV signals: Each image is compared with the previous image, and only the visual information that has changed is transmitted. This savings in information means that more than one program can be transmitted at a time. It also means that, like DVD's, digital TV can display other information, such as captions in different languages.

In 1998, some stations started broadcasting digitally on a second channel while continuing to broadcast on their existing analog channels as well. Under a government plan, all stations were supposed to be broadcasting digitally as well as in analog by 2003, giving the public time to make the switch gradually. In 2006, analog transmissions would cease and all television would be digital—if, that is, at least 85 percent of American homes had digital TV's by then. In reality, the full transition to DTV could take much longer.

Television Controls and Features

One of the most important parts of a television system is the remote control, or, simply, the remote. Remote controls became practical in the mid-1950's, using high-frequency sound or electrical wires to transmit commands. In the 1970's, remote controls began using infrared light to send commands to television sets. And in the 1980's, remote controls could control not only televisions, but also VCR's and sound systems.

By the 1990's, remote controls were virtually in every home. Viewers use them to change channels, adjust the volume (or loudness), and mute the sound of commercials. Many viewers now switch programs at every commercial break. In this way, the remote control has changed the way people watch television, and also the way television programs are produced, as broadcasters struggle to keep viewers on their networks.

Other features developed in the 1980's and 1990's included picture-in-picture (a second program inset in the larger one), closed captioning for the hearing impaired (in which a program's dialogue is displayed on the screen as moving text), and the "V-chip." This term originally referred to a computer chip that would allow parents to block violent or other inappropriate programs, but it later came to mean any technology to achieve that aim. In the United States, the Telecommunications Act of 1995 mandated that such systems eventually be installed in all new TV sets.

▶ THE TELEVISION INDUSTRY

In many countries, television broadcasting is operated by the government. In the United States, the multi-billion-dollar television industry is privately owned. It includes broadcast networks, local television stations, production companies, and distributors such as cable and satellite services.

Commercial Television

For the most part, American broadcasting is a commercial system. That is, much of the cost of producing and distributing programs is paid for by advertising.

Most programs shown on commercial television come from large television networks. For forty years or so, there were three major networks: the Columbia Broadcasting System (CBS), Capital Cities/American Broadcasting Company (ABC), and the National Broadcasting Company (NBC). In the 1980's and 1990's, new networks were launched, such as Fox Broadcasting and the United Paramount Network (UPN). With the rise of cable television, large cable networks arose, such as Home Box Office (HBO), Turner Broadcasting, and the Discovery Channel. The networks distribute programming to affiliate stations all over the country, mostly via satellite. Independent stations are not affiliated with a network and obtain their programming from other sources.

Programming. Generally, the networks purchase the programs they broadcast from independent program producers. Many program producers are located in southern California—in or near Hollywood. News and public affairs programs, however, are usually produced by the networks themselves.

The networks and local stations hire audience research firms to help them determine how popular their programs are. (The process of rating television shows is described in the Wonder Question accompanying this article.) Ratings determine how much money advertisers pay to have their commercials broadcast.

Each broadcast day is divided into periods of time called dayparts. Programs shown during a certain daypart are planned to suit the interests of the audience watching at that time. The most important daypart is prime time, which runs from 8:00 P.M. to 11:00 P.M. That is when audiences are largest, and when advertisers must pay the most money.

Advertising. In the United States, television commercials are designed and produced by advertising agencies. The agencies also help choose the best programs on which to advertise their clients' products.

Educational and Public Broadcasting

Broadcast television in some countries has no advertising at all. Sometimes the government of a country pays for all costs of television. In other cases, noncommercial and commercial networks are in competition.

Public broadcasting in the United States began in the 1950's, when a few stations were created to provide educational programs for the public. These stations, some of which were associated with colleges or universities, broadcast instructional, arts, and public affairs shows. Since then, public broadcasting has played a small but important role.

In 1967, Congress passed a law forming the Corporation for Public Broadcasting (CPB), which in turn created the Public Broadcasting Service (PBS). PBS helps fund new programs and distributes them to more than 300 stations in the United States. Public stations are noncommercial; that is, they do not accept advertising. Money is raised through viewer contributions, grants, and funds from CPB.

Broadcast Regulation

Broadcasting is regulated by the government through an agency called the Federal Communications Commission (FCC), which administers broadcasting laws passed by Congress. Current federal regulation is based on the Communications Act of 1934, which established guidelines for broadcasters, and on later legislation. The Telecommunications Act of 1995 updated the laws to encompass new developments in television, such as digital television. The FCC issues licenses to qualified applicants to operate a television station. According to the law, broadcasters must operate in the public interest.

A television production technician watches several monitors while controlling a console. She is combining video camera images and sounds from a nearby studio.

369

Television Production

Producing a television program combines creative, technical, and business skills. There are three basic types of television production: live, videotape, and film.

Some programs are broadcast live while an event is happening. Live broadcasts include news programs and events such as football games and parades. In the live-on-tape method, a program is videotaped, edited, and then broadcast later. For example, a week's worth of a daily game show might be videotaped on one day. Then the five shows are broadcast one at a time. A third method involves recording scenes on motion picture or video cameras. The recording is edited and then transferred to videotape for later broadcast.

People involved in a television production include the director, writer, producer, lighting director, camera operator, sound director, and editor. To get an idea of the people who work on television productions, read the credits at the end of a program.

Careers in Television

A wide variety of jobs are available in television. But because many people seek careers in the field, competition for jobs is high. Almost all these jobs require a high school education, and many require a college degree. Many schools and colleges offer programs in broadcasting and video production.

The main career areas in television are programming, sales, news, production, engineering, and management. Positions are also available in independent production companies, which hire people to write, produce, and direct television programs. Some companies hire people to produce video programs for businesses, governments, schools, and other groups.

▶ TELEVISION PROGRAMS

When television networks were formed in 1945–46, radio networks were already well established. Many radio programs and personalities simply moved to television.

The period up to 1956 was the era of live television. No videotape machines existed, so shows had to be performed in front of live cameras. During this period, called the Golden Age of television, many excellent live shows were turned out every week. One of the most notable was Milton Berle's comedy and variety show, *The Texaco Star Theater*. "Uncle Miltie" became so well liked by audiences that he earned the nickname Mr. Television.

The early years of television produced several types of programs that, with some variations, have remained popular ever since.

Beginning in the Golden Age, a number of memorable **situation comedies**, or **sitcoms**, were produced. *I Love Lucy*, starring Lucille Ball, may be the most famous, but there were many others—*The Honeymooners*, *Father Knows Best*, *Leave It to Beaver*. Sitcoms have been popular in every decade. Among the hits of the 1970's and 1980's were *All in the Family*, *Cheers*, and *The Cosby Show*. The

---

WONDER QUESTION

What are television ratings?

Television audience ratings try to estimate how many people are watching various television programs. Companies that provide rating services survey a sampling of American families that own television sets. The best-known ratings service in the United States, the A. C. Nielsen Company, uses an electronic measuring device called the "people meter," which it installs in 1,200 American homes.

Ratings are complex, but the basic idea consists of two related concepts: the rating and the share. A **rating** is the percentage of all homes in a sampling that have television sets tuned to a particular program. A **share** compares homes with sets tuned to the program with only other homes whose sets are turned on during that time. For example, a program may have a rating of 19 and a share of 34 for a given week. This means that 19 percent of homes with televisions had the show tuned in that week. Of the homes with sets on while the show was airing, 34 percent were tuned to the program.

Why are ratings so important? They determine which programs get canceled and which remain on the air. Television programs with high ratings can charge advertisers more money to run commercials than can less popular shows. Because commercial television relies on advertising to pay for its costs, low-rated programs usually get canceled.

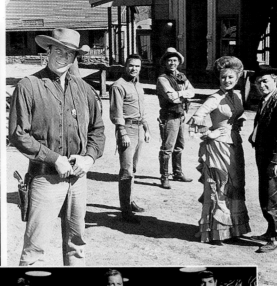

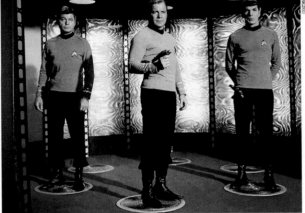

Above: Television's Golden Age produced some memorable situation comedies, or sitcoms, such as *I Love Lucy*. Above right: During the 1950's and 1960's, westerns such as *Gunsmoke* were very popular. Right: The series *Star Trek*, launched in the 1960's, became the most successful science-fiction drama.

most successful sitcom of the 1990's was *Seinfeld*, starring comedian Jerry Seinfeld.

Toward the end of television's Golden Age, a craze developed for **quiz shows**, starting with *The $64,000 Question*, which awarded large sums of money and valuable prizes to winners. Many quiz and game shows, such as *Wheel of Fortune* and *Jeopardy*, continue to draw large audiences.

A great variety of **drama series** have also been produced. In the 1950's and 1960's, western dramas such as *Gunsmoke* were very popular. The 1960's and 1970's saw the rise of police dramas such as *Dragnet* and *Hawaii Five-O*, followed by shows such as *Miami Vice* and *Law & Order* in the 1980's and 1990's. Hospital dramas have also had a faithful following of viewers, from *Marcus Welby, M.D.* in the 1960's to *E.R.* in the 1990's. The most successful science-fiction drama was the 1960's series *Star Trek*, which was revived with new characters in the 1980's and 1990's.

There have also been a number of daytime dramas, such as *The Young and the Restless*. They were originally called **soap operas** because many were sponsored by companies advertising soap and other household products. Dramas known as **miniseries** tell a story in several shows aired over a few days or weeks. One of the most widely watched shows ever was the 1977 miniseries *Roots*, which told the

story of an African-American family from the time of slavery to the present.

The longest-running television show of all time was a **news show**, *Meet the Press*. It started in 1947, featuring interviews with important leaders of American life. The investigative news program *60 Minutes* has had a loyal following since its debut in 1968. Many television stations now carry morning, evening, and late-night shows with local, national, and world news. In addition, there have been various **talk shows**, such as *The Tonight Show*, that include interviews with celebrities. Daytime talk shows, such as *The Oprah Winfrey Show*, also feature interviews with ordinary people who have moving stories to tell.

The 1950's saw the beginning of such **children's programs** as the beloved puppet shows *Kukla, Fran & Ollie* and *The Howdy Doody Show*. *Captain Kangaroo* and *The Mickey Mouse Club* also drew large audiences. Satur-

Above left: The children's show *Sesame Street* was created in the 1960's to both teach and entertain preschoolers. *Far left:* In the 1980's, cable television gave rise to a growing number of specialty channels, such as the Cable News Network. *Above:* In the 1990's, *Seinfeld* became the most widely watched sitcom. *Left:* Medical dramas continued to draw loyal viewers with shows such as *E.R.*

Bernard Shaw
Moscow
CNN LIVE

day morning cartoons first appeared in the 1950's and have remained popular. Cable television gave birth to children's networks such as Nickelodeon, the Disney Channel, and the Cartoon Network. One of the most successful children's programs is PBS's *Sesame Street*, which helps preschoolers learn words and numbers.

Cable television led to the creation of single-purpose **specialty networks**. The Cable News Network (CNN), for example, is dedicated to 24-hour news. ESPN shows only sports-related programs. MTV and VH-1 feature music videos, concert broadcasts, and other shows for popular music fans. In addition, there are networks that are devoted to classic movies, history, cooking, weather, travel, home shopping, and other interests.

▶ **THE FUTURE OF TELEVISION**

With the advent of digital television, the home TV set will likely share more in common with the computer than with television's predecessor, the radio. In addition to offering entertainment programming, television ser-

vices can now provide electronic mail (e-mail) and access to the Internet. Renting videocassettes and DVD's may become obsolete, as viewers "download" movies to their televisions without leaving the living room.

Some experts predict that "smart televisions" could one day scan through many hours of programming each day and pick out clips of particular interest to individual viewers.

Many people wonder about the influence of television. Do programs showing excessive violence make some viewers want to commit crimes? Do commercials make people want things they do not need or cannot afford? Do some programs show lifestyles that conflict with values taught at home and school?

Television is not by itself good or bad; it is merely a powerful communications tool. It is the people behind it, and the people watching it, who will determine whether its effects will be positive or negative.

JOHN P. FREEMAN
Texas Christian University
Reviewed by MARSHALL JON FISHER
Coauthor, *Tube: The Invention of Television*

JUVENILE CRIME

Juvenile crime occurs whenever a young person violates a law. Crime among juveniles is a serious problem in the United States and much of the world. When young people get involved in crime, parents and communities react with great concern.

Young people who break the law are sometimes called juvenile delinquents. In most states a person must be under 18 years of age to receive this designation.

Young people have to obey the same laws as adults. Activities such as scribbling graffiti on a wall, shoplifting, possessing illegal drugs, or driving a car without a license or the owner's permission violate local, state, or federal laws. Moreover, juveniles must follow some rules or laws that do not apply to adults. They may be required to attend school, for example. Age restrictions also prevent juveniles from purchasing guns or alcohol. Societies have more rules for young people because of the widespread belief that children require special protection and care until they become adults.

Ideally, young people are raised to respect the traditions and values of the family and community. When juveniles break laws, these traditions and values are threatened, and people look for ways to help youths become responsible adults. The juvenile justice system was created to deal with youths who disobey laws.

A young person who violates the law can be arrested by police and brought to court. However, the legal process for juveniles is different from that for adults. Early in the process, officials must determine whether a youth is in need of social welfare services or whether a juvenile court should handle the case.

▶ TYPES OF JUVENILE CRIME

Actions that are considered crimes for juveniles and not for adults—such as possessing alcoholic beverages, truancy, or running away from home—are known as **status offenses**. Status offenses account for many of the approximately 2.8 million juvenile arrests in the United States each year. However, young people who commit status offenses are not always formally arrested; they may be referred to the social welfare system. Various studies have found that about 40 percent of

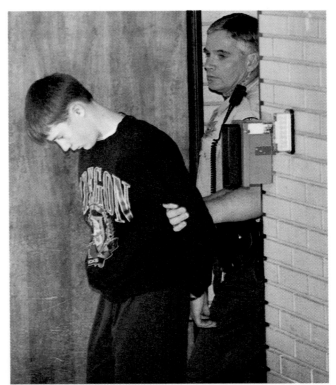

A 15-year-old boy is brought to court on charges of shooting classmates at his high school. Violent crime in schools is of growing concern in the United States.

young people who are detained (held in custody), whether or not they are arrested, are involved in status offenses.

Young people under 18 represent about one-fourth of the U.S. population, but they account for one in three arrests for **property offenses**. Larceny (acts such as shoplifting and purse snatching) is the most frequent property offense, followed by burglary (forced entry into a home or business), motor vehicle theft, and arson (deliberate burning of property). Juveniles account for fully half of all arsons and 40 percent of automobile thefts. They are also involved in many acts of vandalism (destruction of property).

Juveniles account for one in six arrests for **violent crime**. Aggravated assault (attacking someone with the intent to cause serious injury) is the violent crime for which juveniles are arrested most often, followed by robbery (using violence or threats to take something from a person) and, less often, rape and homicide. No more than one in about every 250 young people is arrested each year for a violent crime.

A security guard at a high school scans students for concealed weapons. Keeping firearms out of schools helps ensure the safety of students and teachers.

Juvenile crime rates in the United States decreased or held steady through the 1990's. For example, the juvenile arrest rate for murder declined by 39 percent from 1993 to 1997, and the rate for auto theft declined by 30 percent. However, school violence—particularly several cases of mass shootings by students—sparked intense debate about the accessibility of firearms and the responsibility of all citizens to help identify and find counseling for troubled youths before they resort to crime.

▶ OFFENDERS

Juvenile crime is highest among young people who live in city centers. It is next highest in the suburbs, and lowest in rural areas.

Boys are responsible for about three-fourths of all juvenile arrests.

Counselors from a community youth service talk with young gang members, who are at high risk for becoming involved in crime.

They are more likely to be arrested for murder and robbery than girls. Girls are more likely to be arrested for offenses such as prostitution (having sexual relations for money) and running away from home. Arrests of girls, especially for drug-abuse violations, increased in the early 1990's and thereafter declined more slowly than arrests of boys.

▶ WHY DO YOUNG PEOPLE COMMIT CRIMES?

There is no single explanation for youth involvement in crime. Experts in criminal justice believe that crime arises from a variety of sources, and the importance of various factors varies from child to child. Two children may grow up in similar families and go to the same schools, yet only one may break the law.

Home and Family. The quality of family life may have a lot to do with involvement in juvenile crime. Children raised by caregivers who are psychologically or physically abusive may be more likely to commit crimes. Although single-parent homes are sometimes viewed as a factor contributing to crime, in most such households the children grow up to be law-abiding citizens. What is most important in any home is the quality of care.

Peer Groups. A young person's peer group—people of the same age with whom he or she spends time—is an important influence on behavior. Young people want to be liked by their peers, and they tend to go along with the group. Some may get in trouble as a result.

The influence of peer groups can be seen at work in youth gangs. Gangs exist in every

state and many schools in the United States. Gang members may try to demonstrate their toughness and loyalty to the gang by breaking rules or fighting with other gangs. They are often involved in high-risk behavior, including crime, and they are also more likely to be victims of crime. A gang member may carry weapons, sell drugs, steal property, or commit other crimes to acquire money or as a condition of membership.

Some people believe that gangs make young people commit crimes, but others think that the young people who join gangs would get into trouble anyway. A young person may be attracted by the idea of belonging to a gang, or he or she may join a gang for protection.

Drugs and Alcohol. A great deal of juvenile crime is related to drugs and alcohol. In some places more than half of all arrested juveniles are under the influence of drugs or alcohol. These substances contribute to crime in several ways. Juveniles who are under the influence may commit criminal acts that they might not otherwise. They may harm themselves or others in accidents. Possessing or selling even small amounts of drugs is a very serious offense. Young people may commit crimes to get money to buy illegal drugs. They may also become victims of crime if others try to steal drugs from them.

▶ JUVENILES AND LAW ENFORCEMENT

In the United States, young people who violate laws enter the juvenile justice system in several ways. They may be referred by their families or schools. The most common way, however, is by police arrest.

Arrest. When the police suspect a youth of violating the law, they can deal with the situation in a variety of ways. They may warn the youth or call his or her parents in to discuss the matter. But often the juvenile is arrested. To make an arrest, the police must have reason to believe that an offense occurred and that the juvenile committed it.

Like adults, juveniles who are arrested must be informed of their legal rights. They may be required to appear in a lineup, so that victims can identify them as offenders. They are then booked into a local detention center. Some juvenile cases are handled through local police diversion programs, which are intended to keep young people out of the official juvenile system. However, many cases are referred to the juvenile court system.

Juvenile Court. The first juvenile court in the United States was established in Illinois in 1899. Today there are juvenile courts in every state. The rules of juvenile court differ from those applied to adults. Juvenile court proceedings enable court workers—including probation officers, psychologists, social workers, and other trained

Juvenile offenders may be sent to detention centers or boot camps. Such facilities often promote rehabilitation by requiring inmates to study for their high-school equivalency certificates (*above*) and participate in physical exercise programs (*right*).

workers—to recognize and respond appropriately to the special needs of juveniles.

In court, juveniles have many of the same rights as adults. These include the right to legal counsel, the right to a hearing, the right to cross-examine witnesses, and the right to appeal court decisions. However, juveniles do not have the right to a jury trial, although some states allow it.

Court Decisions. A juvenile court decision is called a **disposition**. The court looks closely at the offense, the circumstances surrounding it, the home life of the youth, and his or her prior problems with family, peers, schools, and the police. Based on this information the court tries to find the best ways to make the youth a responsible and productive citizen.

Juveniles can be sent to a detention center, a ranch or group home for children, a training center, or a similar facility. A few states are attempting to limit costs of holding juveniles in detention by setting up community-based programs for juvenile offenders.

Young people may also be placed on **probation**. They remain free but must meet certain conditions, such as participating in counseling or observing curfews (being home by a certain hour). They are closely monitored by probation officers to ensure that they behave appropriately. If probation is not successful, the juvenile will probably be placed in custody for treatment.

Juveniles cannot be sentenced to prison or jail, which are reserved for adults. Juveniles under 16 cannot be sentenced to death. Those 16 and older may face execution if they commit a capital crime, such as murder, in a state that allows the death penalty.

Rehabilitation (helping offenders become law-abiding citizens) is the primary goal of juvenile justice systems. However, in recent years states have imposed more rules on juvenile court judges. These rules require judges to give the same dispositions to juveniles with similar offenses and prior records, and to give sentences that are geared more toward punishment. Some states have passed laws that require juveniles who commit certain offenses to spend a minimum amount of time in an institution.

▶ **QUESTIONS ABOUT JUVENILE JUSTICE**

The juvenile court system has been criticized by people who feel that it is too easy on juvenile offenders. In response to this criticism, some states have passed or are considering laws that would lower the age at which juveniles can be tried as adults. These **waiver** procedures are generally restricted to older juveniles facing very serious charges. In a **judicial waiver** system, a juvenile court judge decides whether a youth is unfit for juvenile court services. The alternative is a **legislative waiver**, which automatically transfers juveniles to adult courts for certain crimes.

It is important to remember that most young people do not get into trouble with the law, and that those who do usually do not grow up to be criminals. Juveniles who commit crimes hurt themselves, their families, and their communities. But communities attempt to deal with this by finding ways to help them become good citizens. That may involve providing opportunities for education, a job, the support of family, and involvement in community activities.

PATRICK JACKSON
Sonoma State University
Editor, *Western Criminology Review*

Supervised by a police officer, two youths paint over a graffiti-sprayed wall as part of a rehabilitation program for juvenile offenders.

FORENSIC SCIENCE

"Crime Scene: Do Not Cross" say black letters on the yellow tape that surrounds the site of a murder. Inside the area, police methodically search for clues that will help investigators piece together what happened. The officers wear latex gloves and coveralls called bunny suits, which cover them from head to foot. This is to prevent them from leaving their own traces at the crime scene.

What are they looking for? Investigators can extract information about a crime from the most unlikely clues. Saliva found on a cigarette butt may provide a sample of DNA, a substance in cells that is unique to virtually every individual. A candy wrapper may reveal another common clue used to identify a suspect—a latent (invisible) fingerprint that can be made to appear using special powders or lights. A bullet may be marked by grooves, which link it to a certain gun.

Using the tools of science to analyze evidence and help solve crimes is called **forensics**. Some experts in forensics are police, some are scientists working in crime laboratories, and others are outside scientific experts called in when their specialized knowledge is needed. Dentists, chemists, biologists, geologists—they all have expertise that may be needed to crack a particular case.

▶ **GATHERING THE EVIDENCE**

There are two kinds of evidence: information provided by witnesses and other people, and physical evidence. Physical evidence consists of real objects such as guns, fingerprints, blood stains, or documents.

At the Crime Scene

The first forensic experts called to a crime scene are usually police identification officers, often called ident officers for short. Before anything is touched or moved, the officers will videotape and photograph the scene, then take measurements needed to create scale diagrams of the scene on a computer.

Ident officers dust for fingerprints, perhaps using a laser light that makes latent prints glow. They use sticky tape to pick up hairs or tiny fibers that have rubbed off clothing. There may be marks left by tools used to break open a window or a safe, blood splatter on a wall, a charred fragment of paper, or a

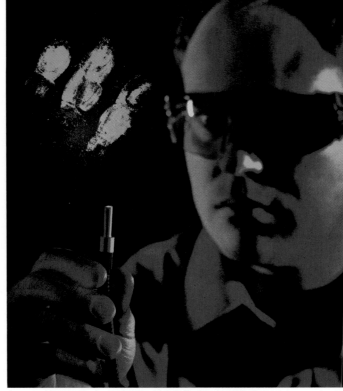

A researcher tests a special lamp that flashes rapidly to reveal fingerprints left on glass. Such forensic tools are used at crime scenes.

shard of broken glass. Most physical evidence is sent to the crime lab for further analysis.

If the crime scene is outdoors, nature itself can provide clues. Soil scientists can detect changes to layers in the soil that indicate someone has been digging in the ground. If a body has been lying at the scene for weeks, a forensic entomologist (an expert on insects) can estimate a time of death by analyzing flies and larvae found on the body.

Every item is identified, photographed, and put in a separate container that is labeled and initialed. Police are very careful to maintain **continuity**—that is, to track each item from the time it is collected until it is presented as evidence in court. Evidence must never be left where somebody might tamper with it.

At the Crime Lab

In the forensic lab, scientists magnify, dissect, identify, and match the pieces of physical evidence using highly sophisticated equipment. For example, chemists determine the types of molecules that make up a stain. A fleck of paint may be traced to a particular make and model of car. Toxicologists look for

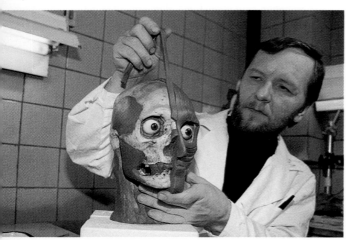

A forensic artist helps identify a murder victim by reconstructing the general appearance of the face from just the skull, using modeling clay and false eyes.

traces of poisons or drugs in a blood sample. In a special room, investigators try to re-create the blood splatter pattern found at the crime scene. Document experts may recover writing that was erased on a forged check.

A very important forensic tool is DNA, which stands for *d*eoxyribo*n*ucleic *a*cid. It is a molecule found in cells of the body and can be extracted from blood stains, hair, urine, or saliva. From a DNA sample, technicians create a DNA **autoradiogram**, or autorad for short. It is a pattern of lines that looks somewhat like a bar-code pattern on goods sold in a store. An autorad of a person's DNA can be compared with autorads of others'. Every person's DNA is unique (except for identical twins). So if a suspect's DNA sample matches DNA found at the scene of the crime, that evidence may link the suspect to the crime.

Examining Victims

If the crime involves a murder, the body may provide important clues. A pathologist will do an **autopsy** (an examination of the body) to determine the time of death and how it occurred.

Identifying a victim may be the first step in finding a criminal. Forensic investigators use the victim's fingerprints, dental records, DNA, old injuries, tattoos, or other identifying features. Forensic anthropologists are experts on bones and can determine a person's height, age, sex, and other characteristics by examining skeleton parts. A forensic artist uses modeling clay on a skull to reconstruct what the victim's face probably looked like.

Examining Suspects

Virtually every suspect will leave some trace of his or her presence at a crime scene, or else take away some trace of the scene. The trace could be as small as a fiber from the victim's sweater found in the suspect's car. Or it could be even smaller—micro-organisms on a wet sock that match those found only in the water where a crime took place.

Even without physical evidence, serial criminals (those who commit a series of similar crimes) may leave clues in their patterns of behavior. Forensic psychologists, who study how criminals think and behave, use these patterns to create a forensic profile of the criminal. It describes whether the criminal is likely male or female, where the criminal lives or works, and what kind of victims the criminal chooses.

▶ SOLVING THE CRIME

One piece of evidence will not usually prove "beyond a reasonable doubt" that a suspect was responsible for committing a crime. It is when investigators find many pieces of evidence linking a suspect to a crime that a case becomes strong enough to lead to a conviction in court.

Forensic evidence is used not only to convict criminals but also to prove innocence. In some famous cases, convicted criminals have been released from prison years later when new DNA evidence has proved that they could not have committed the crime.

Advances in computer and communications technology are helping police share information with other law enforcement agencies across the country or around the world. Police can enter details about unsolved crimes into a computer system that will identify similar crimes committed elsewhere. Possibly the same criminal is at work. Computer databases now give investigators instant access to information on fingerprints, firearms, missing children, glass, and paint.

Technology aside, the most important crime-solving tool is probably still an experienced forensic investigator with patience, persistence, and well-honed reasoning powers.

VIVIEN BOWERS
Author, *Crime Science: How Investigators Use Science to Track Down the Bad Guys*

SUPPLEMENT

Deaths

Independent Nations of the World

The United States

    Senate

    House of Representatives

    Cabinet

    Supreme Court

    State Governors

Canada and Its Provinces and Territories

DEATHS

Blackmun, Harry. Former U.S. Supreme Court Justice; died on March 4, at the age of 90. Blackmun served on the Supreme Court from 1970 to 1994. During his years on the Court, Blackmun fought to preserve such individual liberties as free speech and civil rights. He was best remembered as the author of the Court's decision in *Roe* v. *Wade* (1973), which affirmed a woman's right to terminate a pregnancy.

Chafee, John H. U.S. Senator from Rhode Island; died on October 24, at the age of 77. Chafee, a Republican, focused on issues concerning the environment and health policy during his years in the Senate (1976–99). He also served as governor of Rhode Island (1963–69) and as Secretary of the Navy (1969–72).

Chamberlain, Wilt. American basketball player; died on October 12, at the age of 63. Widely considered the most dominant player in basketball history, Chamberlain set numerous records during his fourteen seasons in the National Basketball Association (1959–73). His record for the most points scored in a single game (100) still stands. Chamberlain was inducted into the Basketball Hall of Fame in 1978.

Farmer, James. American civil rights leader; died on July 9, at the age of 79. As one of the founders of the Congress of Racial Equality (CORE), Farmer was on the front lines of the civil rights movement of the 1950's and 1960's. He led the struggle to integrate public facilities in the South through the use of nonviolent protests.

Funt, Allen. American television host; died on September 5, at the age of 84. Funt was the creator and original host of the hit TV program *Candid Camera*. On the show, people were secretly filmed while reacting to strange or bizarre situations until they finally received the tip-off: "Smile! You're on *Candid Camera!*" *Candid Camera* made its television debut in 1948 and was one of the top-rated series of the 1960's.

DiMaggio, Joe. American baseball player; died on March 8, at the age of 84. Known as "Joltin' Joe" and the "Yankee Clipper," DiMaggio played center field for the New York Yankees from 1936 until his retirement in 1951. He helped the Yankees win ten American League pennants and nine World Series. And in so doing, he amassed some amazing records. He had a career .325 batting average. He hit 361 home runs and batted in 1,537 runs. And in 1941, he got at least one hit in each of 56 straight games—a record that still stands.

DiMaggio left baseball, but he never lost his fans. A quiet man, he was pushed into the public spotlight by his 1954 marriage to film star Marilyn Monroe. The marriage lasted less than a year. But when Monroe died in 1962, it was DiMaggio who made the funeral arrangements. Later, he founded a children's hospital in Florida. In these and other acts, DiMaggio's integrity and kindness made him an American legend.

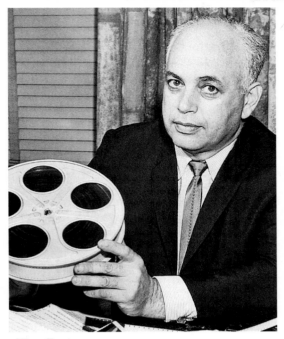

Allen Funt

Gorbachev, Raisa. Last First Lady of the former Soviet Union; died on September 20, at the age of 67. The wife of former Soviet president Mikhail Gorbachev (1985–91), she was the most highly visible first lady in Soviet history. She often accompanied her husband on foreign trips and was noted for her charm, elegance, and self-assured style. Her glamorous image, though widely admired abroad, was harshly criticized in her homeland.

Hussein I. King of Jordan; died on February 7, at the age of 63. The longest-reigning ruler in the Middle East, Hussein ascended the throne in 1953. For many years, he played a prominent role in the Arab-Israeli peace process *(See also page 82.)*

Kelley, DeForest. American actor; died on June 11, at the age of 79. Kelley portrayed the crusty Dr. Leonard "Bones" McCoy on the popular television series *Star Trek* (1966–69). He played the same role in six *Star Trek* feature films that appeared between 1979 and 1991.

Kennedy, John F., Jr. The only son of assassinated U.S. president John F. Ken-

nedy and Jacqueline Kennedy Onassis; died in a plane crash on July 16, at the age of 38, along with his wife, Carolyn Bessette Kennedy, and his sister-in-law, Lauren Bessette. He was the founding editor of *George,* a political magazine. *(See also page 57.)*

Kiley, Richard. American actor; died on March 5, at the age of 76. Kiley was a distinguished actor who appeared in a wide variety of roles on stage, screen, and television during his 50-year career. His signature role was as the idealistic knight Don Quixote in the hit Broadway musical *Man of La Mancha,* which opened in 1965.

Kubrick, Stanley. American film director; died on March 7, at the age of 70. A talented and uncompromising perfectionist, Kubrick created brilliant films that often portrayed a bleak view of humanity. Among his most critically acclaimed works were *Dr. Strangelove* (1964), *2001: A Space Odyssey* (1968), and *A Clockwork Orange* (1971).

Mature, Victor. American actor; died on August 4, at the age of 86. The barrel-

DeForest Kelley

Yehudi Menuhin

chested Mature was a handsome screen hero who starred in numerous movies in the 1940's and 1950's. He was best remembered for his roles in *One Million B.C.* (1940), *Samson and Delilah* (1949), and *The Robe* (1953).

Mellon, Paul. American philanthropist; died on February 1, at the age of 91. The heir to a vast business fortune and a fervent art lover, Mellon used his enormous wealth to support various cultural and environmental causes. Mellon was noted for his generous stewardship of the National Gallery of Art in Washington, D.C., to which he donated more than 900 art works.

Menuhin, Yehudi. American-born British violinist and conductor; died on March 12, at the age of 82. Menuhin was a legendary performer of worldwide renown. A child prodigy, he played his first public concert with the San Francisco Symphony when he was only 7 years old. Over the course of his 75-year musical career, Menuhin played with most of the world's leading orchestras.

Payton, Walter. American football player; died on November 1, at the age of 45. An exceptional athlete, Payton was the star running back for the Chicago Bears for thirteen seasons (1975-87). He set a host of National Football League career records, including rushing yards (16,726), and rushing attempts (3,838). Payton was inducted into the Pro Football Hall of Fame in 1993.

Reese, Pee Wee. American baseball player; died on August 14, at the age of 81. Reese, a shortstop, was the captain of the "Boys of Summer"—the Brooklyn Dodgers of the 1940's and 1950's. He was known as an outstanding leader both on the field and off. Reese welcomed Jackie Robinson as a teammate in 1947, helping to ease Robinson's entry into the major leagues as its first African-American player.

Scott, George C. American actor; died on September 22, at the age of 71. Scott played an extraordinary range of roles on stage, film, and television with a riveting intensity. He won an Academy Award in 1971 for his role as General George S. Patton in the film *Patton*—but he refused to accept it. His best-known films included *The Hustler* (1961) and *Dr. Strangelove* (1964).

Walter Payton

George C. Scott

Silverstein, Shel. American author and illustrator; died on May 9, at the age of 66. Silverstein wrote delightfully zany poems and stories that were considered classics of children's literature. Among his works were *The Giving Tree* (1964), a story; and *Where the Sidewalks Ends* (1974) and *A Light in the Attic* (1981), both collections of poems for children.

Siskel, Gene. American film critic; died on February 20, at the age of 53. The tall, lanky Siskel and his televison-show partner Roger Ebert were a popular team of movie reviewers. Their "thumbs up" or "thumbs down" verdict on a movie often predicted how well it would do at the box office. Their show, *At the Movies,* which later became known as *Siskel & Ebert,* first appeared in 1982.

Springfield, Dusty. British pop singer; died on March 2, at the age of 59. Springfield's soulful singing garnered her a string of hits in the 1960's—"I Only Want to Be With You" (1964), "Wishin' and Hopin'" (1964), and "The Look of Love" (1967). *Dusty in Memphis,* her 1969 album that featured "Son of a Preacher Man," is considered a pop masterpiece.

Steinberg, Saul. Romanian-born artist and cartoonist; died on May 12, at the age of 84. Steinberg's quirky drawings often provided a witty commentary on modern American society. His most famed picture was a satirical image of New York City as the center of the world.

Stewart, Payne. American golfer; died on October 25, at the age of 42. Stewart was always recognizable by the distinctive knickers and tam o'shanter he wore in competition. He won three major PGA tournaments during his 19-year career: the 1989 PGA championship, and the 1991 and 1999 U.S. Opens.

Torme, Mel. American jazz and pop singer; died on June 5, at the age of 73. An immensely accomplished singer, Torme was dubbed "the Velvet Fog" for his smooth vocal style. He often performed such standards as "Blue Moon," "It Might as Well Be Spring," and "Oh, You Beautiful Doll." He co-wrote the popular holiday song "The Christmas Song" (also known as "Chestnuts Roasting on an Open Fire").

Dusty Springfield

INDEPENDENT NATIONS OF THE WORLD

NATION	CAPITAL	AREA (in sq mi)	POPULATION (estimate)	GOVERNMENT
Afghanistan	Kabul	250,000	25,800,000	The Taliban—Muslim fundamentalist group
Albania	Tirana	11,100	3,500,000	Rexhep Mejdani—president Ilir Meta—premier
Algeria	Algiers	919,595	30,800,000	Abdelaziz Bouteflika—president
Andorra	Andorra la Vella	175	100,000	Marc Forne Molne—premier
Angola	Luanda	481,354	12,500,000	José Eduardo dos Santos—president
Antigua and Barbuda	St. John's	171	100,000	Lester Bird—prime minister
Argentina	Buenos Aires	1,068,297	36,600,000	Fernando de la Rúa—president
Armenia	Yerevan	11,500	3,800,000	Robert Kocharyan—president
Australia	Canberra	2,967,895	19,000,000	John Howard—prime minister
Austria	Vienna	32,374	8,100,000	Thomas Klestil—president Viktor Klima—chancellor
Azerbaijan	Baku	33,500	7,700,000	Heydar A. Aliyev—president
Bahamas	Nassau	5,380	300,000	Hubert A. Ingraham—prime minister
Bahrain	Manama	240	700,000	Hamad bin Isa al-Khalifa—head of state
Bangladesh	Dhaka	55,598	125,700,000	Shahabuddin Ahmed—president Sheik Hasina Wazed—prime minister
Barbados	Bridgetown	168	300,000	Owen Arthur—prime minister
Belarus	Minsk	80,154	10,200,000	Aleksandr Lukashenko—president
Belgium	Brussels	11,781	10,200,000	Albert II—king Guy Verhofstadt—premier
Belize	Belmopan	8,867	200,000	Said Musa—prime minister
Benin	Porto-Novo	43,484	6,200,000	Mathieu Kerekou—president
Bhutan	Thimbu	18,147	800,000	Jigme Singye Wangchuck—king
Bolivia	La Paz Sucre	424,165	8,100,000	Hugo Banzer Suarez—president
Bosnia and Herzegovina	Sarajevo	19,800	3,800,000	3-member presidency
Botswana	Gaborone	231,804	1,500,000	Festus Mogae—president
Brazil	Brasília	3,286,478	168,000,000	Fernando Henrique Cardoso—president
Brunei Darussalam	Bandar Seri Begawan	2,226	300,000	Hassanal Bolkiah—head of state
Bulgaria	Sofia	42,823	8,200,000	Petar Stoyanov—president Ivan Kostov—premier
Burkina Faso	Ouagadougou	105,869	11,600,000	Blaise Compaoré—president
Burma (Myanmar)	Rangoon	261,218	48,100,000	Than Shwe—head of government
Burundi	Bujumbura	10,747	5,700,000	Pierre Buyoya—president

NATION	CAPITAL	AREA (in sq mi)	POPULATION (estimate)	GOVERNMENT
Cambodia	Phnom Penh	69,898	11,900,000	Norodom Sihanouk—king Hun Sen—prime minister
Cameroon	Yaoundé	183,569	15,500,000	Paul Biya—president
Canada	Ottawa	3,851,809	30,600,000	Jean Chrétien—prime minister
Cape Verde	Praia	1,557	400,000	Antonio Mascarenhas Monteiro—president
Central African Republic	Bangui	240,535	3,400,000	Ange Patasse—president
Chad	N'Djamena	495,754	7,700,000	Idriss Deby—president
Chile	Santiago	292,257	15,000,000	Eduardo Frei Ruíz-Tagle—president
China	Beijing	3,705,390	1,254,100,000	Jiang Zemin—communist party secretary Zhu Rongji—premier
Colombia	Bogotá	439,736	38,600,000	Andrés Pastrana Arango—president
Comoros	Moroni	838	600,000	Azaly Assoumani—president
Congo (Zaire)	Kinshasa	905,565	50,500,000	Laurent Kabila—president
Congo Republic	Brazzaville	132,047	2,700,000	Denis Sassou-Nguesso—president
Costa Rica	San José	19,575	3,600,000	Miguel Angel Rodríguez—president
Croatia	Zagreb	21,829	4,600,000	Vlatko Pavletic—president
Cuba	Havana	44,218	11,200,000	Fidel Castro—president
Cyprus	Nicosia	3,572	900,000	Glafcos Clerides—president
Czech Republic	Prague	30,469	10,300,000	Vaclav Havel—president Milos Zeman—premier
Denmark	Copenhagen	16,629	5,300,000	Margrethe II—queen Poul Nyrup Rasmussen—premier
Djibouti	Djibouti	8,494	600,000	Ismail Omar Guelleh—president
Dominica	Roseau	290	100,000	Edison James—prime minister
Dominican Republic	Santo Domingo	18,816	8,300,000	Leonel Fernandez Reyna—president
Ecuador	Quito	109,483	12,400,000	Jamil Mahuad Witt—president
Egypt	Cairo	386,660	66,900,000	Mohammed Hosni Mubarak—president Kamal Ahmed al-Ganzouri—premier
El Salvador	San Salvador	8,124	5,900,000	Francisco Flores Pérez—president
Equatorial Guinea	Malabo	10,831	400,000	Teodoro Obiang Nguema Mbasogo—president
Eritrea	Asmara	45,405	4,000,000	Issaias Afeworki—president
Estonia	Tallinn	17,413	1,400,000	Lennart Meri—president
Ethiopia	Addis Ababa	426,372	59,700,000	Negasso Ghidada—president
Fiji	Suva	7,055	800,000	Kamisese Mara—president
Finland	Helsinki	130,120	5,200,000	Martti Ahtisaari—president Paavo Lipponen—premier
France	Paris	213,000	59,100,000	Jacques Chirac—president Lionel Jospin—premier
Gabon	Libreville	103,346	1,200,000	Omar Bongo—president
Gambia	Banjul	4,361	1,300,000	Yahya Jammeh—head of state
Georgia	Tbilisi	27,000	5,400,000	Eduard Shevardnadze—president

NATION	CAPITAL	AREA (in sq mi)	POPULATION (estimate)	GOVERNMENT
Germany	Berlin	137,744	82,000,000	Johannes Rau—president Gerhard Schröder—chancellor
Ghana	Accra	92,099	19,700,000	Jerry Rawlings—president
Greece	Athens	50,944	10,500,000	Costis Stefanopoulos—president Costas Simitis—premier
Grenada	St. George's	133	100,000	Keith Mitchell—prime minister
Guatemala	Guatemala City	42,042	12,300,000	Alvaro Arzu Irigoyen—president
Guinea	Conakry	94,926	7,500,000	Lansana Conté—president
Guinea-Bissau	Bissau	13,948	1,200,000	Malan Bacai Sanha—president
Guyana	Georgetown	83,000	700,000	Bharrat Jagdeo—president
Haiti	Port-au-Prince	10,714	7,800,000	René Préval—president
Honduras	Tegucigalpa	43,277	5,900,000	Carlos Flores Facusse—president
Hungary	Budapest	35,919	10,100,000	Arpád Goncz—president Viktor Orban—premier
Iceland	Reykjavik	39,768	300,000	Olafur Grimsson—president David Oddsson—premier
India	New Delhi	1,269,340	1,000,000,000	Kocheril Raman Narayanan—president Atal Bihari Vajpayee—prime minister
Indonesia	Jakarta	735,358	211,800,000	Abdurrahman Wahid—president
Iran	Tehran	636,293	66,200,000	Ayatollah Ali Khamenei—religious leader Mohammed Khatami—president
Iraq	Baghdad	167,925	22,500,000	Saddam Hussein—president
Ireland	Dublin	27,136	3,700,000	Mary McAleese—president Bertie Ahern—prime minister
Israel	Jerusalem	8,019	6,100,000	Ezer Weizman—president Ehud Barak—prime minister
Italy	Rome	116,303	57,700,000	Carlo Azeglio Ciampi—president Massimo D'Alema—premier
Ivory Coast	Yamoussoukro	124,503	15,800,000	Henri Konan-Bédié—president
Jamaica	Kingston	4,244	2,600,000	Percival J. Patterson—prime minister
Japan	Tokyo	143,751	126,700,000	Akihito—emperor Keizo Obuchi—premier
Jordan	Amman	35,475	4,700,000	Abdullah II—king Abdoul Raouf al-Rawabdeh—prime minister
Kazakhstan	Almaty	1,049,000	15,400,000	Nursultan A. Nazarbayev—president
Kenya	Nairobi	224,959	28,800,000	Daniel arap Moi—president
Kiribati	Tarawa	264	85,000	Teburoro Tito—president
Korea (North)	Pyongyang	46,540	21,400,000	Kim Jong II—president Kim Yong Nam—premier
Korea (South)	Seoul	38,025	46,900,000	Kim Dae Jung—president Kim Jong Pil—premier
Kuwait	Kuwait	6,880	2,100,000	Jabir al-Ahmad al-Sabah—head of state
Kyrgyzstan	Bishkek	76,641	4,700,000	Askar Akayev—president
Laos	Vientiane	91,429	5,000,000	Khamtai Siphandon—president Sisavat Keobounphan—premier

NATION	CAPITAL	AREA (in sq mi)	POPULATION (estimate)	GOVERNMENT
Latvia	Riga	24,600	2,400,000	Vaira Vike-Freiberga—president
Lebanon	Beirut	4,015	4,100,000	Emile Lahoud—president Selim al-Hoss—premier
Lesotho	Maseru	11,720	2,100,000	Letsie III—king Pakalitha Mosisili—premier
Liberia	Monrovia	43,000	2,900,000	Charles G. Taylor—president
Libya	Tripoli	679,362	5,000,000	Muammar el-Qaddafi—head of government
Liechtenstein	Vaduz	61	30,000	Hans Adam II—prince
Lithuania	Vilnius	25,174	3,700,000	Valdas Adamkus—president
Luxembourg	Luxembourg	998	400,000	Jean—grand duke Jean-Claude Juncker—premier
Macedonia	Skopje	9,928	2,000,000	Boris Trajkovski—president
Madagascar	Antananarivo	226,657	14,400,000	Didier Ratsiraka—president
Malawi	Lilongwe	45,747	10,000,000	Bakili Muluzi—president
Malaysia	Kuala Lumpur	127,317	22,700,000	Salahuddin Abdul Aziz Shah—king Mahathir bin Mohamad—prime minister
Maldives	Male	115	300,000	Maumoon Abdul Gayoom—president
Mali	Bamako	478,765	11,000,000	Alpha Oumar Konare—president
Malta	Valletta	122	400,000	Guido De Marco—president Eddie Fenech Adami—prime minister
Marshall Islands	Majuro	70	100,000	Imata Kabua—president
Mauritania	Nouakchott	397,954	2,600,000	Maaouya Ould Sid Ahmed Taya—president
Mauritius	Port Louis	790	1,200,000	Cassam Uteem—president Navinchandra Ramgoolam—premier
Mexico	Mexico City	761,602	99,700,000	Ernesto Zedillo Ponce de León—president
Micronesia	Colonia	271	100,000	Leo Falcom—president
Moldova	Kishiniev	13,000	4,300,000	Petru Lucinschi—president
Monaco	Monaco-Ville	0.6	30,000	Rainier III—prince
Mongolia	Ulan Bator	604,248	2,400,000	Natsagiin Bagabandi—president
Morocco	Rabat	172,413	28,200,000	Mohammed VI—king Abderrahmane Youssoufi—premier
Mozambique	Maputo	309,494	19,100,000	Joaquím A. Chissano—president
Namibia	Windhoek	318,260	1,600,000	Sam Nujoma—president
Nauru	Yaren District	8	11,000	Rene Harris—president
Nepal	Katmandu	54,362	24,300,000	Birendra Bir Bikram Shah Deva—king Krishna Prasad Bhattarai—premier
Netherlands	Amsterdam	15,770	15,800,000	Beatrix—queen Willem Kok—premier
New Zealand	Wellington	103,736	3,800,000	Helen Clark—prime minister
Nicaragua	Managua	50,193	5,000,000	Arnoldo Alemán Lacayo—president
Niger	Niamey	489,190	10,000,000	Mamadou Tandja—president
Nigeria	Abuja	356,667	113,800,000	Olusegun Obasanjo—president

NATION	CAPITAL	AREA (in sq mi)	POPULATION (estimate)	GOVERNMENT
Norway	Oslo	125,056	4,500,000	Harold V—king Kjell Magne Bondevik—premier
Oman	Muscat	82,030	2,500,000	Qaboos bin Said Al Said—sultan
Pakistan	Islamabad	310,404	146,500,000	Pervez Musharraf—head of government
Palau	Koror	192	20,000	Kuniwo Nakamura—president
Panama	Panama City	29,761	2,800,000	Mireya Moscoso de Grubar—president
Papua New Guinea	Port Moresby	178,260	4,700,000	Mekere Morauta—prime minister
Paraguay	Asunción	157,047	5,200,000	Luis González Macchi—president
Peru	Lima	496,222	26,600,000	Alberto Fujimori—president
Philippines	Manila	115,830	74,700,000	Joseph Estrada—president Gloria Macapagal-Arroyo—vice-president
Poland	Warsaw	120,725	38,700,000	Aleksander Kwasniewski—president Jerzy Buzek—premier
Portugal	Lisbon	35,553	10,000,000	Jorge Sampaio—president Antonio Guterres—premier
Qatar	Doha	4,247	500,000	Hamad bin Khalifa al-Thani—head of state
Romania	Bucharest	91,700	22,500,000	Emil Constantinescu—president Mugar Isarescu—premier
Russia	Moscow	6,600,000	146,500,000	Vladimir Putin—acting president
Rwanda	Kigali	10,169	8,200,000	Pasteur Bizimungu—president
St. Kitts and Nevis	Basseterre	105	40,000	Denzil Douglas—prime minister
St. Lucia	Castries	238	200,000	Kenny Anthony—prime minister
St. Vincent and the Grenadines	Kingstown	150	100,000	James F. Mitchell—prime minister
San Marino	San Marino	24	30,000	Gabriele Gatti—head of state
São Tomé and Príncipe	São Tomé	372	200,000	Miguel Trovoada—president
Saudi Arabia	Riyadh	830,000	20,900,000	Fahd ibn Abdul-Aziz al-Saud—king
Senegal	Dakar	75,750	9,200,000	Abdou Diouf—president
Seychelles	Victoria	107	100,000	France Albert René—president
Sierra Leone	Freetown	27,700	5,300,000	Ahmad Tejan Kabbah—president
Singapore	Singapore	224	4,000,000	S. R. Nathan—president Goh Chok Tong—prime minister
Slovakia	Bratislava	18,933	5,400,000	Rudolf Schuster—president
Slovenia	Ljubljana	7,819	2,000,000	Milan Kucan—president
Solomon Islands	Honiara	10,983	400,000	Bartholomew Ulufa'alu—prime minister
Somalia	Mogadishu	246,200	7,100,000	no functioning government
South Africa	Pretoria Cape Town Bloemfontein	471,444	42,600,000	Thabo Mbeki—president
Spain	Madrid	194,896	39,400,000	Juan Carlos I—king José María Aznar—premier
Sri Lanka	Colombo	25,332	19,000,000	C. Bandaranaike Kumaratunga—president

UNITED STATES SUPREME COURT

Chief Justice: William H. Rehnquist (1986)
Associate Justices:
  John Paul Stevens (1975)
  Sandra Day O'Connor (1981)
  Antonin Scalia (1986)
  Anthony M. Kennedy (1988)
  David H. Souter (1990)
  Clarence Thomas (1991)
  Ruth Bader Ginsburg (1993)
  Stephen G. Breyer (1994)

UNITED STATES CABINET

Secretary of Agriculture: Daniel R. Glickman
Attorney General: Janet Reno
Secretary of Commerce: William M. Daley
Secretary of Defense: William S. Cohen
Secretary of Education: Richard W. Riley
Secretary of Energy: Bill Richardson
Secretary of Health and Human Services: Donna E. Shalala
Secretary of Housing and Urban Development: Andrew M. Cuomo
Secretary of Interior: Bruce Babbitt
Secretary of Labor: Alexis M. Herman
Secretary of State: Madeleine K. Albright
Secretary of Transportation: Rodney E. Slater
Secretary of the Treasury: Lawrence H. Summers
Secretary of Veteran Affairs: Togo West

Dennis Hastert, Republican congressman from Illinois, became Speaker of the House in 1999.

STATE GOVERNORS

Alabama	Donald Siegelman (D)	**Montana**	Marc Racicot (R)
Alaska	Tony Knowles (D)	**Nebraska**	Mike Johanns (R)
Arizona	Jane Dee Hull (R)	**Nevada**	Kenny Guinn (R)
Arkansas	Mike Huckabee (R)	**New Hampshire**	Jeanne Shaheen (D)
California	Gray Davis (D)	**New Jersey**	Christine Todd Whitman (R)
Colorado	Bill Owens (R)	**New Mexico**	Gary Johnson (R)
Connecticut	John Rowland (R)	**New York**	George Pataki (R)
Delaware	Thomas R. Carper (D)	**North Carolina**	Jim B. Hunt, Jr. (D)
Florida	Jeb Bush (R)	**North Dakota**	Edward Schafer (R)
Georgia	Roy Barnes (D)	**Ohio**	Bob Taft (R)
Hawaii	Ben Cayetano (D)	**Oklahoma**	Frank Keating (R)
Idaho	Dirk Kempthorne (R)	**Oregon**	John Kitzhaber (D)
Illinois	George Ryan (R)	**Pennsylvania**	Thomas J. Ridge (R)
Indiana	Frank L. O'Bannon (D)	**Rhode Island**	Lincoln Almond (R)
Iowa	Tom Vilsack (D)	**South Carolina**	Jim Hodges (D)
Kansas	Bill Graves (R)	**South Dakota**	William Janklow (R)
Kentucky	Paul Patton (D)*	**Tennessee**	Don Sundquist (R)
Louisiana	Mike Foster (R)*	**Texas**	George W. Bush (R)
Maine	Angus King (I)	**Utah**	Mike Leavitt (R)
Maryland	Parris N. Glendening (D)	**Vermont**	Howard Dean (D)
Massachusetts	Paul Cellucci (R)	**Virginia**	James S. Gilmore III (R)
Michigan	John Engler (R)	**Washington**	Gary Locke (D)
Minnesota	Jesse Ventura (RF)	**West Virginia**	Cecil H. Underwood (R)
Mississippi	**	**Wisconsin**	Tommy G. Thompson (R)
Missouri	Mel Carnahan (D)	**Wyoming**	Jim Geringer (R)

*re-elected in 1999   **election undecided   (D) Democrat (R) Republican (I) Independent (RF) Reform

CANADA

Capital: Ottawa
Head of State: Queen Elizabeth II
Governor General: Adrienne Clarkson
Prime Minister: Jean Chrétien (Liberal)
Leader of the Opposition: Preston Manning (Reform Party)
Population: 30,600,000
Area: 3,851,809 sq mi (9,976,185 km²)

PROVINCES AND TERRITORIES

Alberta
Capital: Edmonton
Lieutenant Governor: H. A. Bud Olson
Premier: Ralph Klein (Progressive Conservative)
Leader of the Opposition: Nancy MacBeth (Liberal)
Entered Confederation: Sept. 1, 1905
Population: 2,969,000
Area: 255,285 sq mi (661,188 km²)

British Columbia
Capital: Victoria
Lieutenant Governor: Garde Gardom
Premier: Dan Miller (New Democratic Party)
Leader of the Opposition: Gordon Campbell (Liberal)
Entered Confederation: July 20, 1871
Population: 4,029,300
Area: 366,255 sq mi (948,600 km²)

Manitoba
Capital: Winnipeg
Lieutenant Governor: Yvon Dumont
Premier: Gary Albert Doer (New Democratic Party)
Leader of the Opposition: Gary Filmon
   (Progressive Conservative)
Entered Confederation: July 15, 1870
Population: 1,143,400
Area: 251,000 sq mi (650,090 km²)

New Brunswick
Capital: Fredericton
Lieutenant Governor: Marilyn Trenholme Counsell
Premier: Bernard Lord (Progressive Conservative)
Leader of the Opposition: Camille Thériault (Liberal)
Entered Confederation: July 1, 1867
Population: 754,700
Area: 28,354 sq mi (73,436 km²)

Newfoundland
Capital: St. John's
Lieutenant Governor: Arthur Max House
Premier: Brian Tobin (Liberal)
Leader of the Opposition: Ed Byrne
   (Progressive Conservative)
Entered Confederation: March 31, 1949
Population: 541,200
Area: 156,185 sq mi (404,517 km²)

Nova Scotia
Capital: Halifax
Lieutenant Governor: J. James Kinley
Premier: John F. Hamm (Progressive Conservative)
Leader of the Opposition: Robert Chisholm (New
   Democratic Party)
Entered Confederation: July 1, 1867
Population: 940,800
Area: 21,425 sq mi (55,491 km²)

Ontario
Capital: Toronto
Lieutenant Governor: Hilary M. Weston
Premier: Mike Harris (Progressive Conservative)
Leader of the Opposition: Dalton McGuinty (Liberal)
Entered Confederation: July 1, 1867
Population: 11,600,000
Area: 412,582 sq mi (1,068,582 km²)

Prince Edward Island
Capital: Charlottetown
Lieutenant Governor: Gilbert R. Clements
Premier: Patrick Binns (Progressive Conservative)
Leader of the Opposition: Paul Connolly (Liberal)
Entered Confederation: July 1, 1873
Population: 137,800
Area: 2,184 sq mi (5,657 km²)

NATION	CAPITAL	AREA (in sq mi)	POPULATION (estimate)	GOVERNMENT
Sudan	Khartoum	967,500	28,900,000	O. Hassan Ahmed al-Bashir—president
Suriname	Paramaribo	63,037	400,000	Jules Wijdenbosch—president
Swaziland	Mbabane	6,704	1,000,000	Mswati III—king
Sweden	Stockholm	173,731	8,900,000	Carl XVI Gustaf—king Göran Persson—premier
Switzerland	Bern	15,941	7,100,000	Adolf Ogi—president
Syria	Damascus	71,498	16,000,000	Hafez al-Assad—president Mahmoud Zubi—premier
Taiwan	Taipei	13,885	22,000,000	Lee Teng-hui—president Vincent Siew—premier
Tajikistan	Dushanbe	55,250	6,200,000	Yakhyo Azimov—premier
Tanzania	Dar es Salaam	364,898	31,300,000	Benjamin Mkapa—president
Thailand	Bangkok	198,457	61,800,000	Bhumibol Adulyadej—king Chuan Leekpai—premier
Togo	Lomé	21,622	4,500,000	Gnassingbe Eyadema—president
Tonga	Nuku'alofa	270	109,000	Taufa'ahau Tupou IV—king Baron Vaea—premier
Trinidad & Tobago	Port of Spain	1,980	1,300,000	A.N.R. Robinson—president Basdeo Panday—prime minister
Tunisia	Tunis	63,170	9,500,000	Zine el-Abidine Ben Ali—president
Turkey	Ankara	301,381	65,900,000	Suleyman Demirel—president Bulent Ecevit—prime minister
Turkmenistan	Ashkhabad	188,455	4,800,000	Saparmurad Niyazov—president
Tuvalu	Funafuti	10	10,000	Ionatana Ionatana—prime minister
Uganda	Kampala	91,134	22,800,000	Yoweri Museveni—president
Ukraine	Kiev	231,990	49,900,000	Leonid M. Kuchma—president
United Arab Emirates	Abu Dhabi	32,278	2,800,000	Zayed bin Sultan al-Nuhayyan—president
United Kingdom	London	94,226	59,400,000	Elizabeth II—queen Tony Blair—prime minister
United States	Washington, D.C.	3,618,467	272,500,000	William J. Clinton—president Albert A. Gore, Jr.—vice-president
Uruguay	Montevideo	68,037	3,400,000	Jorge Batlle—president
Uzbekistan	Tashkent	172,750	24,400,000	Islam A. Karimov—president
Vanuatu	Vila	5,700	200,000	Donald Kalpokas—president
Vatican City	Vatican City	0.17	1,000	John Paul II—pope
Venezuela	Caracas	352,143	23,700,000	Hugo Chávez—president
Vietnam	Hanoi	128,402	79,500,000	La Kha Phieu—communist party secretary Phan Van Khai—premier
Western Samoa	Apia	1,097	200,000	Malietoa Tanumafili II—head of state
Yemen	Sana	203,849	16,400,000	Ali Abdullah Saleh—president Abd al-Karim Iryani—premier
Yugoslavia	Belgrade	39,390	10,600,000	Slobodan Milosevic—president Momir Bulatovic—premier
Zambia	Lusaka	290,585	9,700,000	Frederick Chiluba—president
Zimbabwe	Harare	150,333	11,200,000	Robert Mugabe—president

THE CONGRESS OF THE UNITED STATES

UNITED STATES SENATE
(55 Republicans, 45 Democrats)

Alabama
Richard C. Shelby (R)
Jefferson B. Sessions (R)

Alaska
Ted Stevens (R)
Frank H. Murkowski (R)

Arizona
John S. McCain III (R)
Jon Kyl (R)

Arkansas
Tim Hutchinson (R)
Blanche L. Lincoln (D)

California
Barbara Boxer (D)
Dianne Feinstein (D)

Colorado
Ben Nighthorse Campbell (R)
Wayne Allard (R)

Connecticut
Christopher J. Dodd (D)
Joseph I. Lieberman (D)

Delaware
William V. Roth, Jr. (R)
Joseph R. Biden, Jr. (D)

Florida
Bob Graham (D)
Connie Mack (R)

Georgia
Paul D. Coverdell (R)
Max Cleland (D)

Hawaii
Daniel K. Inouye (D)
Daniel K. Akaka (D)

Idaho
Larry E. Craig (R)
Mike Crapo (R)

Illinois
Richard J. Durbin (D)
Peter Fitzgerald (R)

Indiana
Richard G. Lugar (R)
Evan Bayh (D)

Iowa
Charles E. Grassley (R)
Thomas R. Harkin (D)

Kansas
Sam Brownback (R)
Pat Roberts (R)

Kentucky
Mitch McConnell (R)
Jim Bunning (R)

Louisiana
John B. Breaux (D)
Mary L. Landrieu (D)

Maine
Olympia J. Snowe (R)
Susan Collins (R)

Maryland
Paul S. Sarbanes (D)
Barbara A. Mikulski (D)

Massachusetts
Edward M. Kennedy (D)
John F. Kerry (D)

Michigan
Carl Levin (D)
Spencer Abraham (R)

Minnesota
Paul Wellstone (D)
Rod Grams (R)

Mississippi
Thad Cochran (R)
Trent Lott (R)

Missouri
Christopher S. Bond (R)
John Ashcroft (R)

Montana
Max S. Baucus (D)
Conrad Burns (R)

Nebraska
Robert Kerrey (D)
Chuck Hagel (R)

Nevada
Harry Reid (D)
Richard H. Bryan (D)

New Hampshire
Judd Gregg (R)
Robert C. Smith (R)

New Jersey
Frank R. Lautenberg (D)
Robert G. Torricelli (D)

New Mexico
Pete V. Domenici (R)
Jeff Bingaman (D)

New York
Daniel P. Moynihan (D)
Charles E. Schumer (D)

North Carolina
Jesse Helms (R)
John Edwards (D)

North Dakota
Kent Conrad (D)
Byron L. Dorgan (D)

Ohio
Mike DeWine (R)
George Voinovich (R)

Oklahoma
Donald L. Nickles (R)
James M. Inhofe (R)

Oregon
Gordon Smith (R)
Ron Wyden (D)

Pennsylvania
Arlen Specter (R)
Rick Santorum (R)

Rhode Island
Lincoln D. Chafee (R)*
John Reed (D)

South Carolina
Strom Thurmond (R)
Ernest F. Hollings (D)

South Dakota
Thomas A. Daschle (D)
Tim Johnson (D)

Tennessee
Bill Frist (R)
Fred D. Thompson (R)

Texas
Phil Gramm (R)
Kay Bailey Hutchison (R)

Utah
Orrin G. Hatch (R)
Robert F. Bennett (R)

Vermont
Patrick J. Leahy (D)
James M. Jeffords (R)

Virginia
John W. Warner (R)
Charles S. Robb (D)

Washington
Slade Gorton (R)
Patty Murray (D)

West Virginia
Robert C. Byrd (D)
John D. Rockefeller IV (D)

Wisconsin
Herbert H. Kohl (D)
Russell D. Feingold (D)

Wyoming
Craig Thomas (R)
Michael Enzi (R)

(D) Democrat
(R) Republican

* succeeded J. Chafee, who
died in October

UNITED STATES HOUSE OF REPRESENTATIVES
(222 Republicans, 212 Democrats, 1 Independent)

Alabama
1. H. L. Callahan (R)
2. T. Everett (R)
3. B. Riley (R)
4. R. Aderholt (R)
5. B. Cramer (D)
6. S. Bachus (R)
7. E. Hilliard (D)

Alaska
D. Young (R)

Arizona
1. M. Salmon (R)
2. E. Pastor (D)
3. B. Stump (R)
4. J. Shadegg (R)
5. J. Kolbe (R)
6. J. D. Hayworth (R)

Arkansas
1. M. Berry (D)
2. V. F. Snyder (D)
3. A. Hutchinson (R)
4. J. Dickey (R)

California
1. M. Thompson (D)
2. W. Herger (R)
3. D. Ose (R)
4. J. T. Doolittle (R)
5. R. T. Matsui (D)
6. L. Woolsey (D)
7. G. Miller (D)
8. N. Pelosi (D)
9. B. Lee (D)
10. E. Tauscher (D)
11. R. Pombo (R)
12. T. Lantos (D)
13. F. H. Stark (D)
14. A. Eshoo (D)
15. T. Campbell (R)
16. Z. Lofgren (D)
17. S. Farr (D)
18. G. Condit (D)
19. G. Radanovich (R)
20. C. Dooley (D)
21. B. Thomas (R)
22. L. Capps (D)
23. E. Gallegly (R)
24. B. Sherman (D)
25. H. McKeon (R)
26. H. L. Berman (D)
27. J. E. Rogan (R)
28. D. Dreier (R)
29. H. A. Waxman (D)
30. X. Becerra (D)
31. M. G. Martinez (D)
32. J. C. Dixon (D)
33. L. Roybal-Allard (D)
34. G. Napolitano (D)
35. M. Waters (D)
36. S. Kuykendall (R)
37. J. Millender-McDonald (D)
38. S. Horn (R)
39. E. Royce (R)
40. J. Lewis (R)
41. G. Miller (R)

42. J. Baca (D)*
43. K. Calvert (R)
44. M. Bono (R)
45. D. Rohrabacher (R)
46. L. Sanchez (D)
47. C. C. Cox (R)
48. R. Packard (R)
49. B. Bilbray (R)
50. B. Filner (D)
51. R. Cunningham (R)
52. D. Hunter (R)

Colorado
1. D. DeGette (D)
2. M. Udall (D)
3. S. McInnis (R)
4. R. W. Schaffer (R)
5. J. Hefley (R)
6. T. Tancredo (R)

Connecticut
1. J. Larson (D)
2. S. Gejdenson (D)
3. R. DeLauro (D)
4. C. Shays (R)
5. J. H. Maloney (D)
6. N. L. Johnson (R)

Delaware
M. N. Castle (R)

Florida
1. J. Scarborough (R)
2. A. Boyd, Jr. (D)
3. C. Brown (D)
4. T. Fowler (R)
5. K. Thurman (D)
6. C. B. Stearns (R)
7. J. Mica (R)
8. B. McCollum (R)
9. M. Bilirakis (R)
10. B. Young (R)
11. J. Davis (D)
12. C. Canady (R)
13. D. Miller (R)
14. P. J. Goss (R)
15. D. Weldon (R)
16. M. Foley (R)
17. C. Meek (D)
18. I. Ros-Lehtinen (R)
19. R. Wexler (D)
20. P. Deutsch (D)
21. L. Diaz-Balart (R)
22. E. C. Shaw, Jr. (R)
23. A. L. Hastings (D)

Georgia
1. J. Kingston (R)
2. S. Bishop (D)
3. M. Collins (R)
4. C. McKinney (D)
5. J. Lewis (D)
6. J. Isakson (R)*
7. B. Barr (R)
8. S. Chambliss (R)
9. N. Deal (R)
10. C. Norwood (R)
11. J. Linder (R)

Hawaii
1. N. Abercrombie (D)
2. P. T. Mink (D)

Idaho
1. H. Chenoweth-Hage (R)
2. M. Simpson (R)

Illinois
1. B. Rush (D)
2. J. Jackson, Jr. (D)
3. W. O. Lipinski (D)
4. L. V. Gutierrez (D)
5. R. R. Blagojevich (D)
6. H. J. Hyde (R)
7. D. K. Davis (D)
8. P. M. Crane (R)
9. J. Schakowsky (D)
10. J. E. Porter (R)
11. G. Weller (R)
12. J. F. Costello (D)
13. J. Biggert (R)
14. J. D. Hastert (R)
15. T. W. Ewing (R)
16. D. Manzullo (R)
17. L. Evans (D)
18. R. LaHood (R)
19. D. Phelps (D)
20. J. M. Shimkus (R)

Indiana
1. P. J. Visclosky (D)
2. D. McIntosh (R)
3. T. Roemer (D)
4. M. Souder (R)
5. S. Buyer (R)
6. D. L. Burton (R)
7. E. Pease (R)
8. J. Hostettler (R)
9. B. Hill (D)
10. J. Carson (D)

Iowa
1. J. Leach (R)
2. J. Nussle (R)
3. L. L. Boswell (D)
4. G. Ganske (R)
5. T. Latham (R)

Kansas
1. J. Moran (R)
2. J. Ryun (R)
3. D. Moore (D)
4. T. Tiahrt (R)

Kentucky
1. E. Whitfield (R)
2. R. Lewis (R)
3. A. Northup (R)
4. K. Lucas (D)
5. H. Rogers (R)
6. E. Fletcher (R)

Louisiana
1. D. Vitter (R)*
2. W. J. Jefferson (D)

3. W. J. Tauzin (R)
4. J. McCrery (R)
5. J. Cooksey (R)
6. R. H. Baker (R)
7. C. John (D)

Maine
1. T. Allen (D)
2. J. Baldacci (D)

Maryland
1. W. T. Gilchrest (R)
2. R. L. Ehrlich, Jr. (R)
3. B. L. Cardin (D)
4. A. Wynn (D)
5. S. H. Hoyer (D)
6. R. Bartlett (R)
7. E. E. Cummings (D)
8. C. A. Morella (R)

Massachusetts
1. J. Olver (D)
2. R. E. Neal (D)
3. J. McGovern (D)
4. B. Frank (D)
5. M. Meehan (D)
6. J. F. Tierney (D)
7. E. J. Markey (D)
8. M. Capuano (D)
9. J. J. Moakley (D)
10. W. D. Delahunt (D)

Michigan
1. B. Stupak (D)
2. P. Hoekstra (R)
3. V. Ehlers (R)
4. D. Camp (R)
5. J. Barcia (D)
6. F. S. Upton (R)
7. N. Smith (R)
8. D. A. Stabenow (D)
9. D. E. Kildee (D)
10. D. E. Bonior (D)
11. J. Knollenberg (R)
12. S. M. Levin (D)
13. L. Rivers (D)
14. J. Conyers, Jr. (D)
15. C. C. Kilpatrick (D)
16. J. D. Dingell, Jr. (D)

Minnesota
1. G. Gutknecht (R)
2. D. Minge (D)
3. J. Ramstad (R)
4. B. F. Vento (D)
5. M. O. Sabo (D)
6. W. Luther (D)
7. C. C. Peterson (D)
8. J. L. Oberstar (D)

Mississippi
1. R. Wicker (R)
2. B. Thompson (D)
3. C. W. Pickering, Jr. (R)
4. R. Shows (D)
5. G. Taylor (D)

Missouri
1. W. L. Clay (D)
2. J. Talent (R)
3. R. A. Gephardt (D)
4. I. Skelton (D)
5. K. McCarthy (D)
6. P. Danner (D)
7. R. Blunt (R)
8. J. Emerson (R)
9. K. Hulshof (R)

Montana
R. Hill (R)

Nebraska
1. D. K. Bereuter (R)
2. L. Terry (R)
3. B. Barrett (R)

Nevada
1. S. Berkley (D)
2. J. Gibbons (R)

New Hampshire
1. J. E. Sununu (R)
2. C. Bass (R)

New Jersey
1. R. E. Andrews (D)
2. F. LoBiondo (R)
3. H. J. Saxton (R)
4. C. H. Smith (R)
5. M. Roukema (R)
6. F. Pallone, Jr. (D)
7. B. Franks (R)
8. W. J. Pascrell, Jr. (D)
9. S. R. Rothman (D)
10. D. M. Payne (D)
11. R. Frelinghuysen (R)
12. R. Holt (D)
13. R. Menendez (D)

New Mexico
1. H. Wilson (R)
2. J. R. Skeen (R)
3. T. Udall (D)

New York
1. M. Forbes (D)**
2. R. Lazio (R)
3. P. T. King (R)
4. C. McCarthy (D)
5. G. L. Ackerman (D)
6. G. Meeks (D)
7. J. Crowley (D)
8. J. Nadler (D)
9. A. Weiner (D)
10. E. Towns (D)
11. M. R. Owens (D)
12. N. Velazquez (D)
13. V. J. Fossella, Jr. (R)
14. C. Maloney (D)
15. C. B. Rangel (D)
16. J. E. Serrano (D)
17. E. L. Engel (D)
18. N. M. Lowey (D)
19. S. W. Kelly (R)
20. B. A. Gilman (R)
21. M. R. McNulty (D)

22. J. Sweeney (R)
23. S. L. Boehlert (R)
24. J. McHugh (R)
25. J. T. Walsh (R)
26. M. Hinchey (R)
27. T. Reynolds (R)
28. L. M. Slaughter (D)
29. J. J. LaFalce (D)
30. J. Quinn (R)
31. A. Houghton, Jr. (R)

North Carolina
1. E. Clayton (D)
2. B. R. Etheridge (D)
3. W. Jones, Jr. (R)
4. D. E. Price (D)
5. R. Burr (R)
6. J. H. Coble (R)
7. M. McIntyre (D)
8. R. Hayes (R)
9. S. Myrick (R)
10. T. C. Ballenger (R)
11. C. H. Taylor (R)
12. M. Watt (D)

North Dakota
E. Pomeroy (D)

Ohio
1. S. Chabot (R)
2. R. Portman (R)
3. T. P. Hall (D)
4. M. G. Oxley (R)
5. P. E. Gillmor (R)
6. T. Strickland (D)
7. D. L. Hobson (R)
8. J. A. Boehner (R)
9. M. Kaptur (D)
10. D. Kucinich (D)
11. S. Jones (D)
12. J. R. Kasich (R)
13. S. Brown (D)
14. T. C. Sawyer (D)
15. D. Pryce (R)
16. R. S. Regula (R)
17. J. A. Traficant, Jr. (D)
18. B. Ney (R)
19. S. LaTourette (R)

Oklahoma
1. S. Largent (R)
2. T. Coburn (R)
3. W. Watkins (R)
4. J. C. Watts (R)
5. E. J. Istook (R)
6. F. Lucas (R)

Oregon
1. D. Wu (D)
2. G. Walden (R)
3. E. Blumenauer (D)
4. P. DeFazio (D)
5. D. Hooley (D)

Pennsylvania
1. R. Brady (D)
2. C. Fattah (D)
3. R. A. Borski (D)
4. R. Klink (D)
5. J. E. Peterson (R)

6. T. Holden (D)
7. W. C. Weldon (R)
8. J. Greenwood (R)
9. E. G. Shuster (R)
10. D. Sherwood (R)
11. P. E. Kanjorski (D)
12. J. P. Murtha, Jr. (D)
13. J. Hoeffel (D)
14. W. J. Coyne (D)
15. P. Toomey (R)
16. J. R. Pitts (R)
17. G. W. Gekas (R)
18. M. Doyle (D)
19. W. F. Goodling (R)
20. F. Mascara (D)
21. P. English (R)

Rhode Island
1. P. Kennedy (D)
2. R. A. Weygand (D)

South Carolina
1. M. Sanford (R)
2. F. D. Spence (R)
3. L. Graham (R)
4. J. DeMint (R)
5. J. M. Spratt, Jr. (D)
6. J. Clyburn (D)

South Dakota
J. Thune (R)

Tennessee
1. W. Jenkins (R)
2. J. J. Duncan, Jr. (R)
3. Z. Wamp (R)
4. V. Hilleary (R)
5. B. Clement (D)
6. B. J. Gordon (D)
7. E. Bryant (R)
8. J. S. Tanner (D)
9. H. E. Ford, Jr. (D)

Texas
1. M. Sandlin (D)
2. J. Turner (D)
3. S. Johnson (R)
4. R. M. Hall (D)
5. P. Sessions (R)
6. J. Barton (R)
7. W. R. Archer (R)
8. K. Brady (R)
9. N. Lampson (D)
10. L. Doggett (D)
11. C. Edwards (D)
12. K. Granger (R)
13. W. Thornberry (R)
14. R. Paul (R)
15. R. Hinojosa (D)
16. S. Reyes (D)
17. C. W. Stenholm (D)
18. S. Jackson-Lee (D)
19. L. Combest (R)
20. C. Gonzalez (D)
21. L. S. Smith (R)
22. T. D. DeLay (R)
23. H. Bonilla (R)
24. J. M. Frost (D)
25. K. Bentsen (D)
26. D. Armey (R)

27. S. P. Ortiz (D)
28. C. Rodriguez (D)
29. G. Green (D)
30. E. B. Johnson (D)

Utah
1. J. V. Hansen (R)
2. M. Cook (R)
3. C. Cannon (R)

Vermont
B. Sanders (I)

Virginia
1. H. H. Bateman (R)
2. O. B. Pickett (D)
3. R. C. Scott (D)
4. N. Sisisky (D)
5. V. H. Goode, Jr. (D)
6. R. Goodlatte (R)
7. T. Bliley, Jr. (R)
8. J. P. Moran, Jr. (D)
9. F. C. Boucher (D)
10. F. R. Wolf (R)
11. T. Davis III (R)

Washington
1. J. Inslee (D)
2. J. Metcalf (R)
3. B. Baird (D)
4. D. Hastings (R)
5. G. Nethercutt (R)
6. N. D. Dicks (D)
7. J. McDermott (D)
8. J. Dunn (R)
9. A. Smith (D)

West Virginia
1. A. B. Mollohan (D)
2. R. E. Wise, Jr. (D)
3. N. J. Rahall II (D)

Wisconsin
1. P. Ryan (R)
2. T. Baldwin (D)
3. R. Kind (D)
4. G. D. Kleczka (D)
5. T. Barrett (D)
6. T. E. Petri (R)
7. D. R. Obey (D)
8. M. Green (R)
9. F. J. Sensenbrenner, Jr. (R)

Wyoming
B. Cubin (R)

(D) Democrat
(R) Republican
(I) Independent

* elected in 1999
** switched parties in 1999

NATION	CAPITAL	AREA (in sq mi)	POPULATION (estimate)	GOVERNMENT
Cambodia	Phnom Penh	69,898	11,900,000	Norodom Sihanouk—king Hun Sen—prime minister
Cameroon	Yaoundé	183,569	15,500,000	Paul Biya—president
Canada	Ottawa	3,851,809	30,600,000	Jean Chrétien—prime minister
Cape Verde	Praia	1,557	400,000	Antonio Mascarenhas Monteiro—president
Central African Republic	Bangui	240,535	3,400,000	Ange Patasse—president
Chad	N'Djamena	495,754	7,700,000	Idriss Deby—president
Chile	Santiago	292,257	15,000,000	Eduardo Frei Ruíz-Tagle—president
China	Beijing	3,705,390	1,254,100,000	Jiang Zemin—communist party secretary Zhu Rongji—premier
Colombia	Bogotá	439,736	38,600,000	Andrés Pastrana Arango—president
Comoros	Moroni	838	600,000	Azaly Assoumani—president
Congo (Zaire)	Kinshasa	905,565	50,500,000	Laurent Kabila—president
Congo Republic	Brazzaville	132,047	2,700,000	Denis Sassou-Nguesso—president
Costa Rica	San José	19,575	3,600,000	Miguel Angel Rodríguez—president
Croatia	Zagreb	21,829	4,600,000	Vlatko Pavletic—president
Cuba	Havana	44,218	11,200,000	Fidel Castro—president
Cyprus	Nicosia	3,572	900,000	Glafcos Clerides—president
Czech Republic	Prague	30,469	10,300,000	Vaclav Havel—president Milos Zeman—premier
Denmark	Copenhagen	16,629	5,300,000	Margrethe II—queen Poul Nyrup Rasmussen—premier
Djibouti	Djibouti	8,494	600,000	Ismail Omar Guelleh—president
Dominica	Roseau	290	100,000	Edison James—prime minister
Dominican Republic	Santo Domingo	18,816	8,300,000	Leonel Fernandez Reyna—president
Ecuador	Quito	109,483	12,400,000	Jamil Mahuad Witt—president
Egypt	Cairo	386,660	66,900,000	Mohammed Hosni Mubarak—president Kamal Ahmed al-Ganzouri—premier
El Salvador	San Salvador	8,124	5,900,000	Francisco Flores Pérez—president
Equatorial Guinea	Malabo	10,831	400,000	Teodoro Obiang Nguema Mbasogo—president
Eritrea	Asmara	45,405	4,000,000	Issaias Afeworki—president
Estonia	Tallinn	17,413	1,400,000	Lennart Meri—president
Ethiopia	Addis Ababa	426,372	59,700,000	Negasso Ghidada—president
Fiji	Suva	7,055	800,000	Kamisese Mara—president
Finland	Helsinki	130,120	5,200,000	Martti Ahtisaari—president Paavo Lipponen—premier
France	Paris	213,000	59,100,000	Jacques Chirac—president Lionel Jospin—premier
Gabon	Libreville	103,346	1,200,000	Omar Bongo—president
Gambia	Banjul	4,361	1,300,000	Yahya Jammeh—head of state
Georgia	Tbilisi	27,000	5,400,000	Eduard Shevardnadze—president

NATION	CAPITAL	AREA (in sq mi)	POPULATION (estimate)	GOVERNMENT
Germany	Berlin	137,744	82,000,000	Johannes Rau—president Gerhard Schröder—chancellor
Ghana	Accra	92,099	19,700,000	Jerry Rawlings—president
Greece	Athens	50,944	10,500,000	Costis Stefanopoulos—president Costas Simitis—premier
Grenada	St. George's	133	100,000	Keith Mitchell—prime minister
Guatemala	Guatemala City	42,042	12,300,000	Alvaro Arzu Irigoyen—president
Guinea	Conakry	94,926	7,500,000	Lansana Conté—president
Guinea-Bissau	Bissau	13,948	1,200,000	Malan Bacai Sanha—president
Guyana	Georgetown	83,000	700,000	Bharrat Jagdeo—president
Haiti	Port-au-Prince	10,714	7,800,000	René Préval—president
Honduras	Tegucigalpa	43,277	5,900,000	Carlos Flores Facusse—president
Hungary	Budapest	35,919	10,100,000	Arpád Goncz—president Viktor Orban—premier
Iceland	Reykjavik	39,768	300,000	Olafur Grimsson—president David Oddsson—premier
India	New Delhi	1,269,340	1,000,000,000	Kocheril Raman Narayanan—president Atal Bihari Vajpayee—prime minister
Indonesia	Jakarta	735,358	211,800,000	Abdurrahman Wahid—president
Iran	Tehran	636,293	66,200,000	Ayatollah Ali Khamenei—religious leader Mohammed Khatami—president
Iraq	Baghdad	167,925	22,500,000	Saddam Hussein—president
Ireland	Dublin	27,136	3,700,000	Mary McAleese—president Bertie Ahern—prime minister
Israel	Jerusalem	8,019	6,100,000	Ezer Weizman—president Ehud Barak—prime minister
Italy	Rome	116,303	57,700,000	Carlo Azeglio Ciampi—president Massimo D'Alema—premier
Ivory Coast	Yamoussoukro	124,503	15,800,000	Henri Konan-Bédié—president
Jamaica	Kingston	4,244	2,600,000	Percival J. Patterson—prime minister
Japan	Tokyo	143,751	126,700,000	Akihito—emperor Keizo Obuchi—premier
Jordan	Amman	35,475	4,700,000	Abdullah II—king Abdoul Raouf al-Rawabdeh—prime minister
Kazakhstan	Almaty	1,049,000	15,400,000	Nursultan A. Nazarbayev—president
Kenya	Nairobi	224,959	28,800,000	Daniel arap Moi—president
Kiribati	Tarawa	264	85,000	Teburoro Tito—president
Korea (North)	Pyongyang	46,540	21,400,000	Kim Jong II—president Kim Yong Nam—premier
Korea (South)	Seoul	38,025	46,900,000	Kim Dae Jung—president Kim Jong Pil—premier
Kuwait	Kuwait	6,880	2,100,000	Jabir al-Ahmad al-Sabah—head of state
Kyrgyzstan	Bishkek	76,641	4,700,000	Askar Akayev—president
Laos	Vientiane	91,429	5,000,000	Khamtai Siphandon—president Sisavat Keobounphan—premier

NATION	CAPITAL	AREA (in sq mi)	POPULATION (estimate)	GOVERNMENT
Latvia	Riga	24,600	2,400,000	Vaira Vike-Freiberga—president
Lebanon	Beirut	4,015	4,100,000	Emile Lahoud—president Selim al-Hoss—premier
Lesotho	Maseru	11,720	2,100,000	Letsie III—king Pakalitha Mosisili—premier
Liberia	Monrovia	43,000	2,900,000	Charles G. Taylor—president
Libya	Tripoli	679,362	5,000,000	Muammar el-Qaddafi—head of government
Liechtenstein	Vaduz	61	30,000	Hans Adam II—prince
Lithuania	Vilnius	25,174	3,700,000	Valdas Adamkus—president
Luxembourg	Luxembourg	998	400,000	Jean—grand duke Jean-Claude Juncker—premier
Macedonia	Skopje	9,928	2,000,000	Boris Trajkovski—president
Madagascar	Antananarivo	226,657	14,400,000	Didier Ratsiraka—president
Malawi	Lilongwe	45,747	10,000,000	Bakili Muluzi—president
Malaysia	Kuala Lumpur	127,317	22,700,000	Salahuddin Abdul Aziz Shah—king Mahathir bin Mohamad—prime minister
Maldives	Male	115	300,000	Maumoon Abdul Gayoom—president
Mali	Bamako	478,765	11,000,000	Alpha Oumar Konare—president
Malta	Valletta	122	400,000	Guido De Marco—president Eddie Fenech Adami—prime minister
Marshall Islands	Majuro	70	100,000	Imata Kabua—president
Mauritania	Nouakchott	397,954	2,600,000	Maaouya Ould Sid Ahmed Taya—president
Mauritius	Port Louis	790	1,200,000	Cassam Uteem—president Navinchandra Ramgoolam—premier
Mexico	Mexico City	761,602	99,700,000	Ernesto Zedillo Ponce de León—president
Micronesia	Colonia	271	100,000	Leo Falcom—president
Moldova	Kishiniev	13,000	4,300,000	Petru Lucinschi—president
Monaco	Monaco-Ville	0.6	30,000	Rainier III—prince
Mongolia	Ulan Bator	604,248	2,400,000	Natsagiin Bagabandi—president
Morocco	Rabat	172,413	28,200,000	Mohammed VI—king Abderrahmane Youssoufi—premier
Mozambique	Maputo	309,494	19,100,000	Joaquím A. Chissano—president
Namibia	Windhoek	318,260	1,600,000	Sam Nujoma—president
Nauru	Yaren District	8	11,000	Rene Harris—president
Nepal	Katmandu	54,362	24,300,000	Birendra Bir Bikram Shah Deva—king Krishna Prasad Bhattarai—premier
Netherlands	Amsterdam	15,770	15,800,000	Beatrix—queen Willem Kok—premier
New Zealand	Wellington	103,736	3,800,000	Helen Clark—prime minister
Nicaragua	Managua	50,193	5,000,000	Arnoldo Alemán Lacayo—president
Niger	Niamey	489,190	10,000,000	Mamadou Tandja—president
Nigeria	Abuja	356,667	113,800,000	Olusegun Obasanjo—president

NATION	CAPITAL	AREA (in sq mi)	POPULATION (estimate)	GOVERNMENT
Norway	Oslo	125,056	4,500,000	Harold V—king Kjell Magne Bondevik—premier
Oman	Muscat	82,030	2,500,000	Qaboos bin Said Al Said—sultan
Pakistan	Islamabad	310,404	146,500,000	Pervez Musharraf—head of government
Palau	Koror	192	20,000	Kuniwo Nakamura—president
Panama	Panama City	29,761	2,800,000	Mireya Moscoso de Grubar—president
Papua New Guinea	Port Moresby	178,260	4,700,000	Mekere Morauta—prime minister
Paraguay	Asunción	157,047	5,200,000	Luis González Macchi—president
Peru	Lima	496,222	26,600,000	Alberto Fujimori—president
Philippines	Manila	115,830	74,700,000	Joseph Estrada—president Gloria Macapagal-Arroyo—vice-president
Poland	Warsaw	120,725	38,700,000	Aleksander Kwasniewski—president Jerzy Buzek—premier
Portugal	Lisbon	35,553	10,000,000	Jorge Sampaio—president Antonio Guterres—premier
Qatar	Doha	4,247	500,000	Hamad bin Khalifa al-Thani—head of state
Romania	Bucharest	91,700	22,500,000	Emil Constantinescu—president Mugar Isarescu—premier
Russia	Moscow	6,600,000	146,500,000	Vladimir Putin—acting president
Rwanda	Kigali	10,169	8,200,000	Pasteur Bizimungu—president
St. Kitts and Nevis	Basseterre	105	40,000	Denzil Douglas—prime minister
St. Lucia	Castries	238	200,000	Kenny Anthony—prime minister
St. Vincent and the Grenadines	Kingstown	150	100,000	James F. Mitchell—prime minister
San Marino	San Marino	24	30,000	Gabriele Gatti—head of state
São Tomé and Príncipe	São Tomé	372	200,000	Miguel Trovoada—president
Saudi Arabia	Riyadh	830,000	20,900,000	Fahd ibn Abdul-Aziz al-Saud—king
Senegal	Dakar	75,750	9,200,000	Abdou Diouf—president
Seychelles	Victoria	107	100,000	France Albert Réné—president
Sierra Leone	Freetown	27,700	5,300,000	Ahmad Tejan Kabbah—president
Singapore	Singapore	224	4,000,000	S. R. Nathan—president Goh Chok Tong—prime minister
Slovakia	Bratislava	18,933	5,400,000	Rudolf Schuster—president
Slovenia	Ljubljana	7,819	2,000,000	Milan Kucan—president
Solomon Islands	Honiara	10,983	400,000	Bartholomew Ulufa'alu—prime minister
Somalia	Mogadishu	246,200	7,100,000	no functioning government
South Africa	Pretoria Cape Town Bloemfontein	471,444	42,600,000	Thabo Mbeki—president
Spain	Madrid	194,896	39,400,000	Juan Carlos I—king José María Aznar—premier
Sri Lanka	Colombo	25,332	19,000,000	C. Bandaranaike Kumaratunga—president

UNITED STATES SUPREME COURT

Chief Justice: William H. Rehnquist (1986)
Associate Justices:
  John Paul Stevens (1975)
  Sandra Day O'Connor (1981)
  Antonin Scalia (1986)
  Anthony M. Kennedy (1988)
  David H. Souter (1990)
  Clarence Thomas (1991)
  Ruth Bader Ginsburg (1993)
  Stephen G. Breyer (1994)

UNITED STATES CABINET

Secretary of Agriculture: Daniel R. Glickman
Attorney General: Janet Reno
Secretary of Commerce: William M. Daley
Secretary of Defense: William S. Cohen
Secretary of Education: Richard W. Riley
Secretary of Energy: Bill Richardson
Secretary of Health and Human Services: Donna E. Shalala
Secretary of Housing and Urban Development: Andrew M. Cuomo
Secretary of Interior: Bruce Babbitt
Secretary of Labor: Alexis M. Herman
Secretary of State: Madeleine K. Albright
Secretary of Transportation: Rodney E. Slater
Secretary of the Treasury: Lawrence H. Summers
Secretary of Veteran Affairs: Togo West

Dennis Hastert, Republican congressman from Illinois, became Speaker of the House in 1999.

STATE GOVERNORS

Alabama	Donald Siegelman (D)	**Montana**	Marc Racicot (R)
Alaska	Tony Knowles (D)	**Nebraska**	Mike Johanns (R)
Arizona	Jane Dee Hull (R)	**Nevada**	Kenny Guinn (R)
Arkansas	Mike Huckabee (R)	**New Hampshire**	Jeanne Shaheen (D)
California	Gray Davis (D)	**New Jersey**	Christine Todd Whitman (R)
Colorado	Bill Owens (R)	**New Mexico**	Gary Johnson (R)
Connecticut	John Rowland (R)	**New York**	George Pataki (R)
Delaware	Thomas R. Carper (D)	**North Carolina**	Jim B. Hunt, Jr. (D)
Florida	Jeb Bush (R)	**North Dakota**	Edward Schafer (R)
Georgia	Roy Barnes (D)	**Ohio**	Bob Taft (R)
Hawaii	Ben Cayetano (D)	**Oklahoma**	Frank Keating (R)
Idaho	Dirk Kempthorne (R)	**Oregon**	John Kitzhaber (D)
Illinois	George Ryan (R)	**Pennsylvania**	Thomas J. Ridge (R)
Indiana	Frank L. O'Bannon (D)	**Rhode Island**	Lincoln Almond (R)
Iowa	Tom Vilsack (D)	**South Carolina**	Jim Hodges (D)
Kansas	Bill Graves (R)	**South Dakota**	William Janklow (R)
Kentucky	Paul Patton (D)*	**Tennessee**	Don Sundquist (R)
Louisiana	Mike Foster (R)*	**Texas**	George W. Bush (R)
Maine	Angus King (I)	**Utah**	Mike Leavitt (R)
Maryland	Parris N. Glendening (D)	**Vermont**	Howard Dean (D)
Massachusetts	Paul Cellucci (R)	**Virginia**	James S. Gilmore III (R)
Michigan	John Engler (R)	**Washington**	Gary Locke (D)
Minnesota	Jesse Ventura (RF)	**West Virginia**	Cecil H. Underwood (R)
Mississippi	**	**Wisconsin**	Tommy G. Thompson (R)
Missouri	Mel Carnahan (D)	**Wyoming**	Jim Geringer (R)

*re-elected in 1999   **election undecided   (D) Democrat (R) Republican (I) Independent (RF) Reform

CANADA

Capital: Ottawa
Head of State: Queen Elizabeth II
Governor General: Adrienne Clarkson
Prime Minister: Jean Chrétien (Liberal)
Leader of the Opposition: Preston Manning (Reform Party)
Population: 30,600,000
Area: 3,851,809 sq mi (9,976,185 km²)

PROVINCES AND TERRITORIES

Alberta
Capital: Edmonton
Lieutenant Governor: H. A. Bud Olson
Premier: Ralph Klein (Progressive Conservative)
Leader of the Opposition: Nancy MacBeth (Liberal)
Entered Confederation: Sept. 1, 1905
Population: 2,969,000
Area: 255,285 sq mi (661,188 km²)

British Columbia
Capital: Victoria
Lieutenant Governor: Garde Gardom
Premier: Dan Miller (New Democratic Party)
Leader of the Opposition: Gordon Campbell (Liberal)
Entered Confederation: July 20, 1871
Population: 4,029,300
Area: 366,255 sq mi (948,600 km²)

Manitoba
Capital: Winnipeg
Lieutenant Governor: Yvon Dumont
Premier: Gary Albert Doer (New Democratic Party)
Leader of the Opposition: Gary Filmon
  (Progressive Conservative)
Entered Confederation: July 15, 1870
Population: 1,143,400
Area: 251,000 sq mi (650,090 km²)

New Brunswick
Capital: Fredericton
Lieutenant Governor: Marilyn Trenholme Counsell
Premier: Bernard Lord (Progressive Conservative)
Leader of the Opposition: Camille Thériault (Liberal)
Entered Confederation: July 1, 1867
Population: 754,700
Area: 28,354 sq mi (73,436 km²)

Newfoundland
Capital: St. John's
Lieutenant Governor: Arthur Max House
Premier: Brian Tobin (Liberal)
Leader of the Opposition: Ed Byrne
  (Progressive Conservative)
Entered Confederation: March 31, 1949
Population: 541,200
Area: 156,185 sq mi (404,517 km²)

Nova Scotia
Capital: Halifax
Lieutenant Governor: J. James Kinley
Premier: John F. Hamm (Progressive Conservative)
Leader of the Opposition: Robert Chisholm (New
  Democratic Party)
Entered Confederation: July 1, 1867
Population: 940,800
Area: 21,425 sq mi (55,491 km²)

Ontario
Capital: Toronto
Lieutenant Governor: Hilary M. Weston
Premier: Mike Harris (Progressive Conservative)
Leader of the Opposition: Dalton McGuinty (Liberal)
Entered Confederation: July 1, 1867
Population: 11,600,000
Area: 412,582 sq mi (1,068,582 km²)

Prince Edward Island
Capital: Charlottetown
Lieutenant Governor: Gilbert R. Clements
Premier: Patrick Binns (Progressive Conservative)
Leader of the Opposition: Paul Connolly (Liberal)
Entered Confederation: July 1, 1873
Population: 137,800
Area: 2,184 sq mi (5,657 km²)

Quebec
Capital: Quebec City
Lieutenant Governor: Lise Thibault
Premier: Lucien Bouchard (Parti Québécois)
Leader of the Opposition: Jean Charest (Liberal)
Entered Confederation: July 1, 1867
Population: 7,363,300
Area: 594,860 sq mi (1,540,700 km^2)

Saskatchewan
Capital: Regina
Lieutenant Governor: John N. Wiebe
Premier: Roy Romanow (New Democratic Party)
Leader of the Opposition: Elwin Hermanson
  (Saskatchewan Party)
Entered Confederation: Sept. 1, 1905
Population: 1,028,100
Area: 251,700 sq mi (651,900 km^2)

Yukon
Capital: Whitehorse
Premier: Piers McDonald (New Democratic
  Party)
Leader of the Opposition: Pat Duncan (Liberal)
Commissioner: Judy Gingell
Organized as a Territory: June 13, 1898
Population: 30,700
Area: 186,299 sq mi (482,515 km^2)

Northwest Territories
Capital: Yellowknife
Commissioner: Helen Maksagak
Government Leader: Jim Antoine
Reconstituted as a Territory: Sept. 1, 1905
Population: 41,700
Area: 468,000 sq mi (1,170,000 km^2)

Nunavut
Capital: Iqaluit
Commissioner: Helen Maksagak
Government Leader: Paul Okalik
Organized as a Territory: April 1, 1999
Population: 27,100
Area: 797,600 sq mi (1,994,000 km^2)

Yukon
Northwest Territories
Nunavut
British Columbia
Alberta
Saskatchewan
Manitoba
Ontario
Quebec
Newfoundland
P.E.I.
Nova Scotia
New Brunswick

INDEX

A

B

British Columbia (province, Canada) 394
Broderick, Matthew (American actor) 264
Bronx Zoo (New York City), *picture* 112
Brood pouches (of sea horses) 104
Brown, Curtis (American astronaut) 66
Browne, Anthony (English author)
  Willy the Dreamer (book) 295–96
Bruggen, Coosje van (Dutch-American artist)
  Typewriter Eraser, Scale X (sculpture), *picture* 258
Brunei Darussalam 384
Bt corn 144
Buckles (on shoes) 213
Buffalo Sabres (hockey team) 185–87
Bulgaria 384
Bullock, Sandra (American actress) 264, *picture* 264
Burkina Faso 384
Burma (Myanmar) 384
Burundi 384
Bush, George (president of the United States) 25
Butterflies 143–45
Buttons (on shoes) 213
Butyrskaya, Maria (Russian athlete), *picture* 188

C

Cabbage Patch Kids (dolls) 41
Cabinet, United States 393
Caldecott Medal (children's literature) 294
Calderón Sol, Armando (president of El Salvador) 49
Calendars 198
California
  pandas in American zoos 65
Cambodia 385
Cameroon 385
Camouflage (of sea horses) 103
Canada 385
  Asian long-horned beetles 143
  Bigfoot, *picture* 44
  Canadian football 182
  children's literature awards 295
  Clarkson, Adrienne, *picture* 90
  coins 170–71, *picture* 171
  Gretzky, Wayne 310–12
  Krall, Diana, *picture* 261
  NATO 18
  Nunavut 50, 72–73
  Pan American Games 193–94
  provinces and territories 394–95
  space program 54
  stamps 151–52, 153
  Vincent, Amanda, founder of Project Sea Horse 105
Cantarini, Giorgio (Italian actor), *picture* 251
Cape Hatteras lighthouse (North Carolina) 145
Cape Verde 385
Cardiff Giant (hoax) 218
Careers
  animals, working with 228–35
  law and law enforcement 352–54
Caribou 231
Carnation, Lily, Lily, Rose (painting by John Singer Sargent) 247, *picture* 248

Carolus-Duran (French painter) 246
Cars *see* Automobiles
Carson, Lisa Nicole (American actress), *picture* 268
Cashmere (painting by John Singer Sargent), *picture* 249
Cassiopeia A (supernova) 138, *picture* 138
Cats 94–99
  commemorative coins 171, *picture* 171
  Maine coon cat, *picture* 92–93
  tails 111
Cellular phones, *picture* 30
Central African Republic 385
Cerebral palsy, *picture* 239
Chad 385
Chafee, John H. (American politician) 380
Challenger explosion 29
Chamberlain, Wilt (American basketball player) 380
Chandra X-Ray Observatory 56, 137–38
Chapman, Elizabeth (American student), *picture* 239
Chechnya (Russian province) 87
Cheetahs 108
Chemistry, Nobel Prize in 63
Chernobyl nuclear power plant (Ukraine) 28, 131
Cherry trees, *picture* 115
Chicago (Illinois)
  "Cows on Parade" sculptures, *picture* 258
  Sears Tower, *picture* 36
Children *see* Youth
Child's Treasury of Nursery Rhymes, A (book by Kady MacDonald Denton) 295
Chile 385
China 385
  alleged nuclear-secret theft 53
  Asian long-horned beetles 143
  cats, beliefs about 95
  Chinese embassy bombing in Yugoslavia 52
  cloning experiments 125
  Communism 18, 19
  ferry sinking 64
  50th anniversary of People's Republic of China 62
  foot binding 215
  Macao 66
  population 203
  sea horses in traditional medicine 105
  space program 138
  United States, relations with 84–85
Chinese New Year
  commemorative coins 171
  commemorative stamps 151, 152
Chopines (platform sandals) 213–14, *picture* 212
Christianity
  doomsday predictions 200
Christmas
  commemorative coins 171
  "Visit from St. Nicholas, A" (poem by Clement Clarke Moore) 220–23
Church, Charlotte (Welsh singer) 270, *picture* 224–25
Ciampi, Carlo Azeglio (president of Italy) 53
Citadel, The (military college in South Carolina)
  Mace, Nancy, first woman graduate, *picture* 89
Civil rights 23, 24
  Farmer, James, death of 380
Civil War, United States
  balloning, hot-air 205

H

J

Jaafar bin Abdul Rahman (king of Malaysia) 61

Jackson, Ellen (American author)
Turn of the Century (book) 295

Jackson, Jesse (American civil-rights leader) 52

Jackson, Samuel L. (American actor) 263

Jackson, Shelley (American author)
Old Woman and the Wave, The (book) 296–97

Jagan, Janet (president of Guyana) 59

Jagdeo, Bharrat (president of Guyana) 59

Jagr, Jaromir (Czech athlete) 187, *picture* 186

Jakob the Liar (movie) 267

Jamaica 386
Hannah, Makonnen David Blake (technology consultant), *picture* 239

Japan 19, 386
cloning experiments 125, 126
Little League World Series winning team, *picture* 177
nuclear accident 61
Pokémon, *picture* 236
Princess Mononoke (animated film), *picture* 244–45
World War II 16, 17

Japanese bobtail cats, *picture* 98

Jazz 38
Ellington, Duke, *picture* 261
Krall, Diana, *picture* 261
Torme, Mel, death of 383
word puzzle 154

Jefferson, Thomas (president of the United States) 213

Jeffries, John (American balloonist) 205

Jernigan, Tamara (American astronaut) 54

Jews
Holocaust 16
Israel 17

Joe Camel (advertising character), *picture* 50

Johnson, Lyndon (president of the United States) 23–24

Johnson, Michael (American athlete) 189

Johnson, Randy (American baseball player) 175

Johnston, Kristen (American actress), *picture* 269

Jones, Brian (British balloonist) 48, 204, 206–7, *pictures* 48, 204

Jones, Chipper (American baseball player) 175, *picture* 175

Jones, Paula (American woman who filed civil suit against President Clinton) 68, 71

Jordan 386
Hussein I, death of 82, 381
leadership change 47

Jordan, Michael (American athlete) 180, 195, *picture* 35

Jordan, Vernon (American lawyer) 70

Jupiter (planet) 135

Juvenile crime 373–76
school shootings (Colorado) 51

K

Kafelnikov, Yevgeny (Russian athlete) 190

Kangaroos, *picture* 108
commemorative coin 171, *picture* 171
tails 108

Kansas
tornadoes 52

Kashmir (region in India and Pakistan) 83–84

Kazakhstan 386

Kelley, DeForest (American actor) 381, *picture* 381

Kelly, Scott (American astronaut) 66

Kennedy, Carolyn Bessette (wife of John F. Kennedy, Jr.) 57, *picture* 57

Kennedy, Jacqueline (American First Lady), *picture* 23

Kennedy, John F. (president of the United States) 23, *picture* 23

Kennedy, John F., Jr. (son of American president) 57, 381, *picture* 57

Kenya 386

Key, Francis Scott (American lawyer and author of "The Star-Spangled Banner") 208

Khalifa, Hamad bin Isa al- (leader of Bahrain) 49

Khalifa, Isa bin Salman al- (leader of Bahrain) 49

Khamenei, Ayatollah Ali (Iranian Muslim leader) 83

Khannouchi, Khalid (American athlete) 189

Khatami, Mohammad (president of Iran) 83

Kiley, Richard (American actor) 381

King, Martin Luther, Jr. (American civil rights leader) 24

Kiribati 56, 386

Kismet (robot) 132, *pictures* 116–17, 132

Klebold, Dylan (American student) 51

Koalas, albino, *picture* 101

Korea, North 386

Korea, South 126, 386

Korean War 18

Korn (music group), *picture* 272

Kosovo (region in Serbia) 19, 49, 52, 54, 74–77
refugees, *picture* 42–43

Krakowski, Jane (American actress), *picture* 268

Krall, Diana (Canadian musician), *picture* 261

Kubrick, Stanley (American film director) 381

Kuwait 19, 386

Kwan, Michelle (American athlete) 188

Kyrgyzstan 386

L

Labor
basketball lockout 178
guilds 355–57
robots 130–31
twentieth-century life 20, 33, 34, *picture* 34

Labyrinths (mazes) 252, 253

Lala, Nupur (American student), *picture* 242

Land claims
Nunavut 72

Laos 386

Laptop computers 31, *picture* 31

M

N

O

P

S

ILLUSTRATION CREDITS AND ACKNOWLEDGMENTS

The following list credits or acknowledges, by page, the source of illustrations and text excerpts used in this work. Illustration credits are listed illustration by illustration— left to right, top to bottom. When two or more illustrations appear on one page, their credits are separated by semicolons. When both the photographer or artist and an agency or other source are given for an illustration, they are usually separated by a slash. Excerpts from previously published works are listed by inclusive page numbers.

6 © Karl-Heinz Kreifelts/AP/Wide World Photos; © Gary Torrisi Studio; © Peter Menzel
7 © Lane Stewart/*Sports Illustrated for Kids*; © Claire Hayden/Tony Stone Images; © Stephen Chernin/AP/Wide World Photos
12 © Neil Armstrong/NASA/AP/Wide World Photos
13
14 © AP/Wide World Photos; Corbis-Bettmann
15 © Sovfoto; Courtesy, Staatsbibliothek, Berlin, Germany
16 Margaret Bourke-White/*Life* Magazine © Time Inc.
17 © George Holton/Photo Researchers, Inc.; UPI/Corbis
18 © Tom Stoddart/Woodfin Camp & Associates
19 © Peter Turnely/Black Star
20 The Granger Collection; Stock Montage
21 © FPG
22 The Granger Collection; © AP/Wide World Photos
23 The Granger Collection; © Magnum Photos, Inc.
24 © Bruce Davidson/Magnum Photos, Inc.
25 © Dirck Halstead/Liaison Agency; © Reuters/Peter Morgan/Archive Photos
26 Space Telescope Science Institution; Courtesy, National Institute of Health
27 © Reuters/Ho/Archive Photos; UPI/Corbis
28 © Archive Photos
29 NASA
30 Corbis-Bettmann © Karl-Heinz Groebmair/Seimens Press Photo
31 AP/Wide World Photos; © Jacques M. Chenet/ Liaison Agency; © Gail Oskin/AP/Wide World Photos
32 UPI/Corbis-Bettmann
33 Corbis-Bettmann; Vernon Merritt III/*Life* Magazine, © Time, Inc.
34 National Archives; © Lawrence Migdale/ Photo Researchers, Inc.
35 UPI/Bettmann; © Tom Smart/ Liaison Agency
36 ©2000 Estate of Pablo Picasso/Artists Rights Society (ARS), New York/transparency from Ex-Edward James Foundation, Sussex, UK/Bridgeman Art Library; © Telegraph Colour Library/FPG International
37 Jack Wilkes/*Life* Magazine © Time, Inc.; © Bruce Roberts/Photo Researchers, Inc.
38 The Kobal Collection, Ltd.; © Photofest
39 © Columbia/TriStar Television Distribution/AP/Wide World Photos
40 © Kim Sayer/Corbis-Bettmann; © Frederick Lewis Collection/Archive Photos; UPI/Corbis-Bettmann
41 Corbis-Bettmann; © FPG International; © Carolyn Herter/*The Dallas Morning News*; Courtesy, Mattel, Inc.
42– © Santiago Lyon/AP/Wide World Photos
43
44 © AP/Wide World Photos
45 © Bernd Kammerer/AP/Wide World Photos

46 © Elaine Thompson/AP/Wide World Photos
47 © Jack Smith/AP/Wide World Photos
48 © Khue Bui/AP/Wide World Photos
49 Artist, Natasha Lessnik Tibbott
50 © Michael Newman/PhotoEdit
51 © Michael S. Green/AP/Wide World Photos
52 © J. Pat Carter/AP/Wide World Photos
53 © Greg Baker/AP/Wide World Photos
54 © Keith Gunnar/Bruce Coleman Inc.
55 © Lois Greenfield/Bruce Coleman Inc.
56 © Matthew Borkoski/Stock Boston/PNI
57 © Reuters/Mike Segar/Archive Photos
58 © Karl-Heinz Kreifelts/AP/Wide World Photos; © Zia Mazhar/AP/Wide World Photos
59 © Murad Sezer/AP/Wide World Photos
60 © Princeton University/AP/Wide World Photos
61 Artist, Natasha Lessnik Tibbott
62 © Chung Chien-min/AP/Wide World Photos
63 © Chris Hondros/AP/Wide World Photos
64 © J.C. Cardenas/EFE/AP/Wide World Photos
65 © Ric Feld/AP/Wide World Photos
66 © David Caulkin/AP/Wide World Photos
67 Artist, Natasha Lessnik Tibbott
68 © Chuck Kennedy/Newsmakers
69 © Corbis-Sygma; © Ron Sachs/Corbis-Sygma; © Georges de Keerle/Liaison Agency
70 © Allan Tannenbaum/Corbis-Sygma
71 © Dirck Halstead/Liaison Agency; © Ron Sachs/ Corbis-Sygma
72 © Tom Hanson/AP/Wide World Photos
73 © Stephan Savoia/AP/Wide World Photos; © Canadian Press, Kevin Frayer/AP Photo
74 © Noel Quidu/Liaison Agency
75 © Jerome Delay/AP/Wide World Photos
76 © Boris Grdanoski/AP/Wide World Photos
77 © Daniel Hulshizer/AP/Wide World Photos
78 © Dan Silverstein/Bruce Coleman Inc.
80 © M. Timothy O'Keefe/Bruce Coleman Inc.
81 © Dmitri Messinis/AP/Wide World Photos
82 © Dusan Vranic/AP/Wide World Photos
83 © K.M. Choudray/AP/Wide World Photos
84 © Eugene Hoshiko/AP/Wide World Photos
85 © Louise Gubb/SABA
86 © Erik De Castro/AP/Wide World Photos
87 © Laski Diffusion/Liaison Agency; © ITAR-TASS/AP/Wide World Photos
88 © Tim Graham/Corbis-Sygma
89 © Bebeto Matthews/AP/Wide World Photos; © Mic Smith/AP/Wide World Photos
90 © CP, Fred Chartrand/AP/Wide World Photos; © Bizuayehu Tesfaye/AP/Wide World Photos
91 © Hires/Liaison Agency
92– © Ulrike Schanz/Animals Animals
93
94 © Jerome Wexler/Photo Researchers, Inc.

95 © J. P. Thomas/Jacana/Photo Researchers, Inc.
96 © Melanie Stetson Freeman/*The Christian Science Monitor*
97 © Patti Murray/Animals Animals; © Hans Reinhard/Bruce Coleman Inc.; © Claire Hayden/ Tony Stone Images
98 © Tetsu Yamazaki/Courtesy, Allan Scruggs
99 © Kathi Lamm/Tony Stone Images; © Carolyn A. McKeone/Photo Researchers, Inc.; © Fritz Prenzel/Animals Animals
100 © Zig Leszcynski/Animals Animals; © Joseph Van Wormer/Bruce Coleman Inc.
101 © Patti Murray/Animals Animals; © James H. Robinson/Animals Animals
102 © Pat Canova/Southern Stock/PNI
103 © Jeffrey L. Rotman/Corbis
104 © Rudie Kuiter/Oxford Scientific Films; © George Grall/National Geographic Society Image Collection
105 © Alan Towse/Ecoscene/Corbis
106 © Renee Lynn/Photo Researchers, Inc.
107 © G.C. Kelly/Photo Researchers, Inc.
108 © Charles V. Angelo/Photo Researchers, Inc.; © Jen & Des Bartlett/Bruce Coleman Inc.
109 © Jeff Lepore/Photo Researchers, Inc.
110 © Jeff Lepore/Photo Researchers, Inc.; © Herb Segars/Animals Animals
111 © Robert Winslow/Animals Animals
112 © Mark Lennihan/AP/Wide World Photos
113 © Breck P. Kent/Animals Animals; © Joe Dickson/Indiana State University
114 © Ralph Reinhold/Animals Animals; © Bill Eppridge/*Sports Illustrated*/Time Inc.
115 © Susan Walsh/AP/Wide World Photos; © Pat & Tom Leeson/Photo Researchers, Inc.
116– © Peter Menzel
117
118– Artist, Vince Caputo
123
124 © Roslin Institute; © Dr. Arthur Lesk, Laboratory of Molecular Biology/SPL/ Photo Researchers, Inc.
125 © ProBio America, Inc./ Liaison Agency
126 © Reuters/HO/Archive Photos; © Stephen J. Krasemann/Photo Researchers, Inc.
127 © Reuters/Ishikawa Prefecture/Archive Photos
128 © Reuters/Rickey Rogers/Archive Photos
129 The Granger Collection
130 © Sam Ogden/Science Photo Library/Photo Researchers, Inc.
131 © Hank Morgan/Science Source/Photo Researchers, Inc.; © David Parker/Science Photo Library/ Photo Researchers, Inc.; © Todd Korol
132 © Peter Menzel

133 © Reuters/Toshiyuki Aizawa/Archive Photos
134 NASA/JPL/AP/Wide World Photos; NASA/JPL
135 NASA/AP/Wide World Photos
136 NASA/JPL
137 NASA
138 © Reuters/Joe Skipper/Archive Photos; NASA/
Chandra X-ray Center/AP/Wide World Photos
140 © Eric Vandeville/Liaison Agency
141 Corbis/Bettmann
142 © Chris Gardner/AP/Wide World Photos
143 © Ronen Zilberman/AP/Wide World Photos
144 © Damian Dovarganes/AP/Wide World Photos
145 © Leroy Williamson, Texas Parks and
Wildlife/AP/Wide World Photos; © Bob
Jordan/AP/Wide World Photos
146– Designed and created by Jenny Tesar
147
148– From *Make Cards!* © 1991 by F&W Publications.
149 Used by permission of North Light Books, a
divisionof F&W Publications, Inc.
154 SOLUTION: Duke Ellington
156– © Lane Stewart/*Sports Illustrated for Kids*
157
157 © Joel Thomson
158– © Andy Dappen
160 © Lane Stewart/*Sports Illustrated for Kids*
161 © Joel Thomson; © Lane Stewart/*Sports Illustrated
for Kids*
164– From *Many Friends Cooking: An International Cook
165 book for Boys and Girls*, by Terry Touff Cooper an
Marilyn Ratner. Illustrations by Tony Chen.
Reprinted by permission of Philomel Books, a
division of the Putnam Publishing Group
166– Courtesy, *Crafts 'n Things* magazine. For more
169 detailed information on these craft projects,
write to Crafts 'n Things, 701 Lee St., Suite 1000,
Des Plaines, IL 60016–4570
170 Courtesy, Krause Publications, Inc.
171
172 © Peter Read Miller/*Sports Illustrated*
173
174 © Ron Frehm/AP/Wide World Photos
175 © John Bazemare/AP/Wide World Photos
177 © Rusty Kennedy/AP/Wide World Photos
178 © Andrew D. Bernstein/NBA Photos
180 © David J. Phillip/AP/Wide World Photos
181 © Mark Friedman/Sports Chrome
182 © Michael Zito/Sports Chrome
183 © Mike Segar/Reuters/Archive Photos
184 © Dave Martin/AP/Wide World Photos
185 © Donna McWilliam/AP/Wide World Photos
186 © Keith Srakocic/AP/Wide World Photos
188 © Thomas Keinzle/AP/Wide World Photos
189 © Reuters/Yiorgos Karahalis/Archive Photos
190 © Reuters/Kevin Lamarque/Archive Photos
191 © Kathy Willens/AP/Wide World Photos
192 © Laurent Rebours/AP/Wide World Photos
193 © Reuters Newmedia Inc./Corbis; © Reuters/
Shaun Best/Archive Photos
194 © Eric Risberg/AP/Wide World Photos
195 © Ron Vesely/Focus on Sports; © John Gaps
III/AP/Wide World Photos; © Allsport;
© Focus on Sports
196– © Simon Battensby/Tony Stone Images
197
198– © Gary Torrisi Studio
201
202 © Diana Ong/SuperStock
204 © Fabrice Coffini/AP/Wide World Pictures;
© Yvain Genevay/Sipa
205 © Gary Torrisi Studio

206 © 1999 Time Inc. Reprinted by permission
207 © Yvain Genevay/Sipa
208 © Dennis Cook/AP/Wide World Photos
209 © AFP/Corbis
210 © Tate Gallery/Art Resource; Reprinted with
permission from AP Photo/Copyright/Science Magazine. Copyright 1998 American Association for the
Advancement of Science.
211 © SuperStock
212 © Archive Photos; © Archive Photos; © The Bata
Shoe Museum
213 © Musée du Louvre, Paris/SuperStock; © The Bata
Shoe Museum; © The Bata Shoe Museum
214 © Private Collection/Marilee Whitehouse-Holm/
SuperStock
215 © The Bata Shoe Museum; © Bob Daemmrich/
The Image Works
216– Artist, Vince Caputo
219
220 Corbis-Bettmann
221– The Granger Collection
222
223 Courtesy, Jim Clutter, Northpole.com
224– © John Gurzinski/AP/Wide World Photos
225
226 Courtesy, Gordon Ramel, Earth Life
Communicational; Courtesy, Troy Gilliland,
Executive Producer, Smarty Pants' 3D Yo-Yo Tricks
227 Courtesy, Eric Hein, Vice President of Direct
Marketing, Sovereign Bank; Courtesy, David
Davenport, The Young Writers Club
228 © David Grunfield for Cornell University, College
of Veterinary Medicine
229 © Michael S. Yamashita/Corbis
230 © Douglas Faulkner/Photo Researchers, Inc.
231 Courtesy, Hambleton District Council
232 D. Demello © Wildlife Conservation Society
233 © Grantpix/Photo Researchers, Inc.
234 © Fabricius & Taylor/Liaison Agency
235 © Thomas Nebbia
236 © Stephen Chernin/AP/Wide World Photos;
© Wizards of the Coast/AP/Wide World Photos
237 Courtesty of the Highley Family; © Taro
Yamasaki/*People* Weekly
238 © Doug Levere
239 © Dan Helms; © Ian Howarth
240 © Photofest; © Everett Collection
241 © Phyliss Picardi/Stock South/PNI
242 © Ron Edmonds/AP/Wide World Photos
243 © Blake Little/The Kobal Collection; © Photofest
244– © Miramax Films/Photofest
245
246 The Metropolitan Museum of Art, Arthur Hoppock
Hearn Fund, 1916. (16.53)/Photograph © 1997
The Metropolitan Museum of Art
247 © Tate Gallery, London/Art Resource
248 © Tate Gallery, London/Art Resource; © Art Resource
249 © Private American Collection. National Portrait
Gallery/Sotheby's
250 © Laurie Sparham/Photofest
251 Sergio Strizzi/Photofest; David James © 1998 TM &
Dreamworks; © Everett Collection
252 © Georg Gerster/Photo Researchers, Inc.;
© Victoria & Albert Museum, London/The
Bridgeman Art Library
253 The Granger Collection
254 © Georg Gerster/Photo Researchers, Inc.
255 © Mike Roemer/AP/Wide World Photos
256 © Antonio Calanni/AP/Wide World Photos
257 © Deidre Davidson/SAGA/Archive Photos;
© Dave Caulkin/AP/Wide World Photos

258 © John Zich/Newsmakers; © Dennis Black/Black Star
259 © Everett Collection; Scott Willis © 1999 *San Jose
Mercury News*
260 © Douglas Mason/Woodfin Camp & Associates
261 © Frank Diggs/Archive Photos; © Reglain
Frederic/Liaison Agency
262 © Ron Phillips/Photofest
263 © Lucasfilm Ltd./Photosfest
264 © Everett Collection
265 © Deana Newcomb/Everett Collection
266 © Everett Collection
267 © Suzanne Hanover/20th Century Fox/The
Kobal Collection
268 © Everett Collection
269 © Fotos International/Archive Photos;
© Everett Collection; © Everett Collection
270 © Gregory Pace/Corbis-Sygma
271 © Kevin Frayer/Canadian Press/AP/Wide
World Photos
272 © Gregory Pace/Corbis-Sygma; © Reuters/
Rose Prouser/Archive Photos
273 © Barry King/Liaison Agency; © Reuters/
Andrea Comas/Archive Photos
274 © Evan Agostini/Liaison Agency
275 © Reed Saxon/AP/Wide World Photos
276– From *Night City* by Monica Wellington. Text
277 Copyright © Monica Wellington and Andrew Kupfer,
1998. Illustrations Copyright © Monica Wellington.
1998. Reprinted by arrangement with Dutton
Children's Books, a division of Penguin Putnam, Inc.
278 The Granger Collection
279 © Gary Torrisi Studio
291
292– Artist, Michele A. McLean
293
294 Illustration by Mary Azarian from *Snowflake Bentley*
by Jacqueline Briggs Martin. Illustration copyright
© 1998 by Mary Azarian. Reprinted by permission of
Houghton Mifflin Co. All rights reserved.; Illustration
by Kady MacDonald Denton from *A Child's Treasury
of Nursery Rhymes, page 48. Reprinted by permission
of Larousse Kingfisher Chambers.
295 From *A Sign* by George Ella Lyon, illustrated by Chris
K. Soentpiet. Jacket illustration © 1998 by Chris K.
Soentpiet. Used by permission of Orchard Books,
New York.
296 Illustration from *Willy the Dreamer* by Anthony
Browne; published by Walker Books, Ltd.; Reprinted
with permission from *Turtle Spring*. Copyright
© 1998 by Deborah Turney Zagwyn, Tricycle Press.
297 From *The Old Woman and the Wave* by Shelley
Jackson. Copyright © 1998 Shelley Jackson.
Reprinted with permission by DK Publishing, Inc.;
From *Walter Wick's Optical Tricks*. Copyright
© 1998 by Walter Wick. Reprinted by permission
of Scholastic Inc.
299 © Archivo Iconografico, S.A./Corbis
310 © Paul Chiasson/AP/Wide World Media
311 © Bruce Bennett Studios; © Allsport
312 © Reuters/Mike Blake/Archive Photos
314 © Tim Wright/Corbis
315 © Anthony Bannister/ABPL/Corbis
316 © 1990 Bob Schatz/Liaison Agency
317 © Archive Photos; © Richard Cummins/
Corbis
318 © Hulton Getty/The Liasion Agency;
© David Young-Wolff/PhotoEdit
319 © Photosynthesis/International Stock/Photo
Network; Bettmann-Corbis
320 © Hirz/Archive Photos
321 © Tim Page/Corbis